LENIN

VOLUME XX

THE REVOLUTION OF 1917

FROM THE MARCH REVOLUTION TO THE JULY DAYS

BOOK II

NEW YORK

INTERNATIONAL PUBLISHERS

CONTENTS

CONTENTS

6

ILLUSTRATIONS

PREFATORY NOTE

This book completes the writings and speeches of V. I. Lenin relating to the period from the overthrow of the Tsar in March to the first open conflict with the Provisional Government in July, 1917. The material in Book I covers the period from March to June; the present book extends from the beginning of June to the middle of July, both books constituting Volume XX of Lenin's *Collected Works*. This, however, does not complete Lenin's writings on the Revolution of 1917, since it does not include the period from the July Days to the seizure of power and the establishment of the Soviet Government in November. The material dealing with this period will be found in Volume XXI of the *Collected Works*.

Aside from the explanatory notes which refer exclusively to the text of this book, although they continue the numeration of the notes in Book I, the appendices at the end of the book are for the volume as a whole. The book and page numbers at the end of the biographical notes are intended as an index to the names mentioned in both books. Otherwise, the technical problems in connection with the entire volume have been considered in the general preface published in Book I.

ARTICLES, LETTERS, ETC., TO THE BEGINNING
OF JUNE

THE REVOLUTION OF 1917

THE MEANING OF FRATERNISATION

THE capitalists either poke fun at fraternisation, or wrathfully attack it with lies and calumny, reducing it all to "deception" practiced by the Germans upon the Russians; they threaten—through *their* generals and officers—to punish severely all those guilty of fraternisation.

From the point of view of safeguarding the "sacred property right" of capital and profits, this policy of the capitalists is quite sound: indeed, in order that the proletarian Socialist revolution be crushed at its very inception, it is necessary to regard fraternisation in the light in which the capitalists regard it.

The class-conscious workers and the vast masses of semi-proletarians and poor peasants who, guided by the true instinct of oppressed classes, follow in the steps of class-conscious workers, regard fraternisation with the deepest sympathy. It is obvious that fraternisation is a road to peace. It is obvious that this road leads not to the capitalist governments, not to harmony with them, but, on the contrary, it leads against them. It is obvious that this road develops, strengthens, consolidates the feeling of brotherly confidence among the workers of various countries. It is obvious that this road is beginning to undermine the damnable discipline of the barrack prisons, the discipline requiring the absolute submission of soldiers to "their" officers and generals, to their capitalists (for officers and generals are for the most part either members of the capitalist class or defenders of its interests). It is obvious that fraternisation is the revolutionary initiative of the *masses*, that it is the awakening of the conscience, the mind, the courage of the oppressed classes, that it is, in other words, one of the links in the chain of steps leading towards the Socialist proletarian revolution.

Long live fraternisation! Long live the rising world Socialist revolution of the proletariat!

To expedite fraternisation, to make the attainment of our goal as easy and certain as possible, we must take care that it be well organised and based on a clear political programme.

13

However maliciously the press of the capitalists and their friends may slander us, denouncing us as Anarchists, we still repeat: we are not Anarchists, we are ardent upholders of the best organisation of the masses and of a most firm "state" authority,—but the state we want is not a bourgeois parliamentary republic, but a Republic of Soviets of Workers', Soldiers' and Peasants' Deputies.

We have always counselled and we still counsel that fraternisation be carried on according to an organised plan; that it be tested in the light of the ideas, experiences, observations of the soldiers themselves, so that there may be no deception; that officers and generals, who are for the most part bitterly opposed to fraternisation, be kept away from the meetings.

We are endeavouring to make fraternisation go beyond the limits of general peace parleys. We want it to become an issue on a definite political programme, we want it to turn into a consideration of the question as to how to end the war, how to throw off the yoke of capitalism which is responsible for the war and its prolongation.

Accordingly, our party has issued a proclamation to the soldiers of all the warring countries (see its text in *Pravda*, No. 37), giving our definite and clear answer to these questions, and our precise political programme.

It is well that the soldiers curse the war. It is well that they clamour for peace. It is well that they begin to feel that the war benefits the capitalists. It is well that they, breaking the prison discipline, themselves begin to fraternise on all the fronts. It is all very well.

But this is not enough.

It is necessary that fraternisation be accompanied by the discussion of a definite political programme. We are not Anarchists. We do not think that war can be terminated by a simple "refusal" to fight, a refusal of individuals, groups, or "mobs." We hold that the war should and will be brought to a finish through a *revolution* in several countries, i. e., through the conquests of *state* power by a new class, not the capitalists, not the small proprietors (invariably half-dependent upon the capitalists), but proletarians and semi-proletarians.

In our proclamation to the soldiers of all the warring countries we presented our programme for a workers' revolution in all the countries: transfer of all state power to the Soviets of Workers' and Soldiers' Deputies.

Comrades, Soldiers! Discuss this programme among yourselves together with the German soldiers! Such discussions will help you discover the true, the most effective, and shortest way for the termination of the war and the overthrow of the yoke of capital.

Just a few words about one of the servants of capital, Plekhanov. It is pitiful to see how low this former Socialist has fallen! He puts fraternisation next to "treason"!! His argument is that fraternisation, if successful, will lead to a separate peace.

No, Mr. ex-Socialist, fraternisation, carried on by us on *all* fronts, will lead not to a "separate" peace among capitalists of a few countries, but to a universal peace among the revolutionary workers of all countries, *despite* the capitalists, against the capitalists, for the overthrow of their yoke.

Pravda, No. 43, May 11, 1917.

WHAT THE COUNTER-REVOLUTIONARY STEPS OF THE PROVISIONAL GOVERNMENT LEAD TO

WE have received the following telegram:

> Yeniseisk. The Soviet of Workers' and Soldiers' Deputies has taken cognisance of Minister Lvov's telegram sent to the appointed commissar of the Yeniseisk Province, Krutovsky, for guidance in Yeniseisk.
>
> We protest against the intention of the government again to introduce a bureaucracy; we declare: first, that we will not brook any appointed officers to rule us; second, that the officials driven out by the peasants cannot be returned; third, that we recognise only those local organs that have been created in Yeniseisk County by the people themselves; fourth, that appointed officers can rule here only over our dead bodies.
>
> THE YENISEISK SOVIET OF DEPUTIES.

It appears, then, that the Provisional Government has been appointing "commissars" in Petrograd for the purpose of "guiding" the Yeniseisk Soviet of Workers' and Soldiers' Deputies, or the Yeniseisk organ of self-government. Moreover, this appointment has been made in a form that provoked the Yeniseisk Soviet of Workers' and Soldiers' Deputies to protest against "the intention of the government again to introduce a bureaucracy."

What is more, the Yeniseisk Soviet of Workers' and Soldiers' Deputies declares that "the appointed officers can rule here only over our dead bodies." The behaviour of the Provisional Government has brought this remote province in Siberia, represented by the popularly elected leading organ, to the point of a direct threat of *armed resistance* against the Provisional Government.

The gentlemen of the Provisional Government have certainly managed affairs gloriously!

Yet they will keep on shouting—as they have been shouting all along—denunciations against those malicious people who "preach" "civil war"!

What was the purpose of appointing from Petrograd or from any other centre "commissars" to "guide" elected local governing bodies? Are we to believe that a stranger is more likely to appreciate local needs, is more capable of "guiding" the native inhabitants? What did the people of Yeniseisk do to call forth such an absurd measure?

16

And supposing that the people of Yeniseisk have run counter to the decisions of a majority of citizens in other localities, would it not be better to limit oneself first to an effort at *getting some information* instead of giving cause for talk about "bureaucracy," instead of provoking the justifiable dissatisfaction and resentment of the local population?

To all these questions there can be only one answer. The gentlemen who are representing the landowners and the capitalists and who are in control of the Provisional Government insist on *preserving* the old tsarist government apparatus: officials appointed from above. Excepting for the brief periods of revolution in some countries, this is just the way in which almost all bourgeois-parliamentary republics have always acted. By acting thus, they facilitated and prepared the ground for the return from a republic to a monarchy, for the passing of the republic into the hands of the Napoleons, of military dictators. By acting thus, the Cadet gentlemen insist on repeating those tragic instances.

This is an exceedingly serious matter. Why deceive ourselves? By resorting to such measures, the Provisional Government, no matter whether consciously or not, prepares the ground for a restoration of the monarchy in Russia.

The entire responsibility for any possible—and to a certain extent inevitable—attempts at restoring the monarchy in Russia falls upon the Provisional Government which is endeavouring to carry out such counter-revolutionary measures. For officials "appointed" from above to "guide" the local populations are and always have been a sure step toward the restoration of the monarchy, just exactly as are and always have been the police and the standing army.

The Yeniseisk Soviet of Workers' and Soldiers' Deputies is a thousand times right, both practically and in the matter of principle. The return of the local officials driven out by the peasants must not be countenanced. The introduction of "appointed" officials must not be tolerated. Only those organs of local self-government that have been created by the population itself ought to be recognised.

The idea that it is necessary to "guide" through officials "appointed" from above is, at bottom, false, undemocratic, autocratic, or it is a Blanquist *adventure*. Engels was fully right when, criticising in 1891 the proposed programme of the German Social-Democrats who had become badly infected with bureaucratism, he insistently demanded that there be no supervision from above over local self-government. Engels was right when he referred to the experience of France, which, though governed between the years 1792 and 1798 by local elective bodies without any supervision from above, was, instead of falling apart, instead of "disintegrating," gaining strength through democratic consolidation and organisation.

Silly bureaucratic prepossessions, habitual tsarist red tape, reactionary professorial ideas as to the indispensability of bureaucratism, counter-revolutionary tricks and attempts of landowners and capitalists—these are at the root of such measures of the Provisional Government as we have been discussing.

A sound democratic feeling of workers and peasants indignant over the contemptuous attempt of the Provisional Government to "appoint" officials for the purpose of "guiding" the adult local population, the overwhelming majority, that had carried out a regular election—this is what the Yeniseisk Soviet of Workers' and Soldiers' Deputies has revealed.

What the people needs is a real, democratic, workers' and peasants' republic, a republic in which all officials are elected by the people, and subject to the people's recall. And it is for such a republic that the workers and peasants must fight, resisting all attempts of the Provisional Government to restore the monarchist, the tsarist methods, and the tsarist administrative apparatus.

Pravda, No. 43, May 11, 1917.

I. G. TSERETELI AND THE CLASS STRUGGLE

ALL the newspapers have reprinted, in full or in part, I. G. Tsereteli's speech delivered on May 10 at the special session of the Deputies of all the [four] Imperial Dumas.[182]

Quite a ministerial speech, no doubt about that. It was delivered by a Minister without a portfolio. Still we think that it would not be amiss,—*even* for Ministers without portfolios,—to mention Socialism, Marxism, and the class struggle in their ministerial speeches. Each one must hold to his own. It is proper for the bourgeoisie to avoid all talk of class struggle, to eschew its analysis, its study and its use in determining political lines. It is proper for the bourgeoisie to wave aside these "disagreeable," "tactless topics," as they say in their parlours, and sing hymns of praise to "unity" "of all friends of freedom." It is equally proper for the proletarian party not to forget the class struggle.

Each one must hold to his own.

Two basic political ideas are woven into the speech of I. G. Tsereteli. The first is that a line of demarcation should be drawn between two "parts" of the bourgeoisie. One part "has entered into an agreement with democracy"; the position of this bourgeoisie is "secure." The other represents "irresponsible elements of the bourgeoisie who are inciting to civil war," and includes, as Tsereteli describes them, "many of the so-called moderate centrist elements."

The second political idea stressed by the speaker is that "an attempt to declare (!!?) a dictatorship of the proletariat and the peasantry" forthwith would constitute a "desperate" venture, and that he, Tsereteli, would agree to such a desperate venture only if he could believe for one minute that Shulgin's ideas were really "the ideas of the entire property-owning bourgeoisie."

Let us analyse both political ideas of I. G. Tsereteli, who has assumed—as is becoming a Minister without a portfolio or a candidate for the ministry—a "centrist" position: Neither for reaction, nor for revolution, neither with Shulgin, nor with the advocates of "desperate ventures."

19

What are the class distinctions pointed out by Tsereteli as existing between the two above parts of the bourgeoisie? Absolutely none. It has not even occurred to Tsereteli that it would not be amiss to view politics from the class struggle angle. Both "parts" of the bourgeoisie are, from the point of view of their class position, land-owners and capitalists. Tsereteli never even suggested that Shulgin does not represent the same classes or sub-classes that are represented by Guchkov, one of the most important members of the Provisional Government. Tsereteli considers the ideas of Shulgin to be distinct from the ideas of the "entire" property-owning bourgeoisie, but he offers no reasons for such a distinction. Nor can he offer such reasons. Shulgin stands for the supreme power of the Provisional Government; he is opposed to the control over that government by armed soldiers; he is against "the propaganda antagonistic to Eng-land," against "inciting" the soldiers to oppose their officers, against the propaganda "from Petrogradskaia Storona," [188] etc. These "ideas" are to be found daily on the pages of the *Riech*, in the speeches and manifestos of the Ministers with portfolios, etc.

The only difference between the two is that Shulgin speaks a bit more "brusquely," while the Provisional Government, as a govern-ment, speaks a bit more modestly; Shulgin speaks in a bass voice, Miliukov in a falsetto. Miliukov is for an agreement with the Soviet of Workers' and Soldiers' Deputies; Shulgin, too, has *noth-ing against* such an agreement. Both Shulgin and Miliukov are for "other methods of control" (different from the control of armed soldiers).

Tsereteli has cast overboard all ideas of the class struggle. He has *not* pointed out, nor did he think of pointing out, any serious political or class distinctions between the "two parts" of the bour-geoisie!

In one part of his speech Tsereteli indicated that by "democracy" he meant "the proletariat and the revolutionary peasantry." Let us analyse this class definition. The bourgeoisie has entered upon an agreement with this democracy. The question is, What holds these two together? What class interest?

Not a word about this in Tsereteli's speech! He speaks of a "general democratic platform which at the present moment has proved acceptable to the whole country," *i. e.*, apparently, to the proletarians and the peasants, for the "country" to which he refers, with the exception of the property owners, is really the workers and the peasants.

Does the platform exclude, say, the question of land? No. The platform simply overlooks it. Do the class interests and contradictions vanish because they are overlooked in diplomatic documents, in "covenants," in the speeches and pronouncements of Ministers?

Tsereteli has "forgotten" to mention this question, forgotten a "detail"; he "merely" has forgotten the class interests and the class struggle. . . .

"All the problems of the Russian Revolution," chirps I. G. Tsereteli, "its entire essence (!!??) depends upon the following: Will the propertied classes" (*i. e.*, the landowners and the capitalists) "understand that this platform is the platform of the people as a whole and not merely of the proletariat. . . ."

Poor landowners and capitalists! They are so "stupid." They do not "understand." A special Minister representing democracy is needed to tell them a thing or two. . . .

Has this representative of "democracy" forgotten the class struggle, has he gone over to the position of Louis Blanc, is he resorting to phrases in order to get away from the conflict of class interests?

Is it Shulgin, Guchkov and Miliukov who "do not understand" that by ignoring the land question in their party platform it is possible to reconcile the peasant with the landowner? Or is it I. G. Tsereteli who "does not understand" that this is impossible?

Workers and peasants: Be satisfied with what is acceptable to the landowners and capitalists,—this is the real essence (class, not verbal) of Shulgin's, Miliukov's, and Plekhanov's position. And they understand it much better than Mr. Tsereteli.

We have now come to the second political idea of Tsereteli's: An attempt forthwith to declare a dictatorship (incidentally, a dictatorship is not "declared," but won) of the proletariat and the peasantry would be a desperate venture. First, to speak so simply of this dictatorship now is quite out of place; Tsereteli may yet land in the archives of the "old Bolsheviks" *; second,—and this is the most important point—the workers and peasants constitute the overwhelming majority of the population. And does not "democracy" mean the carrying out of the will of the majority?

How then can one be a democrat, and yet be *opposed to* the "dictatorship of the proletariat and the peasantry"? What reason is

* See my "Letters on Tactics." [Pp. 120-121, Book I of this volume.—*Ed.*]

there to fear that such a dictatorship would bring on civil war? (What sort of civil war? A handful of landowners and capitalists against the workers and peasants? An insignificant minority against an overwhelming majority?)

I. G. Tsereteli is hopelessly confused. Does he not realise that should Lvov and Co. live up to their promise and convoke the Constituent Assembly, the latter would become the "dictatorship" of the majority? Or must the workers and peasants even in the Constituent Assembly be satisfied with what is "acceptable" to the landowners and the capitalists?

The workers and peasants are the vast majority. And here one tells us that for this majority to seize power would be a "desperate venture." . . .

Tsereteli is all mixed up, for he has completely forgotten all about the class struggle. He has abandoned Marxism, and assumed the position of Louis Blanc, using phrases to evade the class struggle.

The task of a proletarian leader is to make clear the difference in class interests and to urge certain strata of the petty bourgeoisie (namely, the poorest peasants) to choose between the capitalists and the workers, to take the side of the latter.

The task of petty-bourgeois Louis Blancs is to attenuate the difference in class interests and to urge certain strata of the bourgeoisie (chiefly the intellectuals and parliamentarians) to "agree" with the workers, to urge the workers to "agree" with the capitalists, to urge the peasants to "agree" with the landowners.

Louis Blanc diligently urged the Parisian bourgeoisie and, as we all know, almost convinced it to give up its methods of wholesale slaughter in the years 1848 and 1871. . . .

N. LENIN.

Pravda, No. 44, May 12, 1917.

THE "CRISIS OF POWER"

ALL of Russia remembers the days of May 2 to May 4, when civil war was about to break out in the streets of Petrograd.

On May 4 the Provisional Government published a new and pacifying little document [184] "explaining" away its predatory note of May first.

Whereupon the majority of the Executive Committee of the Soviet of Workers' and Soldiers' Deputies decided to declare the "incident closed."

Another couple of days passed, and the question of a coalition cabinet came up. The Executive Committee was almost equally divided: 23 against a coalition cabinet, 22 for it. The incident proved to have been "closed" only on paper.

Another two days, and we have a new "incident." The Minister of War, one of the leading members of the Provisional Government, Guchkov, has resigned. There are rumours that the whole Provisional Government has decided to resign. (While writing these lines, we are not yet certain whether the government has resigned.) A new "incident" has come up, and of such a nature that all the preceding "incidents" are likely to pale into insignificance in comparison with it.

What is the source of this multitude of "incidents"? Is there no basic cause that inevitably generates "incident" upon "incident"?

There *is* such a cause. It is the so-called dual power, that unstable equilibrium resulting from the agreement between the Soviet of Workers' and Soldiers' Deputies and the Provisional Government.

The Provisional Government is a capitalist government. It cannot give up its dreams of conquests (annexations), it cannot end the predatory war with a democratic peace, it cannot but protect the profits of its own class (the capitalist class), it cannot but protect the lands of the rich owners.

The Soviet of Workers' and Soldiers' Deputies represents other classes. The majority of workers and soldiers in the Soviet do not want any predatory wars, they are not interested in the profits of

the capitalists or in the preservation of the privileges of the landlords. Nevertheless, they still have faith in the Provisional Government, they want to enter into agreements with it, they wish to be in
contact with it.

The Soviets of Workers' and Soldiers' Deputies themselves are a
power in embryo. Parallel to the Provisional Government, the
Soviets endeavour in certain cases to assert their power. There is
thus an overlapping of power, or, as it is now called, "a crisis of
power."

This cannot keep on very long. Such a state of affairs is bound
to cause new "incidents" and fresh complications. It is easy enough
to inscribe on scraps of paper "the incident is closed." But in life
these incidents will reappear again. And for the very simple reason
that they are not "incidents" at all, not casual happenings, not
trifles. They are the external manifestation of a deep-rooted inner
crisis. They are the results of the perplexity in which humanity
now finds itself. There is no escape from the beastly war, unless
we follow the leadership of the Socialist-internationalists.

The Russian people are offered three ways of bringing an end to
this "crisis of power." Some say: Leave things as they are, place
even greater trust in the Provisional Government. It is possible
that the threat to resign is a trick calculated to make the Soviet
say: We are going to trust you even more. The Provisional Government wants to be implored: Come and rule over us; we shall feel
lost without you. . . .

Others propose a coalition cabinet. Let us share the ministerial
portfolios with Miliukov and Co., they say, let us get a few of our
own people into the cabinet; then the government will change its
tune.

We propose another way: A sweeping change in the policy of
the Soviet, a denial of confidence to the capitalists, a seizure of all
power by the *Soviets of Workers' and Soldiers' Deputies.* A change
of government *personnel* will lead to nothing; the whole *policy* of
government must be changed. Power must pass into the hands of
another class. A government of workers and soldiers would be
trusted by the whole world, for it is obvious that a worker and a
poor peasant would want to rob no one. Only this would put an
end to war, only this would help us live through the period of
economic ruin.

All power to the Soviets of Workers' and Soldiers' Deputies! No confidence in the government of the capitalists!

Every "incident," every day, every hour will confirm the soundness of our slogan.

Pravda, No. 46, May 15, 1917.

FINLAND AND RUSSIA

THE relation of Finland to Russia is the question of the hour. The Provisional Government has not been able to satisfy the Finnish people. The latter do not *as yet* demand separation, all they want is a wider autonomy.

Recently the *Rabochaia Gazeta* formulated and "defended" the undemocratic and annexationist policy of the Provisional Government. The defence was an unconscious condemnation of the defendant. The question is indeed fundamental, it is of importance to the state and deserves close scrutiny.

The Organisation Committee supposes, writes the *Rabochaia Gazeta* in No. 42, that the question of the mutual relations of Finland and the Russian state can be completely settled only by an agreement between the Finnish Diet and the Russian Constituent Assembly. Till then our Finnish comrades (the Organisation Committee was addressing the Finnish Social-Democrats) must remember that should the separation tendencies grow stronger in Finland, they might strengthen the centralist aspirations of the Russian bourgeoisie.

This is the point of view of the capitalists, the bourgeoisie, the Cadets, but under no circumstances that of the proletariat. The Mensheviks have thrown overboard the programme of the Social-Democratic Party, particularly the ninth paragraph,[185] which acknowledges the right of self-determination for all nations included in the composition of a state. The Mensheviks have actually renounced that programme, they have gone over to the side of the bourgeoisie in this question, as well as in the question of substituting for the standing army a general arming of the people.

The capitalists, the bourgeoisie, including the Cadet Party, have never recognised the principle of political self-determination of nations, *i. e.*, the freedom to separate from Russia.

The Social-Democratic Party, in the programme adopted in 1903, *recognises* this right in paragraph nine of the programme.

When the Organisation Committee "refers" the Finnish Social-Democrats to an "agreement" between the Finnish Diet and the Constituent Assembly, it is guilty of desertion to the bourgeoisie.

Fully to convince ourselves of this, all we need is to compare the attitude of *all* the principal classes and parties.

The Tsar, the Rights, the Monarchists, are against an agreement between the Diet and the Constituent Assembly, they want the subjection of Finland to the Russian people. The Republican bourgeoisie is for an *agreement* between the Finnish Diet and the Constituent Assembly. The class-conscious proletariat and the Social-Democrats, *true* to their programme, are for the freedom of Finland, as well as of other non-sovereign nationalities, to separate from Russia. Here we have an unambiguous, clear, and definite picture. Advancing the plan of an "agreement" that solves absolutely nothing—for what are they going to do if *no* agreement be reached?—the bourgeoisie is carrying on the same tsarist policy of subjection, the same tsarist policy of annexations.

For Finland was annexed by the Russian Tsars as a result of a deal with Napoleon, the strangler of the French Revolution. If we are really against annexations, we must come out openly for *Finland's freedom of separation!* After we have said it and practiced it, then, and only then, will "agreement" with Finland have become a truly voluntary, free, and actual agreement, and not a deception.

Only equals can agree. For an agreement to be real and not merely a verbal cover of subjection, it is essential that both parties be given the same rights and privileges, that is to say, both Russia and Finland should have the right not to agree. This is as clear as day.

Only by "freedom to separate" can that right be expressed: only a Finland that is free to separate is really capable of entering into agreements with Russia concerning separation or non-separation. Without such a condition, without the recognition of the right of free separation, all phrases about "agreements" are deceptions.

The Organisation Committee should have told the Finns frankly whether it does or does not recognise the right of separation. Cadet-like it evaded the issue, and thus renounced the principle. It should have attacked the Russian bourgeoisie for the latter's refusal to grant the oppressed nations the right of separation, such refusal being in fact equivalent to annexation. But, instead of doing that, the Organisation Committee attacked the Finns, warning them that "separation" ("separatist" would have been more correct) tendencies might strengthen the centralist aspirations of Russia!! In other words, the Organisation Committee threatens the

Finns with the strengthening of the annexationist Great-Russian bourgeoisie,—this is exactly what the Cadets have always done, it is precisely under such a banner that the Rodichevs and Co. are carrying out their annexationism.

Here is an obvious practical elucidation of the question of annexations, a question that people fear to raise though it is in everybody's mind. He who is against free separation is for annexations.

The Tsars were carrying out their policies of annexation rather crudely, exchanging one people for another by agreement with other monarchs (the partition of Poland, the deal with Napoleon concerning Finland, etc.), like serfowners exchanging their serfs. The bourgeoisie, on becoming republican, is carrying out the same annexationist policy, only more subtly, more covertly. It *promises* "agreement," but *withholds* the only real guarantee for actual equality of the parties entering into agreement, namely, the right of separation. The Organisation Committee is trailing after the bourgeoisie, and in reality takes sides with it. (The *Birzhevka* * was therefore quite right when it reprinted the salient points of the article published in the *Rabochaia Gazeta* and praised the Organisation Committee's answer to the Finns, calling that answer "the lesson" that the Russian democracy taught the Finns. The *Rabochaia Gazeta* has fully deserved this kiss bestowed upon it by the *Birzhevka*.)

The party of the proletariat (the Bolsheviks) has once more passed a resolution relating to national problems, wherein it has affirmed the right of separation.

The grouping of classes and parties is obvious.

The petty bourgeoisie allows itself to be frightened by the phantom of a frightened bourgeoisie,—herein is the gist of the whole policy of the Social-Democratic Mensheviks and the Socialists-Revolutionists. They "fear" separation. Class-conscious proletarians do *not* fear it. Both Norway and Sweden were the gainers after Norway freely separated from Sweden in 1905. The gain was in the increased mutual confidence of the two nations, in their closer voluntary rapprochement, in the disappearance of absurd and harmful friction between them, in the strengthening of economic, political, and cultural *attractions* of the two nations for each other,

* The popular name for the Petrograd newspaper *Birzhevye Viedomosti.—Ed.*

in the consolidation of the fraternal union between the workers of the two countries.

Comrades, workers and peasants! Do not be carried away by the annexationist policy of the Russian capitalists, Guchkov, Miliukov, and the Provisional Government, with regard to Finland, Courland, Ukraine, etc.! Do not fear to recognise the right of these nations to separation. It is not by violence that we should draw these people into a union with the Great-Russians, but by a truly voluntary, truly free agreement which is *impossible* without freedom of separation.

The greater the freedom in Russia, the more decidedly our republic recognises the right of non-Great-Russian nations to separate, the more powerfully will other nations be drawn into a union with us, the less friction will there be, the more rarely will actual separation occur, the shorter the period of separation of some nations from us, the closer, the more permanent—in the long run—the brotherly union of the workers' and peasants' republic of Russia with the republic of any other nation.

Pravda, No. 46, May 15, 1917.

DEFENCE OF IMPERIALISM DISGUISED BY NICE PHRASES

THIS is precisely what the appeal of the Executive Committee of the Petrograd Soviet of Workers' and Soldiers' Deputies to the Socialists of the world,[186] published in to-day's paper, is. Of words denouncing imperialism there is no end, but all these words are nullified by one little phrase which reads:

> The Provisional Government of revolutionary Russia has adopted this platform (*i. e.*, peace without annexations and indemnities on the basis of self-determination of nations).

This phrase contains the gist of the matter. And this phrase is a defence of *Russian* imperialism; it is its condonement and whitewashing. For, as a matter of fact, our Provisional Government has not only not "adopted" the platform of peace without annexations, but it is trampling upon it daily and hourly.

Our Provisional Government has "diplomatically" renounced the policy of annexations, just as the government of the German capitalists, the blackguards, Wilhelm and Bethmann-Hollweg, have renounced it. In words, *both* governments have renounced annexations. In deed, *both* of them adhere to the policy of annexations. The German government uses force in keeping Belgium, a part of France, Serbia, Montenegro, Poland, Danish provinces, Alsace, etc.; the Russian capitalist government keeps part of Galicia, Turkish Armenia, Finland, the Ukraine, etc. The English capitalist government is the most annexationist government in the world, for it forcibly retains the greatest number of nationalities as parts of the British empire: India (three hundred million), Ireland, Turkish Mesopotamia, the German colonies in Africa, etc.

The proclamation of the Executive Committee, covering with sweet words its lies about annexations, is most harmful to the cause of the proletariat and the revolution. First of all, the proclamation does not differentiate between renunciation of annexations in words (in this sense, all capitalist governments, without exception, have "adopted" the "platform of peace without annexations") and renunciation of annexations in deeds (in this sense not one capitalist

30

government in the world has abandoned the policy of annexations).
Secondly, the proclamation whitewashes—without any justification,
without any basis, contrary to truth—the Russian Provisional Government of the capitalists when, in point of fact, it is not a whit
better (and, probably, not worse) than other capitalistic governments.

To cover up an unpleasant truth with nice words is most harmful
and most dangerous to the cause of the proletarian struggle, to the
cause of the toiling masses. The truth, however bitter, must be
faced squarely. A policy not in conformity with this truth is a
ruinous policy.

The truth about annexations is this: *All* capitalist governments,
the Russian Provisional Government included, deceive the people
with *promises*—they renounce the policy of annexations in words,
they adhere to it *in deeds*. Any literate person can convince himself
of the truth of our contention, if he take the trouble to make a complete list of the annexations of, say, three countries: Germany,
Russia, and England.

Try to do it, gentlemen!

Whoever refuses to do it, whoever whitewashes his own government, while blackening the others, is actually turning into a defender
of imperialism.

In conclusion we should note that the end of the proclamation,
too, contains a "spoonful of tar," * namely, the assurance that
"whatever the disagreements that, in the course of three years of
war, have been rending Socialism asunder, no faction of the proletariat should decline to participate in the general struggle for peace."

These, too, we regret to say, are utterly empty and meaningless,
saccharine words. Plekhanov and Scheidemann both assert that they
are "fighting for peace," for "peace without annexations" to boot.
Can any one fail to see, however, that each of them is fighting to
defend his own imperialist, capitalist government? Of what benefit
to the cause of the working classes is sugar-coated untruth? Why
hide the fact that the Plekhanovs and the Scheidemanns have taken
the side of their respective capitalists? Is it not obvious that such
attenuation of facts is equivalent to embellishing imperialism and its
defenders?

Pravda, No. 47, May 16, 1917.

* A Russian adage says that one spoonful of tar would spoil a barrelful of
honey.—*Ed.*

A SORRY DOCUMENT

THE proclamation issued by the Petrograd Soviet of Workers' and Soldiers' Deputies to the army, and published in last night's papers,[187] signifies a new step of the Soviet leaders, Narodniks and Mensheviks, to the side of the Russian imperialist bourgeoisie.

The logical inconsistency of this proclamation is simply amazing. Only people whose minds are crammed with "revolutionary" phrases are capable of not noticing it.

> . . . The toiling masses did not need the war. They did not begin it. It was started by the Tsars and the capitalists of all the countries. . . .

Correct. That is just it. And when the proclamation "calls upon the workers and peasants of Germany, Austria, and Hungary to rebel, to revolt," we greet it whole-heartedly, for it is a sound slogan.

But how can one utter along with the above indubitable truth the following *flagrant untruth:*

> . . . You (Russian soldiers) are defending with your bodies not the Tsar, not the Protopopovs and the Rasputins, *not the rich landowners and capitalists.* . . .

The words we have italicised are an utter and flagrant untruth.

If the toiling masses "did not need" the war, if the war was started *not only* by the Tsars, but also, by "the capitalists of *all* the countries" (as was recognised very definitely in the proclamation issued by the Soviets), then, obviously, any people which, while engaged in this war, tolerates a government of capitalists, is *actually* "defending" the capitalists.

One or the other: *either* the Austrian and German capitalists alone are "responsible" for this war; if the Narodnik and Menshevik leaders of the Petrograd Soviet think so, they sink to the level of Plekhanov, the Russian Scheidemann—then we should eliminate, as untrue, the words which declare that "the capitalists of all the countries" have "started" the war; in that case we should throw overboard, as untrue, the slogan "peace without annexations," for the appropriate slogan for the true policy would be: take away from

32

the Germans the German annexations; preserve and multiply the English and Russian annexations. *Or* this war was actually started by "the capitalists of all the countries," then, if the Narodnik and Menshevik leaders of the Soviet do not deny this unquestionable truth, the revolting lie that the Russian soldiers, while tolerating their capitalist government, are *not* defending the capitalists, cannot be tolerated—then the Russian soldiers too (not only the Austrian and the German) should be told the truth: Comrades, soldiers, one must say to them, while you and we tolerate respectively our capitalist governments, while the secret treaties of the Tsar are regarded as sacred, we are carrying on an imperialist war for acquisitions, we are *defending* predatory treaties concluded by ex-Tsar Nicholas with the Anglo-French capitalists.

That is the bitter truth. But it is the truth. The people should be told the truth. Only thus can the people's eyes be opened; only thus can the people learn to struggle against untruth.

Look at this matter from another angle, and you will convince yourselves once more of the utter untruthfulness of the Soviet proclamation. It calls upon the German workers and peasants to "revolt." Very well. But to revolt against whom? Is it only against Wilhelm?

Imagine that Wilhelm is displaced by the German Guchkovs and Miliukovs, *i. e.*, by the representatives of the German capitalist class, would this change the predatory character of the war in so far as Germany is concerned? Clearly, not. Every one knows,—and the Soviet proclamation admits it,—that the war was "started by the Tsars and the capitalists of all the countries." It follows that the overthrow of Tsars, when power passes into the hands of the capitalists, does not affect the nature of the war in the least. The annexation of Belgium, Serbia, etc., will not cease being annexation because the German Cadets have taken the place of Wilhelm, just as the annexations of Khiva, Bokhara, Armenia, Finland, the Ukraine, etc., remain annexations despite the fact that the Russian Cadets, the Russian capitalists, have taken the place of Nicholas.

One more hypothesis: suppose that the Soviet proclamation calls upon the German workers and peasants to revolt not only against Wilhelm but also against the German capitalists. We should then say that the appeal is correct and sound. We sympathise with it. But then we should ask the esteemed fellow citizens, Chernov, Chkheidze, Tsereteli: is it just, is it rational, is it decent to call upon the Germans to rise against their capitalists, while *you your-selves are supporting the capitalist government here?*

Are you not at all apprehensive, honourable fellow citizens, that the German workers may accuse you of prevarication and even (God forbid) of hypocrisy?

Are you not at all afraid that the German workers may turn around and say to you: Our revolution has not yet broken out, we have not as yet reached the point where our Soviets of Workers' and Soldiers' Deputies can openly negotiate with the capitalists in the matter of power. If you, our Russian brothers, have already come to such a point, then why do you preach to us "revolt" (a thing difficult, burdensome, and bloody), while you yourselves refrain from taking over by peaceful means the power from Lvov and Co., who have expressed their willingness to relinquish it? You refer us to the Russian Revolution, but, Citizens Chernov, Chkheidze, and Tsereteli, you have all studied Socialism, and you surely realise that *so far* your revolution has given power only to the *capitalists.* Is it not trebly insincere, when, in the name of the Russian Revolution that has given power to the Russian capitalists-imperialists, you call upon us, Germans, to revolt against the German capitalists-imperialists? Does it not look as if your "internationalism," your "revolutionism" were for foreign consumption only; that for the German, they mean *revolution* against the capitalists, while for the Russian (despite the seething revolution in Russia) they mean *agreement* with the capitalists?

Chernov, Chkheidze, and Tsereteli have sunk to the level of defending Russian imperialism.

It is sad, but true.

Pravda, No. 47, May 16, 1917.

BOURGEOIS BUGABOOS TO SCARE THE PEOPLE

THE capitalist newspapers with the *Riech* at the head do their utmost to frighten the people with the phantom of "anarchy." Not a day passes without the *Riech* raising a howl about anarchy, without its spreading exaggerated rumours and reports concerning individual, absolutely insignificant cases of disorder, without its scaring the people with phantoms born in the minds of a panic-stricken bourgeoisie.

The *Riech* and the other capitalist papers are followed by the papers published by the Narodniks (the Socialists-Revolutionists among them) and the Mensheviks. They, too, have become frightened. The leading article in to-day's *Izvestia* shows that the leaders of the Petrograd Soviet of Workers' and Soldiers' Deputies, all of whom are members of the above-mentioned parties, have definitely taken sides with the disseminators of "bourgeois bugaboos." They have even been carried away into making the following—I am trying to find a less harsh expression—obviously exaggerated statement:

> The army is disintegrating. In certain localities there are disorderly seizures of land, and destruction and plunder of live stock and other farm property. Mob rule is rampant.

By mob rule the Narodniks and the Mensheviks, the parties of the petty bourgeoisie, mean, among other things, that the peasants in various localities are seizing the entire land without waiting for the Constituent Assembly. Mob rule is what Minister Shingarev once called it in his famous, widely published telegram. (See *Pravda*, No. 33.*)

Mob rule, anarchy,—what terrifying words! However, let the Narodnik or the Menshevik with an inclination to think reflect for a minute over the following question:

Up to the Revolution the land belonged to the landlords. That was *not* called anarchy. And what has that led to? To destruction all along the line, to "anarchy" in the fullest sense of the word, to

* See p. 192, Book I of this volume.—*Ed.*
35

the devastation of the land, to the ruin of the majority of the population.

Is there any other escape, except the widest application or energy, initiative, and determination by the majority of the population? There is obviously none.

What, then, is the conclusion?

1. The Tsar's partisans stand for the absolute reign of the landowners in the village, and for their continued hold on the land. They are not afraid of the actual "anarchy" that has resulted from such a state of affairs.

2. The Cadet Shingarev, representing the capitalists and the landowners (with the exception of a small group of tsarists), advocates "agricultural chambers of conciliation for the purpose of effecting voluntary agreements between the agricultural workers and the landowners" as "adjuncts of the volost supply committees" (see his telegram). The petty-bourgeois politicians, the Narodniks and Mensheviks, follow in Shingarev's footsteps; they urge the peasant "to wait" for the Constituent Assembly; they denounce the immediate confiscation of the land by the peasant as "anarchy."

3. The party of the proletariat (Bolsheviks) stands for the immediate seizure of the land by the peasants of each locality, the seizure to be carried out in the best organised manner. We fail to see "anarchy" in a decision arrived at and carried out by the *majority* of the population in each locality.

Since when has the decision of the majority come to be called "anarchy"? Would it not be more appropriate to bestow this name upon a decision arrived at by a *minority*, a decision such as suggested in various forms by the tsarists as well as by the Shingarevs?

For when Shingarev wants to force the peasants "voluntarily" to come to agreements with the landowners, does he not propose a decision in accordance with the wishes of the minority, since there are about three hundred peasant families for every one family of the rich landowners. When we tell three hundred families "voluntarily" to "agree" with *one* family of a rich exploiter, we are actually deciding in favour of the minority, we are making an anarchist decision.

You, Messrs. Capitalists, by shouting "Anarchy" are protecting the interests of one against the interests of three hundred. This is the crux of the matter.

Some may object, saying: You wish the whole thing to be settled by the people in separate localities, without waiting for the Constituent Assembly! And that is what we mean by anarchy!

Our reply is: How about Shingarev, what does he want? Is not what he advocates also a settlement by the people ("voluntary agreements" between the peasants and the landlords), without waiting for the Constituent Assembly?

On this point there is no disagreement between us and Shingarev. We both stand for a final settlement by the Constituent Assembly and for a preliminary settlement—and realisation of the settlement in practice—by local people. The difference between us and Shingarev is the following: We say, three hundred people shall decide and one person shall submit; while Shingarev says, if three hundred people decide, that would be mob rule; let therefore the three hundred "agree" with the one.

How low the Narodniks and Mensheviks must have fallen to help Shingarev and Co. disseminate bourgeois bugaboos.

It is fear of the people that guides these alarmists.

There is no reason to fear the people. The decision of the majority of workers and soldiers is not anarchy. Such a decision is the only possible assurance of democracy and of a successful escape from economic disintegration.

Pravda, No. 48, May 17, 1917.

ON THE EVE

THE "coalition" machine is working at full speed. The Narodniks and the Mensheviks are labouring in the sweat of their brows over the selection of a new cabinet. We are on the eve of a "new" cabinet. . . .

Alas! There will be very little new in it. To the government of the capitalists there will be added a handful of petty-bourgeois Ministers, Narodniks and Mensheviks, who have allowed themselves to be lured into the support of the imperialist war.

Now we shall have more glittering phrases, more fireworks, magnificent promises, and oral tinsel work about "peace without annexations"—and a complete absence of firmness even in such a small matter as presenting a precise, direct, and honest list of *actual* annexations effected, say, by three countries: Germany, Russia, England.

To deceive oneself with the utopia that the peasants will support the capitalists (prosperous peasants are not the whole of the peasantry . . .), with the utopia of an "offensive" at the front (in the name of "peace without annexations" . . .)—how long will it last, gentlemen of the old and the new cabinet?

Pravda, No. 49, May 18, 1917.

FORGETTING THE MAIN THING

MUNICIPAL PLATFORM OF THE PARTY OF THE PROLETARIAT

ELECTIONS to borough councils being close at hand, the two petty-bourgeois democratic parties, the Narodniks and the Mensheviks, have issued high-sounding platforms. These platforms are of precisely the same nature as are the platforms of the European bourgeois parties that are forever busy luring the gullible uneducated mass of petty-bourgeois electors, as for instance, the "Radical" and the "Radical-Socialist" parties of France. The same high-sounding phrases, the same gorgeous promises, the same vague formulation, the same silence on or forgetfulness of the main thing, namely, a discussion of the objective circumstances under which those promises are realisable.

At the present moment the actual conditions are as follows: 1. The imperialist war. 2. The existence of a capitalist government. 3. The impossibility of taking serious measures leading to an improvement in the life of the workers and the toiling masses without revolutionary encroachment on the "sacred rights of capitalist private property." 4. The impossibility of carrying into life the reforms promised by these parties while the old organs and apparatus of administration remain, while there is in existence the police which cannot but aid and abet the capitalists, which cannot but place a thousand and one obstacles in the way of such reforms.

For example, the Mensheviks write: "To regulate rents during the war period on habitable buildings" . . . "the requisition of such supplies" (that is, supplies of necessities in commercial houses or in the hands of private individuals) "to meet the needs of the community," . . . "organise communal stores, bakeries, restaurants, and kitchens." And the Narodniks (the Socialists-Revolutionists) echo: "To pay proper attention to sanitation and hygiene."

Excellent wishes, to be sure, but the trouble is that to realise them one must first of all stop supporting the imperialist war, stop supporting the Loan (which is profitable to the capitalists), stop supporting the capitalist government which safeguards capitalist profits, remove the police which otherwise is sure to impede, thwart, and kill any such reform, even if the government and the capitalists themselves fail to take a firm stand against the reformers (and they certainly will do so as soon as capitalist profits are involved).

The trouble is that once we forget the crude and cruel conditions of capitalist domination, then all such platforms, all such outlines of high-sounding reforms are nothing but empty words which in practice turn out to be either harmless "pious wishes," or simple deception of the masses by shrewd bourgeois politicians.

We must look the truth squarely in the face. We must not attenuate it, we must tell it to people in a straightforward manner. We must not conceal the class struggle, but rather explain its relation to the beautifully sounding, plausible-appearing, delightful "radical" reforms.

Comrades, workers, and all citizens of Petrograd! In order to put into life all those necessary, ripe, and pressing reforms of which the Narodniks and the Mensheviks speak, one must refuse to support the imperialist war, the loans, the capitalist government, the principle of the inviolability of capitalist profits. To realise those reforms, one must not allow the police to be re-established, which is being done by the Cadets; on the contrary, one must replace it by a universal militia. This is what the party of the proletariat should tell the people at elections, this is what it must say *against* the petty-bourgeois parties of the Narodniks and the Mensheviks. This is the essence of the proletarian municipal platform that is being glossed over by the petty-bourgeois parties.

Foremost in this platform, preceding the enumeration of reforms, there must be, as a basic condition for their actual realisation, the following three fundamental points:

1. No support whatever to be given to the imperialist war (either in the form of a loan, or generally in any other form whatsoever).

2. No support whatever to the capitalist government.

3. The police must not be re-established. A universal militia should take its place.

Unless attention is fixed on these basic demands, unless it is shown that the municipal reforms are contingent upon them,—the municipal program inevitably becomes (at best) an innocent wish.

Let us examine the third point.

In all bourgeois republics, even the most democratic, the police (like the standing army) is the chief instrument for the oppression of the masses, and for the restoration of monarchy, which is always possible. The police beats the common people in the police stations of New York, Geneva, and Paris, and favours the capitalists either because it is bribed to do so (America and other countries), or because it gains promotion through "pulls" and "backings" (Switzerland), or because of a combination of both (France). Being detached from the people, forming a professional caste, made up of persons accustomed to practice violence upon the poor, of persons receiving somewhat higher wages and the privileges that go with authority (to say nothing of "side" incomes), the police in any democratic republic inevitably remains, while the bourgeoisie is in power, the bourgeoisie's most unfailing weapon, its chief support and protection. While the police is in existence it is impossible, objectively impossible, to carry out any serious and fundamental reforms for the benefit of the toiling masses.

Universal militia, instead of a police force and a standing army, is the first prerequisite for successful municipal reforms in the interests of the toilers. In revolutionary times this prerequisite can be realised. And it is on this that we must concentrate the whole municipal platform, for the other two fundamental points deal with the state as a whole, not only with municipal governments.

Just how this universal militia can be brought into existence is something which experience will show. To enable the proletarians and the semi-proletarians to serve in this militia, it is necessary to force the employers to pay them their full wages for the days and hours they spend in service. This can be done. Whether we should *first* organise a workingmen's militia by drawing upon the workers from the largest factories, *i. e.*, the workers that are best organised and most capable of fulfilling the task of militiamen, or whether we should *immediately* organise a general compulsory service of all adult men and women, who would devote to this service one or two weeks a year, is a question of no fundamental importance. It would not matter if various boroughs adopted different procedures—in fact that would enrich our experience, we would learn more, we would come closer to life.

A universal militia would mean a real education of the masses in the practices of democracy.

A universal militia would mean that the poor are governed, not through the rich, not through their police, but by the people themselves, predominantly by the poor.

A universal militia would mean that control (over factories, dwellings, the distribution of products, etc.) would be real and not only on paper.

A universal militia would mean that the distribution of bread would be without bread lines, with no privileges for the rich.

A universal militia would mean that the series of earnest and radical reforms enumerated by the Narodniks and the Mensheviks would not remain mere pious wishes.

Comrades, workers of Petrograd! Go to the elections of the borough councils. Stand up for the rights of the poor population. Oppose the imperialist war, oppose the capitalist government, oppose the restoration of the police, demand that the police be replaced by a universal militia.

Pravda, No. 49, May 18, 1917.

INSTRUCTIONS TO THE DEPUTIES ELECTED TO THE SOVIET OF WORKERS' AND SOLDIERS' DEPUTIES FROM FACTORIES AND REGIMENTS [188]

OUR Deputy must be unconditionally opposed to the present predatory, imperialist war. This war is waged by the capitalists of all countries, of Russia, Germany, England, etc., for profits, and in order to stifle the weak peoples.

While a capitalist government is at the head of the Russian people —there must be no support of the government that is carrying on a predatory war, not even one kopeck!

Our Deputy must stand for the immediate publication of the secret predatory treaties (relating to the stifling of Persia, the partition of Turkey, Austria, etc.), which were concluded by former Tsar Nicholas with England, France, etc.

Our Deputy must stand for the immediate abrogation of all these treaties. The Russian people, the workers and the peasants, do not wish to oppress and will not oppress any people; they do not wish to and will not hold by force within the boundaries of Russia a single non-Russian (non-Great-Russian) people. Freedom for all the peoples, a brotherly union of the workers and peasants of all nationalities!

Our Deputy must stand for the Russian Government's proposing openly, immediately and unconditionally, without equivocation and without the least delay, conditions of peace to all the warring countries on the basis of freedom for all the oppressed and non-sovereign nationalities without any exception.

This means that the Great-Russians shall not forcibly retain either Poland, or Courland, or the Ukraine, or Finland, or Armenia, or any other people. The Great-Russians propose a brotherly union to all the peoples, they propose to form a common state on the basis of the voluntary consent of each individual people, and under no circumstances on the basis of violence, direct or indirect. The Great-Russians obligate themselves by the terms of such a peace immediately to withdraw their armies from Galicia, Armenia, Persia, leaving it to the peoples of those countries, as well as to

43

all other peoples without exception, freely to determine whether they wish to live as a separate state, or in union with whomsoever they please.

Germany, by the terms of such a peace, must relinquish not only all the territories she has occupied since the beginning of the war, all without exception, but she must also release the peoples forcefully held within the German boundaries: the Danes (Schleswig), the French (part of Alsace and Lorraine), the Poles (Posen), etc. Germany must agree immediately, and simultaneously with Russia, to withdraw her armies from all the regions that she has seized, as well as from all the regions enumerated above, and must leave it to each people to determine freely, by universal voting, whether it wishes to live as a separate state, or in union with whomsoever it pleases. Germany must unconditionally and unequivocally renounce all her colonies, for colonies are oppressed peoples.

England, by the terms of such a peace, must renounce, immediately and unconditionally, not only the lands that she has seized from others (the German colonies in Africa, etc., the Turkish lands, Mesopotamia, etc.), but also all her own colonies. England, like Russia and Germany, must immediately withdraw her armies from all the lands she has occupied, from her colonies, and also from Ireland, leaving it to each people to determine by a free vote whether it wants to live as a separate state, or in union with whomsoever it wishes.

And so on: all the belligerent countries, without exception, must be offered immediate peace on the same clearly defined terms. The capitalists of the world should no more deceive the peoples by promising, in words, "peace without annexations" (*i. e.*, without seizures of territory), while holding on to their own annexed territories and continuing the war in order to take away from the enemy its annexed territories.

Our Deputy must not give any support, or vote for any loan, or give a kopeck of the people's money, to any government, unless it solemnly agrees immediately to offer to all the peoples its terms for an immediate peace, and to publish its offer within two days so that everybody may know it.

Written May 18-19, 1917.
First published in the *Lenin Collection*, Vol. IV, 1925.

CLASS COLLABORATION WITH CAPITAL, OR CLASS STRUGGLE AGAINST IT?

It is thus that the question is put by history, not history in general, but the present economic and political history of Russia.

The Narodniks and the Mensheviks, Chernov and Tsereteli, have moved the Contact Commission from the adjacent room (a room next to the one where the Ministers met) into the ministerial chamber proper. This and only this is the purely political significance of the advent of the "new" cabinet.

Its economic and class significance is this: When everything goes well (for the stability of the cabinet and the preservation of capitalist domination) the upper strata of the peasant bourgeoisie, headed by Peshekhonov since 1906, and the petty-bourgeois "leaders" of the Menshevik workers, may offer the capitalists their class collaboration. (When things go wrong for the capitalists, the whole change may have a purely personal or clique significance, without any class meaning at all.)

Let us suppose that everything goes well. Even so there is not the shadow of a doubt that those who have promised will not be able to carry out their promises. "We shall help—in league with the capitalists—to bring the country out of its crisis, to save it from ruin, to rid it of war"—this is what the entrance into the ministry of the leaders of the petty bourgeoisie, the Chernovs and Tseretelis, actually means. Our answer is: Your help is not sufficient. The crisis has advanced infinitely farther than you imagine. Only the revolutionary class, by taking revolutionary measures against capital, can save the country—and not our country alone.

The crisis is so deep, so widely ramified, so world-wide in its scope, so closely bound up with capital, that class struggle against capital must inevitably take the form of political domination by the proletariat and semi-proletariat. There is no other escape.

You wish to see revolutionary enthusiasm in the army, Citizens Chernov and Tsereteli? But you can not arouse it, because the revolutionary enthusiasm of the masses does not spring from the change of "leaders" in Cabinets, from high-sounding words and

45

declarations, from promises to take steps toward the revision of our treaties with English capitalists—it springs from facts of a revolutionary policy visible to every one, undertaken every hour everywhere *against* the omnipotence of capital, against capitalists' war profits, and *for* a radical betterment of the living conditions of the impoverished masses.

Even if you should forthwith give the land to the people, it would not make it possible to end the crisis without resorting to revolutionary measures against capital.

Do you wish an offensive, Citizens Chernov and Tsereteli? You cannot inveigle the army into an offensive, for at present the people cannot be forced. Unless force is used against the people, the army would undertake an offensive only for the great interests of the great revolution against world capital, and then it would have to be not merely a promised or announced revolution, but a revolution, actually in the process of realisation, a revolution carried into life in a manner obvious to and felt by all.

Do you wish the organisation of supply deliveries, Citizens Peshekhonovs and Skobelevs? Do you wish to supply the peasants with manufactured goods, the army with bread and meat, the industry with raw material, etc.? Do you wish control over, and even partial organisation of production?

You cannot accomplish all this without the revolutionary enthusiasm of the proletarians and semi-proletarians. Such enthusiasm can be awakened only by revolutionary measures against the privileges and profits of capital. Without such measures your promised control remains a dead bureaucratic-capitalist half-measure.

The experiment of class collaboration with capital is now being undertaken by Chernov and Tsereteli, by certain strata of the petty bourgeoisie, on a new, gigantic, all-Russian, national scale.

These lessons will prove all the more useful to the people, when the people become convinced of the futility and hopelessness of such collaborations—and this will, obviously, happen very soon.

Pravda, No. 50, May 19, 1917

FIRM REVOLUTIONARY POWER

WE stand for firm revolutionary power. Regardless of what the capitalists and their satellites may try to shout about us, their lies remain lies.

It is very essential not to let phrases obscure the mind and dim the consciousness. When one speaks of "revolution," of the "revolutionary people," of "revolutionary democracy," etc., nine times out of ten it is a lie and self-deception. One should ask oneself, who is carrying on this revolution? *What class?* A revolution *against whom?*

Is it against tsarism? In that case the majority of landowners and capitalists in Russia are revolutionists now. When a revolution is accomplished, even reactionaries acquiesce in its conquests. There is no more frequent, more contemptible, and more harmful deception of the masses at the present time than the deception practiced by praising the revolution against tsarism.

Is it against the landowners? In that case the majority of peasants, even the well-to-do peasants, *i. e.*, at least nine-tenths of the population of Russia, are revolutionists. Nay, even a certain section of the capitalists is ready to become revolutionary, on the ground that the landowners are beyond salvation under any conditions, and that if they, the capitalists, side with the revolution, they may have a chance to save the inviolability of capital.

Is it against the capitalists? This really is the main question. This is the crux of the matter, for, without a revolution against the capitalists, the prattle about "peace without annexations" and about a speedy termination of the war by such a peace is either naïveté and ignorance, or stupidity and deception. Had it not been for the war, Russia could have existed for years and even for decades without a revolution against the capitalists. With the war, it is a question of either ruin, or a revolution against the capitalists. Thus the question stands. Thus is it propounded by life itself.

Instinctively, emotionally, temperamentally, the majority of Russia's population, the proletarians and semi-proletarians, *i. e.*, the workers and the poorest peasants, are in sympathy with a revolution against the capitalists. But so far there is no clear idea with regard to that, no determination. To develop these is our task.

The leaders of the petty bourgeoisie—the intelligentsia, the well-to-do members of the peasantry, the present parties of the Narodniks (the Socialists-Revolutionists among them) and the Mensheviks, —are at present opposed to a revolution against the capitalists, and their opposition is at times most harmful to the people. The coalition cabinet is the kind of "experiment" that is going to help the entire people rapidly to overcome the illusions concerning a petty-bourgeois agreement with the capitalists.

The conclusion is obvious: Only the assumption of power by the proletariat, supported by the semi-proletarians, can give the country a really firm, a truly revolutionary power. It will be really firm, for it will be backed by a vast and class-conscious majority of the people. It will be firm, because it will not be based upon a shaky "agreement" of the capitalists with the little proprietors, the millionaires with the petty bourgeoisie, the Konovalovs and Shingarevs with the Chernovs and Tseretelis.

It will be a truly revolutionary power for it alone is capable of demonstrating to the people that in times of the greatest suffering inflicted upon the masses, the government does not stop in trepidation before capitalist profits. It will be a truly revolutionary power, for it alone can generate, encourage, enhance the revolutionary enthusiasm of the masses. The latter will see, actually feel, experience every day, every minute of the day, that the government trusts the people, does not fear the people, helps the poor to improve their lot right now, compels the rich to carry an equitable portion of the heavy burden of popular suffering.

We stand for a firm revolutionary power.

We stand for the only possible and the only reliable revolutionary power.

Pravda, No. 50, May 19, 1917.

SWEETMEATS TO THE NEWLY BORN, THE "NEW" GOVERNMENT

THE *Riech* in a very "serious" editorial says:

> Let us hope that no great convulsions in our relations with the Allies will be needed to prove to the adherents of the formula "without annexations and indemnities" (read: the new government) its inapplicability in practice.

And right they are, too, the capitalists who speak through the *Riech*. This formula is really "inapplicable in practice" . . . unless a revolution against capital actually occurs.

From a speech by Miliukov, who did not go himself but was made to go:

> No matter what beautiful declarations we write with regard to our friendship for the Allies, once our army remains inactive, we will actually be guilty of repudiating our obligations. And, conversely, no matter what terrible declarations we may write emphasising our disloyalty, once our army is actually fighting, then that, of course, will be actual fulfillment of our obligations with regard to the Allies. . . .

Correct! Citizen Miliukov does at times understand the essence of things. Citizens Chernov and Tsereteli, is it possible that you do not understand what follows from the above as regards your *actual* attitude toward the imperialist war?

From a speech by Shulgin delivered at a conference of the counter-revolution that is organising its forces: [189]

> We prefer to be paupers, but paupers in our own land. If only you can save our country, and preserve it, then take away our last shirts, we shall not shed a tear.

You will not frighten us, Mr. Shulgin. Even when we are in power, we shall not take away your "last shirt," we shall guarantee you good clothes and good food, on the one condition that you work, in a capacity for which you are fit and to which you are

49

used! You can frighten the Chernovs and the Tseretelis—you cannot scare us.

From a speech by Maklakov at the same conference ("of the members of the Imperial Duma"):

Russia has proven unworthy of the freedom she has won.

Read: the workers and the peasants do not satisfy the Maklakovs. These gentlemen wish that the Chernovs and the Tseretelis "reconcile" the masses with the Maklakovs. It won't work!

From the same speech:

There are many who deserve to be reproached, but we cannot get on in Russia unless we have both the bourgeoisie and the proletariat, a multiplicity of factions and individual leaders.

We beg pardon, Citizen Maklakov, but "we" (the party of the proletariat) "can get on in Russia" "without the bourgeoisie." If you live long enough you will acknowledge that yourself, you will recognise that there was no other escape from the imperialist war.

From the same speech:

We see a great many evil instincts brought to the surface: we see reluctance to work, reluctance to realise one's duty to one's country. We see that in a time of fierce war Russia has become a country of festivities, meetings, and talk,—a country that rejects all governmental power and refuses to submit to it.

Correct! A great many "evil instincts," particularly on the part of the landowners and the capitalists. The petty bourgeoisie has evil instincts too—for instance, the instinct to enter into a coalition ministry with the capitalists. Evil instincts are also exhibited by the proletarians and the semi-proletarians—for instance, the slow emancipation from petty-bourgeois illusions, the slow ripening of the conviction that "power" must be completely taken over by themselves.

From the same speech:

Power will gravitate more and more toward the Left while the country advances more and more toward the Right.

By the "country," Maklakov means the capitalists. In this sense he is right. But the "country" of the workers and the poor peasants, I assure you, citizen, is a thousand times more to the Left than the Chernovs and Tseretelis, and about a hundred times more to the Left than ourselves. If you live long enough you will see.

Pravda, No. 50, May 19, 1917.

THE "NEW" GOVERNMENT IS LAGGING NOT ONLY BEHIND THE REVOLUTIONARY PROLETARIAT, BUT ALSO BEHIND THE PEASANT MASSES

HERE is the evidence:

The evening edition of the *Russkaia Volia* (The Will of Russia!) of May 17, has the following communication concerning the state of mind of the delegates of the Peasant Congress now in session:

> The chief complaint of the delegates, over a grievance alleged to be felt by the peasants, is that all classes are already gathering the fruits of the revolution while the peasants alone are still waiting for their share. Only the peasants, they complain, are told to wait for the convocation of the Constituent Assembly which will settle the land question.
>
> "No, that shall not be," they say, "we refuse to wait, just as others have refused to wait. We want land directly, immediately."

There is no doubt that the reporter of the *Russkaia Volia*, a paper serving the worst capitalists, does not slander the peasants in this case (for in this case there is nothing to be gained by lying), but tells the truth, warns the capitalists. This truth is being confirmed by all the news coming from the Congress.

Compare this truth with paragraph five in the draft of the declaration of the "new" government:

> Leaving it to the Constituent Assembly to settle the question of transferring the land to the toilers, the Provisional Government will take . . . measures, etc. (the "old" Provisional Government also kept on "taking measures" . . .).

The "new" government is hopelessly behind even the Peasant Congress!!

A fact not anticipated by many, but a fact.

And facts are stubborn things, as the saying goes.

Pravda, No. 50, May 19, 1917.

TRYING TO FORESTALL

YESTERDAY, May 18, two large morning papers, the *Volia Naroda* and the *Riech,* published an announcement on their front pages which deserves serious attention. The same announcement was reprinted in the Guchkov-Suvorin evening paper, the *Vecherneie Vremia.*[190]

The announcement informs the public that in Petrograd there has been organised, "in accordance with an agreement arrived at by the Soviet of Workers' and Soldiers' Deputies and the Union of Engineers, as authorised by the Provisional Government," a "Central Committee for the purpose of reviving and keeping up the normal progress of work in industrial enterprises."

The Central Committee, the announcement reads, regards as its main tasks the development and co-ordination of all measures relating to the revival and maintenance of the normal progress of work in industrial enterprises and the organisation of a steady and active *social control* over all industrial enterprises.

The words "social control" were italicised in the announcement.

They remind one of the Senate and other bureaucratic committees of the "good old" tsarist times. No sooner would some scoundrel from among the Tsar's Ministers, governors, leaders of the nobility, etc., be caught red-handed at some thievery, no sooner would some institution directly or indirectly connected with the Tsar's government conspicuously disgrace itself throughout Russia or throughout the whole of Europe, than a committee of notables and most highly placed officials of rich and most affluent "personages" would be appointed to "take charge" and thus "allay popular apprehension."

And those personages usually managed to "allay" popular apprehension most successfully. The more high-sounding the phrases used by "our wise Tsar" as regards the allaying of "popular apprehension," the more certain was the death of the "social control" principle at the hands of the committee.

So it was, so it will be, one feels like saying as one reads the bombastic announcement about the new Central Committee.

The capitalists are trying to forestall things. There is growing among the workers the consciousness of the necessity of *proletarian* control over factories and syndicates. The "great" leaders of the business world, now in ministerial and near-ministerial circles, have been struck with a "great" idea: to forestall this tendency, to take the Soviet of Workers' and Soldiers' Deputies in tow. This ought not to be difficult to accomplish, they thought, as long as the Soviet was still headed by the Narodniks and the Mensheviks. Let us get up a "social control," they said to themselves. It will look so important, so wisely statesmanlike, so ministerial, so appropriate . . . it will destroy all possible actual control, all *proletarian* control so surely, so quietly. . . . A great idea! Complete "allaying" of the "popular conscience"!

How, then, should the new Central Committee be composed?

Well, of course, on democratic lines. Are we not *all* "revolutionary democrats"? If any one presumed that democracy implies proportional representation, that 200,000 workers are entitled to 20 representatives and 10,000 engineers, capitalists, etc., to one representative, he would be guilty of "anarchist" delusions. No, real democracy means to imitate the manner in which "revolutionary democracy" has made up its "new" government: the workers and peasants are "represented" by six Mensheviks and Narodniks while eight Cadets and Octobrists represent the landowners and the capitalists. Indeed, do not the latest statistical researches, conducted by the new Ministry of Labour in conjunction with the old Ministry of Industry prove that the majority of the population in Russia belongs to the class of landowners and capitalists?

Here, look at this *complete* list of "representatives" of the organisations that have united in the new Central Committee in consequence of the agreement between "revolutionary democracy" and the government.

The Central Committee is composed of representatives from the following organisations: 1. The Executive Committee of the Soviet of Workers' and Soldiers' Deputies. 2. The Provisional Committee of the Imperial Duma. 3. The All-Russian Union of Zemstvos.[191] 4. The All-Russian Union of Cities. 5. The Petrograd Municipal Administration. 6. The Union of Engineers. 7. The Soviet of Officers' Deputies. 8. The Council of Congresses of Representatives of Industry and Commerce. 9. The Petrograd Society of Shop and Factory Owners. 10. The Central War Industries Committee.[192]

11. The Committee of Zemstvos and Cities. 12. The Committee of Technical War Aid. 13. The Free-Economic Society.[198] . . .

Is this all?

Yes, all.

Is it not quite ample for the pacification of the popular conscience?

What matter if the same large bank, the same syndicate of capitalists is represented five or ten times, through its shareholders, in these ten or twelve institutions?

Why quibble about "details," when the main objective is to secure "a steady and active *social control*"!

Pravda, No. 51, May 20, 1917.

OPEN LETTER TO THE DELEGATES OF THE ALL-RUSSIAN SOVIET OF PEASANT DEPUTIES [194]

COMRADES, peasant deputies!

The Central Committee of the Russian Social-Democratic Labour Party (Bolsheviks), to which I have the honour to belong, wished to give me authority to represent our party at the Peasant Congress. As, until now, illness has prevented me from fulfilling this commission, I take the liberty of addressing this open letter to you, in order to greet the All-Russian Union of the Peasantry and briefly to point out the far-reaching differences of opinion which separate our party from those of the "Socialists-Revolutionists" and the "Mensheviks."

These far-reaching differences of opinion concern three highly important questions, those of the land, the war, and the structure of the state.

The whole land must belong to the people. All landed property must be handed over to the peasants without any compensation. This is clear. The question in dispute is: Shall the peasants in each locality take possession of the land at once, without paying rent to the landowners and without waiting until the Constituent Assembly is called, or shall they not?

Our party holds to the point of view that the peasants should adopt the former plan, and recommends the peasants settled in a locality to take possession of the land at once, to carry out these measures as systematically as possible, permitting in no circumstances any destruction of property, and using every effort to increase the production of grain and meat, for our soldiers at the front are suffering terribly from hunger. The Constituent Assembly will work out the final laws with regard to the soil. Preliminary regulations must, however, be made by the local institutions at once, before the spring sowing; for our Provisional Government, the government of the landowners and capitalists, is postponing calling the Constituent Assembly and has not yet announced the date for which it will be summoned.

The provisional land measures can be taken only by the local institutions. The cultivation of the fields is absolutely essential. The majority of the resident peasants will know how best to administer and work the soil systematically. This is necessary in order to improve the provisioning of the soldiers at the front. For this reason it is out of the question to wait until the Constituent Assembly is called. We do not in any way dispute the right of the Constituent Assembly to determine in detail the final laws regarding the handing over of the land to the whole people and the forms of its administration. For the time being, however, now, this spring, the peasants on the spot must themselves take the initiative. The soldiers at the front can and must send delegates to the villages.

Further, a close alliance between the urban proletariat and the poorest peasants (semi-proletarians) is necessary if the whole land is to be placed in the hands of the toilers. Without such an alliance it is impossible to defeat the capitalists, and unless they are defeated the transfer of the land into the hands of the people will not save the people from distress. The soil cannot be eaten, and it is impossible, without money, without means, to get hold of tools, cattle, and seed for the sowing. The peasants must not put their trust in the capitalists nor in the rich peasants (for they are capitalists too), but only in the urban proletariat. Only in alliance with the latter, can the poor peasants insist on the lands, the railways, the banks, and the factories being recognised as the property of all toilers; without such measures, the mere handing over of the land to the people will not remove misery and distress.

In some districts of Russia the workers are introducing a kind of supervision (control) of the factories. This supervision on the part of the workers greatly benefits the peasants, for in this way production is increased and the goods become cheaper. The peasants, to the best of their ability, must support this action of the workers, and refuse to believe the calumnies spread by the capitalists concerning the workers.

The second question is that of the war.

This war is a war of conquest. The capitalists of all countries are carrying it on in order to make conquests and to increase their own profits. This war can and will bring nothing but destruction, horror, devastation and brutalisation to the working people. That is why our party, the party of the class-conscious workers and the poorest peasants, condemns this war positively and unqualifiedly;

it refuses to support the capitalists of one country against those of another; it refuses to support the capitalists of any country. It attempts to bring about a speedy end of the war by overthrowing the capitalists in all countries, by kindling the proletarian world revolution.

Ten of the Ministers in our present new Provisional Government belong to the parties of the large landowners and capitalists, six to the parties of the "Narodniks" ("Socialists-Revolutionists") and the "Mensheviks." In our opinion, the Socialists-Revolutionists and the Mensheviks are committing a serious and fatal mistake in taking part in a government of the capitalists and altogether consenting to support it. Men like Tsereteli and Chernov hope to persuade the capitalists to put an end to this criminal war of conquest as soon and as honestly as possible. The leaders of the Narodniks and the Mensheviks, however, are in error; for, in reality, they are helping the capitalists to prepare a new offensive against Germany, which means that they are helping to prolong the war and to multiply tenfold the terrible sufferings of the Russian people caused by the war.

We are convinced that the capitalists of all countries are deceiving the people; they promise an early and a just peace, and nevertheless they prolong the war of conquest. The Russian capitalists, who were supreme in the old Provisional Government and who have the new government in their hands, even refused to publish the secret predatory treaties concluded by the former Tsar, Nicholas Romanov, with the capitalists of England, France, and other countries,—treaties from which it is evident that he intended to rob the Turks of Constantinople, the Austrians of Galicia, the Turks of Armenia, etc. The Provisional Government has ratified and is continuing to ratify these treaties. In the opinion of our party, these treaties are just as criminal and predatory as are those of the German criminal capitalists and their bandit Kaiser Wilhelm and his accomplices.

The blood of the workers and peasants must not flow in order that these predatory aims of the capitalists be realised.

This terrible war must be terminated as soon as possible—not by a separate peace with Germany but by a general peace, not by a peace concluded by the capitalists, but by one forced on the capitalists by the working masses. There is only one way to do this, that of transferring the whole power of the state into the hands of the Soviets of Workers', Soldiers', and Peasants' Deputies in Russia and other countries. Such Soviets alone are capable of putting an end to the frauds of the capitalists and of preventing the capitalists from prolonging the war.

This brings me to the third and last question I raised, that of the form of government.

Russia must be a democratic republic. Even the majority of the landowners and capitalists agree to this,—they who were always in favour of the monarchy, but have now realised that the people of Russia will never permit the monarchy to be re-established. The capitalists are now exerting every effort to make the republic resemble a monarchy as closely as possible, so that, at any given moment, the monarchy can be restored (we have examples enough of this sort of thing in many countries). For this reason, the capitalists wish to maintain the officialdom which is to be *above* the people; they wish to maintain the police and standing army which is to be separated from the people and under the command of generals and officers. Unless, however, the generals and officers are chosen by the people, they will certainly be recruited from the class of capitalists and landowners. This we know from the experiences of all the republics in the world.

Our party, the party of the class-conscious workers and poorest peasants, is therefore aiming at a different kind of democratic republic. We aim at a republic in which there is no police hostile to the people, in which all officials, from the highest to the lowest, are elected and are liable to be dismissed at any time if the people demand it, their salary not being higher than the wages of a skilled worker. We demand that the officers in the army be elected and that the standing army which is alien to the people and is commanded by a class hostile to the people, should be replaced by a general arming of the people, by a people's militia.

We aim at a republic in which the whole power of the state, from top to bottom, belongs exclusively and entirely to the Soviets of Workers', Soldiers', and Peasants' Deputies.

The workers and peasants form the majority of the population. Power must belong to them, not to the landowners and capitalists.

The workers and peasants form the majority of the population. Power and administration must be entrusted to *their Soviets* and not to the officials.

These are our views, comrades, peasant delegates! We are

firmly convinced that experience will soon show the broad masses that the policy of the Narodniks and the Mensheviks is wrong. The masses will soon learn from experience that the salvation of Russia, which is on the edge of a precipice just as are Germany and the other belligerent countries, that the rescue of the peoples, tortured by the war, cannot be achieved by working in common with the capitalists. All peoples can be saved only if the power of the state is transferred into the hands of the majority of the population.

N. LENIN.

May 20, 1917.
Soldatskaia Pravda, No. 19, May 24, 1917.

"A VIRTUAL TRUCE"

THE *Novaia Zhizn* of May 18 publishes interviews with the Ministers of the "new" government. Prime-Minister Lvov has declared that "the country must express its mighty will and send the army into battle."

This is the essence of the new government's "programme." An offensive, an offensive, an offensive!

Defending this imperialist programme, now accepted by the Chernovs and the Tseretelis, Minister Lvov in tones of deepest moral indignation rages against "the virtual truce that is being established at the front"!

Let every Russian worker, let every peasant think well over the offensive laid out in the programme; let them think well over those thunderous diatribes against a "virtual truce."

Millions of people have been killed and maimed in the war. Unheard-of sufferings have fallen to the lot of the people, particularly the toiling masses, in consequence of the war. While the capitalists are reaping scandalously high profits, the soldiers are being cruelly maimed and tortured.

What wrong is there in a virtual truce? What harm is done if the slaughter ceases? What wrong is there in the soldiers' getting a brief respite?

We are told that truce has been made on one front only, and that it carries the danger of a separate peace. The objection is clearly without any foundation. If neither the Russian Government, nor the Russian workers and peasants want a separate peace with the German capitalists (our party, through the *Pravda* and in resolutions passed by the conference which spoke in the name of the party as a whole, has repeatedly protested against such a peace)—if no one in Russia wants a separate peace with separate capitalists, how then, from where, by what miracle can such a peace come?? Who can impose it upon us?

The objection is clearly a baseless and evident fiction, an attempt to throw sand into our eyes.

61

Moreover, why does a virtual truce on one front necessarily imply the "danger" of a separate peace on that front, and not the danger of such a truce spreading to all fronts?

A virtual truce is, by its very nature, unstable and transitional. This is incontrovertible. Where does a truce lead? It cannot lead to a separate peace so long as there is no mutual consent between two governments or two peoples. But why could not such a truce lead to a virtual truce on *all* fronts? Surely this is exactly what *all* peoples agree to, despite all or most of their governments!

Fraternisation on one front can lead only to fraternisation on all fronts. A virtual truce on one front is bound to and will lead to a virtual truce on all fronts.

The nations would thus gain a respite from the carnage. The revolutionary workers in all the countries would raise their heads still higher; their influence would spread; faith in the necessity and possibility of a proletarian revolution in all the advanced countries would become strengthened.

Is there anything bad in such a change? Why should we not help to accomplish this change as far as it is in our power?

We may be told that a virtual truce on all the fronts would at the present moment aid the German capitalists, for they have gathered in more loot than the others. This is not true, for the English capitalists have grabbed more loot (the German colonies in Africa, German islands in the Pacific, Mesopotamia, part of Syria, etc.) and, unlike the German capitalists, have lost nothing. This is first. And secondly, even if the German capitalists should evince a greater stubbornness than the English capitalists, the growth of the revolution in Germany would only be accelerated. The German revolution is rising. An offensive by the Russian army would hamper its growth. The "virtual truce" hastens the rise of the German revolution.

Thirdly, from the point of view of hunger, ruin, and devastation, Germany is worse off than any other country. It is in desperate, hopeless straits, particularly since the United States has entered the war. A "virtual truce" would not remove *this* fundamental source of Germany's weakness; on the contrary, it is rather likely to better conditions in the other countries (freedom of transporting supplies) while affecting the situation of the German capitalists for the worse (no chance for imports; greater difficulty in hiding the truth from the people).

The Russian people has the choice of two programmes. One is the programme of the capitalists, adopted by the Chernovs and the Tseretelis. This is the programme of the offensive, the programmes for continuing the imperialist war, continuing the slaughter.

The second programme is the programme of the revolutionary workers of the world. In Russia it is advocated by our party. The programme says: stimulate fraternisation (but do not permit the Germans to deceive the Russians); fraternise by means of proclamations; extend fraternisation and virtual truce on all fronts; aid the growth of fraternisation in every possible way; accelerate thereby the proletarian revolution in all the countries; thus bring at least temporary respite to the soldiers of all the warring nations; hasten in Russia the transfer of power to the Soviets of Workers', Soldiers', and Peasants' Deputies; hasten thereby the conclusion of a really just, really universal peace for the benefit of the toilers, and not for the benefit of the capitalists.

Our government, together with the Chernovs and Tseretelis, the Narodniks and the Mensheviks, is for the first programme.

The majority of the Russian people and of all the peoples within Russia (and out of Russia), i. e., the majority of the workers and poor peasants, are undoubtedly for the second programme.

Every day brings the success of the second programme nearer and nearer.

Pravda, No. 52, May 22, 1917.

THE SECRETS OF FOREIGN POLICY

IT is a pity that the masses can read neither books dealing with the history of diplomacy, nor the leading articles in the capitalist papers! And it is a still greater pity—incidentally, this word is too weak in this connection—that the Ministers of the Socialist-Revolutionist and Social-Democratic Menshevik parties, together with their ministerial colleagues, are passing over in silence these historical facts and these articles written by the "great men" of the diplomatic world, so well known to the above-mentioned Ministers.

The *Riech* cites what is in its opinion an authentic communication to the *Birzhevka*, the real meaning of which is that England is not at all averse to giving up "the dismemberment of Turkey and the partitioning of Austria-Hungary"; *i. e.*, England is ready to agree that Russia should not obtain the annexations promised it by the old treaties (Constantinople, Armenia, Galicia). It is in this sense, and in this sense only, that England is ready to revise the treaties.

And the *Riech* is indignant:

> Here then is the first result of the success of the new slogan (*i. e.*, the slogan: Peace without annexations or indemnities). The revision of the treaties is most likely taking place; "preliminary steps" toward such a revision are now being made not by us, but by our allies. The result of this revision, however, will not be a complete (hear! hear!) renunciation of all the serious objectives set before themselves by all the Allies, but a one-sided (well, isn't this a gem?) renunciation of the objectives in Southeastern Europe (read: in Austria and in Turkey, *i. e.*, renunciation of the plan to loot Armenia, Constantinople, and Galicia) in favour of objectives advanced not by us but by our allies in other places and in the colonies.
>
> In point of fact, the press has already mentioned the possibility of the Allies' giving up their objectives in Asia Minor. True, the declarations alleged to have been made in this respect by Albert Thomas in the Soviet of Workers' and Soldiers' Deputies have not been officially confirmed as yet. However, as far as England is concerned, it is difficult to expect such renunciation. England holds to the correct view that what you wish to get, you must first occupy, (hear! hear!) and the English army is already occupying those spots in Mesopotamia and Palestine that are of vital interest to her (read: to her capitalists). Under such circumstances, England's refusal to fight for the vital interests of the *rest* (italics in the *Riech*) of the Allies in that region, would also, of course, have a one-sided character, and be of benefit to her only.[195]

Really, Miliukov, or whoever was the author of these lines, though still alive, deserves a monument for . . . frankness. Bravo,

bravo, the diplomats on the *Riech* are frank! (And why are they frank? Because they are resentful over Miliukov's loss of his portfolio). . . .

All that has been said in the above-quoted lines is true, and is confirmed by the whole history of diplomacy, the whole history of capitalist foreign investments within recent years. England will certainly not give up the idea of grabbing (annexing) Palestine and Mesopotamia. She is, however, willing to punish the Russians (for the "virtual truce" on the Russo-German front) by depriving them of Galicia, Constantinople, Armenia, etc. This is the simple and clear meaning of the above-quoted lines, expressed in plain, not diplomatic, Russian.

And the Russian capitalists, whose mouthpiece is the *Riech*, can hardly restrain their anger; they blurt out the secrets of our foreign policy; they hiss and rage, and say mean things to the English capitalists. You are, they say, "one-sided"; you want things only for yourselves.

Comrades, workers! Comrades, soldiers! Ponder these remarkably candid, these remarkably truthful statements made by the all-knowing diplomats and former Ministers on the *Riech*. Ponder this excellent exposé of the real aims of the war pursued by the capitalists, the Russian as well as the English.

Comrades! Russian soldiers! Do you wish to fight so that the English capitalists may be able to seize Mesopotamia and Palestine? Do you wish to support the Russian Government of Lvov, Chernov, Tereshchenko, and Tsereteli, a government that is bound by capitalist interests, a government that is afraid to admit the truth, blurted out by the *Riech?*

Pravda, No. 53, May 23, 1917.

ONE OF THE SECRET TREATIES

EVERYBODY knows that the first statement made by the "revolutionary" Provisional Government on its foreign policy was the declaration that all secret treaties concluded by the former Tsar Nicholas II with the "Allied" capitalists remain in force, and that new Russia shall regard them as sacred and inviolable.

Furthermore, it is well known that our "defencists" vehemently support the refusal of the Miliukov followers to publish the secret treaties. These wretched Socialists have come to the point where they are defending secret diplomacy, the secret diplomacy of the former Tsar, to boot.

Why do the supporters of the imperialist war watch over the secret treaties so diligently?

Do you wish to know why, comrades, workers and soldiers?

Familiarise yourselves with at least one of these noble treaties: we are referring to "our" treaty with Italy (i. e., with the Italian capitalists) signed in the beginning of 1915.

The bourgeois democrat, Mr. V. Vodovozov, basing himself on the material published in the *Novoie Vremia*, informs us in the *Dien* (May 19, 1917) of the contents of that treaty:

> The Allies, he writes, have guaranteed Italy Southern Tyrol and Trient, the entire coast-line, the northern part of Dalmatia with the cities Zara and Spalato, the central part of Albania with Valona, the islands in the Ægean Sea near Asia Minor; in addition to the above Italy receives a profitable railroad concession in Asiatic Turkey,—this is the blood money which Italy exacts from the Allies. These territorial annexations exceed many times any national claims ever advanced by Italy. Besides regions with an Italian population (Southern Tyrol and Trieste) amounting to nearly 600,000, Italy, according to the treaty, is to receive territories with over a million population absolutely alien to Italy ethnographically and in point of religion. Dalmatia, for instance, contains 97 per cent Serbs and only slightly over 2 per cent Italians. It is quite obvious why the treaty with Italy, which was concluded not only without the advice, but even without the knowledge of Serbia, should have provoked such bitterness and exasperation in the latter country. Pashich in the Skupshchina expressed the hope that the rumours concerning the treaty were false, since Italy herself, he thought, had only recently united in the name of the principle of nationalism, and she therefore could not perpetrate anything in direct contradiction to that principle. But Pashich was wrong; the treaty had been concluded.

66

Of all the treaties dealing with the present war, this is the only one the contents of which we know, and this treaty is barbarously predatory. Whether similar predatory instincts are or are not reflected in the other treaties, we do not know. At any rate, democracy which inscribes on its banner "peace without annexations" is entitled to have this very important information.

Is it true that "we do not know" to what extent the other secret treaties are predatory?   No, Mr. Vodovozov, we know it very well: the secret treaties concerning the partition of Persia, Turkey, the seizure of Germany, Armenia are just as vile and predatory as the rapacious treaty with Italy.

Comrades, soldiers and workers!   You are told that you are defending "freedom" and the "revolution"!   In reality you are defending the shady treaties of the Tsar, which are being concealed from you as one conceals a shameful disease.

Pravda, No. 53, May 23, 1917,

MINISTERIAL TONE

THE editors of the *Izvestia* of the Petrograd Soviet of Workers' and Soldiers' Deputies are assuming a ministerial tone. They do not like the *Pravda*; they condemn it for its "sharp attacks directed against the Provisional Government."

To criticise what he doesn't like is the sacred right of every publicist. But why make oneself ridiculous by condemning our "attacks" in a ministerial way without criticising the issues we raise? Would it not be better to analyse our arguments? Even one of our resolutions? Even one of our references to the class struggle?

"The country is perishing to-day," writes the *Izvestia* in its editorial. Correct. That is just why it is not wise to-day to rely on the agreement of the petty bourgeoisie, the Narodniks, and the Mensheviks with the capitalists. The country cannot be saved from ruin in such a way.

Pravda, No. 53, May 23, 1917.

IN SEARCH OF A NAPOLEON

THE newspaper of former Minister Miliukov is angry at the Mensheviks and the Socialists-Revolutionists who have forced certain individuals out of the cabinet, and for that reason allows itself to be carried away into making the following not quite "cautious" statement.

> Is it possible to suffer this criminal propaganda? . . .—we read in an unsigned article of May 22 relating to fraternisation—will this never be stopped? Is it possible that we cannot get along without a Napoleon? Is it possible that we are going to be satisfied with mere talk about iron discipline?!! [196]

A delicate, very delicate reference to Kerensky's notorious words about iron discipline.

The *Riech* gives its readers a truthful and correct picture of what is going on in "our" "new" government. We thank the *Riech* most sincerely for this truthfulness which is exceptionally rare in such a newspaper and which has been called forth by exceptional circumstances.

In the "new" government Kerensky, supported by Chernov and Tsereteli, proclaims "iron discipline" for the army (in order to carry out the imperialist programme for an offensive).

And the landowners and the capitalists who have ten out of the sixteen posts in the cabinet, hiss maliciously at Kerensky: "Is it possible that we are going to be satisfied with mere talk about iron discipline?"

Is it not clear that this phrase is calculated to inspire Kerensky or "corresponding" generals to assume the rôle of a Napoleon? The rôle of a strangler of freedom? The rôle of an executioner of the workers?

Pravda, No. 53, May 23, 1917.

NOTHING HAS CHANGED

Now that "Socialists" [197] have become members of the cabinet, things will take a different turn, the defencists have been assuring us. Only a few days have passed, and the falsity of these assurances has become manifest.

The indignation aroused among the soldiers and workers by ex-Minister Miliukov's declaration that he neither wished nor was he going to publish the secret treaties which Tsar Nicholas II concluded with the English and French capitalists, is well known. Well, then, what does Mr. Tereshchenko, the *new* Minister of Foreign Affairs, the associate of Skobelev and Tsereteli, say with regard to this question?

Tereshchenko admits that "this question" (*i. e.*, the secret treaties) "arouses passions." But what does he do to allay these passions? He simply *repeats* what Miliukov, who has just been deposed, said before him.

"The immediate publication of the treaties would be equivalent to a break with the Allies," declares Tereshchenko in a statement to the press.

And the "Socialist" Ministers are silent and condone the system of secret diplomacy.

The coalition cabinet has brought no changes. The Tsar's secret treaties remain sacred.

And do you, gentlemen, wish that this should not "arouse passions"? What do you take the class-conscious workers and soldiers to be? Do you really regard them as "rebellious slaves"?

Pravda, No. 54, May 24, 1917.

A GRIEVOUS DEPARTURE FROM THE PRINCIPLES
OF DEMOCRACY

To-day's *Izvestia* carries information concerning the conference of the soldiers' section of the Soviet of Workers' and Soldiers' Deputies. Among other things the conference considered the question "of the advisability of soldiers performing the duties of militiamen." The Executive Commission proposed to the conference the following resolution:

In view of the fact that soldiers must perform *specific* tasks, the Executive Commission of the Soviet of Soldiers' Deputies wishes to place itself on record as *opposed to the soldiers' participation* in the militia, and proposes that all soldiers who are members of the militia *be immediately returned to their respective regiments.*

After a short discussion, the resolution was passed with an *amendment* granting to soldiers *discharged from active service as well as to wounded soldiers the right to perform militia duties.*

It is to be regretted that the exact texts of the resolution and the amendment have not been published. What is still worse, the Executive Commission proposed and the conference adopted a resolution which represents a complete abandonment of the basic principles of democracy.

There is hardly a democratic party in Russia that does not include in its program a demand for the general arming of the people as a substitute for the standing army. There is hardly a Socialist-Revolutionist or a Social-Democrat Menshevik who would dare oppose such a demand. But the trouble is that "nowadays" it is "customary" under the guise of high-sounding phrases about "revolutionary democracy" to accept democratic (and of course Socialist) programs "in principle," but to ignore them in practice.

To oppose the participation of soldiers in the militia on the ground that "soldiers must perform specific tasks" means to forget completely the principles of democracy and involuntarily, unconsciously, perhaps, to adopt the idea of a standing army. The soldier is a professional; his specific task is *not* at all social service, —this is the point of view of those who are for a standing army. It is not a democratic point of view. It is the point of view of the Napoleons. It is the point of view of the supporters of the old régime, of the capitalists, who dream of a slow retrogression from a republic back to a constitutional monarchy.

A true democrat is opposed to such a view in principle. The participation of soldiers in the militia tends to tear down the wall separating the army from the people. It tends to break with the accursed barrack-like past where a specific group of citizens, detached from and in opposition to the people, was drafted, trained, and armed for the special task of following a military profession. The participation of soldiers in the militia involves a radical re-education of the "soldiers" into citizen-militiamen, a re-education of the population of smug residents into citizen-militiamen. Democracy will remain an empty, lying phrase, or merely a half measure, unless the *entire* people is given the immediate opportunity to learn how to handle arms. Without the systematic, constant, and widespread participation of the soldiers in the militia the people will never learn how to use arms efficiently.

It may be objected that it would not be advisable to *draw* the soldiers away from their *immediate* duties. But this is self-evident. It is as ridiculous and superfluous to speak of it as it is to maintain that a physician busy at the bedside of a dangerously ill person has no right to abandon that person and go off to cast his vote at the polls, or that a worker, engaged in production which admittedly must not be interrupted, has not the right to abandon his task and go off to exercise his political rights before he is replaced by another worker. This is so obvious, that even the mention of it strikes one as unnecessary and even disingenuous.

Participation in the militia is one of the cardinal and basic principles of democracy, one of the most substantial guarantees of freedom. We might add, parenthetically, that there is no better way of enhancing the purely military strength and capacity of the army, than by substituting the universal arming of the people for the standing army, and by using the soldiers to instruct the people; this method has ever been used and ever will be used in every truly revolutionary war. Immediate, unconditional, universal organisation of a people's militia and unlimited participation of soldiers in that militia,—this, we hold, is of the greatest importance to the workers, peasants, and soldiers, that is to say, to the vast majority of the population, the majority that is not interested in safeguarding the profits of the landowners and the capitalists.

Pravda, No. 55, May 25, 1917.

ON THE CALLING OF AN INTERNATIONAL QUASI-SOCIAL-IST CONFERENCE WITH THE PARTICIPATION OF THE SOCIAL-CHAUVINISTS

THE *Izvestia* of the Petrograd Soviet of Workers' and Soldiers' Deputies publishes to-day the "rulings" of the Executive Committee pertaining to the organisation of a commission for the convocation of an International Conference.[198] Incidentally our party is asked to send a representative to the commission. It goes without saying that our party will take part neither in the commission, nor in the Conference, that is being called and that will include quasi-Socialist Ministers who have deserted to the side of the bourgeoisie. This must be perfectly well known to any one who has taken an interest in our party, who has read our resolution dealing with the state of affairs in the International.

The Central Committee of our party unanimously decided a few days ago to send a delegate to the Zimmerwald Conference that is now being called, with instructions to leave the Conference and secede from the Zimmerwald Alliance, should the Conference express itself in favour of any rapprochement or of any discussion of affairs together with the social-chauvinists.

Pravda, No. 55, May 25, 1917.

THE PARTY OF THE PROLETARIAT AT THE ELECTIONS TO THE BOROUGH COUNCILS

OUR party enters the elections with its own independent tickets. According to advance information received by the secretariat of the Central Committee, in four out of twelve boroughs (the Moskovsky, the Rozhdestvensky, the Kolpinsky, and the Porokhovskoi), the tickets have been made up without blocs. In all the other boroughs we have formed blocs with Internationalists only; namely, in six boroughs (the Second City Borough, the Narvsky, the Petrogradskaia Storona, the Moskovsky, the First City Borough, and the Vasilieostrovsky), with the "interboroughites" * (who have condemned, as we all know, most definitely the entrance of the Narodniks and the Mensheviks into the capitalist cabinet); then, in four boroughs (the Viborgsky, the Nevsky, First City Borough, and Vasilieostrovsky), with the Mensheviks-Internationalists, the opponents of "Socialist" ministerialism; and in one borough (the Nevsky) also with Internationalists from the party of the Socialists-Revolutionists, who have been condemning the "ministerialism" of their party.

Such a union with Internationalists from other parties is in full accord with the decisions of our conferences (the Petrograd and the All-Russian), as well as with the principles of the proletarian party opposed to the petty-bourgeois defencism and ministerialism of the Mensheviks and the Narodniks.

The propaganda in favour of the "Left bloc," carried on, by the way, also in the *Novaia Zhizn*, could not of course alter the decision of our party. Wrong, basically wrong, is the opinion that municipal elections "do not bear such a definite political character" (as the elections to the Constituent Assembly). It is just as wrong to maintain that "the municipal programmes of the different Socialist (??) parties differ very little from one another." To make such queer statements, without answering the arguments of the *Pravda*, as such, means to avoid the analysis of the most important question, or simply to give up.

* Mezhraiontsy, see note 206.—*Ed.*

74

To narrow down the elections in the capital in times of revolution to a purely (or even predominantly) "municipal" issue is something monstrously absurd. This means making sport of the experience of all revolutions. This means jeering at the common-sense of the workers who know full well that the rôle of Petrograd is a leading one, and at times even a decisive one.

The Cadets unite all the Right elements, the entire counter-revolution, all the landowners and the capitalists. They are for the government, they wish to reduce revolutionary Petrograd to playing second fiddle to the capitalist government, which consists of ten capitalist ministers to six Narodniks and Mensheviks.

Against the Cadets, the chauvinists, the supporters of war for the sake of the Straits, there stands out the party of the proletariat, unqualifiedly opposed to imperialism, the only party capable of breaking with the interests of capital, of taking serious revolutionary measures, without which it is impossible to help the toiling masses at the moment when a great catastrophe is approaching and is already quite near. Without revolutionary measures there is no salvation. Without a workers' militia, as a step towards the immediate creation of a people's militia, it is impossible, even with the best of intentions, to carry out such measures, it is particularly impossible to get rid of "queues" and the disorganisation of supplies.

And as far as the "middle course" is concerned, the path of the petty bourgeoisie, the Mensheviks and the Narodniks, who proclaim their good intentions but render themselves impotent by agreements with the capitalists and by surrendering to the capitalists (six Ministers against ten!!), it is devoid of vitality. The masses will soon learn from experience that this is so, even if they should believe for a time in "agreements" with the capitalists.

He who stands for measures intended to satisfy the interests of the toiling masses, he who stands for the elimination of the police, for the substitution of a people's militia for the police, he who stands for serious revolutionary measures that will lead the country out of the unheard-of crisis, of the unheard-of débâcle, must vote for the ticket of the proletarian party, the Russian Social-Democratic Labour Party (Bolsheviks).

Pravda, No. 56, May 26, 1917.

PRE-REVOLUTIONARY PRONOUNCEMENTS OF OUR PARTY WITH REGARD TO THE WAR

Of particular interest are the declarations which anticipated the victory of a chauvinist ("defencist") revolution. In the *Social-Democrat*, the Central Organ of the Russian Social-Democratic Labour Party, published in Geneva under the editorship of Zinoviev and Lenin, in No. 47, October 13, 1915, there appeared the following statement of the editors: *

. . . 8. We regard those as revolutionary chauvinists who want a victory over tsarism for the purpose of obtaining a victory over Germany, for the purpose of robbing other countries, for the purpose of strengthening the domination of the Great-Russians over the other peoples in Russia, etc. The basis of revolutionary chauvinism is the class position of the petty bourgeoisie. The latter always fluctuates between the bourgeoisie and the proletariat. At the present moment it fluctuates between chauvinism (which does not permit it to be consistently revolutionary even in the sense of a democratic revolution) and proletarian internationalism. The political exponents of the petty bourgeoisie in Russia are at present the Trudoviks, the Socialists-Revolutionists, the *Nasha Zaria*, the Chkheidze fraction, the Organisation Committee, Mr. Plekhanov, etc. 9. Should the revolutionary chauvinists in Russia be victorious, we would then be against the defence of *their* "fatherland" in the present war. Our slogan is: oppose the chauvinists, even though they be revolutionists and republicans, oppose them and advocate the union of the international proletariat for a Socialist revolution. 10. To the question whether the proletariat can assume a leading rôle in the bourgeois revolution in Russia, our answer is that it can *if* the petty bourgeoisie swings to the Left at the decisive moment; and it is being pushed to the Left not only by our propaganda, but also by a series of external causes, economic, financial (the burdens of the war), military, political, etc. 11. To the question what would the proletarian party do should the revolution put it in power during the present war, our answer is that we would propose peace to *all* the warring nations, on condition that the colonies and all dependent, oppressed, and non-sovereign peoples become free. Neither Germany nor England and France would accept, under their present governments, such a condition. We would then have to make ready and conduct a revolutionary war, *i. e.*, we would not only carry out, through a series of decisive measures, our entire minimum programme, but we would also begin to arouse to insurrection all the peoples that are at present oppressed by the Great-Russians, all the colonies, all the dependent Asiatic countries (India, China, Persia, etc.). Moreover, we would arouse the Socialist proletariat of Europe to insurrection against the various governments despite the social-

* See "A Few Theses. The Editors." V. I. Lenin, *Collected Works*, Vol. XVIII.—*Ed.*

chauvinists. There is not a shadow of a doubt that the victory of the proletariat in Russia would make conditions favourable for the growth of revolution in Asia as well as Europe. This was proved even as far back as the year 1905. And the international solidarity of the revolutionary proletariat is a *fact*, despite the turgid effervescence of opportunism and social-chauvinism.

Pravda, No. 56, May 26, 1917.

ECONOMIC CHAOS IS IMMINENT

NEWS, arguments, apprehensions, and rumours with regard to an imminent catastrophe are becoming more frequent. The capitalist newspapers are trying to frighten the people, they are fulminating against the Bolsheviks, parading as they do Kutler's cryptic references to "one" factory, to "some" factories, to "one" enterprise, etc. Remarkable methods, strange "proofs" . . . why not name a definite factory, why not give the public and the workers a chance to verify the rumours calculated to arouse uneasiness?

It should not be difficult for the capitalists to understand that, unless they present exact data and correctly named enterprises, they only make themselves ridiculous. You are the government, gentlemen capitalists, you have ten out of sixteen Ministers, yours is the responsibility, and you are the administration. Is it not ridiculous that people who are managing the affairs of the state and who have a majority in the government, should confine themselves to Kutler's enigmatic references, should be afraid to come out openly and straightforwardly, and should try to shift responsibility to other parties that are not at the helm of the state?

The newspapers of the petty-bourgeois parties, the Narodniks and the Mensheviks, are also complaining, but in somewhat different tones. They do not so much accuse the terrible Bolsheviks (although, of course, they do not leave them alone) as they heap good wishes upon one another. The *Izvestia*, the editorship of which is in the hands of the two above-named parties, is in this respect particularly typical. Number 63 (May 24) contains two articles dealing with the struggle against economic chaos. The articles are of identical nature. One of them has, mildly speaking, an extremely incautious heading (quite as incautious as the entrance of the Narodniks and Mensheviks into the imperialist cabinet): "What Does the Provisional Government Want?" [199] It would be more correct to say: "What Does the Provisional Government *Not* Want and What Does It Promise?"

The second article deals with "the resolution of the economic department of the Executive Committee of the Soviet of Workers'

78

and Soldiers' Deputies." [200] Here are a few quotations which will best give an idea of its content:

> Many branches of industry have reached the point where they are ripe for a state trade monopoly (bread, meat, salt, leather) ; others are ready to be organised into trusts regulated by the state (coal mining, oil drilling, production of metal, sugar, paper), and finally, nearly all branches of industry are in need, considering contemporary conditions, of state supervision in the matter of distributing raw materials and finished products, as well as in the matter of fixing prices. . . . Simultaneously with the above, it is necessary to put under state and public control all credit institutions with the view of preventing speculation in goods subject to state regulation. . . . Along with that, most energetic measures should be taken to eliminate loafing; compulsory labour should be instituted if necessary. . . . The country is already in a state of catastrophe, and the only thing that will save it is the creative effort of the entire people *under the guidance of the government* which has voluntarily assumed (hem . . . hem . . . !?) the grandiose task of salvaging a country ruined by war and the Tsar's régime.

With the exception of the last phrase (beginning with the italicised words), which, with purely philistine gullibility, makes the capitalists "assume" tasks which they are incapable of carrying out, the programme is splendid. Here we have control, state regulated trusts, a struggle against speculation, labour conscription—for Mercy's sake! in what sense does it differ from "terrible" Bolshevism? Is there anything more that the Bolsheviks want?

This is just the point, this is the gist of the whole matter, and this is precisely what the bourgeoisie and the philistines of all descriptions stubbornly refuse to see: they are *forced* to adopt the programme of "terrible" Bolshevism, because no other programme offers an escape from the impending terrible catastrophe. *But* . . . the capitalists "recognise" this programme (see the famous third paragraph of the proclamation issued by the "new" Provisional Government) [201] *in order not to carry it out.* And the Narodniks and the Mensheviks "have confidence" in the capitalists, and unfortunately they also teach the people to have confidence in them. This is the crux of the whole situation.

To exercise control over the trusts, to publish their full accounts, to call conferences of all their employés, with the obligatory participation of the *workers themselves* in supervising the business of the trusts, with the admission of representatives of each important political party to independent control over them,—all this can be brought into life by a decree, for the drafting of which *one day* would suffice.

What is in the way, then, citizens Shingarevs, Tereshchenkos, Konovalovs? What is stopping you, citizens, near-Socialist Ministers Chernov and Tsereteli? What is interfering with you, citizens, Narodnik and Menshevik leaders of the Executive Committee of the Soviet of Workers' and Soldiers' Deputies?

Neither we, nor anybody else, proposed or could propose anything except the *immediate* establishment of such control over trusts, banks, commerce, *parasites* (a remarkably apt word came— for a change—to the pens of the editors of the *Izvestia* . . .), and foodstuffs. "The creative effort of the entire people,"—no one could suggest anything better than that . . .

Only we must not have confidence in the words of the capitalists, nor must we have faith in the naïve (at best, naïve) hope of the Mensheviks and the Narodniks that the capitalists would be able to introduce such control.

Chaos is imminent. A catastrophe is near. The capitalists have brought and are continuing to bring all countries to ruin. There is one road to salvation: revolutionary discipline, revolutionary measures by the *revolutionary class*, the proletarians and semi-proletarians, the passing of all power to the class that would really be able to institute such control, that would actually be able to carry to a victorious conclusion the fight upon "parasitism."

Pravda, No. 57, May 27, 1917.

CONTEMPTIBLE METHODS

A WHOLE congress of delegates from the front unanimously adopted a resolution on May 26 [202] denouncing the despicable methods of the *Riech* in lying about our Comrade Zinoviev for the purpose of sowing discord between the army and the Bolsheviks. The gentlemen of the *Riech* have never thought of publishing the resolution passed by the congress from the front, despite the fact that the congress mailed a copy of the resolution to that paper. Instead, that sheet is keeping up its campaign of insinuations against our paper and against our Comrade Zinoviev in an attempt to instigate a little pogrom.

"The *Pravda* is systematically publishing information concerning Germany which is not to be found in any other paper. From where and how does the *Pravda* receive its special (!) news?"— the *Riech* queries significantly in an article under the suggestive heading "Queer Omniscience."

From where, Messrs. Calumniators?

From telegrams and letters mailed to us by our Comrade Radek, the Polish Social-Democrat, who spent a number of years in the Tsar's prisons, who has been active for over ten years in the ranks of German Social-Democracy, who has been driven from Germany because of his revolutionary agitation against Wilhelm and against the war, and who has purposely gone to Stockholm to supply us with information. From letters and telegrams, Messrs. Cadets, which your servants who are lording it over the Russian-Swedish border are not always successful in intercepting; from newspaper clippings and underground German newspapers and proclamations that are supplied to us by our friends, the followers of Karl Liebknecht. The same is true of our French news,—information is sent to us by the *French* Socialist-Internationalist, Henri Guilbeaux, a friend of Romain Rolland and an adherent of the famous French Internationalist, Comrade Loriot.

"The German General Staff has forbidden fraternisation," we wrote in the *Pravda* on the basis of information printed recently in all the Russian newspapers. The slanderers in the *Riech* pretend to

81

be surprised, and try to "offset" that statement with the statement of the Russian War Minister that "all those sectors of the front where fraternisation took place have already been destroyed by the artillery of the enemy."

We do not know, of course, whether the information concerning the destruction of those sectors is authentic. But *if* it is authentic, then it confirms rather than contradicts the information that the German General Staff is opposed to fraternisation. For it is obvious that by destroying the sectors where fraternisation occurred the German General Staff is discouraging the Russian soldiers, as well as those honest German soldiers who do not wish to use fraternisation as a trap, from becoming friendly.

Somehow your lies are not very convincing, Messrs. Cadet counterfeiters!

In conclusion, one more of their lies: "As is well known," writes Miliukov's organ, "at the Peasant Congress, Zinoviev was not given a chance to finish his speech." "As is well known," you lie again, Messrs. Cadets, just as you have lied about the congress from the front. Things must be pretty bad with you, gentlemen, if you are forced to resort to such shameful, such contemptible lies.

Pravda, No. 58. May 29, 1917.

UNAVOIDABLE CATASTROPHE AND BOUNDLESS PROMISES

I

THE question of imminent economic ruin, of a gigantic, unheard-of catastrophe, is so important that we must dwell on it more and more if we want to understand it fully. In the last issue of the *Pravda* we already pointed out that the *programme* of the Executive Committee of the Soviet of Workers' and Soldiers' Deputies cannot at present be distinguished *in any way* from the programme of "terrible" Bolshevism.*

To-day we must point out that the programme of the Menshevik Minister Skobelev goes one step beyond Bolshevism. Here is the programme as reported in the ministerial paper, the *Riech:*

> Minister (Skobelev) declares that . . . our state economy is on the brink of a precipice. We must intervene in the various domains of the economic life of the country, for there is no money in our treasury. We must better the living conditions of the toiling masses, and to do this we must take away the profits from the treasuries of the business men and the bankers. (*Voice in the audience:* "By what method?") By ruthless taxation of property, replies the Minister of Labour Skobelev. This method is known to the science of finance. The rate of taxation must be increased for the propertied classes to one hundred per cent of their profits. (*Voice in the audience:* "This means everything.") Unfortunately, declares Skobelev, many corporations have already distributed their dividends among their shareholders, that is why we must levy a progressive personal tax on the propertied classes. We will go even further. If capital wishes to preserve the bourgeois method of doing business, then let it work without interest, so as not to lose the clients. . . . We must introduce obligatory labour duty for the shareholders, bankers, and factory owners, who have been in a lackadaisical mood ever since the incentives that had once stimulated them to work have disappeared. . . . We must force the gentlemen-shareholders to submit to the state; they, too, must be subject to labour duty.[208]

We urge the workers to read and re-read this programme, to discuss and try to grasp the conditions prerequisite for its realisation.

The main things are the conditions for its realisation, the immediate efforts toward its realisation.

* See p. 79 of this book.—*Ed.*

This programme in itself is not only excellent and in accord with our Bolshevik programme, but in one particular, i. e., in the matter of "taking away the profits from the treasuries of the bankers" to the extent of "100 per cent," it even goes a step further than we do.

Our party is more moderate. In its resolution it demands much less, namely, the instituting of control over the banks and the "gradual" (Hear! hear! the Bolsheviks are in favour of gradualness) "transition to a more just and progressive tax on incomes and property."

Our party is more moderate than Skobelev.

Skobelev hands out immoderate, nay, boundless promises, without understanding the conditions which would render their practical realisation possible.

This is the crux of the matter.

To think of actually realising the programme proposed by Skobelev is absurd, since not even one serious effort toward its realisation can be made either through the ten Ministers of the landowners and the capitalists or through the bureaucratic, official-ridden machine to which the government of the capitalists (plus a few Mensheviks and Narodniks) is perforce limited.

Fewer promises, Citizen Skobelev, and more action. Fewer high-sounding phrases, and more understanding as to how to get down to business.

We can and must get down to business immediately without losing a day, in order to save the country from an otherwise unavoidable and gruesome disaster. The crux of the matter is that the "new" Provisional Government does not want to get down to business; and even if it wanted to it could not, for it is fettered by a thousand chains designed to safeguard the interests of capital.

We can and must, in one day, call upon the people to commence to work; in one day we can publish a decree which would immediately convoke the following:

1. Soviets and congresses of bank employés in individual banks as well as on a national scale; they are to be directed to work out at once practical measures for insuring the merger of all banking and credit establishments into one general state bank, and for establishing the most scrupulous control over all banking operations; the results of such control to be published forthwith;

2. Soviets and congresses of employés of all syndicates and trusts, with instructions to work out measures for control and

accounting; the results of such control to be published forthwith;

3. This decree is to grant the right of control not only to all the Soviets of Workers', Soldiers', and Peasants' Deputies, but also to the Soviets of workers in every big factory, as well as to the representatives of every large political party (by a large party we mean, for example, a party that had on May 25 independent electoral tickets in not less than two Petrograd boroughs); all books, all documents to be open to such control;

4. The decree must call upon all shareholders, directors and members of the managing boards of all concerns to publish the names of all shareholders who own no less than 10,000 (or 5,000) rubles' worth of stocks; the various shares and the various companies in which the listed individuals are interested, to be indicated; incorrect statements (discovered through the control of banking and other employés) to be punished by the confiscation of the guilty party's entire property, and by imprisonment for not less than five years;

5. The decree must call upon the whole people to establish immediately, through the local organs of self-government, universal obligatory labour duty, for the control and realisation of which there must be established a universal people's militia (in the villages—directly; in the cities—through the workers' militia).

Without such universal, obligatory labour duty, the country cannot be saved from ruin. And without a people's militia, universal obligatory labour duty cannot be established. This can be grasped by any one who has not fallen into ministerial lunacy or been hypnotised into credulity by ministerial eloquence.

He who actually wants to save from ruin tens of millions of people, must come to the defence of such measures.

In the next article we will discuss gradual transition toward a more equitable tax, also the method whereby it may be possible to bring to the fore and gradually place in ministerial positions those really gifted organisers (from among the workers as well as from among the capitalists) who have manifested their ability in the kind of work described above.

II

When Skobelev, in a moment of ministerial abandon, threatened to deprive the capitalists of 100 per cent of their profits, he really offered us in that speech a sample of a phrase calculated to impress. It is just such phrases that are always used to deceive the people in bourgeois parliamentary republics.

But here we have something worse than a mere phrase. "If capital wishes to preserve the bourgeois method of doing business, then let it work without interest, so as not to lose the clients," says Skobelev. This sounds like a "terrible" threat directed at the capitalists; in point of fact, however, it is an attempt (unconscious, most likely, in the case of Skobelev, but conscious, no doubt, in the case of the capitalists) to preserve the all-powerful rule of capital by a temporary sacrifice of profits.

The workers are taking "too much"—reason the capitalists—let us shift to them all responsibility, without giving them either the power or the opportunity actually to manage all production. Let us, capitalists, sacrifice for a time our profits, but by preserving "the bourgeois method of doing business," by not losing "our clients," we shall hasten the fall of this intermediate stage in industry, we shall disorganise it in all kinds of ways, and we shall put the blame on the workers.

We have facts to prove that this is how the capitalists figure. The coal operators in the South are actually disorganising industry, are "deliberately neglecting and disorganising it" (see *Novaia Zhizn* for May 29, report of statements made by a workers' delegation).[204] The picture is clear: The *Riech* is lying brazenly when it puts the blame on the workers.

The coal operators are "deliberately disorganising industry"; and Skobelev is twittering in nightingale fashion that "if capital wishes to preserve the bourgeois method of doing business, then let it work without interest." The picture is clear.

It is to the advantage of the capitalists and the bureaucrats to make all kinds of "boundless promises," and thus to divert the attention of the people from the main thing, namely, from the transfer of actual control to the workers.

The workers must sweep aside all high-sounding phrases, promises, declarations, projects evolved in the centre by bureaucrats ready every minute to apply themselves to drawing up the most effective plans, regulations, statutes, rules. Down with all this lying! Down with all this fracas of bureaucratic and bourgeois project-mongering that has collapsed everywhere with a crash. Down with this habit of procrastination! The workers must demand the immediate establishment of actual control, to be exercised only by the workers themselves.

This is imperative for the success of the cause, the cause of averting a catastrophe. If this is lacking, the rest is sheer deception. Once we have this, we will not at all be in a hurry to take "100 per cent" of the capitalists' profits. We can and we must be more moderate, we must pass gradually to a more equitable tax; we shall differentiate between small and large shareholders, taking very little from the former, taking a great deal (but not necessarily everything) only from the latter. The number of large shareholders is insignificant; but the rôle they play and the wealth they possess are tremendous. It may be safely said that a list of five or even three thousand (or perhaps even one thousand) names of the richest men in Russia, or an insight (by means of control exercised from below by bank, syndicate, and other employés), into all the threads and ties of their finance capital, their banking connections, would expose the whole knot of capitalist domination, the main body of wealth accumulated at the expense of others' labour, all the really important sources of "control" over social production and distribution of goods.

It is this control that must be handed over to the workers. It is these ties, these sources, that the capitalist interests are eager to conceal from the people. Better forego for a time "all" our profits, or 99 per cent of our income, rather than disclose to the people these roots of our power—says the capitalist class and its unconscious servant, the government official.

Under no circumstances will we renounce our right and our demand that the chief fortress of finance capital be opened to the people, that just this fortress be placed under workers' control, say, and will say, the class-conscious workers. And every passing day will prove the soundness of this argument to ever greater masses of the poor, to an ever growing majority of the people, to an ever greater number of sincere men and women honestly seeking an escape from the impending disaster.

The chief fortress of finance capital must be seized. Unless this is done, all phrases, all projects of how to avert disaster are sheer deception. As to the individual capitalists, or even the majority of capitalists, not only does the proletariat not intend to "strip" them (as Shulgin has been "scaring" himself and his ilk), not only does it not intend to deprive them of "everything," but, on the contrary, it intends to place them at useful, honourable tasks, subject to the control of the workers themselves.

When unavoidable disaster is approaching, the most useful and most indispensable task confronting the people is that of organisation. Marvels of proletarian organisation—this is our slogan at present, and shall become our slogan and our demand to an even greater extent, when the proletariat is in power. Without the organisation of the masses it is absolutely impossible either to introduce the needed universal obligatory labour duty, or to establish a relatively serious control over banks, syndicates, and the production and distribution of goods.

That is why it is necessary to begin, and begin immediately, with a workers' militia, in order that we may advance, firmly, efficiently, gradually, towards the establishment of a universal militia, toward the displacement of the standing army by a universal army of the people. That is why it is necessary to bring forward gifted organisers from all strata of society, from all classes, not excluding the capitalists, who *at present* have more of the required experience and more talented organisers. There are many such talents among the people. These forces lie dormant in the peasantry and the proletariat, for lack of application. They must be mobilised from below, by practical work, by efficiently eliminating waiting lines, by a skilful organisation of house committees, by organising the domestic servants, by creating model farms in the country, by putting on a sound basis the factories taken over by the workers, etc., etc. After we have brought these forces to the surface, into practice, after we have tested their ability in actual work, we can make them all into "Ministers"—not in the old sense, not in the sense of rewarding them with portfolios, but in the sense of appointing them as instructors of the people, travelling organisers, assistants in the work of establishing everywhere the strictest order, the greatest economy in human labour, the strictest comradely discipline.

This is what the party of the proletariat must preach to the people as a means to avert a catastrophe. This is what it must partly begin to do now, in those localities where it is gaining power. This is what it must carry out fully when it becomes the state power.

Pravda, Nos. 58 and 59, May 29 and 30, 1917.

ON THE PROBLEM OF UNITING THE INTERNATIONALISTS

THE All-Russian conference of our party has recognised the necessity of a rapprochement and consolidation of all the groups and movements that are really international in their outlook, on the basis of a break with the policy of petty-bourgeois betrayal of Socialism.[205]

The question of unity has also been discussed at the conference of the Mezhraiontsy organisation of the united Social-Democrats in Petrograd.[206]

In compliance with the decision of the All-Russian conference, the Central Committee of our party, recognising the great desirability of uniting with the Mezhraiontsy [Interboroughites] came forward with the following proposals (which were first made to the Mezhraiontsy in the names of Comrade Lenin and several other members of the Central Committee; subsequently, however, were approved by the majority of the members of the Central Committee) :

Immediate unity is desirable. It will be proposed to the Central Committee of the Russian Social-Democratic Labour Party that to each staff of the two papers (the present *Pravda* which is to be converted into an All-Russian *popular* newspaper, and the Central Organ which is to be established in the near future) be added one representative of the Mezhraiontsy!

It will be proposed to the Central Committee that it create a special organisation commission to be charged with the task of convoking (in a month and a half hence) a party congress.

The Mezhraiontsy conference has a right to send two delegates to that commission. Should the Mensheviks, the followers of Martov, break with the "defencists," then the inclusion of their delegates in the above-mentioned commission would be desirable and indispensable.

Free discussion of controversial questions is to be insured by the publication of discussion leaflets in the *Priboi* and by a free discussion in the periodical *Prosveshchenie* which is to resume publication.[207]

This draft was read by N. Lenin on May 23, 1917, in his own name and in the name of several members of the C. C.

The Mezhraiontsy, on their part, have passed another resolution. It reads:

On Unity. Realising that only the closest consolidation of all the revolutionary forces of the proletariat

1. Can make it the foremost fighter for the clearing of the way toward Socialism;

2. Will enable it to become the leader of the Russian democracy in its struggle against the survival of a semi-feudal régime and the heritage of tsarism;

3. Will make it possible to carry on the revolution to a forceful end and to settle the questions of war and peace, confiscation of the land, the eight-hour day, etc.;

The conference declares:

a. That such a consolidation of forces, so indispensable to the proletariat, can be achieved only under the banner of Zimmerwald and Kienthal, and upon the party programme and decisions of the years 1908 and 1910, 1912 and 1913;

b. That every workers' organisation, be it a trade union, an educational club, or consumers' league, every proletarian newspaper or periodical should be enlisted under that banner;

c. In addition to the above, the conference declares itself as the most determined and ardent advocate of unity on the basis of the above resolutions.

Which resolution is most likely to lead to unity, is a question for all the international workers to discuss and decide.

The political resolutions of the Mezhraiontsy basically follow the sound policy of breaking away from the "defencists."

Under such circumstances, any division of forces would, in our opinion, be utterly unjustifiable.

Pravda, No. 60, May 31, 1917.

CONFUSION

ONCE MORE ABOUT ANNEXATIONS

THE editors of the *Izvestia,* a paper controlled by a bloc of the Narodniks and the Mensheviks, are beating all records at making a mess of things. In No. 67, May 29, they attempt to engage the *Pravda* in a polemic. They, of course, do not mention the *Pravda,* thus acting in accord with the bad "ministerial" manner. The *Pravda,* you see, has a vague, misleading conception of annexation.[208]

We beg pardon, citizen Ministers and ministerial editors. The fact nevertheless remains that our party was the *only* one to define annexation in careful official resolutions. Annexation (seizure) is the forceful retention of an alien people within the confines of a given state. No one who reads and understands Russian could fail to understand this on reading the supplement to No. 13 of *Soldatskaia Pravda* (resolutions of the All-Russian Conference held May 7-12, 1917).

What objections do the Narodnik and Menshevik editors of the *Izvestia* offer? Only this, that according to our view, they claim, it would be necessary "to keep on fighting until Germany is reduced to the Duchy of Brandenburg . . . Russia—to the Grand Principality of Moscow"!! Annexation,—the editors of the *Izvestia* inform their readers,—"is the forceful seizure of territory that is a part of the domain of another state on the day when war is declared" (in brief: without annexations means status quo, *i. e.,* the re-establishment of conditions as they were before the war).

The Narodnik and Menshevik leaders of the Executive Committee are quite reckless in entrusting the responsibilities of editing a paper to people with such a hodgepodge in their heads. Really, they are quite reckless.

Let us apply to *their* definition the objections they offer to *ours:* Would it be necessary "to keep on fighting until Russia gets back Poland, and Germany Togoland and its colonies in Africa"? Palpable nonsense, nonsense from the theoretical as well as from the practical point of view; the soldiers of any country would send packing any editor who reasoned in such a slovenly manner.

91

Here is the flaw in their argument:

1. The theoretical definition of annexation involves the conception of an "alien" people, *i. e.*, a people that has preserved its peculiarities, and its will for independent existence. Ponder this, fellow citizens; and if it is still not clear to you, then read Engels' and Marx's discussions relating to Ireland, the Danish districts in Germany, the colonies,—you will then realise how confused you were. Neither the Duchy of Brandenburg nor the principality of Moscow has anything to do with it. 2. It is absurd to confuse one's conception of annexation with the question of how long "to keep on fighting," for that means that one does not grasp the connection between war and the interests and domination of certain classes; it means that one is deserting the standpoint of the *class-struggle* and is adopting the philistine standpoint of "no classes." For while the capitalist class is in power, the peoples inevitably must "keep on fighting" as long as that class wants it. 3. While the capitalists are in power, *their* peace is bound to be "an exchange of annexations": Armenia for Lorraine, colony for colony, Galicia for Courland, and so on. It is pardonable when an uneducated man fails to see this, it is unpardonable when the editors of the *Izvestia* make the same error. 4. When the proletariat is in power—a state of affairs to which the war is leading and bringing us closer day by day—then and only then will "peace without annexations" become possible.

When our party speaks of "peace without annexations" it takes pains to explain,—anticipating the lack of understanding on the part of the people with a hodgepodge in their heads,—that that slogan must be taken as inseparably connected with the proletarian revolution. Only in connection with the revolution is it true and useful, it indicates the revolution's path, it aids its development and growth. Whoever vacillates helplessly between faith in the capitalists and faith in the proletarian revolution, condemns himself to confusion and impotence in the question of annexations.

P.S.—The *Dielo Naroda* of May 30 agrees with the *Izvestia* in that "without annexations" is equivalent to "status quo." Gentlemen, Socialists-Revolutionists and Mensheviks, why not try to state your ideas on this subject in a clear, precise, and straightforward manner, in the name of your party, your Petrograd Committee, your congress!

Pravda, No. 60, May 31, 1917.

MORE COMMISSIONS AS A MEANS OF STRUGGLE AGAINST ECONOMIC CHAOS

THE *Izvestia* of May 30 publishes a long, dull and foolish resolution passed by its economic department * on the struggle against economic chaos.[209]

Some struggle! Splendid ideas, excellent plans stifled in a net of bureaucratic, dead institutions. "The economic department shall be changed" . . . (hear! hear!)—"into a department for the organisation of national economy."

Excellent! We are on the right track! Our country may rest secure. The department has been renamed.

But is it possible to "organise the national economy" without state power at your command? This the Executive Committee forgot to consider.

. . . The department comprises six "sub-departments." . . . This is the first paragraph of the resolution. The second promises to establish "close organisation ties"; the third, to work out "basic principles" for regulation; the fourth, to establish "close organisational intercourse" with the Ministers (upon my word, this is not taken from a fable of Muzhik Vredny,** but from the *Izvestia*, No. 68, of May 30, page 3, column 3, paragraph 4 . . .); the fifth lets us know that "the government forms commissions"; the sixth, that "in the nearest future a bill will be prepared"; the seventh urges forthwith to start "determining the basic propositions of the bills" divided into five sub-titles.

Oh, wise men! Oh, lawgivers! Oh, Louis Blancs!

Pravda, No. 60, May 31, 1917.

---

* Of the Executive Committee of the Petrograd Soviet.—*Ed.*
** The former pseudonym of the popular Communist poet E. A. Pridvorov, now writing under the name of Demian Biedny.—*Ed.*

ONE MORE DEPARTURE FROM DEMOCRATIC
PRINCIPLES

THE Narodniks and the Mensheviks who are editing the *Izvestia* wish to be considered Socialists, yet they do not even know how to be democrats. In Number 68 (May 30) of their paper, they advocate "caution" with regard to the "slogan of partial re-elections." "Deputies ought to be elected," they instruct the workers, "for a definite term, for two or three months, for instance, but under no circumstances (!!) are they to be elected for a week, or for the interval of time between meetings." [210]

Is it proper for an official body to worry about re-elections and to recommend "caution"? . . . Caution as to what? As to the expression of popular distrust in *that body!*

That is the first question.

The second question: Should not an intelligent democrat regard the question of caution in the matter of re-elections (if it ought to be regarded at all) from the point of view of *party principles?* Is it not his duty, for instance, to say: We, Narodniks and Mensheviks, consider our policy correct on such and such grounds, and that of the Bolsheviks wrong for such and such reasons? Why then, do the editors, in flagrant violation of democratic principles, resort not to party principles but to the queer argument that mistakes at elections are "exceptions"? Is it really possible that they do not know that the "mistake" of having the Skobelevs and the Chernovs enter the capitalist cabinet is being weighed and discussed by the workers everywhere, that such mistakes are not at all "exceptions"?

Will not the editors of the *Izvestia*, if they still reckon with the opinions of the founders of scientific Socialism, Marx and Engels, recall what those real Socialists said with regard to such a right?

Pravda, No. 60, May 31, 1917.

94

HOW THE CAPITALISTS ARE SCARING THE PEOPLE

THE *Finansovaia Gazeta* (May 30) writes in a leading editorial:

The political change, so much hoped for and expected, is taking on the unprecedented form of a social revolution. The "class struggle," legitimate and natural in a free country, is taking on the character of a class war. Financial bankruptcy is ahead. The collapse of industry is inevitable.

To accomplish a political revolution, all that was necessary was to force the abdication of Nicholas II and to arrest a dozen of his Ministers. That was easily accomplished in one day. A social revolution, however, implies that tens of millions of citizens give up their property rights; it also implies the arrest of all non-Socialists. This cannot be accomplished in decades.

Untrue, worthy citizens, flagrantly untrue! The passing of *control* over industry into the hands of the workers, you choose to call "social revolution." In doing this you are guilty of three monstrous errors:

First, the revolution of March 12 was also a social revolution. Every political change, when it is not a mere change of cliques, is a social revolution. It is only a question as to *which class* is involved in that social revolution. The revolution of March 12, 1917, took the power out of the hands of the feudal landowners headed by Nicholas II, and gave it to the bourgeoisie. That was the social revolution of the *bourgeoisie*.

The *Finansovaia Gazeta*, by using clumsy and unscientific terms, by confusing "social" with "Socialist" revolution, is endeavouring to conceal from the people the obvious fact that the workers and peasants cannot be satisfied with the seizure of power by the bourgeoisie.

The capitalists are deceiving themselves and the people when they gloss over this simple and clear fact.

Secondly, "unprecedented" has also been the imperialist war of 1914-1917. "Unprecedented" have also been the devastation, the bloody horrors, the misery, the *breakdown of our entire civilisation*. It is not anybody's impatience, or propaganda, but objective forces and the unparalleled wreck of civilisation that impel the proletariat to assume control over industry and distribution, over banks, factories, etc.

Without such a step, the ruin of tens of millions of people is inevitable. And this is no exaggeration.

In view of the freedom resulting from the "political change" of March 12, in view of the existence of the Soviets of Workers', Peasants', etc., Deputies, such control is *impossible* without the preponderance of the workers and the peasants, without the minority submitting to the majority. Fulminate as you may, you cannot change an established fact.

Thirdly,—and this is the most important point,—even a Socialist revolution does *not* by any means imply that "tens of millions of citizens give up their property rights." Even Socialism (and the control over banks and factories does *not yet* mean Socialism) does not imply anything of the sort.

This is the vilest libel on Socialism. No Socialist has ever proposed to deprive "tens of millions," that means the small peasant proprietors, of their property (to make tens of millions "give up their property rights").

Nothing of the kind!

Socialists have always and everywhere denied such nonsense.

All we Socialists want is to make the landowners and the capitalists give up their property rights. In order to deal a finishing blow to the sport made of the people by the capitalists, for instance, by the coal operators who disorganise and spoil production, all we have to do is to make a *few hundred* people, at the most one to two thousand millionaires, bankers, manipulators of commerce and industry, give up their property rights.

This would be quite sufficient to break the resistance of capital. And even this handful of rich people must not necessarily be deprived of *all* their property rights; they may retain the ownership of a few personal possessions, and of enough property to secure them a certain modest income.

To break the resistance of a few hundred millionaires—this is the whole problem. This is the only condition under which we should be able to save ourselves from ruin.

Pravda, No. 61, June 1, 1917.

ONE MORE CAPITALIST CRIME

IT was only recently that the Petrograd report of the delegation from the Donetz workers exposed the gentlemen coal-mine proprietors of the Donetz, who are criminally disorganising production, who are stopping it, who (to safeguard their "divine" right to enormous profits) are condemning the workers to unemployment, the country to hunger, industry to a crisis because of the lack of coal.

To-day we received a telegram informing us of another equally brazen attempt of a criminal group of coal-mine proprietors in another part of Russia. Here is the telegram sent to the Soviet of Workers' and Soldiers' Deputies and to three Ministers:

The Soviet of Soldiers' Deputies and the union of employés in Mikhelson's Sudzhensk mines on May 12 removed nine persons from the administration of the mines because of their criminal and provoking manner of managing the business, which might have led to the shutting down of the mines. The management has been placed in the hands of a council of engineers, a technical council under the direct control of the Soviet of Workers' and Soldiers' Deputies. A commission of the leading Sudzhensk organisations has, upon investigation, approved our decision.

Mikhelson, in a telegram dated May 24, refused to settle with the workers; we demand complete restoration; restoration is impossible; * the mines are threatened with anarchy, the workers with misery. Take immediate measures by sending half a million rubles, determine the fate of the mines, confiscate them. The mines are working for national defence, the daily output is 135,000 poods—stoppage may imperil the movement of trains, the functioning of factories. So far the work is normal. Wages for March and April have not been fully paid.

(Signed) Soviet of Workers' and Soldiers' Deputies, and the Union of Employés.

It is impossible to find a more fitting expression than the one used by the Soviet of Workers' and Soldiers' Deputies and the Union of Employés in their telegram: "criminal and provoking manner of managing the business" by the capitalists.

And all the members of the Provisional Government, the so-called Socialist Ministers included, will be accomplices of this crime, if

---

* The meaning is not clear. Does the telegram aver that, once the mines are shut down, it would be difficult to start work again?

97

they continue to "grapple" with the approaching collapse by means of resolutions, commissions, conferences with the employers, if they continue to waste words, where they should use force against the capitalists.

Pravda, No. 61, June 1, 1917.

LETTER TO THE EDITOR

THE newspapers have again published an untruth when they said that for some unexplained reason I have not appeared at the Peasant Congress, that I have declined to attend, etc. As a matter of fact I was to appear on Wednesday and was prepared to do so when I was notified that on Wednesday the organisation problem was to be discussed instead of the agrarian question, deliberations on which were temporarily discontinued; the same thing occurred to-day, *i. e.*, Thursday. Once more I beg you not to believe the papers, except the *Pravda*.

N. LENIN.

Pravda, No. 61, June 1, 1917.

HAS DUAL POWER DISAPPEARED?

No. Dual power is still here. The basic question of every revolution, the question of state power, is still in an indefinite, unstable, and transitory state.

Compare the papers of the cabinet, the *Riech*, for instance, on the one hand, with the *Izvestia, Dielo Naroda, Rabochaia Gazeta*—on the other. Look through the scanty—alas, too scanty—official reports relating to the proceedings at the meetings of the Provisional Government, observe how the government "postpones" the discussion of the most essential questions, because of its inability to follow a definite course. Ponder the resolutions of the Executive Committee of the Soviet of Workers' and Soldiers' Deputies, passed on May 29, which deal with a most essential, most important matter, the question of how to forestall economic ruin and an imminent breakdown —and you will be convinced that dual power has remained fully intact.

Every one realises that the country is on the brink of an abyss,— yet all we do about it is engage in bureaucratic dallying.

Is it not bureaucratic dallying, when a resolution pertaining to such a grave question as an economic catastrophe, at such a grave moment, merely piles up commissions upon commissions, departments upon departments, and sub-departments upon sub-departments; when the same Executive Committee, in the outrageous and unparalleled case of the Donetz coal operators that were exposed as guilty of deliberate disorganisation of production, passes a resolution expressing nothing but pious wishes? [211] To fix prices, to regulate profits, to establish a minimum wage, to begin the formation of state-controlled trusts—all well and good. But how? through whom? "Through central and local institutions in the Donetz-Krivorozhsky basin. These institutions must be of a democratic character and must be formed with the participation of workers' representatives, employers, the government, and democratic, revolutionary organisations!"

This would be comic if it were not tragic.

For it is well known that such "democratic" institutions have existed and still exist in the localities concerned, as well as in Petrograd (the very same Executive Committee of the Soviet of Workers' and Soldiers' Deputies), but they have proved unable to do anything. Since the early part of March—March!—these conferences between the Donetz workers and industrialists have been going on. More than a month and a half has passed. The result is that the Donetz workers have been forced to the conclusion that the industrialists are engaged in deliberately disorganising industry!

And the people are treated again to promises, commissions, meetings of workers' and industrialists' representatives (in equal numbers?), and again an endless yarn begins!

The root of the evil is in the dual power. The root of the error of the Narodniks and the Mensheviks is in their not understanding the class-struggle, which they want to displace, disguise, attenuate with phrases, promises, make-shifts, commissions "with the participation" of representatives . . . of the same dual government!

The capitalists have reaped unheard-of outrageous profits during this war. They have on their side the majority of the government. They want exclusive power; they cannot, in view of their class position, but try to obtain complete control, they cannot but fight for it.

The working masses, comprising an overwhelming majority of the population, having the Soviets at their disposal, sensing their power as a majority, meeting everywhere with promises for the "democratisation" of life, knowing that democracy means the rule of the majority over the minority (*and not the reverse*—which is what the capitalists want), striving to better their lives since the revolution only (and then not everywhere), and not since the beginning of the war,—the working masses cannot but aspire towards a situation where all power is in the hands of the people, *i. e.*, the majority of the population, *i. e.*, a situation where affairs are managed according to the will of the majority of workers as opposed to the minority of capitalists, and not according to "an agreement" between the majority and the minority.

Dual power is still with us. The government of the capitalists remains a government of the capitalists, despite the small addition, in a minority capacity, of a few Narodniks and Mensheviks. The Soviets remain the organisation of the majority. The Narodniks and Menshevik leaders are helplessly tossing about hither and thither, trying to take up a position "on the fence."

And the crisis is growing. It has reached a point where the

capitalist coal operators are perpetrating incredibly brazen *crimes* —they are *disorganising and stopping* production. Unemployment is spreading. There is talk of lock-outs. Lock-outs are actually *beginning*—in the form of disorganisation of production by the capitalists (for, after all, coal is the food of industry!!), in the form of increasing unemployment.

The sole responsibility for this crisis, for the approaching catastrophe, falls upon the Narodnik and Menshevik leaders. For it is they who are at the present moment leaders of the Soviets, *i. e.*, of the majority. That the minority (the capitalists) should be unwilling to submit to the majority is inevitable. He who has not forgotten all the lessons of science and world-wide experience, he who has not forgotten the class-struggle, will not wait confidently for an "agreement" with the capitalists in such a basic, burning question.

The majority of the population, *i. e.*, the Soviets, *i. e.*, the workers and peasants, would have every possibility of saving the situation, of preventing the capitalists from disorganising and stopping production, of placing production, immediately and in practice, under their own control if it were not for the "conciliatory" policy of the Narodnik and Menshevik leaders. It is they who are responsible for the crisis and the catastrophe.

But there is no way out except through the determination of the majority of workers and peasants to act against the minority of capitalists. Delays will not help, they will make the malady more acute.

Viewed from a Marxist angle, the "conciliatory" attitude of the Narodnik and Menshevik leaders is a manifestation of petty-bourgeois indecision. The petty bourgeoisie is afraid to trust the workers, and is afraid to break with the capitalists. Such wavering is inevitable, as inevitable as our struggle, the struggle of the proletarian party, to overcome indecision, to explain to the people the necessity for rebuilding, organising, increasing production despite the capitalists.

There is no other escape. Either we go backward to a situation where all power is in the hands of the capitalists, or we go forward towards real democracy, towards decisions by the majority. The present situation of dual power cannot last long.

Pravda, No. 62, June 2, 1917.

ON THE "UNAUTHORISED SEIZURE" OF LAND

THE WEAK ARGUMENTS OF THE SOCIALISTS-REVOLUTIONISTS

THE *Izvestia* of the All-Russian Soviet of Peasant Deputies (No. 10, June 1) has published a report by S. Maslov, containing a discussion of "land seizures."

> In certain localities, says S. Maslov, the peasants are endeavouring to establish their right to the land by unauthorised seizures of the lands belonging to the neighbouring landowners. The question arises as to the expediency of such a procedure.[212]

S. Maslov regards it as inexpedient, and he supports his contention by four arguments. Let us examine them carefully.

Argument one. Reserve lands in Russia are unequally distributed in the various regions and provinces. Pointing out this incontestable fact, S. Maslov says:

> If every province or region were to lay claim to all the land within its confines and seize it for its own use, we can easily see how complications might arise which would interfere with a sound settlement of the land question. This can be easily foreseen, for the peasants of various villages might occupy the lands of the neighbouring landowners, leaving other peasants without land.

This argument deviates from the truth in an obvious and striking way. It hits at those who may conceive the idea of counselling the peasants to seize—and seize haphazardly—the lands as *private property*. Grab, divide—and hold.

This would, indeed, be the height of Anarchism, the height of absurdity.

We do not know who, what party, ever suggested such nonsense. If this is what S. Maslov has in mind, then he is simply fighting windmills. It is ridiculous.

Our party, the Russian Social-Democratic Labour Party (Bolsheviks), has proposed in a carefully framed resolution that *all property* in land be vested in the people as a whole. This means that we are *opposed* to any seizure of land as private property.

But this is not what S. Maslov is talking about, and he betrays

103

himself when he makes mention of the essential, the cardinal point: the seizure of the lands belonging to the *landowners*. This is the crux of the matter. Here is where the trouble lies. This is the question that makes S. Maslov writhe and purr.

Private estates must be confiscated *immediately*, *i. e.*, they must immediately be taken from the owners *without any compensation*.

But how about possession of these lands? Who should forthwith take hold of them, cultivate them? The local peasants, in an organised way, *i. e.*, in accordance with the decision of the majority. This is what our party counsels. The local peasants are to have the immediate use of the land; the ownership, however, is to remain with the people as a whole. The final right of ownership will be settled by the Constituent Assembly (or by the All-Russian Soviet of Soviets, should the people turn the latter into a Constituent Assembly).

What has the unequal distribution of reserve lands in various regions to do with all this? Obviously, nothing. Whatever the plan, be it that of the landowners, of S. Maslov, or of our party, this unequal distribution is bound to persist until the coming together of the Constituent Assembly.

S. Maslov is simply diverting the attention of the peasants from the matter in hand. He is concealing the essential point behind a flood of empty words that have nothing to do with the subject.

The essential point is the question of the private estates. The landowners wish to retain them. We wish to transfer them directly to the peasants without any compensation, *free of charge*. Maslov wants to procrastinate the matter by having it referred to "chambers of conciliation."

This is harmful. Delays are harmful. The landowners must submit to the will of the majority of peasants immediately. There is no need of conciliating the majority (the peasants) with the minority (the landowners). Such conciliation constitutes an illegitimate, unjust, undemocratic privilege granted to the landowners.

S. Maslov's second argument:

> The peasants are endeavouring to seize the land in the hope that if they succeed in sowing a crop the land will remain in their permanent possession. But this can be accomplished only by such peasant households as are equipped with a sufficient number of horses and labourers. Households that have no horses, families that have given most of their labour power to the army, will not be in a position to utilise this method of land seizure. It is clear, therefore, that this method can be of advantage to the more powerful, to the more prosperous, even, but not to those who are most in need of land.

This argument, too, is a crying falsehood.   Again S. Maslov diverts the attention of the peasants from the essential point, from the question of private estates.   For, were the peasants to take the private estates not by "seizing" (*i. e.*, free of charge, as we propose) the lands, but *by leasing, i. e.*, paying *rent* for them (as is proposed by the landowners and by S. Maslov), would the situation change in any way?   Does not the cultivation of lands leased from the owners require horses and labourers?   Can families that have given their labourers to the army lease lands on a par with large families?

On this point, the whole difference between our party, the Bolsheviks, and Maslov is this: he proposes that the land be taken from the landowners on a basis of payments and "conciliation" agreements, while we propose that the land be seized immediately and free of charge.

The question of rich *peasants* has nothing to do with the matter. Moreover, it is better for the poor that the land be seized without compensation.   For the rich it is easier to pay.

What measures are possible and necessary to prevent the rich peasant from injuring the poor one?

1. Majority rule (there are more poor peasants than rich ones). This is what we propose;

2. A *separate* organisation of poor peasants, where they *themselves* can consider *their own* interests.   This is what we propose;

3. Collective cultivation of lands; the livestock and implements on the landowners' estates to be held in common; the management to be in the hands of Soviets of Agricultural Workers' Deputies. This is what we propose.

And it is the last two measures, the most important ones, that the Party of "Socialists-Revolutionists" does not uphold.   What a pity.

The third argument:

At the beginning, during the first days of the Revolution, when rumours began to circulate among the soldiers that at home a division of land was taking place, many soldiers, for fear of being left without land, began to abandon the lines; desertions increased.

This argument bears upon the immediate division of land on the basis of private property.   No one has proposed such a division. Again S. Maslov shoots off the mark.

Fourth argument:

Finally, land seizures threaten to cause a reduction in planting. Cases are known, when, upon seizing private estates, the peasants have planted them poorly, using small quantities of seed, or have not planted their own lands. Now that our country is in such need of provisions, such a situation is absolutely inadmissible.

Well, this is altogether a poor argument, and is only likely to make people laugh! It turns out, then, that if the landowners are paid for their lands, the lands will be better cultivated!!

Do not disgrace yourself with such arguments, worthy citizen S. Maslov!

If the peasants do plant the fields poorly, then the peasants must be helped. And it is the poorest peasants that must be helped by means of collective cultivation of the large estates. There is no other way of helping the poorest peasants. Unfortunately, however, S. Maslov ignores the only remedy. . . .

We should add, in justice to S. Maslov, that he himself apparently feels the inadequacy of his arguments, for he himself hastens to remark:

Now after what I have said, I feel that some of you are ready to object: Are we being advised to leave everything as of old, after all we have suffered as a result of the lands belonging to the rich landowners? I do not undertake to propose to you any remedy at all.

Just so! From S. Maslov's words we gather that (though he does *not* want it) he would like to leave everything as of old. There is something wrong with his arguments somewhere.

The peasants must themselves decide. The business of the various parties is to make suggestions. Our party suggests what I have presented in the foregoing and what is carefully and precisely worked out in our resolutions [213] (Published as a supplement to No. 13 of the *Soldatskaia Pravda*, price 5 kopecks.)

N. LENIN.

Pravda, No. 62, June 2, 1917.

THE FIRST ALL-RUSSIAN CONGRESS OF PEASANT DEPUTIES

FROM MAY 17 TO JUNE 10, 1917

First published in 1917 in the pamphlet *Materials on the Agrarian Question* (in Russian).

THE FIRST ALL-RUSSIAN CONGRESS OF PEASANT DEPUTIES

I

1. ALL lands belonging to landowners and other private proprietors, as well as appanage and church lands, etc., must be immediately turned over, without compensation, to the people.

2. The peasantry must seize all the lands immediately, in an organised manner, through their Soviets of Peasant Deputies, and manage them economically, without, however, in the least prejudicing the final settlement of the land question by the Constituent Assembly or by the All-Russian Soviet of Soviets, should the people decide to place the power of the state in the hands of such a Soviet of Soviets.

3. Private ownership in land must be generally abolished, i. e., the right of ownership of all the lands must be vested in the people as a whole; the management of the land, however, must rest with local democratic institutions.

4. The peasants must reject the advice of the capitalists, the landowners, and the Provisional Government relating to "an agreement" with the landlords in each locality upon the question of the immediate management of the lands; the management of the lands should be determined by the organised will of the majority of local peasants, and not by an agreement of the majority, i. e., the peasants, with an insignificant minority, i. e., the landowners.

5. The landowners and the capitalists who wield tremendous monetary power, and exercise a vast influence on the still benighted masses through the newspapers, the numerous officials accustomed to the domination of capital, and through other agencies, are fighting and will fight with all means at their disposal, against the transfer, without compensation, of all privately owned lands to the peasants. That is why the transfer, without compensation, of all privately owned land to the peasantry cannot be completely carried out, nor made permanent unless the confidence of the peasant

masses in the capitalists has been undermined, unless close ties between the peasantry and the city workers have been established, unless all state power has completely passed into the hands of the Soviets of Workers', Soldiers', Peasants', etc., Deputies. It is only through such power placed in the hands of such Soviets and governing the state not through a police, nor a bureaucracy, nor a standing army alien to the people, but through a general, universal, armed militia of workers and peasants, that the above-stated agrarian reforms demanded by the entire peasantry can be secured.

6. Hired agricultural workers and the poorest peasants, *i. e.*, such peasants who for the lack of land, cattle and implements are obtaining their means of subsistence partly by hiring themselves out, must strain every effort to form independent organisations, either special Soviets or special groups within the all-peasant Soviets, in order that they may defend their interests against the rich peasants who inevitably tend towards a union with the capitalists and landowners.

7. As a result of the war, Russia, as well as all the other warring and many neutral countries, is threatened with ruin, catastrophe and hunger because of the lack of working hands, coal, iron, etc. Only the assumption of control and supervision over all production and distribution of goods by the Workers' and Peasants' Deputies can save the country. It is therefore necessary to begin working out agreements between the Soviets of Peasants' Deputies and the Soviets of Workers' Deputies with regard to the exchange of food and other products of the land for implements, shoes, clothing, etc., without the aid of the capitalists who are to be removed from the management of the factories. With the same purpose in view, the passing of the landowners' cattle and implements into the hands of peasant committees must be encouraged, such cattle and implements to be used in common. Similarly, the turning of each large private estate into a model farm must be encouraged, the land to be cultivated collectively with the best implements, under the direction of agriculturists, and in accordance with the decisions made by the local Soviets of Agricultural Workers' Deputies.

II

SPEECH ON THE AGRARIAN QUESTION

(June 4, 1917)

COMRADES! The resolution which I have the honour of submitting to your attention in the name of the Social-Democratic fraction of the Peasant Soviet has been printed and copies of it distributed among the delegates. If not all have received copies we will see to it that an additional number be printed to-morrow to be distributed among all desirous of having it.

In a short report I can take up, of course, only the main, the fundamental problems which interest the peasantry and the working class most. Whoever wishes more details about the question, I would recommend to him the resolution of our party, the Russian Social-Democratic Labour Party (Bolsheviks), which was published as a supplement to No. 13 of the paper *Soldatskaia Pravda* * and repeatedly commented upon in our paper, the *Pravda*. At present I shall have to limit myself to an examination of the most important, most controversial and most misunderstood points of my resolution and of our party programme on the agrarian question. One of such controversial and misunderstood points is the question touched upon at yesterday's or the day before yesterday's session of the Main Land Committee, a session of which you have all probably heard or read in yesterday's or the day before yesterday's papers.[215] At the session of the Main Land Committee there was present one of the representatives of our party, a fellow member of mine in the Central Committee, Comrade Smilga. Comrade Smilga moved that the Main Land Committee express itself in favour of an immediate organised seizure of the landowners' land by the peasantry. For this motion a number of objections were showered on Comrade Smilga. (*Voice: Here, too.*) I hear that here too many comrades object to this motion. The more reason why I should dwell on the examination of this point of our programme for it seems to me that the major part of the objections raised against our programme are based either on a misunderstanding or on an incorrect interpretation of our views.

What do all the resolutions of our party, all the articles of our paper, the *Pravda*, say? We say that the land must all without ex-

* See Note 160, Book I of this volume.—*Ed.*

ception pass into the ownership of the whole people. This conclusion we have reached on the basis of studying, particularly, the
peasant movement of 1905, the declaration of the peasant deputies
in the first and second Imperial Dumas where peasant deputies from
all parts of Russia could express themselves with comparative
freedom.

All the land must be the property of all the people. It follows
from this that when we stand for an immediate and free transfer
of all the landowners' lands into the hands of the local peasants, we
by no means stand for the seizure of those lands as private property, we by no means advocate the division of those lands. We only
propose that the land must be taken for a year's planting by the
local peasantry after a decision has been reached by a majority of
the local and peasant delegates. We have never insisted that the
land should become the property of those peasants who take it at
present for a year's planting. All such objections against our proposal which I have come across in the columns of the capitalist
papers are obviously based on an incorrect interpretation of our
views. Once we say—and I repeat, we say it in all our resolutions—
that the land must be the property of all the people and pass to
them free of charge, then it is obvious that the settlement of the
final distribution of this land, the final establishment of land regulations must be the business of the central state power alone, *i. e.*,
the Constituent Assembly or the All-Russian Soviet of Soviets, if
such a power, the Soviet of Soviets, were to be created by the
peasant and workers' masses. There are no differences of opinion
on this score.

The differences of opinion begin when one objects to our saying:
"If that is the case, then every immediate, uncompensated passage
of the landowners' land into the hands of the peasantry will be an
arbitrary act." This view, expressed most precisely and with the
greatest weight and authority by Minister of Agriculture Shingarev
in his well-known telegram, we consider most erroneous, detrimental to the peasantry, detrimental to the tillers of the land, detrimental to the cause of providing the country with bread, and unjust
besides. I take the liberty to read to you that telegram, in order
that you may see what it is that we object to most.

. . . An independent solution of the land question in the absence of a
general state law is inadmissible. Arbitrary action will lead to a national
calamity . . . the lawful solution of the land question is the business of

the Constituent Assembly. Pending that there will be formed in each locality as adjuncts of the volost supply committees agricultural chambers of conciliation . . . [by] the land tillers and land owners.

This is the salient passage of the government's declaration on this question. If you acquaint yourself with the resolution recently adopted by a conference of the members of the Imperial Duma, you will realise that both resolutions proceed from the same view. They accuse of arbitrary acts those peasants who insist on putting into practice the immediate and uncompensated transfer of the land to local land committees. They proceed from the idea that only a voluntary agreement between the peasants and the landowners, between the tillers of the land and the proprietors of the land, is compatible with the general needs and interests of the state. It is this that we deny, it is this that we dispute.

Let us analyse the objections advanced against our proposal. The usual objection is that the land in Russia is distributed very unequally, both among individual, small units, like villages and volosts, and between large units, like provinces and regions. It is said that if the local population, by its own decision, by a majority of votes, were to take the land into its own hands without reckoning with the landowners' will, and without compensation at that, the inequality in the distribution would remain, and there would be even a danger of that inequality becoming permanent. We reply to such an objection that it is based on a misunderstanding. Unequal distribution of the land will remain in any case, until the Constituent Assembly or the central state power, whatever it may be, has finally established a new order. Pending the establishment of this order, no matter whether the question is solved peasant-fashion or landowner-fashion, whether, as we wish it, the land is immediately transferred into the hands of the peasants or, as the landowners wish it, the land is rented at high rentals and the peasant lease-holder and landowner retain their rights,—whatever the case, unequal distribution remains. This is why such objection is obviously incorrect and unjust. We say that it is necessary as quickly as possible to create a central state power not only based on the will and decisions of a peasant majority but also directly expressing the opinion of that majority. There is no difference of opinion on this score. When we hear objections against the Bolsheviks, when we see them attacked in the capitalist papers, when people say that we are Anarchists, we repudiate this most categorically.

We look upon such attacks as the dissemination of malicious lies and calumny.

People who deny the necessity of state power are called Anarchists, whereas we say that it is absolutely necessary, and not only for Russia at the present time, but also for every state, even when it is directly introducing Socialism. A strong state power is absolutely necessary! We only desire that this power should be entirely and fully in the hands of a majority of workers', soldiers', and peasants' deputies. This is wherein we differ from other parties. We by no means deny the necessity of strong state power, we only say that all the landowners' land must pass without compensation into the hands of the peasants after the local peasant committee has, by a majority of votes, adopted a resolution in this respect, and under the conditions that there be no damage to inventory. This has been indicated in our resolution most precisely. We decidedly repudiate objections to our view which claim that this is arbitrary action.

No, in our opinion, if the landowners nold the lands to their advantage or take rentals for them, this is arbitrary; but if a majority of the peasantry says that the landowners' land must not remain with the landowners, that the peasants for long decades, nay, for centuries, have seen nothing but oppression on the part of those landowners, those masters, then it is not arbitrary action; it is a right restored, and we cannot wait with the restoration of a right. If the land right now passes to the peasants, this will not do away with inequality between regions; there is no doubt about that, but this inequality will not be done away with by anybody until the Constituent Assembly convenes. If we were to ask Shingarev, the man who objects to us and brands in official papers the adherents of our views for "arbitrary acts,"—if we were to ask him what is his remedy for the inequality, he would not be able to answer. He proposes nothing, and cannot propose anything.

He says: "Voluntary agreements between the peasants and the landowners." What does that mean? Let me present two basic figures concerning landownership in European Russia. Those figures show that at one end of the Russian village we have the richest landowners, including the Romanovs, the richest and worst landowners, at the other end the poorest peasants. My figures will show you what significance there is to Shingarev's preaching, to the preaching of all landowners and capitalists. If we take the richest landowners of European Russia, we find that, numbering less than 30,000, they possess something like seventy million desiatinas. This amounts to an average of two thousand desiatinas for each. In other words, if we take the upper strata of the rich Russian landowners without distinction of class origin (most of them are nobles, but there are also other landowners), we find them numbering 30,-000. Their possessions equal seventy million desiatinas! When we take the poorest peasantry, then, according to the same 1905 census which offers the latest information uniformly collected all over Russia,—information not deserving in substance very much credence, like all statistics collected under the Tsar by the Tsar's officials, but still offering data approaching the truth, data capable of comparison,—if we take the poorest peasantry, we find 10,000,000 of households with seventy to seventy-five million desiatinas. In other words, one has over two thousand desiatinas, another seven desiatinas and one-half per household. And still they say that it would be arbitrary action if the peasants do not enter into a voluntary agreement! What does this "voluntary agreement" mean? It means that maybe the landowners will yield land for good rentals, but will not give it to anybody for nothing. Is this just? No, it is unjust. Is this of advantage to the peasant population? No, it is to their disadvantage. In which way the final landownership will be settled is the business of the future central power, for the present, however, all the landowners' land must without compensation pass into the hands of the peasantry under the conditions of organised seizure. Minister Shingarev, arguing against my Comrade Smilga in the Main Land Committee, said that the words "organised seizure" are mutually contradictory; these two words, he said, nullify each other, for if it is seizure it is not organised, and if it is organised it is not seizure. I think that this criticism is incorrect. I think that once the peasantry adopts a majority decision in a village or volost, in a county, in a province—and in some provinces, if not in all, the peasant congresses have established local power representing the interests and the will of the majority of the population, i. e., of the majority of the tillers of the land,—once the peasants adopt a decision locally, then it is the decision of the power which they recognise. This is the power for which the local peasants cannot fail to have full respect. Let the peasant know that he takes the landowners' land; if he pays, let him pay into the peasants' county fund; let him know that his money will go to improve agriculture, to lay pavements, roads, etc. Let him know that he takes his own land,—not the landowners', but the people's, the land which the Constituent Assembly will finally dispose of. This is why from the very beginning of the revolution, from the moment the first land committee was established, there must be no right of landowner to the land, and there must be no payments collected for that land.

We differ from our opponents fundamentally as to what constitutes order, and what is law. Up to now, it was accepted that order and law is what is good for the landowners and the officials. We say that order and law is what is good for the majority of the peasantry! As long as there is no All-Russian Soviet of Soviets, as long as there is no Constituent Assembly, all of the local power, the county committees, the province committees, are the embodiment of the highest order and law! Arbitrary action we call the fact that one landowner, on the basis of centuries-old rights, demands a "voluntary" agreement with 300 peasant families, each of which has on the average seven and one-half desiatinas! We say: "Let decisions be adopted by a majority; we wish that the peasants should receive the landowners' lands right now, without losing a single month, a single week, a single day!"

Another objection: "If the peasantry were to seize the land right now, then it may happen that it will be seized by the more prosperous who have cattle, implements, etc. Will that not be dangerous from the point of view of the poorest peasantry?" Comrades, I must dwell on this objection because our party in all its decisions, programmes, and appeals to the people declares: "We are a party of wage-workers and poorest peasants; we wish to safeguard their interests; through them, and through them alone, through these classes can humanity get out of the horrors into which it was precipitated by this war of the capitalists."

This is why we are very attentive to objections which claim that our decisions are not in accord with the interests of the poorest peasants. We invite you to dwell on them with particular attention, because these objections touch upon the very essence of the matter, the very root of the question. The essence is how the interests of the wage-workers in city and village, the interests of the poorest peasants, can and must be defended in the developing revolution against the interests of the landowners and the rich peasants, who are also capitalists under a different name. Of course, this is the crux of the question, this is its real essence! And it is here that we are told that if we advise the peasants immediately to seize the land, then it will be seized first of all by those who have implements and cattle, and the poor will remain empty-handed. I ask you now: Will a voluntary agreement with landowners help?

You know perfectly well that the landowners will not be eager to rent their land to those peasants who have not a kopeck in their pocket. On the contrary, the landowners resort to "voluntary" agreements when they see a prospect of good payments. The landowners have never given away their land for nothing. It seems to me nobody has ever seen a thing like this in Russia.

A voluntary agreement with the landowners means that the privileged, preferred position, the advantages of the rich peasants, will be much more enhanced, increased, strengthened, for they certainly can pay the landowners, and the rich peasant is in the eyes of every landowner a solvent person. The landowner knows that he can pay, that the rent can be collected, this is why when such "voluntary" deals with the landowners take place, the rich peasants will certainly gain more than the poor. On the contrary, if there is a way of helping the poor peasantry right now, it is only through the measure that I propose, namely, that the land must immediately pass over to the peasants free of charge.

Landlords' private ownership has been and will be the greatest injustice. The free holding of this land by the peasants, if it is done by majority decision, is no arbitrary act; it is a right restored. This is how we look upon the matter, and this is why the argument that the poorest peasantry may lose is in our opinion a great injustice. Can you call it "voluntary" agreement—only Shingarev can do so—when one landowner has two thousand desiatinas while three hundred peasants have seven and one-half desiatinas each? To call such an agreement voluntary is to mock at the peasant! It is not a voluntary agreement; it is a compulsory one for the peasantry, and compulsory it will remain until every peasant committee, volost, province or county, and the All-Russian Soviet will have declared that landowners' private property is a great injustice, the removal of which cannot wait a single hour, a single minute.

Property in land must belong to the whole people, and its establishment is the task of the state power. As long as there is none, the local powers, I repeat, take the landowners' land, and this they must do by majority decision, in an organised way. It is not true that disorder reigns in Russia, as the papers lament! It is not true; in the villages there is more order than ever, for decisions are made by a majority vote; there has been almost no violence against landowners; cases of injustice and violence against the landowners are sporadic and very rare; in fact, their number is insignificant and hardly exceeds, taking Russia as a whole, the number of acts of violence that occurred before.

Let me now touch upon one more argument which I happened to hear and which I analysed in our paper, the *Pravda,* in connection with the question of the passing of the lands into the hands of the peasantry.* The argument is that if the peasant is advised immediately to take the landowners' lands into his hands free of charge, this will call forth dissatisfaction, irritation, suspicion, and perhaps even revolts on the part of the soldiers at the front who may say: "If the peasants take the land now while we are at the front, we will remain without land." The soldiers, one says, might start an exodus from the front and there would be chaos and anarchy. To which we reply that the objection does not meet the main question in the least: for in either case, whether the land is taken and remuneration made after an agreement with the landowners or by a decision of a majority of the peasantry, the soldiers will remain at the front as long as the war is going on, and of course they will stay at the front and cannot go home. Now, if the soldiers at the front are not afraid that the landlords, under the guise of a voluntary agreement, may impose on them unfavourable conditions, why must they be afraid of what the peasantry would decide by a majority vote against the landowners? Incomprehensible! Why must the soldier at the front have confidence in the landowner, in the "voluntary" agreement with the landowner? I understand when this is said by a party of landowners and capitalists, but that a Russian soldier at the front should look this way, I do not believe. If there is a "voluntary" agreement with the landowner, the soldier will not call it order, he will have no confidence in it. He will rather think that the old disorder of landowners' rule continues.

The soldier will have more confidence in what is happening when he is told that the land goes over to the people, that the local peasants rent it and do not pay to the landowner, but contribute to their committee for satisfying general needs, including the soldiers' front,

* See p. 105 of this book.—*Ed.*

but nothing for the landowners. When this is decided by a majority, the soldier at the front will learn that there can be no more "voluntary" agreements with the landowners, but that the landowners are citizens with the same rights as others, and that nobody wishes to harm them. The land belongs to the whole people, this means it belongs to the landowner as well, but not on the basis of the privileges of nobility, only on the same basis as it belongs to every citizen. There must be no privileges for the landowners from the very day of the overthrow of the power of the Tsar, who was the largest landowner and oppressor of the masses. With the establishment of freedom, the landowners' power must be considered overthrown once and for all. The soldier at the front will lose nothing from this conception; on the contrary, he will have much more confidence in the state power, he will have a serene confidence in the future of his home, knowing that his family will not be injured, will not remain unaided.

There is one more argument advanced against our proposal. The argument is that if the peasants were to seize the landowners' land immediately, such immediate hardly-prepared seizure might entail a worsening in the cultivation of the land. That is to say, the crops would be worse. I must repeat here that the power of the majority, the central state power, has not been created as yet. The peasants have not yet gained sufficient confidence in themselves, and have not yet lost confidence in the landowners and capitalists. I think that with every day we approach this state of affairs, with every day the peasantry is losing confidence in the old state power and is beginning to understand that the government in Russia must consist of persons elected by the peasants, soldiers, workers, and nobody else.

I think that with every day we come closer to such a state of affairs, not because one or the other party has counselled it, for never will millions of people follow the advice of parties if that advice does not coincide with what they are taught by the experience of their own life. We are rapidly approaching a situation when there will be no other power in Russia but that of persons elected by the peasants and the workers. And when I am told that maybe the seizure of the land would lead to bad cultivation, to bad planting, I. must admit that our peasants, due to their backwardness, due to centuries-old oppression by landlords, cultivate the land very badly. Of course, there is a terrible crisis in Russia as in all other belligerent countries, and there is no salvation for Russia, if one does not pass to better cultivation, to the greatest economy in human labour. But can the "voluntary" agreement with the landowners change anything as far as the first crop is concerned? What does it mean? Will the landowners look after the cultivation of the land better, will the peasants plant the land worse if they know that they plant not on the landowners' but on the people's land, that they pay not to the landowner but to peasant funds? This is such nonsense that I am astonished when I hear such arguments. The proposition is entirely inconceivable and is nothing but a landowner's ruse.

The landowners understand that it is impossible to rule any longer by the club; this they now understand well; they therefore try to adopt a method of ruling which, for Russia, is a novelty, which in western Europe, however, has been in existence for a long time. That it is impossible to rule by the club any longer was shown in our country by two revolutions, in western Europe by dozens of revolutions. Those revolutions teach the landowners and capitalists a lesson: they tell them that it is necessary to rule people by fraud and flattery; that it is necessary to adapt oneself, to attach a red badge to the coat and, though one may be a village shark, to say: "We are revolutionary democrats if you please, you just wait a little and all will be done for you." The argument that the peasants will plant their land worse when they do it not on the landowners' but on the people's land, is nothing but a mockery at the peasants, an attempt to retain the landowners' rule by fraud.

I repeat, there must be no landowners' property at all. To hold does not yet mean to own; holding is a temporary measure; holding changes every year. The peasant who rents a little piece of land does not dare to think that the land is his. The land is neither his nor the landowner's but the people's. The planting cannot be worse this year or this spring on account of the seizure. Such a proposition is so monstrous, so unbelievable, that I can tell you only this: beware of the landowners, do not trust them, do not allow yourselves to be deceived by friendly words and promises. Remember that the decisions of a majority of the peasants, who are very cautious in their decisions, are lawful decisions pertaining to the whole state. One may rely on the peasants in this respect. Here, for instance, I have before me the decision of the Penza peasants

which from the first to the last point is based on the spirit of unusual caution; the peasants do not undertake in it any immediate
reform for all of Russia; what they want is not to be driven into
intolerable bondage and in this they are right. The greatest bondage
has been and is that imposed by the landowners, the bondage under
those who own the land and use it for oppression. This is why one
must not wait a summer with the removal of this bondage. Still,
every seizure must be organised seizure, not made for the sake of
private property, not for the sake of distributing, but for the sake
of using in common the common land of the people. I could finish
now with this question of seizure. I could say that the objections
to our proposition are, on the part of landowners and capitalists,
based on fraud, and that on the part of non-landowners and non-
capitalists, on the part of people who wish to defend the interests
of the toilers, they are based on a misunderstanding, on an excess
of confidence in what the capitalists and the landowners fraudu-
lently say against us. If we analyse our arguments, it appears that
the just demand for an immediate abolition of the landowners'
private property, as well as for the transfer of the landed property
to the people, cannot be realised until the central state power is in
existence; that, nevertheless, we recommend in the most urgent
fashion the transfer of landholding to the peasants immediately,
in every locality with the understanding that there must not be the
slightest disturbance of order. This we counsel in our resolutions,
and it even may be that this counsel is superfluous, for the peasants
practice it in life anyway.

Let me now pass to the second question to which attention must
be particularly directed, namely, to the question of how we desire,
and how it is best in the interests of the labouring masses, to deal
with the land once it has become the property of all the people,
once private property has been abolished. This hour is very near
in Russia. The strength of the landowners' power is undermined,
if not destroyed. Once the land is held by all the peasants, once
there are no landowners, what then? How shall the land be distributed? It seems to me that a general view on this question must
be established, since it is quite obvious that it will always be in the
power of the peasants to dispose of the land locally. It cannot be
otherwise in a democratic state. This is so obvious that it is superfluous to discuss it. As to the question, what shall be done so that
the land shall be transferred to the toilers, we say: "We wish

to defend the interests of the wage-workers and the poorest peasants." This our party, the Russian Bolshevik Social-Democratic Party, considers its task. Still, we ask ourselves: if we say that the land will be transferred to the people, is it the same as to say that the land will be transferred to the toilers? Our answer is no, it is not the same! If we say that the land will be transferred to the people, it means that the landowners' private property will be destroyed; it means that all the land will belong to all the people; it means that every one who takes the land, takes it on the basis of renting it from the whole people. Once this order is established, it means that there is no difference in landownership any longer, that all the land is on the same plane, or as the peasants often say: "All the old fences have been removed; the land is unfenced; there is free land and free labour."

Does that mean, that the land is transferred to all the labourers? No, it does not mean that. Free labour on free land means that all old forms of ownership have been reduced to naught, that there is no landownership other than that of the state as a whole; that every one rents the land from the state; that there is a general state power, the power of all the workers and peasants; that the peasant as a lease-holder rents land from this power; that there are no middlemen between the state and the peasant; that everybody rents land on an equal footing. This is what is meant by free labour on free land.

But does that mean, that the land is transferred to all the toilers? No, it does not mean that. You cannot eat the land; to conduct a farm enterprise one must have implements, cattle, improvements, money; without money, without implements, one cannot till. This is why when you establish the order of free labour on free land, when there is no landowners' private property any longer, when there are no classes in relation to the land, when, on the contrary, the land is the property of the whole people and free peasants rent it from the state, it will not mean yet that the land is transferred to all the toilers, it will only mean that every peasant manages the land freely, that every one who wishes to do so will freely take from the nationalised land. In comparison with the tsarist, landowners' Russia this will be a long step forward, since under landowners', tsarist Russia seventy million desiatinas were in the hands of 30,000 Markovs, Romanovs and similar landowners, whereas in this new Russia there will be free labour on free land. This latter has already been accomplished in many localities. Russia has already made strides to combat old tsarist, landowners' Russia, but this is not a transfer of the land to the toilers; it is a transfer of the land to the man who conducts an agricultural enterprise; because if the land belongs to the state as a whole, and it is taken by those who wish to conduct an enterprise on it, the wish to conduct an enterprise is not sufficient in itself, one must know how to do it, and knowledge is not sufficient either. Every agricultural labourer and every peasant has the knowledge, but he has no cattle, implements, capital. This is why, no matter what you decide, no matter what you say, we shall not establish in this way real free labour on free land. Even if we post signs about free land in every volost council, the matter will improve in favour of the labourers as little as prisons of the western European republics bearing the inscription "Liberty, Equality, and Fraternity" cease being prisons. If we inscribe the legend, "Liberty, Equality, and Fraternity" on a factory, as is done in America, the factory will not cease being hell for the workers and paradise for the capitalists.

It follows that we must think now of the further steps, we must think how to secure more than free labour. The latter is a step forward but does not yet safeguard the interests of the toilers; it is a step towards liberation from landowners' rapacity, from landowners' exploitation, liberation from the Markovs, from the police, but it is not a step towards safeguarding the interests of the toilers, since without cattle, without implements, without capital the poor peasant, the economically weak peasant cannot get hold of the land. This is why I very much mistrust the proposition of two measures or two norms, the labour norm and the food norm. I know that the Narodnik parties have discussed and interpreted this point about two norms. I know that those parties assume the necessity of establishing those two norms, those two measures: the labour norm, i. e., the maximum amount of land above which no family is allowed to cultivate, and the food norm, the minimum amount below which starvation must ensue. I say that I have misgivings about this proposition concerning two norms or measures; I think it is a bureaucratic plan which will be of no value, which cannot be introduced in life even if you were to decide upon that plan. That is the main thing! That plan can give no appreciable relief to the wage-workers and poorest peasants. This plan, even if you accept it, will remain on paper as long as capitalism rules. This plan will not help find the right way for passing from capitalism to Socialism.

When one speaks about those two measures, those two norms, one pictures the situation as if there were only land and citizens, and nothing else in the world. If that were so, the plan would be good. However, it is not so. There is the power of capital, the power of money, without money there can be no enterprise on the freest land possible under any possible "measures," for as long as money reigns, hired labour remains. And that means that the rich peasants, of whom there are no less than a million families in Russia, oppress and exploit the wage-workers and will oppress them also on "free" land. Those rich peasants, always, as a rule and not as an exception, resort to hiring labourers for a year, for a season or by the day, which means that they exploit the poorest peasants, the proletarians. Side by side with them there are millions and millions of peasants who have no horses, who cannot exist without selling their labour power, without going to other provinces to seek seasonal work. Whatever "norms" are established, as long as the power of money remains, the norms will at best be unfitted to practical life because they do not reckon with the chief factor, namely, that property, implements, cattle, money are unequally distributed. They do not reckon with the fact that there is wage labour subject to exploitation. This is the fundamental fact in the life of present-day Russia; it cannot be circumvented; if we establish one or the other "measure," life will circumvent them and the "measures" will remain on paper. This is why in order to defend, and win victory for, the interests of the impecunious and the poorest peasants in this greatest transformation of Russia which you are now carrying out and which you will undoubtedly carry out when private property in land is abolished, when a step forward is made, nearer to a better, a Socialist future,—in order to safeguard the interests of the workers and the poorest peasants in this great transformation which you are only beginning and which will proceed far ahead, since there is no power to stop it,—we cannot go along the road of establishing norms and measures, we must seek another way.

My comrades and myself, members of the party in whose behalf I have the honour to speak here, know that there are two such ways for safeguarding the interests of the agricultural wage workers and poorest peasants. Those two ways we submit to the attention of the Peasant Soviet.

The first way is to organise the agricultural wage-workers and

poorest peasants. This is why we recommend that in every peasant
committee, in every volost, county, province, a special fraction or
a special group of agricultural wage-workers and poorest peasants
be formed. This fraction is to ask itself the following: Should the
land to-morrow become the property of the whole people—and this
will inevitably happen because it is the will of the people—what
shall we do? We who have no cattle or implements, where shall
we get them? How shall we till the land? How shall we defend
our interests? How shall we see to it that the land, becoming
the property of the whole people, shall not fall into the hands of
the propertied peasants alone? If it were to fall into the hands of
those who have enough cattle and implements, what will we gain
by it? Is it for this that we have accomplished this great change?
Is it this that we need?

The land will belong to the "people." But this is not sufficient
for defending the interests of the agricultural wage-workers. The
main line cannot be mapped out by establishing here, from above,
or through a peasant committee, a "norm" for individual landholding. Those measures will be of no avail as long as capital rules;
they will not lead us away from the rule of capitalism. To get out
from under the yoke of capitalism so that the people's land should
be transferred into the hands of the toilers, only one main road is
open: This is the road of organising the agricultural wage-workers
who will be guided by their experience, by their observations, by
their distrust of all that the village sharks say, even when they be-
deck themselves with red bows and call themselves "revolutionary
democracy."

Only an independent organisation established locally, only experience will teach the poorest peasants. This experience will not
be easy, we do not and cannot promise that there will be rivers
of milk and banks of honey. No, the landowners will be overthrown because such is the will of the people, but capitalism will
remain. Its overthrow will be much more difficult, its overthrow
will be reached by a different road. This is the road of independent, separate organisations of agricultural wage-workers and poorest peasants.

This is what our party proposes in the first place. Only along
this road can one expect a gradual, not a very easy, but a certain
transfer of the land into the hands of the actual toilers.

The second step recommended by our party is that every large farm, say every large landowner's estate, of which there are 30,000 in Russia, should be organised as quickly as possible into model farms to be worked by agricultural workers jointly with trained agriculturists, with the application for this purpose of the landowners' cattle, implements, etc. Without such common work under the leadership of the Soviets of Agricultural Workers, the land will not be in the hands of the toilers. Of course, common labour is a difficult thing; of course, if anybody imagines that such common tillage can be established and foisted from above, that would be madness, since the centuries-old habit of individual enterprises cannot disappear at once, since money is needed for such an undertaking, an adaptation to the new foundations of life is needed. Were these plans, these opinions concerning common tillage, common inventory, common cattle, with the best application of implements jointly with agriculturists,—were all these plans an invention of one or the other party, things would be rather in bad shape, since no changes in the life of a people are accomplished by the planning of one or the other party, since tens of millions of people do not go into a revolution because parties have planned it, since such a change will be a much greater revolution than the overthrow of the imbecile Nicholas Romanov. I repeat, tens of millions of people do not make a revolution to order, but they do so when there is bitter privation, when the people finds itself in an impossible situation, when the general onslaught, the determination of tens of millions of people shatters all the old partitions and is in reality capable of creating a new life. If we propose such a measure, if we propose to approach it with caution, although we say that it is necessary, we conclude this not from our programme, not from our Socialist doctrine, but we do so because, being Socialists and observing the life of the western European peoples, we have reached that conclusion. We know that there have been many revolutions in those countries, that democratic republics were organised by those revolutions; we know that in 1865 the slaveholders were defeated in America,[216] and that then hundreds of millions of desiatinas of land were distributed among the farmers, free or almost free of charge; nevertheless capital is ruling there as nowhere else, and it is crushing the labouring masses as much if not more than in other countries. This is the Socialist doctrine; these are our observations of other peoples that have led us to the firm conviction that, outside of common tillage of the land by agricultural workers under the condition of applying the best machines and using the advice of trained agriculturists, there is no way out from the yoke of capitalism. If, however, we were to base ourselves only on the experience of the western European states, we would be in a bad shape in Russia, because the Russian people is capable in its mass of taking an earnest step on a new road only when extreme necessity arises. We say, a time has come when this extreme necessity knocks at the door of the entire Russian people. This extreme necessity is the fact that you cannot cultivate your land in the old manner. If we continue, as of old, in small households, even as free citizens on free land, we are still threatened with unavoidable ruin, since economic chaos is looming larger every hour, every minute. Everybody speaks about that; it is a fact resulting not from the ill-will of individual persons, but from the annexationist World War, from capitalism.

The war has destroyed large numbers of people; all the world is flooded with blood; all the world has been brought to the brink of ruin by the war. This is no exaggeration. Nobody can vouch for the coming day; everybody speaks about that. Take, for instance, the *Izvestia* of the Soviet of Workers and Soldiers' Deputies; everybody says there that the capitalists resort to sabotage and lock-outs. The pretext is that there is no work, and the workers are being discharged in great numbers. This is what this criminal war has brought, not only upon Russia, but upon all the countries.

We say therefore that an agricultural enterprise on individual plots, even if it be "free labour on free land," is still no way out of the terrible crisis, out of the world destruction; it is no salvation. Universal labour duty is required. The greatest caution in utilising human labour is required. An unusually strong and firm power is required, which shall be in a position to introduce this universal labour duty. This cannot be introduced by state bureaucrats; it can be introduced only by the Soviets of Workers', Soldiers', and Peasants' Deputies, because they are the people themselves, they are the mass of the people; because this is not a bureaucratic power; because knowing the peasant life from top to bottom they can establish labour duty, they can establish safeguards for human labour whereby the peasants' labour shall not be squandered and the transition to common tillage would thus be accomplished gradually and cautiously. It is a difficult task, but it is necessary to undertake common tillage on the large model farms. Outside of this there is no way out of economic ruin, out of the truly desperate situation in which Russia finds itself. It would, however, be the greatest error to think that a reform of such colossal dimensions can be made by one stroke. No, it demands a tremendous amount of labour, it demands exertion, determination, and endurance on the part of every individual peasant and worker in the locality and in the work which he knows best, and in the production which he has been conducting for decades. This cannot be done by somebody's order, but done it must be, because the annexationist war has brought all humanity to the brink of ruin, because tens of millions of lives have perished, and many more will perish in this terrible war, if we do not exert all our efforts, if all the organisations of the Soviets of Workers,' Soldiers' and Peasants' Deputies will not undertake common, determined action on the road to common tillage of land without capitalists and without landlords. Only thus will the land actually pass into the hands of the toilers.

ARTICLES, SPEECHES, ETC., ON THE EVE OF THE
ALL-RUSSIAN CONGRESS OF SOVIETS

PARTIES IN THE ELECTIONS FOR THE BOROUGH COUNCILS
OF PETROGRAD

THE lists of candidates for members of the Borough Councils have recently been made public (free supplement to the Bulletin of the Public City Administration, May 30).[217] It is to be regretted that the information published covers only ten boroughs. Still we get a very clear and striking picture of *party alignments*—a picture that deserves close study, because of the propaganda value it has, and because of the light it throws on the relation of parties to *classes*.

The existence of parties is both a condition for and an index of political enlightenment. The more politically enlightened, educated and intelligent a certain population or a certain class the higher, as a rule, is its party adherence. This general rule is corroborated by the experience of all civilised countries. From the point of view of the class struggle, it is obvious that this is as it should be: absence of parties, or inadequate party crystallisation and party organisation signifies class instability (this is at best; at worst, such inadequacy signifies the deception of the masses by political char-latans—a phenomenon quite usual in parliamentary countries).

What, then, do the lists of the Petrograd candidates reveal to us in the matter of parties?

There are altogether seventy-one lists in the ten boroughs; these actually indicate a division into *five* large groups.

1. The R.S.-D.L.P.—The *Bolsheviks*. Lists were presented for each of the ten boroughs. Our party and two other groups, the Mezhraiontsy-Interboroughites and the Mensheviks-Internationalists have formed a bloc. This bloc is based on principles, openly pro-claimed in resolutions passed by the Petrograd and the All-Russian conferences of our party. The basic problem in the contemporary political life in Russia, as well as in the political life of the rest of the world, is that of the struggle of proletarian internationalism against the chauvinism (or "defencism") of the big and the petty bourgeoisie. Accordingly, our party has publicly declared its determination to bring about the "rapprochement and consolidation" of all internationalists. (See the resolution passed by the All-

131

Russian conference pertaining to the consolidation of all internationalists in their opposition to the petty-bourgeois defencist bloc.)

The party of the proletariat has taken a clear, frank, honest stand on the issues involved in the elections.

2. The "People's Freedom" Party, *i. e.*, the Cadets, the party of the counter-revolutionary bourgeoisie, shows its class physiognomy no less clearly. Here we also have ten regular party lists for the ten boroughs. As is well known, *all* the parties of the landowners and the capitalists are at present supporting the Cadets; this, however, is still being done covertly.

3. In respect of clear party alignments, the third place belongs to the newly formed radical-democratic party which has put up its lists in six out of the ten boroughs. This party, known to no one, is also clearly capitalist, and hopes to "pull" votes by means of promises that commit to nothing—it is something in the nature of a Cadet party in disguise.

4. The fourth place belongs to a group that has put up seventeen lists in nine boroughs; it is made up of a motley crowd of Narodniks (Trudoviks, Socialists-Revolutionists, People's Socialists), Mensheviks and the notorious *Yedinstvo* group.

A perfect specimen of petty-bourgeois confusion and petty-bourgeois want of principle, *not one* of these parties has dared to come out in advance with an open declaration of principles as regards rapprochement and consolidation of the groups composing it. They have been dragged along by events, they are trailing after the chauvinists. All of them have fallen into the same mire, and are floundering in it in true philistine fashion, trying to "insinuate" themselves into the confidence of the voters of each borough by various methods. By hook or crook but we must get in,—this is their motto.

If they are all of one mind on "defencism" or on supporting the coalition cabinet,—then why do they not combine into one real, open political bloc appearing in the present election campaign with a set of definite principles?

The point is that the petty bourgeoisie, *i. e.*, the Narodniks and Mensheviks, have neither principles, nor party cohesion! All of them are defencists and "coalitionists." Yet they do not trust one another. Here the Socialists-Revolutionists run independently, there they have entered into a bloc with the People's Socialists and the

Trudoviks (people who approve of compensation for confiscated land!!), with parties whom in 1906-1907 the Socialists-Revolutionists Vikhliaiev, Chernov and Co. had openly accused of worshipping at the shrine of private property!! Most often they are found in fusion with the Mensheviks, at times with the *Yedinstvo* adherents, the same *Yedinstvo* of which the *Dielo Naroda* writes in so hostile and contemptuous a tone.

Never mind! The smug citizen will swallow everything! The petty bourgeois bothers little about parties or principles. In our paper "we" are opposed to the *Yedinstvo*, but in order to get into the Council "we" are *for* it.

Nor are the Mensheviks a whit better. In their paper they attack the *Yedinstvo*, at their All-Russian conference they met the notorious Deutsch with shouts of disapprobation, which incident made the *Yedinstvo* complain bitterly. But it does not matter, the smug citizen is forgetful. Let us act accordingly. "In matters of principle" we are opposed to the Deutsches and the Yordanskys, in the presence of workers we shun them, but, when it comes to obtaining political berths for ourselves, we run with these gentlemen on the same tickets!

Let all class-conscious workers know, let them spread among the labouring masses, that the bloc of the Socialists-Revolutionists, the Narodniks and the Mensheviks is composed of people who stealthily work for the election of the *Yedinstvo* heroes, *people who are ashamed of their allies!*

In two boroughs, the Kazansky and the Spassky, there are no Socialists-Revolutionists and Mensheviks at all: they *have concealed* themselves apparently, in the lists of the borough Soviets of Workers' and Soldiers' Deputies, *i. e.*, in non-partisan lists (in each borough there is a very incomplete number of candidates: 38 and 28 candidates respectively against 54 and 44 of the Cadet Party and 43 and 46 of our party). In two boroughs, therefore, the petty-bourgeois parties have not only not overcome their gaudy party hybridism, but they have landed in the mire of non-partisanship: "Who cares for parties, as long as we are elected?" This is the usual motto of bourgeois parliamentarians.

5. In the fifth group non-partisanship reigns supreme. There are 28 lists in ten boroughs, and, what is more, most of these groups are purely local, restricted to one borough. This is worse than mere philistinism, it is philistinism at its narrowest. What a crowd!

Here is a "house administration," here is a "group of employés in educational institutions," here the "honesty, responsibility and justice" group, here "democratic republicans and Socialist functionaries nominated by non-partisan toilers, democratic republicans active in house committees." . . .

Comrades, workers! Let us all become active, let us make our rounds through the poorest quarters, let us awaken and educate the domestic servants, the most backward workers, etc., etc. Let us agitate against the capitalists and the Cadets parading under the cloaks of "radical democrats." Let us agitate against the petty-bourgeois "defencist" mire of the Narodniks and Mensheviks, against their bloc that represents no party and no principle, against their cowardly methods of trying to secure the election of Trudoviks, advocates of compensation for confiscated lands, and the heroes of Plekhanov's *Yedinstvo*, gentlemen with whom even the *Dielo Naroda* and the *Rabochaia Gazeta*, ministerial organs, are ashamed to join hands.

Pravda, No. 64, June 6, 1917.

DRAFT RESOLUTION ON MEASURES TO OVERCOME ECONOMIC CHAOS [218]

1. THE utter disorganisation of the economic life of Russia has now reached a point where a catastrophe is inevitable, a catastrophe of unheard-of dimensions, a catastrophe that will bring to a stop a great number of most essential industries, that will prevent the farmer from conducting farming on the proper scale, that will interrupt railroad communications, that will stop the delivery of food to many millions of the industrial population and to the cities in general. Moreover, economic disintegration has already begun, and has already affected many branches of industry. Successfully to contend with this disintegration there must be the greatest exertion of the people's strength, recourse must be had to immediate revolutionary measures, in each locality as well as in the seat of supreme state power.

2. Neither by the bureaucratic method, *i. e.*, by creating institutions with a preponderance of capitalists and bureaucrats, nor by the method of safeguarding the profits of the capitalists, their domination of industry, their rule as the rule of finance capital, their commercial secrets as regards their banking, commercial and industrial affairs, can there be found a way to avert the impending catastrophe. This has been amply demonstrated by a series of partial manifestations of the crisis in various branches of industry.

3. The way to avert a catastrophe is to establish a real workers' control over the production and distribution of goods. To establish such control it is necessary (1) to make certain that in all the basic institutions there is a majority of workers, not less than three-fourths of all the votes, and that all owners who have not deserted their business, as well as the scientifically and technically trained personnel, are compelled to participate; (2) that all the shop and factory committees, the central and local Soviets of Workers', Soldiers' and Peasants' Deputies, as well as the trade-unions, be granted the right to participate in such control, that all commercial and bank accounts be open to their inspection and that the management be compelled to supply them with all the data; and (3) that the representatives

135

of all the more important democratic and Socialist parties be granted the same right.

4. Workers' control, already recognised by the capitalists in a number of cases where conflicts arose, should be immediately developed, by way of a series of carefully considered and gradual, but immediately realisable measures, into complete regulation of the production and distribution of goods by the workers.

5. Exactly in the same way and on the same basis the workers' control should be extended to financial and banking operations: the financial situation should at the same time be made perfectly clear, and councils and conferences of bank employés, syndicate employés and others, to be organised forthwith, should participate in the control.

6. To save the country from a catastrophe it is first of all necessary that the workers and peasants be inspired, not by words, but by deeds, with absolute and unqualified confidence that the leading and ruling institutions, local and central, do not hesitate to place the greater portion of the profits, the incomes and the property of the great banking, financial, commercial and industrial magnates of capitalist economy in the hands of the people. Unless this measure is actually carried into effect, it is futile to demand or expect real revolutionary measures and actual revolutionary exertion of energy from the masses of workers and peasants.

7. In view of the complete disorganisation of the whole financial and monetary systems, in view of the impossibility of restoring order while the war lasts, the aim of the state organisation should be to organise on a wide regional, and later on a national scale, the exchange of agricultural implements, clothes, shoes and other products for bread and other agricultural products. City and village co-operatives should be drawn into a wide participation in this matter.

8. Only upon the complete realisation of the foregoing measures will it be possible and necessary to introduce universal labour duty. This measure, in turn, requires the establishment of a workers' militia, in which the workers are to serve without remuneration after their regular eight-hour day, and which is to be developed into a universal militia where the workers and the employés shall be paid by the capitalists. Only such a workers' militia and the universal militia that is to grow out of it could and should establish universal labour duty, not by bureaucratic means, nor in the interests of

the capitalists, but for the sake of actually saving the people from ruin. And only such a militia could and should introduce real revolutionary discipline, could and should elicit from the entire people the maximum of exertion in order to save the country from the impending catastrophe.   Only a universal labour service is capable of effecting the greatest economy in the utilisation of people's labour power.

9. One of the most important tasks among the measures calculated to save the country from ruin should be to engage large numbers of workers in the production of coal and raw materials, as well as in the field of transportation.   It is equally important gradually to transfer workers from war industries into industries engaged in producing commodities essential to the restoration of the economic life of the country.

10. A well-regulated and successful introduction of the foregoing measures can be accomplished only upon the passing of the power of the state into the hands of the proletarians and semi-proletarians.

Social-Democrat, No. 64, June 7, 1917.

COMING TO TERMS WITH THE CAPITALISTS OR OVER-THROWING THE CAPITALISTS?

HOW TO END THE WAR

EVERY one thinks, every one speaks of how to end the war.

Almost all workers and peasants agree that the war has been brought on by the capitalists, and that it is the capitalists of the world who need it. Indeed, this idea has been expressed in the resolutions passed by the Soviets of Workers, Soldiers' and Peasants' Deputies.

And this is undoubtedly true.

Disagreements arise when we come to the question of the various roads that would *lead* to peace (that the war cannot be brought to an end at once, every one realises). Ought we to come to terms with the capitalists, and if so, to what kind of terms? Or ought we to advance in the direction of the proletarian revolution, *i. e.*, of the overthrow of the capitalists? This is the main, the basic question.

It is on this question that our party has parted ways with the Petrograd Soviet of Workers' and Soldiers' Deputies and with the All-Russian Soviet of Peasants' Deputies, both of which *seem to be inclined to settle the question in favour of the capitalists and with the aid of the capitalists.*[219]

This has been very strikingly confirmed by the resolution on the war adopted by the All-Russian Soviet of Peasants' Deputies. In accord with the notorious—and similarly confused—proclamation to the peoples of the world (March 27), this resolution, too, demands:

> . . . peace without annexations and indemnities, and the right of each people, within whatever state it might be found, to determine its own destiny.

Here the question of annexations (seizures) is put in a manner different from that recently put by the *Izvestia* of the Petrograd Soviet of Workers' and Soldiers' Deputies and the *Dielo Naroda* (see *Pravda*, No. 60, May 31 *).

* See page 91 of this book.—*Ed.*

138

These two latter organs, directed by the bloc of Narodniks and Mensheviks, have gone hopelessly astray, declaring that "without annexations" means *status quo ante bellum*—the Latin for "as it was before the war."

Such a solution of the problem, we may as well tell the truth, means to strike bargains with the capitalists and among the capitalists. It means: Let us retain the old seizures (made before the war), but let us have no new ones.

First of all such a solution cannot be accepted by a Socialist who does not wish to betray Socialism. It is not the business of a Socialist to make peace among the capitalists on the basis of the old division of spoils, of annexations; this is obvious. Secondly, such a solution is in any event not practical, unless, of course, a revolution *against capital* takes place, at least against Anglo-Japanese capital, for any one in his senses can see that *without a revolution* Japan will not give up Kiaochow, nor England Bagdad and the colonies in Africa.

The peasant resolution has defined seizures (annexations) *differently*. It proclaimed the right of *"each"* people (this also includes peoples annexed, *i. e.*, subjugated, before the war) to be free, "to determine its own destiny."

From the standpoint of a real consistent democrat, particularly a Socialist, this is the only sound solution of the problem. No Socialist, no honest Socialist, can view this question of annexations (seizures) in any different light, no one can deny any people the right to self-determination, the right to separation.

But we must not deceive ourselves; such a demand implies a revolution against the capitalists. And the first ones to decline to meet such a demand (unless there be a revolution) will be the English capitalists who have annexed (seized) more territories than any other nation in the world.

Either demand, either wish, whether it be the wish to renounce all annexations in the sense of a return to the *status quo ante bellum*, or the wish to renounce both old and new annexations, *i. e.*, all annexations, cannot be carried out without a revolution against capital, without the overthrow of the capitalists. We must deceive neither ourselves nor the people in this matter.

Either we must preach and await some arrangement with the capitalists—and this would be equivalent to inspiring the people with faith in its worst enemies—or we must have confidence in the proletarian revolution only, concentrating all our efforts on the task of overthrowing the capitalists.

We must make our choice between the two ways of ending the war.

Pravda, No. 65, June 7, 1917.

THE CAPITALISTS MUST BE EXPOSED

V. BAZAROV, universally recognised as an authority on the state of affairs in our industries, wrote in the *Novaia Zhizn* of June 6:

> The war and the resulting economic and financial disorganisation have created a state of affairs in which the efforts of private enterprise are directed not towards strengthening and developing the productive forces of the country, but towards destroying them. It is much more profitable at the present moment—in expectation of higher prices—to keep all the material elements of capital inactive, than to put them into circulation: it is more profitable to produce, on terms ruinous to the country, absolutely useless military supplies, than to serve conscientiously the immediate needs of the people; and it is most profitable to build new war supplies factories which will never be utilised, and which would be in a position to start work only two or three years hence. Is it any wonder that our so-called "national economy" has degenerated into a bacchanalia of pillage, into industrial anarchy, into a systematic spoliation of national wealth? . . .
>
> . . . Why should an ignorant, and, for that matter, even a fully class-conscious worker, forego an "excessive" increase in wages amounting to three or four rubles, when he sees hundreds of millions of rubles looted before his very eyes? [220]

No honest person would venture to deny the absolute truth of V. Bazarov's statement.

A "bacchanalia of pillage"—there are no other words to characterise the behaviour of the capitalists during the war.

This bacchanalia is leading the country to wreck and ruin.

We must not keep still. We must not tolerate it.

Let every worker, who knows and understands what is going on in "his" factory; let every employé, whether he works in a bank, a factory or a commercial house, who cannot remain indifferent to the ruin of his country; let every engineer, statistician, accountant, do everything in his power to *collect* accurate—if possible, documented—data concerning this bacchanalia of pillage, *i. e.,* concerning *prices and profits*. Even partial data would be of use.

We must not keep still. We must not tolerate it. We are not children, after all, and we will not permit ourselves to be lulled to sleep by promises made by near-Socialist Ministers or commissions, or departments, or sub-departments of bureaucrats.

Were not the Russian government in capitalist captivity, were it made up of people who wanted and could act decisively, act to save their country from ruin, it would immediately,—without procrastinating even for one day, even for one hour,—issue a decree ordering the publication of *all* prices charged on war contracts, of *all* data pertaining to *profits*.

To chatter about the impending collapse, about saving the country from ruin, yet not to follow the above suggestions, means to stoop to the level of deceivers of the people, or of playthings in the hands of tricksters.

To expect a government of capitalists, of Messrs. Lvov, Tereshchenko, Shingarev and Co., and their impotent, toylike "appendages" in the persons of Chernov, Tsereteli, Peshekhonov, Skobelev, to issue such a decree, and thus to expose the capitalists, would be childish and naïve. Only those who suffer from a "ministerial softening of the brain" are likely to expect that.

All the more energetically therefore must we stimulate private initiative. Comrades and citizens! All those who truly wish to save the country from hunger, must immediately collect and publish all accessible data *pertaining to prices and profits*.

Exposing the capitalists is the first step towards curbing the capitalists.

The first step in our fight against the pillagers is to expose the bacchanalia of pillage.

Pravda, No. 67, June 9, 1917.

REPORTS ON ECONOMIC CHAOS

THE cardinal and basic question at the present time is the impending catastrophe. We must collect as much data on it as possible. Here are some of the most instructive quotations taken out of the papers of our opponents, the combined Narodniks and Mensheviks (*Izvestia* No. 70, June 1):

> The calamity of mass unemployment is drawing nearer. The resistance of the united employers to the demands of the workers is growing. The employers are resorting to the peculiar method of calling Italian strikes and to secret lock-outs.[221]

And further:

> . . . The capitalists do nothing to help the state out of its economic difficulties. . . .
> . . . Tenaciously holding on to their profits, the capitalists are the actual disorganisers and counter-revolutionists. But the revolution will not and should not perish. If the capitalists do nothing to meet its wishes voluntarily, the revolution must lay its hands on them.[222]

One can hardly express oneself more eloquently. The situation therefore must be really critical. "The revolution" must "lay its hands on the capitalists"—*what* revolution? the revolution of *which* class? *how* should it lay its hands?

Here are the answers given by those who reported to the Executive Committee on May 29: [223]

> A number of reports revealed a depressing picture of wide-spread chaos in the country . . . the bourgeois press is silent concerning the real causes of our hardships, *i. e.*, the war and the selfish conduct of the bourgeoisie.

From the report of the Menshevik ministerialist Cherevanin:

> The economic ruin we are now going through is too grave for any individual palliative, for any separate concrete measure effectually to improve conditions. What we need is a general plan, what we need is state regulation of our economic life. . . .
> In order that our plan be carried out in practice, it is necessary to create a special Economic Council as an adjunct of the cabinet.

A mountain has given birth to a mouse. Instead of the revolution's laying its hands on the capitalists, we have a purely bourgeois prescription.

From a report by Avilov:

> The basic cause of the present economic breakdown is the shortage in the most essential industrial products. . . .
> . . . With the rise in prices the workers in many fields find themselves on the verge of chronic hunger. . . .
> . . . The employers, despite their enormous profits, refuse to make any concessions to the workers, unless there is a simultaneous rise in the prices of their products. . . .
> . . . The only escape from the present situation is the fixing of prices on commodities. But this cannot be carried into practice unless there is public control of the distribution of commodities.
> Along with such compulsory distribution of commodities with fixed prices, there must also be control of production, otherwise production may be slowed down or even completely stopped. . . .
> Together with the above there must be state control of all the sources upon which industry draws for means of subsistence and turnover, i. e., all credit institutions.

Comrade Avilov has apparently forgotten that the "state" is a machine that is being pulled in opposite directions by the working class and the capitalists. Which class is at the present moment able to carry out state control?

From Bazarov's report:

> Fixed prices are effectually evaded; state monopolies exist on paper; regulations tending to supply factories with coal and metal have not only failed to direct production so as to serve the interests of the state, but have not even overcome the anarchy that reigns on the market, they have not even curbed the wild speculation of the middlemen.
> What is needed is compulsory state trustification of industry.
> Only by drafting the administration of the various enterprises and the capitalists into compulsory state service, can the suppression of anarchy which the industrialists are deliberately creating in production be achieved.

The government of the capitalists (who are deliberately creating anarchy) must draft the capitalists into compulsory state service, which is equivalent to making the capitalists forget all about the class-struggle.

From a report by G. V. Shuba:

> Despite our ceaseless demands lasting for two months, the general problem, the problem of organising the national economic life and labour, has made no progress at all. We have been simply shifting from one foot to another. The situation at present is as follows: we have succeeded, in spite of opposition, in passing a series of measures and laws; we already have a law pertaining to the monopoly on bread. . . . But it all remains on paper. . . .

. . . We have arrived at a theoretical solution of the problem regarding the municipalisation of agricultural machinery. But this cannot be realised, since there are practically no machines to speak of. The factories that would normally produce agricultural machinery are turning out absolutely unessential articles for the army. In addition to regulating the entire economic life of the country, we must demolish and rebuild the entire executive apparatus of the government. . . .

This gets us a little nearer to the point, to the heart of the matter! "To demolish and rebuild the entire executive apparatus of the government"—this is perfectly sound. But is it not obvious that the question relating to the *apparatus* of the government constitutes only a small part of the larger question relating to the *class* which is in power?

From a report by Kukovetsky:

The financial situation of the country is in an abominable state. We are rapidly advancing toward financial bankruptcy. . . .
Purely financial measures will not help. . . .
We must take steps to enforce a compulsory allotment of government loan bonds, and if this does not yield the desired results, we must resort to a compulsory loan.
The second measure is the compulsory regulation of industry, the fixing of prices on goods.

"Compulsion" is a very good thing, but the question is which class will do the compelling, and which one will be compelled?

From a report by Groman:

Everything that is taking place in all the countries at present may be characterised as a process of disintegration of the national economic organism. This is everywhere counteracted by the principle of organisation. The state has everywhere begun to organise economic life and labour. . . .
Neither the government nor the country at large has up to now developed a central organ which would regulate the economic life of the country. There is, so to speak, no economic brain. It must be created. . . . A powerful executive organ must be organised. An economic council must be built up. . . .

A new bureaucratic institution,—this is what Groman's ideas are reduced to! Sad, indeed.

All admit that an unheard-of catastrophe is inevitable. But they do not understand the main thing, *i. e.,* that *only the revolutionary class* is able to lead the country out of it.

Pravda, No. 67, June 9, 1917.

"SLEIGHT OF HAND" MANIPULATIONS, AND MANIPULATIONS OF UNPRINCIPLED POLITICIANS

THE expression "sleight of hand" we take from the leading editorial in to-day's *Dielo Naroda*. This paper of the "Socialists-Revolutionists," in which Kerensky and Chernov take part, thus exposes the game played by the French representatives "of Socialism tamed by the bourgeoisie":

. . . These are old, very old sleight-of-hand manipulations. With us it is Mr. Plekhanov, who repeatedly but unsuccessfully amuses himself with them, for he really deceives no one. . . .

Is it only Plekhanov, my dear fellows?

Are you not in an election bloc with this very Plekhanov's *Yedinstvo?* Are you not pulling him through, are you not saving him?

And it was in your paper (No. 44, May 22) that S. Mstislavsky wrote of Plekhanov:

When the erstwhile intellectual leader of Russian Social-Democracy is applying himself to exactly the same counter-revolutionary attacks (as the *Russkaia Volia* and the *Novoie Vremia*) it is with profound regret and sincere sorrow that we are forced to speak of this fact, for we were really reluctant to believe that the disintegration of the International had advanced so far.

We add: and the disintegration of the Socialists-Revolutionists who have entered into a bloc with this *Yedinstvo!*

And in an unsigned, *i. e.*, editorial, note in No. 48 of the *Dielo Naroda* (May 26) we read:

The political unity of the *Yedinstvo* with the liberal bourgeoisie is a well-known fact. . . .

Hear! Hear! The "Socialists-Revolutionists" and the Mensheviks are in unity with that very *Yedinstvo* whose unity with the liberal bourgeoisie is a well-known fact. Do not forget it, men and women, comrade workers and comrade soldiers!

The Menshevik *Rabochaia Gazeta* in a leading editorial for May 3 (No. 35) said:

We are against the English imperialists. The *Yedinstvo* is against the English Socialists. Herein is the whole difference. Herein lies the reason why the *Yedinstvo* has to argue in a Hottentot manner. . . . The Russian workers very well remember how Plekhanov during the tsarist (there is a typographical error in the text; it should read: during the tsarist-republican) régime was trying in all manner of ways to dissuade them from declaring strikes. Then, too, Plekhanov was trying to scare us with things even more terrible; he was assuring us that such conflicts were of benefit to the general staff of the German army.

And in No. 57 (May 29) of the same paper the most moderate ministerialist Cherevanin wrote:

Plekhanov and his *Yedinstvo* do everything in their power to compromise here, too, the principle of defencism which has been sufficiently compromised on an international scale by the efforts of the majority of the German, French and other Socialists.

This is how the *Yedinstvo* is appreciated, this is how it is being shunned, this is how the Narodniks and the Mensheviks are ashamed of it!!

But all the same they enter into a bloc (union) with it for the elections,—and Plekhanov accepts places from people who publicly honour him with such names as "trickster," "bourgeois-tamed," "Hottentot," "he who has compromised himself," "he who is united with the liberal bourgeoisie."

Which side is worse in such a bloc?

Workers and soldiers! Not one vote to the bloc of the Narodniks and the Mensheviks, who are shielding and smuggling through members of the *Yedinstvo*, which is "united with the liberal bourgeoisie"!

Pravda, No. 67, June 9, 1917.

COUNTER-REVOLUTION TAKING THE OFFENSIVE

"JACOBINS WITHOUT THE PEOPLE"

THE counter-revolution has gathered enough strength to begin an offensive. With the aid of the Narodnik and Menshevik Ministers, the capitalists are organising an attack on liberty.

The decision to disband the "45th, 46th, 47th and 52nd regiments" of the 12th and 13th divisions; the decision to "arraign before the court" the "instigators" (what a queer word! Are "instigators" more significant than "perpetrators" in war?); moreover, the *arrest* of Ensign Krusser *for a speech he had delivered at a meeting* in Skuliany; finally, the unusually rude tone employed by the Provisional Government as regards Cronstadt (for example, the decrees "must be obeyed absolutely": is this the way to talk to citizens who so far have not been accused of anything, not of a single act of disobedience?) [224]—all taken together, and illumined by the fireworks of the maliciously jeering defender of the counter-revolutionary capitalists, the *Riech* ("The government has finally begun to use the language of power")—clearly indicates that the counter-revolution is taking the offensive.

This "offensive" creates a strange impression. Those at the front who are accused of "instigating insubordination" are arraigned before the court. Four regiments are disbanded (four out of the eight regiments forming the two divisions mentioned in the telegram; although, according to the same telegram in No. 76 of the *Izvestia* of the Petrograd Soviet, only *one* out of the eight regiments "advanced in full force," and another one in "almost full force"). Since, gentlemen of the government, you do inform the people of your disbanding some regiments, since you do find it useful, since you do let telegrams concerning this matter reach the public, then why do you not inform us, clearly and truthfully, at least in a few lines, as to what has prompted the insubordination of those whom you are arraigning before the court?

You, gentlemen, must do one of two things: either carry on your work in darkness (you have military censors), not bothering about informing the people and not bothering the people with your information; or, if you decide to inform the people, then come out with the whole truth as to how, why and wherefore and whether it is some particular or a general question that is involved in the behaviour of those whom you have arraigned before the court.

Vagueness is harmful.

As far as Krusser's arrest is concerned, the affair is quite simple. To hustle a man off to prison *for a speech he has delivered at a meeting,*—is that rational? Does it not signify that you have simply lost your heads? But you, gentlemen, Cadets and Rights combined in a cabinet with the Narodniks and the Mensheviks, you have ten times, or perhaps a hundred times as many daily newspapers as your opponents have!! Having such a tremendous advantage in possessing the chief means of propaganda, you nevertheless hustle a man off to prison for "a speech at a meeting"!! Gentlemen, are you insane with fear?

We are not opposed to revolutionary violence when resorted to for the benefit of the majority of the people.

When Plekhanov recently mentioned the Jacobins of 1793 with their *direct* declaration: "Such and such persons are enemies of the people," we thought in that connection: No party should refuse to follow the example of the Jacobins of 1793 in the instance cited by Plekhanov.

The trouble is that there are Jacobins and "Jacobins." A witty French expression, which twenty years ago Plekhanov, then still a Socialist, liked to quote, pokes fun at the "Jacobins without the people" (*Jacobins moins le peuple*).

The historical greatness of the real Jacobins, the Jacobins of 1793, is based on the fact that they were "Jacobins *with* the people," with the revolutionary *majority* of the people, with the *revolutionary* advanced class of *their* time.

They are ridiculous and pitiful, the "Jacobins without the people," they who only ape the Jacobins, they who are *afraid* to come out in a clear, straightforward manner and openly denounce as enemies of the people the exploiters, the oppressors, the servants of monarchies in various countries, the defenders of the landowners in all countries.

You have studied history, Messrs. Miliukovs and Plekhanovs, and you cannot deny that the *great* Jacobins of 1793 were not afraid to denounce all the representatives of the reactionary exploiting *minority* of their time as enemies of the people.

You, the present-day government, its assistants, its defenders, its servants, can you declare openly, directly and officially which *classes* you regard as the "enemies of the people" *throughout the world?*

You certainly dare not! You are Jacobins without the people. You are only make-believe Jacobins. You look more like mediocre representatives of the mediocre reaction of landowners and capitalists.

Workers and soldiers! Toilers! The counter-revolution of the landowners and the capitalists is taking the offensive! Not one vote for any of the parties that support the government,—that participate in the government!

Vote for the Bolsheviks!

Pravda, No. 68, June 10, 1917.

A QUESTION OF PRINCIPLE

"FORGOTTEN WORDS" OF DEMOCRACY

THE flood of lies and calumny poured out by the capitalist newspapers upon the Cronstadt comrades has once more revealed the dishonesty of those papers. They have seized upon a very ordinary and insignificant incident and puffed it up to the dimensions of a "state" affair, of "secession" from Russia, and so on and so forth.

No. 74 of the *Izvestia* contains information with respect to the liquidation of the Cronstadt affair; as was to be expected, Ministers Tsereteli and Skobelev found it easy to come to terms with the Cronstadtians on the basis of a compromise resolution. Of course, we hereby express our hope and confidence that this compromise resolution, provided both sides faithfully live up to it, will make possible a long period of harmonious revolutionary work in Cronstadt as well as in the rest of Russia.

From the point of view of principle the Cronstadt incident is significant in two respects.

It first of all proved that, as we had stated long before and officially recognised in the resolutions (on the Soviets), passed by our party, outside of Petrograd the revolution has advanced much further than in Petrograd. Not only the Cadets, but the Narodniks and the Mensheviks as well, have allowed themselves to be swept away by current revolutionary phrases, and they, therefore, did not wish to, or could not, fathom the full significance of this fact.

Secondly, the Cronstadt incident has brought to the fore a very important question pertaining to principle and programme which no honest democrat, to say nothing of a Socialist, can afford to treat with indifference. The question is whether the central government has or has not the right to ratify the election of officials by the local population.

The Mensheviks, to which party Ministers Tsereteli and Skobelev belong, are still pretending that they are Marxists. Tsereteli and Skobelev advanced a resolution advocating such ratification by the government. Did they stop to think of their obligations as Marxists?

151

Should the reader regard this question as rather naïve, and say that in point of fact the Mensheviks have become now a petty-bourgeois, and, what is more, a defencist (*i. e.*, chauvinist) party, and that it would, therefore, be ridiculous to speak of Marxism, we would have no objections. All we would say, though, is that Marxism pays very close attention to all questions involving democracy; and it is hardly possible to deny citizens Tsereteli and Skobelev the name of democrats.

Have they stopped to think, while advancing the resolution relating to the "ratification" by the Provisional Government of officials elected by the Cronstadt population, of their obligations as democrats, of their "title" as democrats?

Obviously, not.

To show that our conclusion is correct, we shall quote the opinion of a writer who, we hope, has not entirely lost his standing as a scientific and Marxian authority even in the eyes of Tsereteli and Skobelev. This writer is Friedrich Engels.

In 1891, in criticising the proposed programme of the German Social Democrats (the so-called Erfurt Programme), Engels wrote that the German proletariat was in need of a single and indivisible republic.

But not such a republic, added Engels, as the present French Republic, which in reality is an empire founded in 1798 but without an emperor. From 1792 up to 1798 every French department, every community had home-rule on the American model. It is this that we, too, (*i. e.*, the German Social-Democratic Party) must accomplish. How home-rule should be organised, how the development of a bureaucracy might be avoided, has been demonstrated to us by America, by the First French Republic, by Australia, Canada and other English colonies. Such regional and communal autonomy affords much more freedom than does, for instance, Swiss federalism, where each canton is really independent of the "Union" (*i. e.*, of the central government), but is at the same time the supreme authority in so far as the minor subdivisions of each canton, the districts (*Bezirk*) and the communes are concerned. The canton governments appoint the district commissioners (*Stadthalter*) and prefects. In English-speaking countries the right of appointing local officers is completely unknown, and in the future we also must politely abolish this right (*i. e.*, appointments from above), just as we must abolish the Prussian *Landrats* (district administrators) and *Regierungsrats* (governors).[225]

Such was Engels' opinion regarding the right of a democracy to appoint officers from above. And in order to express these views more definitely, more directly, and more precisely, he proposed that the German Social-Democrats incorporate into their programme the following demand:

Complete home-rule of the communes, counties and regions through officers elected by a universal suffrage; *abolition of all State-appointed local and district officials.*

The italicised words are decisive and clear.

Worthy citizen Ministers, Tsereteli and Skobelev! You are, no doubt, quite pleased that your names shall be mentioned in history text-books. But are you pleased to think that every Marxist—and every honest democrat—shall be forced to say: Ministers Tsereteli and Skobelev helped the Russian capitalists to build a republic that, strictly speaking, was no republic at all, but *a monarchy without a monarch?*

P. S. The above article had been written before the Cronstadt incident entered its last stage, as presented in to-day's papers. The Cronstadtians have *not* broken the compromise agreement. Not a single instance that would even remotely suggest a breach of the agreement has been cited. The references made by the *Riech* to newspaper articles are mere trickery, for it is by deeds and not by newspaper articles that agreements are broken. The fact, then, remains: Ministers Tsereteli, Skobelev and Co. have allowed themselves to be scared for the hundredth and thousandth time by the shouts of the frightened bourgeoisie, and have resorted to *violent threats* against the Cronstadtians. Crude, absurd threats, calculated to aid the counter-revolution.

Pravda, No. 68, June 10, 1917.

THE BLACKS ARE FOR THE CADETS, THE MENSHEVIKS AND THE NARODNIKS ARE IN ONE GOVERNMENT WITH THE CADETS

WHO does not know the newspaper *Novoie Vremia*? Who does not know that for decades and decades this paper made itself "famous" by defending the tsarist power, by defending the capitalists, by baiting Jews, and by baiting revolutionists?

Who does not know that everything that was honest in Russia turned away with indignation and contempt from the *Novoie Vremia*, and that this paper, even now, after the revolution, has not changed its policy even by one iota?

Well, we have the first elections in free Russia. On the first day of the elections, the *Novoie Vremia* writes: "Vote for the ticket of the People's Freedom Party."

The fact stares one in the face: All the landowners and the capitalists, all the dark forces, all those who are trying to restore tsarism, are for the Cadets.

And the Mensheviks and the Narodniks have given six of their Ministers as hostages to the *ten Cadet* Ministers.

The Mensheviks and the Narodniks have allowed themselves to be fooled by empty promises, of which not one has been fulfilled. Not one step towards stopping the war, towards rejecting annexations (seizures of territory *), towards curbing the capitalists who are making outrageous profits and leading the country to ruin. *Not one such step has been taken* by the government.

The war is dragging on, ruin is imminent, the capitalists are growing richer, the Mensheviks and the Narodniks are chattering and threatening, threatening and chattering . . . but things do not change in the least.

Workers and soldiers and all toilers! Not one vote for the Cadets, the Mensheviks and the Narodniks!

Vote for the Bolsheviks!

Pravda, No. 68, June 10, 1917.

* Towards the publication of the secret treaties, towards an open, honest, direct proposal of peace to all the peoples on definite and clear terms.

154

DISGRACEFUL BLOC OF THE MENSHEVIKS AND THE NARODNIKS WITH THE *YEDINSTVO*

To-day is the second and most important day of the elections. Besides the Cadets, it is the Mensheviks and the Narodniks that are most pertinacious in offering themselves to the voter.

What answer can they make to our accusation as to their disgraceful bloc with the *Yedinstvo?* What principle could they invoke in defence of such a bloc?

As a matter of fact, they have no principle.

The *Rabochaia Gazeta,* in reply to our suggestion that a bloc with the *Yedinstvo* is indecent, refers us . . . to whom do you think? . . . to the provocateur Malinovsky, to the fact that he was elected into the Duma with the aid of the secret police!

The disingenuousness of such quasi-polemics is exposed by us in a separate note.* Here we are concerned not so much with the honesty of the *Rabochaia Gazeta,* as with its *logic.* Well, well, gentlemen! When we refer to "your" *Yedinstvo,* you reply by pointing at "our" provocateur Malinovsky. What does that mean? Apparently that you place the *Yedinstvo* on the same level with a provocateur!!

That is how the wiseacres of the *Rabochaia Gazeta* are "defending" the bloc with the *Yedinstvo.* Clever, isn't it? When they are told that they *have* in *free* Russia such a disgraceful colleague as Plekhanov's *Yedinstvo,* they reply: And the Bolsheviks, didn't they have in *tsarist* Russia a provocateur Malinovsky!!

Isn't it a gem of a defence?

The *Dielo Naroda* is also hobnobbing with the *Yedinstvo.* The paper of Kerensky, Chernov and Co. prints on the front page of the issue of June 9, the first day of the elections, an appeal to the people to vote for the lists which are pulling along the *Yedinstvo.*

On the second page of the same number of the *Dielo Naroda,* we run across a lengthy denunciation of the "social-patriot" Plekhanov and his *Yedinstvo.* Here we read the following "venomous remark":

* See p. 157 of this book.—*Ed.*

155

We will gladly inform our readers what other liberal imperialists and social-imperialists, the *Riech*, the *Russkaia Volia* and the *Yedinstvo*, think about the Italian seizure of Albania.

Is it not a gem?

The Socialists-Revolutionists call upon the people to vote for lists in which are concealed the candidates of the same *Yedinstvo* which the Socialists-Revolutionists themselves, on the very day of the elections, call "social-imperialists," *i. e.*, Socialists in words, imperialists in deeds, and which they place on a level with the *Riech* and the *Russkaia Volia*.

The wise *Rabochaia Gazeta*, together with the still wiser *Dielo Naroda*, have certainly "defended" the *Yedinstvo* very eloquently!

And Plekhanov accepts alms from people who unwittingly place him alongside of Malinovsky, or who on election day declare him to be a "social-imperialist."

Such are the ethics of this disgraceful bloc, these Mensheviks plus the Narodniks plus the *Yedinstvo*. . . .

Workers and Soldiers! Toilers! Not one vote to the "social-imperialists," the Narodniks, the Mensheviks!

Vote for the Bolsheviks!

Pravda, No. 68, June 10, 1917.

LACKING A CLEAN WEAPON OF PRINCIPLE, THEY RESORT TO A DIRTY ONE

THE *Rabochaia Gazeta*, the organ of the Menshevik ministerialists, is trying to hurt us by recalling the fact that in 1911 the secret police arrested the Bolshevik-conciliationist Rykov in order to afford "freedom" of action to the Bolsheviks of our party "on the eve of the elections for the Fourth Duma." (This is emphasised by the *Rabochaia Gazeta*.)

But what does that fact prove? It proves that the secret police was clearing the way for Malinovsky, who subsequently turned out to be a provocateur, to get into the Duma. Naturally, the secret police was taking care of its provocateurs.

Does this imply a reproach to our party? No. Honest people do not reproach Chernov and Co. for their erroneous exoneration of Azef, or Yonov (a member of the Bund, a colleague of the *Rabochaia Gazeta*) and Co. for exonerating in 1910, in the name of the combined Central Committee, the provocateur Zhitomirsky ("Otsov"), just as they do not reproach those Mensheviks who in 1904 had for some time tried to defend the provocateur Dobroskokov, just as they do not reproach those Cadets among whom, we now know, there have also been provocateurs.

All parties, without exception, have made mistakes in failing to recognise provocateurs. This is a fact. And when the *Rabochaia Gazeta*, while entering into a bloc with Minister Chernov, does not make any mention of his old errors, but does dwell on the mistakes of its present opponents, then it is guilty of methods obviously unfair, obviously dishonest. The blow which the *Rabochaia Gazeta* aims at us, falls upon itself; the *Rabochaia Gazeta* itself would never admit before the whole world that it is honest to keep silent about Azef while shouting, for selfish factional reasons, about a similar provocateur, Malinovsky.

Pravda, No. 68, June 10, 1917.

POSTSCRIPT TO PAMPHLET *THE TASKS OF THE PROLETARIAT IN OUR REVOLUTION* *

My pamphlet is now out of date due to the present economic chaos and because of the disorganisation of the printing shops in Petrograd. The pamphlet was written on April 23, 1917; it is now June 10, and the pamphlet has not yet appeared!

The pamphlet was intended as a draft platform expressive of my views before the calling of the All-Russian Conference of our party, the R.S.-D.L.P. (Bolsheviks). Several typewritten copies were distributed among members of the party, before and during the Conference. Thus the pamphlet did accomplish at least some of its purpose. But the Conference of May 7-12, 1917, is long since over, its resolutions have been published for some time (see supplements to No. 13 of *Soldatskaia Pravda*), and the attentive reader can easily discern that my pamphlet is in many cases the original outline of these resolutions.

Still, I hope that the pamphlet will be of some use in connection with and as an elucidation of these resolutions. Besides, there are two points that I wish to take up.

I suggested ** that we remain at Zimmerwald only for the purpose of obtaining information. The Conference did not agree with me on this point, and I had to vote against the resolution relating to the International. Now it is already becoming evident that the Conference made a mistake and that the course of events will soon rectify it. By remaining in Zimmerwald, we participate (though unwillingly) in delaying the creation of the Third International; indirectly we hinder its creation, for we are weighed down by the dead weight of the politically and ideologically dead Zimmerwald.

Our present position among the labour parties of the world is such that we must immediately found the Third International. There is no one else to do it, and delays are harmful. Had we remained in Zimmerwald for information only, we would have freed our hands to begin the building of the International right

* See p. 130, Book I of this volume.—*Ed.*
** See p. 152, Book I of this volume.—*Ed.*

then (while at the same time we would have been in a position to utilise Zimmerwald, in case such utilisation were possible).

Now, however, owing to the mistake made by the Conference, we are forced to wait passively at least till July 18, 1917 (the date for which the Zimmerwald Conference is called; that is, if it is not postponed a second time! It has already been postponed once . . .).

The unanimous decision of the Central Committee of our party, made after the Conference, and published in No. 55 of the *Pravda* (May 25) partly rectified the mistake: it was decided that we withdraw from Zimmerwald, in case it confers with the Ministers.* Let us hope that the rest of the mistake will be rectified, as soon as we call a conference of all the "Lefts" ("the third tendency," "Internationalists in fact").**

The second point I wish to discuss is the formation of the "coalition cabinet" on May 19, 1917. It may seem that the pamphlet is particularly out of date on this point.

It is on this point, however, that the pamphlet is not at all out of date. It is all built on a *class analysis* of which the Mensheviks and the Narodniks, who have given six Ministers as hostages to the ten capitalist Ministers, are in mortal fear. And just because the pamphlet bases everything on a class analysis it has not become obsolete; for the entrance of Tsereteli, Chernov and Co. into the cabinet has changed to an insignificant degree only the *form* of the compact between the Petrograd Soviet and the government of the capitalists, while I have advisedly emphasised that "I have in mind not so much formal agreement, as practical support." ***

Day by day it becomes ever clearer that Tsereteli, Chernov and Co. are simply hostages of the capitalists, that of all its gorgeous promises the "renovated" government does not wish to, and cannot, fulfill anything with regard to either its foreign or its domestic policy. Chernov, Tsereteli and Co. have committed political suicide, have become the aides of the capitalists who are actually stifling the revolution, Kerensky has sunk to the point where he uses violence against the masses: "Guchkov only threatens to use force against the soldiers," **** while Kerensky really had to carry out those threats. . . . Chernov, Tsereteli and Co. have politi-

* See p. 73 of this book.—*Ed.*
** See pp. 146-148, Book I of this volume.—*Ed.*
*** See p. 134, Book I of this volume.—*Ed.*
**** See p. 135, Book I of this volume.—*Ed.*

cally destroyed themselves as well as their parties, the Menshevik and the Socialist-Revolutionist parties. Every day will make this clearer to the people.

The Coalition Cabinet represents only a transition period in the development of the basic class contradictions in our revolution as I have analysed them in my pamphlet. This cannot last very long. Either backward—toward counter-revolution all along the line, or forward—towards the passing of power into the hands of other classes. In times of revolution, in the midst of an imperialist world-war, it is impossible to stand pat.

Petrograd, June 10, 1917.
Published in 1917 in the pamphlet *The Tasks of the Proletariat in Our Revolution*, by the "Priboi" firm.

SESSION OF THE PETROGRAD COMMITTEE OF THE R.S.-D.L.P., JUNE 12, 1917 [226]

I

SPEECH CONCERNING AN ORGAN FOR THE PETROGRAD COMMITTEE

THE desire of the Petrograd Committee to have its own organ is news to the Central Committee. It is difficult to understand why this question has arisen at a time when we are about to have our printing press, and when there have begun negotiations with the *Mezhraiontsy* as to the possibility of getting Comrade Trotsky to edit a popular organ.

In Europe, in the capitals or in great industrial centres, the loca. and the central organs are not published separately. Such a separation is harmful because of the waste of energy it entails. It is not advisable to have a Petrograd Committee organ independent of the Central Organ. Petrograd does not exist as a distinct locality. Petrograd is the geographical, political, and revolutionary centre of the whole of Russia. The life of Petrograd is being watched by entire Russia. Every step made by Petrograd becomes an example to be followed. It follows that the life of the Petrograd Committee cannot be treated as a local affair.

Why not accept the suggestion of the Central Committee concerning the formation of a press commission? The history of the press in Europe where there have been such commissions, reveals, of course, occasional misunderstandings between the editorial staff of an organ and the commission; such misunderstandings, however, have arisen only because of disagreement as to policy. What reasons are there for any disagreement as to policy between the Petrograd Committee and the Central Committee? Whether we want it or not, the organ of the Petrograd Committee will always be the leading organ of the party.

The experience of establishing an independent organ will soon convince the Petrograd Committee that it cannot confine itself to purely local matters. The Central Committee does not deny the necessity of devoting considerable space in the newspapers to the

161

needs of the Petrograd organisation. The Central Committee does not deny the need for a popular organ that would explain our slogans to the masses. But the establishment of a popular newspaper is a complicated matter and requires a great deal of experience. That is why the Central Committee is trying to induce Comrade Trotsky, who has succeeded in establishing his own popular organ, the *Russkaia Gazeta*, [227] to participate in the founding of a popular organ.

In the history of Europe the question of a popular organ has never been so vital a problem as it is with us. The general level of the masses in Western Europe rose more evenly, thanks to the cultural and educational work of the liberals. In such countries as Bohemia there are such popular organs. The task of a popular organ is to elevate the reader to an understanding of the leading party organ. If we do not establish a popular organ, the masses will be attracted by other parties which will try to make political capital out of that. A popular organ ought not to be local in character, but in view of the difficulties in postal deliveries, it will of necessity serve the needs of Petrograd above everything else. In order that local needs be adequately served, the Petrograd Committee must obtain a proper representation on the editorial staff of the organ.

II

TWO RESOLUTIONS SUBMITTED AT THE SESSION OF THE PETROGRAD COMMITTEE

FIRST RESOLUTION

THE Central Committee is to publish two papers in Petrograd, the Central Organ and a popular paper, with one editorial staff. The Petrograd Committee has a consultative voice in the editorial staff of the Central Organ, and a vote on the editorial staff of the popular organ. The Central Committee is to allot a certain number of columns in both papers to material of purely local interest.

SECOND RESOLUTION

The Petrograd Committee resolves to take part in both papers published by the Central Committee, on the conditions proposed by the Central Committee. It resolves to make every effort to serve more fully and widely the needs of local activities and to develop in greater detail the general line of the party. Having reason to fear that the Central Committee or the editorial staff appointed by it may place too much confidence in the comrades-internationalists who in the past repeatedly disagreed with Bolshevism, that the Central Committee may interfere with the freedom and independence of action of the local comrades, that the Central Committee may not give them the opportunity to exert the influence accorded to leaders of local activities, the Petrograd Committee is to elect a commission which shall formulate the exact guarantees of the rights of the Petrograd Committee in the local departments of both papers.

Printed from the minutes of the Petrograd Committee of the R.S.-D.L.P., and first published in *Krasnaia Lietopis* [Red Annals], No. 3 (14), 1923.

THE HARM OF PHRASES

THE answer of the French and the English governments offers convincing proof of the soundness of our repeated assertions that neither the Russian, nor the French, nor the English, nor the German government is in a position to give up the policy of annexations, and that all such promises are intended to deceive the peoples.[228]

We are fighting in order to seize Alsace-Lorraine, we are fighting for victory, replied the French. Please live up to your treaty obligations and fight for Russian and German Poland, replied the Englishmen.

The bitter truth—the fact that capitalism cannot be reconciled to a non-annexationist policy—is exposed once more. The failure of the policy of the "conciliators," of those who wish to make peace between the capitalists and the proletariat, the policy of the ministerialists, of the Narodniks and the Mensheviks—is most obvious. All their hopes relating to a coalition government have been blown to pieces, all their promises have been exposed as mere rhetoric.

And what is most harmful for the cause of the revolution and for the interests of the toiling masses, is the attempt to cover up the whole matter with phrases. Two varieties of the same stream of phrases have appeared, and truly "both are worse."

The *Rabochaia Gazeta*, the organ of the ministerialist Mensheviks, lets the stream flow in Cadet fashion.[229] "On this basis," it says (on the basis of the answers of the two allied governments), "there can be no agreement between them and us" . . . When they say "us," do they mean the Russian *capitalists?* The theory of the class struggle is apparently thrown overboard, for it is much more profitable to spout phrases about "democracy" in general, and all the time trample under foot the elementary truth of Marxism that it is precisely *within* a "democracy" that the chasm between the capitalists and the proletarians is deepest.

On the other hand, the *Rabochaia Gazeta* wishes to bring about "an attempt at revision" (of the agreements and the treaties) "through a specially called conference of representatives from the allied governments." The same old thing: agreement with capitalists, which, in fact, signifies the *deception of the workers* by make-believe negotiations with their class foes.

"The pressure of the rank and file of the English and French democracies, even the pressure of the English and the French proletariat alone upon their respective governments . . ." writes the *Rabochaia Gazeta*.

In Russia the Mensheviks are supporting *their own* imperialist government, but in other countries they want *pressure* to be brought to bear . . . Are these not lying phrases from beginning to end?

"We are preparing for it" (peace on an international scale) "by calling together an international Socialist conference . . ." with the participation of Ministers from among those ex-Socialists who have deserted to the side of *their* governments!! Some wonderful "preparation!" Deception of the people on a large scale prepared by a series of deceptions on a small scale.

The *Dielo Naroda* spouts phrases "in Jacobin fashion." It affects an austere tone, impressive revolutionary exclamations . . . "we know enough" . . . "faith in the victoriousness of our Revolution" (with a capital R, to be sure); "upon this or that step . . . of the Russian revolutionary democracy . . . depend the destinies . . . of the *entire* Insurrection (capital I, of course) of the workers so happily and so victoriously begun."

Of course, writing the words Revolution and Insurrection with capital letters makes the thing look "awfully" terrible, makes it appear Jacobin. Lots of effect at small expense. For this is done by people who in reality are helping to stifle the Revolution and to impede the growth of the uprising of the toilers by supporting the *Russian* Government of imperialists, by supporting their methods of concealing from the people the secret treaties, by supporting their methods of delaying the immediate abolition of the landowners' property in land, by supporting their methods of a military "offensive," their violent threats against local representative bodies, their presumption to appoint local officers or to confirm officers elected by the local population, etc., etc.

Gentlemen, heroes of the phrase! Gentlemen, knights of revolutionary grandiloquence! Socialism implies a distinction between a capitalist democracy and a proletarian democracy, between a bourgeois revolution and a proletarian revolution, between the rise of the rich against the Tsar and the rise of the toilers *against the rich*. Socialism demands that we distinguish our bourgeois revolution that has come to a close (the bourgeoisie now is counter-revolutionary) from the growing revolution of the proletarians and the poorest peasants. The former revolution is *for* war, *for* the preservation of the landowners' property in land, *for* "subjection" of local self-government to the central government, *for* secret treaties. The latter revolution has begun to smother the war by revolutionary fraternisation, by abolishing the power of the landowners in the different localities, by increasing the number and enhancing the power of the Soviets, by introducing everywhere the elective principle.

The ministerialist Narodniks and Mensheviks are spouting phrases about "democracy" in general, "Revolution" in general, in order to *conceal* their agreement with the definitely counter-revolutionary imperialist bourgeoisie of their country,—an agreement that is assuming the nature of a struggle *against* the revolution of the proletarians and the semi-proletarians.

Pravda, No. 69, June 13, 1917.

CAPITALIST MOCKERY OF THE PEOPLE

THE conference of representatives of the capitalists and workers of the southern mining industry ended on June 5.[280]

The results of the conference are *nil*. The capitalist gentlemen declared all the demands of the workers to be unacceptable. The workers' delegation that participated in the conference issued a statement *disclaiming all responsibility for possible complications*.

The case is as clear as day. The crisis has not been averted in the least. The employers have not been curbed.

It would be funny, were it not sad. We now read that it has been decided to appoint a committee made up of representatives of the government and the two conflicting parties(!!) and that the employers have asked for an *immediate* increase in prices!!!

To illustrate to the readers the extent to which the gentlemen capitalists would go in making sport of the people, we hereby present a few passages from a certain ministerial paper (*i. e.*, an organ of a party that has representatives in the cabinet): [281]

The workers' delegation (from the southern mining industry) presented to the Economic Department of the Executive Committee of the Soviet of Workers' and Soldiers' Deputies information relating to the actual state of affairs. Utilising this information, we are now in a position to announce that the figures quoted by N. N. Kutler on the basis of statements made by the capitalists deserve no credence whatever.

. . . The coal operators had been making enormous profits before the revolution, and yet, just before its outbreak, they were bargaining with the old government concerning a rise in the fixed prices on coal. In addition to the three kopecks which the government was willing to grant, the coal dealers were asking five more kopecks. From the revolutionary Provisional Government, on the other hand, the operators succeeded, during the very first days of the revolution, in obtaining a rise of eight kopecks, applying the new rate to shipments delivered to the railroads, and to government purchases, dating as far back as the beginning of January. They later managed to get three kopecks more, making a total of eleven kopecks.

Before the revolution the fixed price was eighteen kopecks; now it is twenty-nine kopecks. Government contracts at that time brought twenty-two kopecks per pood, while now they are thirty-three and thirty-four and even more. . . .

Is this not a most outrageous capitalist mockery of the people? Taking advantage of the revolution, the capitalist government, styling itself "revolutionary" and deceiving the benighted people with this "fine" appellation, is handing to the capitalists greater and greater profits! It places in their pockets more and more millions!

The country is on the verge of ruin, while the ten capitalists—members of the Provisional Government—are aiding the employers who are looting the land, robbing the people, and adding to the colossal profits of capital.

> The Ministry of Commerce and Industry is the captive of the congress of the South Russian mine operators. Faced by the catastrophe towards which industry in the South is heading, it takes no steps to avert the calamity; on the contrary, it systematically submits in its actions to the pressure of the southern industrialists.

Thus wrote the very same ministerial paper, the organ of the Mensheviks, the *Rabochaia Gazeta*, on May 27, 1917, *i. e.,* one week after the forming of the coalition cabinet.

Since then absolutely nothing has changed.

But the ministerial paper has been forced to admit even more damaging facts. Hear! Hear!

> . . . The operators are sabotaging. They deliberately refuse to take measures to assure the functioning of the industry. If a pump is needed, it cannot be found. If wire gauze is needed, for the miners' safety lamps, it is not supplied. The operators do not want increased production. They are also reluctant to spend money on necessary repairs, on replacing the worn-out parts. The machines are too old, and will soon be out of commission. Frequently the workers themselves, when told that this or that article cannot be obtained, venture forth to purchase the necessary tools, and they generally find what they need. The operators make no effort to ship the products, such as coal, cast-iron, etc. Tens and hundreds of millions of rubles' worth of these products lie idle, while the country is in dire need of them.

Thus wrote the ministerial paper, the paper that belongs to the same Menshevik party to which belong Tsereteli and Skobelev.

This is mockery; the capitalists are trifling with the people. This is a veritable madhouse: the capitalists are in collusion with the bourgeois portion of the Provisional Government (among the members of which are Mensheviks and Socialists-Revolutionists)—the capitalists are *blocking* industry, are *interfering* with the work, are *not making any effort* to ship their products, without which the country is facing *ruin.*

Without coal, the factories and railroads cannot function. Unemployment is spreading. There is a shortage of goods. The peasants cannot part with their bread without getting anything in return. Famine is imminent.

For all this the capitalists who are in collusion with the government are responsible!!

And all this is tolerated by the Narodniks, the Socialists-Revolutionists, and the Mensheviks!! They are getting off with words. They wrote about these crimes of the capitalists *as far back as May 27.* It is June 13 now. More than two weeks have passed. Everything remains as it was before. Famine is steadily approaching.

To cover up the crimes of the capitalists, to distract the attention of the people, all the capitalist newspapers: the *Riech*, the *Dien*, the *Novoie Vremia*, the *Russkaia Volia*, the *Birzhevka*, the *Yedinstvo*, pour their daily slops of lies and calumny upon the Bolsheviks. . . . The Bolsheviks are responsible for the collusion between the capitalists and the government, for the damaging and blocking of production!

This indeed would resemble a madhouse, were it not that the theory and the universal experience of the class-struggle have proven that the capitalists and *their* government (supported by the Mensheviks) do not stop at anything when it comes to the protection of their profits.

How long will it keep up? Is it necessary to wait until calamity descends upon every nook and corner of this land, until hundreds and thousands of people begin to die of hunger?

Pravda, No. 69, June 13, 1917.

LETTER TO THE BOROUGH COMMITTEES OF THE PETRO-GRAD ORGANISATION OF THE R.S.-D.L.P.

DEAR COMRADES:

I herewith enclose a resolution of the Petrograd Committee concerning the issuance of a paper and two resolutions introduced by me in the name of the Central Committee of the Russian Social-Democratic Labour Party, at a session of the Petrograd Committee on Tuesday, June 12.* I would ask that you consider all the three resolutions and present your conclusion and reasons for same in the most detailed manner.

There is a conflict growing between the P.C. and the C.C. on the question as to whether the P.C. needs a separate paper. It is extremely important and highly desirable that the greatest possible number of members of our party in Petrograd should take an active part in the discussion of this crucial question and help us with their decision to settle it.

The Executive Commission of the P.C. has expressed itself unanimously in favour of a separate organ for the P.C. in Petrograd, contrary to the decision of the C.C. to the effect that, instead of the *Pravda*, which is obviously inadequate, two papers should be established: the old *Pravda* as the Central Organ of the party, and a small *Narodnaia Pravda* (the names of both papers have not yet been definitely decided upon), as a popular organ for the masses. The editorial staff, according to the C.C., is to be one for both papers, and each paper is to have a representative of the P.C. on its editorial staff (with a voice without vote on the staff of the Central Organ and one *with* a vote on the staff of the popular organ). There is to be created a "press commission" (of workers most closely connected with the masses in the boroughs), and a definite number of columns in each paper is to be devoted to the needs of the local labour movement.

This is the plan of the C.C.

The Executive Commission of the P.C., instead of this, wants its own paper, a separate paper for the P.C. The Executive Commission has unanimously decided upon it.

* See pp. 161-163 of this book.—*Ed.*

At the meeting of the P.C. on June 12, after the report and the concluding word by Comrade M. Tomsky, after my speech and the discussion in which many comrades participated, there was an equal division of votes: Fourteen for the Executive Commission, fourteen against it. My motion was rejected by a vote of sixteen to twelve.

It is my conviction that, as a matter of principle, the P.C. does not need a separate paper. For in the *capital,* in view of its guiding influence on the whole country, we must have one organ of the party, namely, the Central Organ, and a popular paper, to be put out in a particularly popular form, under the same editorial staff.

A special organ of the P.C. would inevitably make impossible complete harmony in our work, it may even give birth to a different, or slightly different, policy. The harm therefrom, particularly in revolutionary times, may be very serious.

Why should we diffuse our efforts?

We are all fearfully overloaded with work, we have few workers; the writers are mostly deserting us for the defencists. Is it permissible under such conditions to diffuse our efforts?

We must concentrate our efforts instead of diffusing them.

Is there any reason for mistrusting the C.C. for fearing that it will not select the proper editorial staff or that it will not give enough space in both papers to local activities, or that it will show a disregard for the editors from the P.C. who are in a minority, and . . . .*

In the second draft resolution I purposely enumerate many similar objections (which I heard at the session of the P.C. on June 12), in order to put the matter frankly before all the members of the party, to urge them to weigh carefully each of the two arguments and to decide in a responsible way.

If you, comrades, have weighty and serious reasons for not trusting the C.C., say so openly. That is the duty of every member of our democratically organised party, and then it would be the duty of the C.C. of our party to give your distrust especial consideration, to report it to the party congress, to enter into negotiations with a view to removing this deplorable lack of confidence in the C.C. by a local organisation.

But if there is no such lack of confidence, then it is unjust and

* Omission in the text.—*Ed.*

wrong to attempt to take away from the C.C. the power which was vested in it by the party congress to direct the activities of the party generally and the activities in the capital particularly.

Does our C.C. demand too much when it insists on directing the Petrograd papers? No. In the German Social-Democratic Party, in its best days, when Wilhelm Liebknecht was at the head of the party for many decades, he was the editor of the Central Organ of the party. The C.O. was published in Berlin. The Berlin organisation never had a special Berlin paper. There was a "press commission" of workers, there was a department of local affairs in the Central Organ of the party. Why should we depart from this good example set by our comrades in other countries?

If you, comrades, wish special guarantees from the C.C., if you want certain points changed (in the plan of the C.C. relating to the publication of two papers), I ask you in the name of the C.C. carefully to consider and to present your views. The decision of the Executive Commission of the P.C. to create a special newspaper in Petrograd is, in my opinion. exceedingly wrong, undesirable, it splits our forces and injects into our party a number of issues that may cause friction. In my opinion (and on this point I merely represent the opinion of the C.C.) it is desirable that the Petrograd organisation should support the decision of the C.C., that it should wait until it has had an opportunity to see the results of our experience with the two papers as published according to the plan of the C.C., and that, if necessary, it should then adopt any decision it may wish regarding the results of that experiment.

With comradely Social-Democratic greetings,

N. LENIN.

June 13, 1917.
Printed from the minutes of the Petrograd Committee of the R.S.-D.L.P., and first published in *Krasnaia Lietopis*, No. 3 (14), 1923.

SPEECH DELIVERED AT THE FIRST PETROGRAD CONFER-
ENCE OF FACTORY-SHOP COMMITTEES,
JUNE 13, 1917.[232]

A BRIEF NEWSPAPER REPORT

COMRADE AVILOV's resolution shows a complete forgetfulness of the class-struggle. In his resolution B. V. Avilov, it would seem, has conceived the aim of collecting and concentrating all the faults of all the resolutions of petty-bourgeois parties.[233]

In the first part of his resolution, Avilov lays down the proposition, by now incontrovertible to any Socialist, that the predatory rule of the capitalists has brought Russia to complete economic and industrial ruin; but further on he advances a hasty formula for the control of industry by "state power," with the participation of broad strata of democracy. Nowadays everybody speaks a great deal about control; even those who in former days threw up their hands at the mere hearing of the word "control," are now admitting that control is indispensable.

But through the very use of this general word "control," they, as a matter of fact, want to reduce control to zero.

The coalition government, which includes "Socialists," has done nothing as yet in the way of carrying this control into practice. We therefore can readily understand why the factory committees demand actual proletarian control, and not control on paper.

In endeavouring to elucidate the concept "control" as well as the question as to when and by whom such control should be effected, one must not forget for a moment the class character of the present state, which is merely the organisation of class rule. The same class analysis should be applied to the concept "revolutionary democracy." This analysis should be based on the real correlation of social forces.

Avilov's resolution, which starts out with a promise to give everything, ends in fact with the proposition that everything be left as of old. In his entire resolution there is not a shadow of revolutionism.

In revolutionary times, more than at any other time, it is necessary correctly to analyse the question as to the very essence of the state, as to which interests it shall protect, and as to how it shall be constructed so that it may really protect the interests of the toilers. But this is not at all made clear in Avilov's resolution.

Why has the new coalition government, which now includes "Socialists," not carried control into practice during the past three months? Not only has it not carried it into practice, but in the conflict between the mine owners and the workers of Southern Russia, the government openly sided with the capitalists.

To render industrial control really practicable, the control must be exercised by the workers, all the responsible institutions must have a majority of workers, and the administration must give an account of all its actions to all of the most authoritative workers' organisations.

Comrade workers, you must try to secure actual, not imaginary, control. Reject all such resolutions and propositions as would establish a fictitious control, a control on paper only.

Pravda, No. 72, June 16, 1917.

DISGRACE JUSTIFIED

THE Department of International Relations of the Executive Committee of the Petrograd Soviet of Workers' and Soldiers' Deputies has sent to Huysmans, the well-known secretary of the bankrupt Second International, the members of which are now supporting their "own" national governments, a note that has been reprinted in No. 78 of the *Izvestia*.[284]

This note endeavours to prove that the entrance of the Russian Narodniks and Mensheviks into the bourgeois imperialist government cannot be "compared" with the entrance of the West-European Socialist-traitors into "their" governments. The proofs adduced by the "Department" are so weak and pitiful, so ludicrously impotent, that it is necessary to expose them in all their futility, over and over again.

Argument 1. In other countries the entrance into the government took place "under entirely different conditions." Untrue! The difference between England, France, Denmark, Belgium, Italy, etc., on the one hand, and present-day Russia, on the other, are entirely unessential. Every one who has *not* betrayed Socialism knows that the essential point is the *rule* of the bourgeoisie. In *this* respect conditions in all the above-named countries are not "different," but the same. National peculiarities do not affect in the least the basic question of bourgeois rule.

Argument 2. "Our" Ministers have entered a "revolutionary" government. This is the most shameful deception of the people by the use of the great word "Revolution" to which the Mensheviks and the Narodniks resort to hide their treason. Every one knows that ten Ministers (out of sixteen in the present "revolutionary" government) belong to the parties of the landowners and the capitalists, and stand for the imperialist war and the non-publication of the secret treaties. Every one knows that these parties are now pursuing a *counter-revolutionary* policy. This was made evident by the elections to the Borough Councils of Petrograd on June 9-11, when *all* the Black Hundred elements joined hands to vote for the majority in our "revolutionary" government.

Argument 3. "Our" Ministers have entered "with a definite mandate to achieve universal peace by encouraging reconciliation among peoples, and not to protract the imperialist war in the name of liberating the nations by force of arms." First of all, this mandate is not at all "definite," for it does not signify any definite *programme*, or any definite *acts*.

These are meaningless words. Imagine a secretary of a labour union becoming an executive member of an association of capitalists at a salary of 10,000 rubles on the basis of a "definite mandate" to work for the welfare of the toilers and oppose the continuance of capitalist domination. Secondly, *all* imperialists, Wilhelm, and Poincaré, and the rest, are also striving for "reconciliation among peoples"; this, too, is an empty phrase. Thirdly, as far as Russia is concerned, the war, after May 19, 1917, is clearly being "protracted," among other things, by the failure of our imperialist government to proclaim or propose precise and clear conditions for a peace of reconciliation.

Argument 4. "Our" aim "is not the cessation of the class-struggle, but its continuation by means of the instruments of political power." Magnificent! So, everything is well, vileness is justifiable, so long as it can be concealed by a smoke-screen of virtuous professions, so long as the aims are praiseworthy!!

Participation in a bourgeois imperialist government which is actually carrying on an imperialist war, may, don't you see, also be called "continuation of the class-struggle by means of the instruments of political power." This is simply a gem. We suggest that the workers, the people at all their meetings, shout "Hurrah" in honour of Chernov, Tsereteli, Peshekhonov, Skobelev, who are carrying on a *"class-struggle"* against Tereshchenko, Lvov and Co.

They will kill you with ridicule, gentlemen of the "Department," if you defend ministerialism by such arguments. Incidentally, you are not original at all: the famous Vandervelde, the friend of Plekhanov (whom you scold, although, since your entrance into the cabinet, you have not the slightest moral right to do so), said long ago that he had joined the cabinet for "the continuation of the class-struggle."

Argument 5. "Our" Ministers entered the cabinet after the overthrow of tsarism and upon the expulsion of "the enemies of the Russian proletariat" (*i. e.*, of Miliukov and Guchkov) "by a revolutionary mass movement on May 3-4."

What fault is it of the French if they overthrew their autocracy

125 years ago, instead of 100 days ago? and the English, if they did it over 260 years ago? and the Italians, a few decades ago? On May 3, Miliukov was driven out, and Tereshchenko took his place, *i. e.*, nothing was really changed as far as class or party rule is concerned. New promises do not mean a new policy.

If we were to drive out the Metropolitan * and recognise the Pope in his place, that would not mean that we ceased being clericals.

Argument 6. In Russia "there is complete freedom for the proletariat and the army." Untrue, not complete. It is more nearly complete than in other countries; the disgrace, therefore, is so much greater when we allow this young, this fresh freedom to be marred by this unsavoury business of participating in a bourgeois-imperialistic government.

The difference between the Russian Socialist-traitors and the European ones is not greater than that between one who violates and one who rapes.

Argument 7. "Moreover the Russian proletariat is possessed of means for the complete control of those it elects."

Untrue. The organisation along party lines is so new in Russia, disintegration among the Mensheviks and the Socialists-Revolutionists is so evident (Martov half splitting away from his party, Kamkov protesting, joining us at the elections against his party, the Mensheviks and the Socialists-Revolutionists forming a bloc with the *Yedinstvo* group which they themselves call *imperialists,* etc.) that, not only is there no "complete" control, but there is in fact *no* way at all whereby the "proletariat" may effectually control the Ministers.

Furthermore, "proletariat" is a *class* concept which the Mensheviks and the Narodniks have no right to use at all, because they rather lean on the support of the *petty bourgeoisie.* Once *you* speak of classes, be precise!

Argument 8. "The entrance of the representatives of the Russian Socialist (??) proletariat (???) into the government did not imply a weakening of the ties that bind the Russian proletariat to the Socialists of other countries who are fighting against imperialism; on the contrary, it signified a strengthening of those ties in a joint struggle for universal peace."

Untrue. A mere phrase, an untruth.

* The head of the Greek-Catholic Church, formerly the State church in Russia.—*Ed.*

Everybody knows that the entrance of "Socialists" into the Russian cabinet has strengthened the ties among the *supporters* of imperialism, the social chauvinists, the *social-imperialists* of all countries, such as Henderson and Co., Thomas and Co., *Scheidemann* and Co.

Yes, Scheidemann, too! For he understands that *German* social-imperialism and its deleterious influence upon the working class movement of the world are safe, as long as even the Russians, their very considerable freedom and their revolution notwithstanding, have entered into a disgraceful alliance with *their* imperialist bourgeoisie.

Pravda, No. 70, June 14, 1917.

A PETTY-BOURGEOIS POSITION ON THE QUESTION OF ECONOMIC CHAOS

THE *Novaia Zhizn* publishes to-day a resolution introduced by Comrade Avilov at the conference of the factory committees. Unfortunately, this resolution cannot but be viewed as an example of an un-Marxian, un-Socialist, and petty-bourgeois attitude towards this question. And just because this resolution brings out in strong relief all the weak spots of the usual Menshevik and Narodnik Soviet resolutions, this resolution is typical and worthy of attention.

The resolution begins with an excellent general statement, with a splendid indictment of the capitalists: "The present-day economic havoc . . . is the result of the war and the predatory anarchistic rule of the capitalists and the government . . ." Correct! That capital oppresses, that it is a beast of prey, that it is the real source of anarchy, in this the petty bourgeois is ready to agree with the proletarian. But the difference between the two begins immediately: The proletarian regards capitalist rule as predatory, he therefore wages a class struggle against it, he builds his entire policy on the unconditional distrust of the capitalist class, he distinguishes, as far as the state is concerned, which class the "state" serves, which class interests it protects. The petty bourgeois does at times wax "mad" at capital, but he soon recovers from this attack of madness and returns to faith in the capitalists, to hopes placed in the "state" of the capitalists!

So it is with Comrade Avilov.

After an excellent, decisive, formidable introduction, which accuses the capitalists of "rapacity," and not only the capitalists, but also the capitalist government, Comrade Avilov, throughout his entire resolution, in all its concrete matter, in all its practical suggestions, forgets the class point of view, and like the Mensheviks and the Narodniks stoops to phrases about the "state" in general, about "revolutionary democracy" in general.

Workers! The rapacity of predatory capital causes anarchy and economic chaos, while the capitalist government administers the country in anarchic fashion. Salvation lies in control "of the

179

state with the participation of revolutionary democracy." This is the content of Avilov's resolution.

Have you no fear of God, Comrade Avilov! Should a Marxist forget that the government is an organ of class rule? Is it not ridiculous to appeal to a capitalist government to restrain "capitalist rapacity"?

Should a Marxist forget that the capitalists have also repeatedly been "revolutionary democrats,"—in 1649 in England, in 1789 in France, in 1830, 1848, 1870 also in France, in March, 1917, in Russia?

Have you really forgotten that it is necessary to differentiate between the revolutionary democracy of the capitalists, of the petty bourgeoisie and of the proletariat? Is it not clear from the history of all the above-mentioned revolutions that there is a difference of classes within "revolutionary democracy"?

He who after the experience of March, April, May, 1917, continues to talk in Russia about "revolutionary democracy" in general, is deceiving the people, whether willingly or unwillingly, consciously or unconsciously. For the "moment" of a general fusion of classes against tsarism has already come and passed. The first agreement between the first "Provisional Committee" of the Duma and the Soviet definitely signified the end of the class fusion and the beginning of the class struggle.

The May crisis (May 3), and that of May 19, then June 9-11 (elections) and so on and so forth, have definitely drawn the lines between the various classes in the Russian Revolution within Russian "revolutionary democracy." To ignore this means to sink to the helplessness of a petty bourgeois.

To appeal now to the "state" and to "revolutionary democracy" particularly as regards the rapacity of the capitalists, means to drag the working class backward, means in fact to preach complete cessation of the revolution. For our "state," now, after April, after May, is a state of (rapacious) capitalists who have tamed, in the persons of Chernov, Tsereteli and Co., a goodly portion of "revolutionary (petty-bourgeois) democracy."

This state hinders the revolution everywhere, in all the realms of foreign and domestic policy.

To let this state carry on the struggle against capitalist "rapacity" means to throw the shark into the water.

Pravda, No. 70, June 14, 1917.

A MOTE IN YOUR NEIGHBOUR'S EYE

ALGERIA is at fault. . . . Our ministerial "Socialists-Revolutionists" had all but succeeded in befogging themselves and their audiences with phrases concerning their belief in "peace without annexations" (*i. e.*, without seizure of foreign lands),—when suddenly the question of Algeria came up! The paper *Dielo Naroda*, with two Socialists-Revolutionists, members of the cabinet, Kerensky and Chernov, on its staff, was guilty of carelessly starting a discussion with three Allied Ministers (also near-Socialists) concerning Algeria. How fearful the carelessness of this paper of the Kerenskys and the Chernovs is, the reader may realise from the following:

Three Ministers of the Allied countries, Henderson of England, Thomas of France, and Vandervelde of Belgium, had declared that they did not want "annexations," but "the liberation of territories." The paper of the Kerenskys and the Chernovs denounced the statement—and quite justly—as "sleight-of-hand" performed by the "bourgeois-trained Socialists," and hurled at the latter the following angry and sarcastic tirade:

"True, they" (the three Ministers) "demand the liberation of territories only 'in accordance with the wishes of the population.' Splendid! But in that case we must demand of them and of ourselves logical consistency, we must allow for the 'liberation of the territories' of Ireland and Finland on the one hand, of Algeria and Siam on the other. It would be exceedingly interesting to hear the opinion of the Socialist Albert Thomas on the 'self-determination' of Algeria."

Yes, indeed, it would also "be exceedingly interesting to hear the opinion" of Kerensky, and Tsereteli, and Chernov, and Skobelev on the "self-determination" of Armenia, Galicia, the Ukraine, and Turkestan.

Gentlemen, Russian Ministers, Narodniks and Mensheviks, you yourselves have exposed the disingenuousness, the falseness of your attitude and actions by citing the examples of Ireland and Algeria. You yourselves have proved that in speaking of "annexations" one

181

must not limit oneself to territories seized only during the present war. You have defeated yourselves, as well as the *Izvestia* of the Petrograd Soviet, which, proudly ignorant, had only recently declared that "annexations" meant seizures of territories effected during the present war. But who does not know that Ireland and Algeria were seized decades and centuries before the present war?

The *Dielo Naroda* is exceedingly careless, for it has revealed the utter confusion that reigns in its own mind, as well as in the minds of the Mensheviks and the *Izvestia* of the Petrograd Soviet on the question of annexations, a very important and very fundamental question.

But this is not all. Once you question Henderson about Ireland, and Albert Thomas about Algeria, once you counterpose the opinion of the French *people* to that of the "French bourgeoisie that is in power," once you do call Henderson and Albert Thomas "bourgeois-trained Socialists,"—then why is it that you have forgotten all about yourselves?

How about you, Messrs. Kerensky, Tsereteli, Chernov, and Skobelev? Are you not also "bourgeois-trained Socialists"? Have you raised in the cabinet of the "Russian bourgeoisie that is in power" any questions about *Russia's* Ireland, *Russia's* Algeria, etc., *i. e.*, about Turkestan, the Ukraine, Armenia, Finland, etc.? Has this question ever been raised? Why should you not tell the Russian people something about it? Why do you not denounce as "sleight-of-hand" the method of the *Russian* Narodniks and Mensheviks who prate in the Soviet, in the cabinet and before the people, spouting gorgeous phrases about "peace without annexations," while not raising, in a clear, precise and unambiguous manner, the question about the Russian annexations of the type of Ireland and Algeria?

The Russian ministerial Narodniks and Mensheviks are hopelessly confused; each day discloses it more and more.

Their usual and "final" argument is: we have a revolution. But this argument is disingenuous, through and through. For our revolution has *thus far* given power only to the *bourgeoisie*, as in France and in England, with an "innocuous minority" of "bourgeois-trained Socialists,"—as in France and England. What our revolution will bring to-morrow,—whether the restoration of the monarchy, or the strengthening of the bourgeoisie, or the transfer of power to more advanced classes,—we know not, nor does anybody know. Hence to base one's arguments on the "revolution" as such, means shamefully to deceive oneself as well as the people.

The question of annexations is an acid test for the Narodniks and the Mensheviks who have lost themselves in a maze of lies and falsehoods. They are just as confused as are Plekhanov, Henderson, Scheidemann and Co. The two groups differ *only in theory,* in practice both are lost to the cause of *real* Socialism.

Pravda, No. 70, June 14, 1917.

IT IS NOT DEMOCRATIC, CITIZEN KERENSKY

THE Petrograd Telegraph Agency reports:

Kiev, May 30. At the session of the All-Ukrainian Peasant Congress, a telegram from War Minister Kerensky was read. In it he declares that, in view of the military situation, he deems the convocation of a second Ukrainian army congress untimely. The congress, considering the Minister's order to be an infringement of the right of free assembly in the Ukraine, despatched the following telegram to the Provisional Government and to the Petrograd Soviet of Workers' and Soldiers' Deputies:

"We call attention to the first case of infringement of the right of free assembly, resorted to by Minister Kerensky in the case of the Ukrainian army congress. We renounce all responsibility for any possible consequences that may arise as a result of this infringement of the democratic principles of the new life in the Ukraine, and, expressing our resolute protest, we await the Provisional Government's immediate reply to the demands made by the delegation of the Ukrainian Central Rada."

This news will no doubt stir up a great commotion in the ranks of the Socialist workers.

The War Minister deems the congress of Ukrainians "untimely," and prohibits it on his own authority! Not so very long ago citizen Kerensky was trying to discipline Finland, he has now decided to do the same with the Ukrainians. And it is all done in the name of "democracy."

A. I. Herzen once said that when one beholds the antics of the ruling classes of Russia, one begins to feel ashamed of being a Russian. This was said when Russia was groaning under the yoke of serfdom, when the knout and the rod held sway over our land.

Now in Russia tsarism is no more. Now in the name of Russia speak the Kerenskys and the Lvovs. And the treatment which Russia of the Kerenskys and the Lvovs accords to her subject nationalities brings back to mind the bitter words of A. I. Herzen.

It is not our wish to stress the point that Kerensky with his "great-nation" policy manages to inflame and to strengthen the very "separatist" aspirations which the Kerenskys and the Lvovs are endeavouring to crush.

But we do ask whether such treatment of oppressed nationalities is compatible with the dignity, let alone of Socialism, but even of

184

simple democracy?   We ask: Are there any limits to the "mischief" of Kerensky and his backers?

We ask the party of the Socialists-Revolutionists whether it subscribes to the step taken by its honourable member, citizen Kerensky, in forbidding the Ukrainian congress?

We are informed that the Executive Committees of the Soviet of Workers' and Soldiers' Deputies decided yesterday to invite citizen Kerensky to a conference on the question of self-determination of nations, as well as on other questions of national policy.

And still there is talk about the "demise" of the "contact commission."   Not at all, gentlemen!   Dual power is still with us. There is no other escape from the present situation, except through the transfer of all power to the Soviets of Workers' and Soldiers' Deputies.

Pravda, No. 71, June 15, 1917.

BOLSHEVISM AND THE "DISINTEGRATION" OF THE ARMY

EVERYBODY is howling for "firm authority." There is salvation in dictatorship, in "iron discipline," in forcing all the non-conformists, the "Rights" and the "Lefts" to shut their mouths and submit. We know whom they wish to force into silence. The Rights do not make noise, they *work*. Some of them work in the government, others, in factories. They threaten lock-outs, they order regiments to be disbanded, they threaten people with hard labour. The Konovalovs and the Tereshchenkos, with the aid of the Kerenskys and the Skobelevs, are organised to work for their own benefit. There is no need of making them keep still. . . .

But we have at our disposal *only* the right to speak.

And it is of this right that we are to be deprived. . . .

The *Pravda* is not permitted to reach the front. The "agents" in Kiev have decided not to distribute the *Pravda*. The "Union of Zemstvos" is not selling the *Pravda* on its stands. Now, finally, we are being promised a "systematic struggle against Leninist propaganda . . ." (*Izvestia* of the Soviet of Workers' and Soldiers' Deputies). On the other hand, every elemental protest, every excess, whatever its origin, is blamed on us.

This, too, is a method of fighting Bolshevism.

It is a well-tried method.

Not given the chance to obtain clear and definite directions, feeling instinctively how false and unsatisfactory is the position of the official leaders of democracy, the masses are forced to feel out their own way. . . .

The result is that many dissatisfied, class-conscious revolutionists, many indignant fighters who yearn for their home cottages but who see no end to the war, many men even who simply try to save their own skins are drawn to the banner of Bolshevism.

Where Bolshevism has a chance to appear in the open, there we find no disorganisation.

Where there are no Bolsheviks, or where they are not permitted to talk, there we find excesses, disintegration, and pseudo-Bolsheviks. . . .

And this is just what our enemies need.

They need a pretext for saying that "the Bolsheviks are disorganising the army," later to shut the mouths of the Bolsheviks.

In order that we may once for all fence ourselves off from the calumnies spread by our "enemies" and from the absurd distortions of Bolshevism, we quote the concluding part of a proclamation spread by one of the delegates in the army on the eve of the All-Russian Congress.

Here it is:

Comrades, it is for you to say the word.

There must be no agreements with the bourgeoisie!

All power to the Soviet of Workers' and Soldiers' Deputies!

This does not mean that we are forthwith to proceed to overthrow or disobey the present government. While the majority of the people still follow it and still believe that five Socialists will be able to overcome the rest, we cannot afford to fritter away our forces in desultory uprisings.

Never!

Conserve your strength! Gather into meetings! Pass resolutions! Demand the transfer of all power to the Soviet of Workers' and Soldiers' Deputies! Convince the refractory ones! Forward your resolutions to me in Petrograd, in the name of your regiment, so that I may be able there to refer to your voice!

But beware of provocateurs who, posing as Bolsheviks, will attempt to lure you into disorders and riots, and thus hide their own cowardice! Know that, though they are with you now, they will sell you to the old régime at the first intimation of danger.

The real Bolsheviks appeal to you not to make riots, but to carry on a class-conscious revolutionary struggle.

Comrades! The All-Russian Congress will elect representatives to whom the Provisional Government will be accountable pending the convocation of the Constituent Assembly.

Comrades! At that Congress I shall demand:

First, the transfer of all power to the Soviet of Workers' and Soldiers' Deputies;

Second, the immediate offer of peace without annexations or indemnities, in the name of our people, to the peoples and governments of all the belligerent nations, our allies as well as our enemies. Let then any government dare to refuse—it will be overthrown by its own people.

Third, the taking over for state needs of all money made by war profiteering, i. e., confiscation of the war profits of the capitalists.

Comrades! The war can be terminated only by the transfer of power to the peoples of Russia, Germany, France, only by the overthrow of the present bourgeois governments in all the countries.

Our revolution is beginning—our next task is to give the world revolution a further impulse by a peace offer made by a real, authorised, popular government of Russia to all the governments of Europe and by strengthening our ties with the revolutionary democracies of Western Europe.

Woe to the bourgeois government that will insist on continuing the war.

Together with its people we shall wage a revolutionary war against such a government.

I have been elected as your delegate to the Petrograd Congress, in order that I may say all this to our government at Petrograd.

Member of the Army Committee of the XI Army, delegate of the Central Committee of the Russian S.-D. Labour Party (Bolsheviks) to the congress of the South-Western front, Ensign Krylenko.

No one who has taken the trouble to read the resolutions of our party can fail to see that Comrade Krylenko has correctly expressed their true essence.

It is not to disorder and riots but to a class-conscious revolutionary struggle that the Bolsheviks summon the proletariat, the poorest peasants, the toiling and exploited masses.

Only real people's power, *i. e.*, power belonging to the majority of the people, is capable of pursuing the right path that leads humanity to the overthrow of the capitalist yoke, to freedom from the horrors and misery of the imperialist war, to a just and lasting peace.

Pravda, No. 72, June 16, 1917.

DISORGANISATION AND THE STRUGGLE OF THE PROLETARIAT AGAINST IT

WE are publishing in this issue the resolution on the economic measures to be taken for combating economic disorganisation, passed by the Conference of Shop and Factory Committees.

The fundamental purpose of the resolution is to indicate the conditions necessary for *actual* control over capitalists and over production, in contradistinction to the current *phrases* about control used by the bourgeoisie and the petty-bourgeois officials. The bourgeois are lying when they try to make us believe that the systematic measures taken by the state to ensure threefold or even tenfold profits for the capitalists are "control." The petty bourgeoisie, partly from naïveté, partly from economic interest, is placing its faith in the capitalists and the capitalist state, and is resting fully satisfied with the emptiest bureaucratic projects in the matter of control. The resolution passed by the workers places the main emphasis on what is to be done (1) to prevent the actual "safeguarding" of capitalist profits; (2) to expose the commercial secrets; (3) to ensure for the workers a majority in the controlling bodies; (4) to make certain that the organisation (of control and direction), since it is an organisation on a "national scale," should be not under the guidance of the capitalists but under that of the Soviets of Workers', Soldiers', and Peasants' Deputies.

Without the foregoing, all talk of control and regulation is either empty babble or outright deception of the people.

Against this truth, which is accessible to any thinking class-conscious worker, the leaders of our petty bourgeoisie, the Narodniks and the Mensheviks (*Izvestia, Rabochaia Gazeta*) have declared war. Unfortunately, the writers on the *Novaia Zhizn*, who frequently vacillate between us and them, have this time sunk to their level.

Comrades Avilov and Bazarov are trying to disguise their "fall" into the mire of petty-bourgeois trustfulness, compromise, and bureaucratic project-making by resorting to Marxist-sounding arguments.

Let us examine these arguments.

189

Because we of the *Pravda* defend the resolution of the Organisation Bureau (accepted by the Conference), they accuse us of swerving from Marxism to Syndicalism. Shame on you, Comrades Avilov and Bazarov! Such lack of attention (or such trickery) would be expected from the *Riech* or the *Yedinstvo!* We do not suggest anything resembling the ludicrous passing of the railroads into the hands of the railwaymen, of the leather factories into the hands of the leather workers: What we do advocate is *workers' control,* which is gradually to develop into complete proletarian regulation of production and distribution of goods, into a "nation-wide organisation" of the exchange of grain for manufactured products, etc. (whereby "extensive use is made of urban and rural co-operatives") ; what we demand is "the passing of all state power into the hands of the Soviets of Workers', Soldiers', and Peasants' Deputies."

Only people who have not read the resolution, or who are altogether illiterate, could, with a clear conscience, discover any Syndicalism in it.

And only pedants, whose conception of Marxism is like that of Struve and of all liberal bureaucrats, are capable of asserting that "skipping state capitalism is Utopian," that "in our country, too, regulation must retain the character of state capitalism."

If we take the sugar syndicate, or the state railways in Russia, or the naphtha magnates, etc., what is it but state capitalism? How can we "skip" a stage that already exists?

The truth is that those people have turned Marxism into a kind of rigid bourgeois doctrine. Those people disdain the concrete problem confronting them in actual life in Russia where we have syndicates in industry and small peasant-holdings in the villages; they evade these living problems by advancing their quasi-learned, in reality very primitive, arguments about a "permanent revolution," "introduction" of Socialism, and other nonsense.

To business! To business! Fewer excuses, and closer to the practical reality! Are the profits made on war supplies, profits amounting to 500 per cent or so, to remain untouched? Yes or no? Is commercial secrecy to remain intact? Yes or no? Are the workers to be given the opportunity to control affairs? Yes or no?

To all these practical questions Comrades Avilov and Bazarov can give no answer; they use "Struveist," "almost-Marxian" arguments, and without themselves realising it, stoop to the rôle of helpmates of the bourgeoisie. There is nothing the bourgeois desires more than to meet people's queries about scandalous war profiteering, about disorganisation in our national economy, with "learned" arguments about the "Utopian character" of Socialism.

These arguments are ridiculously stupid. What makes Socialism objectively impossible is the petty economy which we do not pretend to be able to expropriate, or even to regulate or control.

That "state regulation" of which the Mensheviks, the Narodniks, and all the bureaucrats (who have enticed Comrades Avilov and Bazarov to follow them) speak to avoid action, which they project to *safeguard* capitalist profits, which they are grandiloquent about to preserve commercial secrecy,—that very state regulation we are endeavouring to make a reality, not a delusion. This, worthy near-Marxists, and not the "introduction" of Socialism, is the essence of the whole matter.

Not regulation and control of the workers by the capitalist class, but vice versa—this is the essence of the matter. Not confidence in the "state," worthy of a Louis Blanc, but the demand for a state under the control of the proletarians and semi-proletarians—this is how we must cope with economic disorganisation. Any other decision is a mere phrase and a deception.

Pravda, No. 73, June 17, 1917.

THE THOUSAND AND FIRST LIE OF THE CAPITALISTS

In to-day's leading article the *Riech* writes:

> If Germany had its own Lenin acting with the kindly foreign co-operation of the Robert Grimms and the Rakovskys, we would be forced to suppose that the International does not wish to keep the great Russian Revolution from spreading and strengthening its position and, chiefly, from growing in depth. But so far the Germans have politely replied that they are not in need of a republic and that they are satisfied with Wilhelm. Even more amiable are the arguments of the *Vorwaerts* [235] to the effect that Russian democracy ought not to suffer secret treaties; but of the duty of the German democracy in this respect the Socialist organ modestly fails to mention.[236]

That the "Robert Grimms and the Rakovskys" have in any way "co-operated" with the Bolsheviks (with whom they have never been in agreement), is a lie.

To confuse the German Plekhanovs (it is just they who are writing in the *Vorwaerts*) with the German revolutionary internationalists, hundreds of whom (like Karl Liebknecht) now find themselves in German prisons, is the most loathsome and brazen lie which the *Riech* and the capitalists in general have been repeating for the thousand and first time.

There are two Internationals: 1. The International of Plekhanov, *i. e.*, the International of the betrayers of Socialism, *i. e.*, the International of people who have gone over to the side of their governments: Plekhanov, Guesde, Scheidemann, Sembat, Thomas, Henderson, Vandervelde, Bissolati and Co.; 2. The International of the revolutionary internationalists who, even in war time, fight everywhere in a revolutionary manner against their governments, against their bourgeoisie.

"The Great Russian Revolution" can become "great," can "strengthen its position" and "grow in depth," only if it ceases to support the imperialist "coalition" government, the imperialist war conducted by it, and the capitalist class in general.

Pravda, No. 75, June 17, 1917.

THE FIRST ALL-RUSSIAN CONGRESS OF SOVIETS OF WORKERS' AND SOLDIERS' DEPUTIES, JUNE 16–JULY 6, 1917 [287]

THE FIRST ALL-RUSSIAN CONGRESS OF SOVIETS

I

COMRADES! In the short time allotted to me, I am able—and I deem it more advisable—to dwell only on those questions of fundamental principle that have been brought up by the speaker from the Executive Committee and by the speakers that followed him.

The first fundamental question we have been confronted with is this: *Where* are we? What are these Soviets that have assembled here in an All-Russian Congress? What is this revolutionary democracy that has been discussed here so endlessly as to conceal the speakers' ignorance of its meaning and their absolute abandonment of its principles? For to speak of revolutionary democracy before the All-Russian Congress of Soviets and to overlook the nature of the latter, its class composition, its part in the revolution, to say nothing about this and still claim to be democrats,—is rather strange! One shows us a programme for a bourgeois parliamentary republic, the kind known all over Western Europe; one shows us a programme of reforms, the kind accepted now by all bourgeois governments—and still one speaks of revolutionary democracy!

To whom does one say it? To the Soviets. Let me ask you this: Is there any European country, bourgeois, democratic, or republican, where anything resembling our Soviets exists? Your answer is bound to be—no. There is no other place where such institutions do or can exist, and for this reason: there can be *either* a bourgeois government with such reform "plans" as have been exhibited to us here and as have dozens of times been proposed in all countries only to remain on paper; or an institution like the one we are now appealing to, a new type of "government," created by the revolution and having its prototypes in the history of the greatest revolutionary upheavals, as, for example, in France in 1792 and 1871, in Russia in 1905. The Soviets are an institution that does not and cannot

195

exist within, or alongside of, the ordinary bourgeois-parliamentary state. They are the new, the more democratic type of state which we in our party resolutions call the workers' and peasants' democratic republic, where all authority should belong to the Soviets of Workers' and Soldiers' Deputies. Vain is the thought that this is only a theoretical question, vain is the attempt to regard this matter as something that can be easily side-tracked, vain is the argument that we have at the present moment certain institutions of certain kinds existing side by side with the Soviets of Workers' and Soldiers' Deputies. Yes, they do exist side by side. But this is just the cause of an unheard-of number of misunderstandings, conflicts and frictions. This is just the thing that is pulling the Russian Revolution from its initial ascent, from its first forward movement, down to stagnation, back to the reaction now observable in our coalition government and its entire domestic and foreign policy connected with the impending imperialist offensive.

It is one thing or the other: either we have an ordinary bourgeois government—then there is no need for peasants', workers', soldiers', or any other kind of Soviets, then they will be dispersed by the generals, the counter-revolutionary generals, who control the army, paying no heed whatever to Minister Kerensky's oratory, then they will die an ignominious death otherwise,—or we have a real government of the Soviets. There is no other way open for these institutions; they can neither go backward nor remain in the same place if they are to live; they can only exist going forward. Here is a type of state not of the Russian's invention but created by the revolution itself which could not be victorious in any other way. Friction, party struggle for power within the All-Russian Soviet are inevitable. But that will mean that the masses themselves are overcoming possible errors and illusions through their own political experience (*Noise*) and not through reports by Ministers who quote what they said yesterday, what they are going to write to-morrow and what they are going to promise the day after to-morrow. This, comrades, is ridiculous, if one looks at things from the point of view of this institution which sprang from the revolution itself and is now facing the question: to be or not to be. The Soviets cannot continue to exist as they exist now. Adult people, workers and peasants, must come together, pass resolutions, listen to reports, without being able to verify them by studying the original documents! Institutions of this kind are a transition to a republic which, in deeds, not in words, will establish a firm power without police, without a standing army,—the kind of power that cannot as yet exist in Europe, that is, however, indispensable for a victory of the Russian Revolution if we mean by it a victory over the landowners, a victory over imperialism.

Without such a power, we cannot even dream of ourselves ever gaining such a victory; and the more we ponder the programme that is being urged upon us here, and the facts confronting us, the more crying appears the basic contradiction. We have been told by the main speaker and the other orators that the first Provisional Government was no good! But when the Bolsheviks, the ill-fated Bolsheviks, said: "Neither support nor confidence to this government," how many accusations of "Anarchism" were hurled against us. Now everybody says that the former government was bad, but what about the coalition government of near-Socialist Ministers? Wherein does it differ from the former one? Has not there been enough talk about programmes and projects? Haven't we had enough of it? Isn't it high time to get down to work? A whole month has passed since the coalition government was formed on the nineteenth of May. Look at the state of affairs, see the economic chaos spreading in Russia and in the other countries involved in this imperialist war!

How can this chaos be accounted for? Capitalist depredation. Here we have real anarchy! This is evident from admissions published not by our paper, not, God forbid, by a Bolshevik sheet, but by the ministerial *Rabochaia Gazeta*. It appears that prices on coal contracts have been raised by the "revolutionary government." The coalition government has made no change in this respect, either. We are told that it is impossible to introduce Socialism in Russia, to make radical changes at once; this, comrades, is an idle excuse. The doctrine of Marx and Engels, as they themselves always expounded it, is: "Our teaching is not a dogma, but a guide to action." Pure capitalism transformed into pure Socialism does not and cannot exist anywhere in time of war. What does exist is something intermediate, something new, unheard-of, caused by the fact that hundreds of millions of people, drawn into this criminal war among the capitalists, are perishing. It is not a question of promising reforms—these are empty words; it is a question of taking the step that must be taken now.

If you wish to refer to *"revolutionary"* democracy, then please differentiate between this conception and that of *reformist* democracy under a capitalist cabinet, for it is high time we passed from phrases about "revolutionary democracy," from mutual congratulations upon "revolutionary democracy," to a class characterisation as taught by Marxism and scientific Socialism in general. What we are offered is a reformist democracy under a capitalist cabinet. This may be excellent from the point of view of the ordinary patterns of Western Europe. Now, however, a number of countries are on the verge of ruin, and those practical measures, which, according to the preceding orator, citizen-Minister of Posts and Telegraphs,[238] are so complicated that it is difficult to introduce them, that they need special study,—those measures are perfectly clear. He said that there is no political party in Russia that would express willingness to take all state power into its hands. I say: "Such a party exists! No party has a right to refuse power, and our party does not refuse it. Our party is ready at any moment to take all power into its hands." (*Applause, laughter.*)

You may laugh, but if the citizen-Minister confronts us with this question side by side with a party of the Right, he will receive the proper reply. No party has a right to refuse power. At the present time while we still have freedom, while the threats of arrest and Siberian exile, made by the counter-revolutionists with whom our near-Socialist Ministers sit in one cabinet, are only threats as yet,—at this moment each party should say: give us your confidence, and we shall give you our programme.

Our Conference of May 12 gave such a programme. Unfortunately, one does not reckon with it, one is not guided by it. Apparently it needs a more popular presentation. I shall try to give to the citizen-Minister of Posts and Telegraphs a popular explanation of our resolutions, our programme. With regard to the economic crisis, our programme demands that all the unheard-of profits, reaching 500-800 per cent, which the capitalists get, not in the open market, under conditions of "pure" capitalism, but on army contracts, be immediately made public, without any delay. This is exactly where workers' control is needed and possible! This is exactly the kind of measure which you, who claim to be "revolutionary" democrats, must carry out in the name of the Soviet, and which can be carried out within a day or two. This is not Socialism. It simply means opening the eyes of the people to the real anarchy, to the imperialist game that is being played with the people's wealth, with hundreds of thousands of lives which are to perish to-morrow as a result of our continued oppression of Galicia. Make the profits of the capitalists known, imprison 50 or 100 of the biggest millionaires. It would be sufficient to keep them a few weeks under the same conditions as Nicholas Romanov, to make them disclose all the wire-pulling, the fraudulent transactions, the filth, the greed that cost our country even under the new government thousands and millions of rubles daily. This is the basic cause of anarchy and ruin, this is why we say: everything with us has remained as of old, the coalition cabinet has changed nothing, it has only added a heap of declarations and pretty pronunciamentos. However sincere these people be, however sincerely they might wish for the toilers' welfare, matters have remained unchanged—the *same class* has remained in power. The policy that is being carried on now is not a democratic policy.

We are being told of the "democratisation of the central and local governments." Is it possible that you do not know that these words are new only in Russia, and that in other countries dozens of near-Socialist Ministers have been giving their countries similar promises? What value have they in face of a concrete fact like this: while local populations elect their own government, the ABC of democracy is being destroyed by the pretensions of the central government to the right of appointing or confirming local officials. Capitalist depredation of the people's wealth is still going on. The imperialist war is still going on, while we are being promised reforms, reforms, and reforms, which cannot at all be realised within the present framework, for the war crushes, weighs down everything, determines everything. Why do you not agree with those who maintain that the war is *not* fought for capitalist profits? What is the criterion? The criterion is, first of all: which class is in power, which class continues to rule, which class continues to make hundreds of millions in banking and financial operations? The same old capitalist class does it, and the war therefore continues to be an imperialist war. Both the first Provisional Government and the government embracing near-Socialist Ministers have changed nothing. The secret treaties are still secret. Russia is fighting for the Straits, for a continuation of Liakhov's policy in Persia,[239] etc.

I know that you do not want these things, that the majority of you do not want them, that the Ministers do not want them, because it is impossible to want them, because they mean the slaughter of hundreds of millions of people. But look at the offensive, so much talked of now by the Miliukovs and Maklakovs. They understand perfectly well what it is in essence. They know that the offensive is tied up with the question of power, with the question of the revolution. We are told to distinguish between politics and war strategy. It is ridiculous even to bring this up. The Cadets know full well that this is a political question.

That the revolutionary struggle for peace begun from below may lead to a separate peace is sheer calumny. Our first step, were we in power, would be to arrest the biggest capitalists, to sever all the threads of their intrigues. Unless this is done, all talk about peace without annexations and indemnities is sheer piffle. Our second step would be to address ourselves to all peoples, over the heads of their governments, and to tell them that we consider all capitalists as robbers: both Tereshchenko (who is not a whit better than Miliukov, only a little more foolish) and the capitalists of France, England, and all other countries.

Your own *Izvestia* is off the track, for instead of peace without annexations and indemnities it proposes the *status quo*. No, it is not thus that we understand peace "without annexations." Much nearer the truth in this respect is the Peasant Congress, which speaks of a "federated" republic, thereby expressing the idea that the Russian republic does not wish to oppress any people either in the old or in the new way, that it does not wish to live on a basis of violence either with our own people, or with Finland, or with the Ukraine, with which countries our War Minister quarrels for no reason, creating inadmissible and unforgivable conflicts. We want a single indivisible Russian republic, with a firm government, but firm government can be achieved only through the consent of the peoples. "Revolutionary democracy" are big words, but we are applying them to a government which by petty annoyances is complicating the situation with the Ukraine and Finland, who do not even wish to break away, who merely say: "Do not postpone the application of the ABC of democracy until the Constituent Assembly!"

Peace without annexations and indemnities cannot be concluded unless you yourselves renounce your own annexations. This is simply ridiculous, it is a joke! The workers of Europe laugh at it, they say: "In words they are eloquent, they call upon the nations to overthrow the bankers, but they themselves put their native bankers into the cabinet." Arrest them, expose their tricks, uncover their machinations! You do not do this, although you have the organisations of power which cannot be resisted. You have lived through the years of 1905 and 1917, you know that a revolution is not made to order, that revolutions in other countries have proceeded along the hard and bloody road of insurrection, while in Russia there is no such group, there is no such class that could offer resistance to the authority of the Soviets. In Russia this revolution is possible, by way of exception, as a peaceful revolution. Let our revolution offer this day peace to all the peoples by way of a breach with all the capitalist classes, and within the shortest time we would receive the consent of the peoples of Germany, as well as of France, because these countries are perishing, because the situation of Germany is hopeless, because it cannot save itself, because France. . . .

(CHAIRMAN: Your time is up.)

I'll be through in half a minute. . . . (*Noise, requests that the speech be continued, protests, applause.*)

(CHAIRMAN: The presidium proposes to the Congress that the time of the speaker be extended. Any objections? The majority is for extending the time.)

I have maintained that if revolutionary democracy in Russia were democratic in deeds and not merely in words, then, instead of entering into an agreement with the capitalists, it would move the revolution forward; instead of talking about peace without annexations and indemnities, it would abolish annexations within Russia and declare directly that it regarded all annexations as criminal and predatory. Then would it be possible to avoid the imperialist offensive which, to achieve the division of Persia and the Balkans, threatens to ruin thousands and millions of people. Then would the road to peace be open. We do not say that it would be an easy road; no, it would not exclude a real revolutionary war.

We do not put this question the way Bazarov puts it in to-day's *Novaia Zhizn.* All we saw is that Russia has been placed in such a position that its tasks toward the end of the imperialist war are easier than they may seem. Russia is so situated geographically that powers venturing to attack the Russian working class and its semi-proletarian ally, the poorest peasantry, in the name of capital and its predatory interests—powers undertaking such a step— would encounter an exceedingly difficult problem. Germany is on

the brink of ruin, and since America which wants to gobble up
Mexico, and will to-morrow probably wage a struggle against Japan,
has entered the war, Germany's situation is hopeless: Germany will
be destroyed by France which is so placed geographically that she
suffers most and that her exhaustion has reached the limit. France
may be less hungry than Germany, but in human material she has
lost incomparably more. Under such conditions, had your first step
been to curb the profits of the Russian capitalists and to deprive
them of the opportunity of raking-in hundreds of millions; had you
offered peace to *all* peoples against the capitalists of *all* countries
thereby announcing that you refused to enter into any negotiations
or dealings with the German capitalists or with any one who directly
or indirectly approved of them or hob-nobbed with them, that you
refused to have any relations with the French and English capitalists,—then this would have been an indictment of the capitalists
before the workers. You would not have regarded as a victory the
issuance of a passport to MacDonald,[240] a man who has never carried
on a revolutionary struggle against capitalism, and who is permitted
to pass because he has never expressed the ideas, or principles, or
practice, or experience of that revolutionary struggle against the
English capitalists for which our Comrade MacLean and hundreds
of other English Socialists are in prison, for which our Comrade
Liebknecht, who said, "German soldiers, fight against your Kaiser,"
has been sentenced to hard labour.

Would it not be more proper to put the imperialist capitalists into
the same prisons which the majority of the members of the Provisional Government, together with the Third—but I really do not
know whether it is the Third or the Fourth—Duma especially re-
established for that purpose, have daily been threatening with and
preparing? And are they not busily engaged in writing laws for
that purpose in the Ministry of Justice? MacLean and Liebknecht—
these are names of Socialists who put the idea of revolutionary
struggle against imperialism into life. This is what we ought to
say to all governments, if we want to fight for peace! We must
indict them before the peoples. Thus could you place all the imperialist governments in an embarrassing position. Now it is you
who have become embarrassed when on March 27 you said to the
people in a proclamation: "Overthrow your Tsars, your kings, and
your bankers," while you yourselves, being in possession of such
an extraordinary organisation, rich in numbers, in experience, in

material strength, as the Soviet of Workers' and Soldiers' Deputies, are forming a bloc with your bankers, forming a coalition near-Socialist government, writing projects for reforms such as Europe has been writing for many decades. Over there, in Europe, they laugh at such struggles for peace! There they will understand us only when the Soviets seize power and act in a revolutionary manner.

Only one country in the world will be able to take steps toward stopping the imperialist war immediately through class means, in opposition to the capitalists, without a bloody revolution,—only one country, and that is Russia. It will be in such a position as long as the Soviet of Workers' and Soldiers' Deputies exists. The latter cannot long exist beside a Provisional Government of the ordinary type. It will exist as hitherto only until the offensive has become a fact. For the offensive constitutes a break in the entire policy of the Russian Revolution: it means transition from the policy of waiting, of preparing peace through a revolutionary uprising from below, to a renewal of the war. We have had in mind another transition: from fraternisation on one front to fraternisation on all fronts, from spontaneous fraternisation where people give a crust of bread to a starved German proletarian in exchange for a penknife,—for which exchange they are threatened with hard labour,—to fraternisation that is consciously planned,—this is the road that suggested itself.

When we seize power we shall curb the capitalists, then the war will be entirely *different* from the one now waged,—for the nature of a war is determined by the class that conducts it, and not by what is written on scraps of paper. Anything can be written on scraps of paper. But as long as the capitalist class has a majority in the government, the war will remain an imperialist war, no matter what you write, no matter how eloquent you are, no matter how many near-Socialist Ministers you may have. This everybody knows and everybody sees. In fact, the example of Albania, the examples of Greece and Persia [241] have shown it so clearly, so palpably, that I am astonished to see everybody attacking our written declaration concerning the offensive,[242] while nobody says a word about concrete examples! Promises of projects are easily made, while concrete measures are continually postponed. Declarations about peace without annexations are easily written, yet the cases of Albania, Greece, and Persia have occurred *after* the coalition cabinet had come into life. It was in reference to these cases that the *Dielo*

Naroda, an organ not of our party, an organ of the government, an organ of the cabinet, said that Russian democracy is being made sport of, that Greece is being stifled. That very Miliukov whom you picture to be God knows what,—he is a rank and file member of his party, and Tereshchenko in no way differs from him,—has written that Allied diplomacy pressed on Greece. The war remains an imperialist war and, however great your desire for peace, however sincere your sympathy with the toilers, however sincere your desire for peace,—and I am fully convinced that, with the masses, it can be nothing but sincere,—you are powerless because the war cannot be terminated except by a further development of the revolution. When the revolution started in Russia, the revolutionary struggle for peace started from below. Were you to take power into your hands, were the revolutionary organisations to seize power for the purpose of waging a struggle upon the Russian capitalists, then the toilers of the other countries would trust you, then you would be able to offer peace. Then our peace would be secure, at least on two flanks, with respect to two peoples, Germany and France, both of which are bleeding to death and are in desperate straits. Should conditions have forced us then into a revolutionary war—nobody knows whether it would be so, nor do we forswear it—our answer would be: "We are no pacifists, we do not refuse to wage war once the revolutionary class is at the helm, once it has actually removed the capitalists from having any influence on the situation, once they cannot aggravate economic ruin which allowed them to make hundreds of millions in profits." The revolutionary power would then proclaim to all the peoples of the world the right of every people to be free; it would make clear that just as the German people has no right to wage war in order to retain Alsace-Lorraine so has the French people no right to wage war in order to retain its colonies. For if France fights for its colonies, then Russia has Khiva and Bokhara, also something in the nature of colonies, and the distribution of colonies begins. But how distribute them? According to what norm? Power. But power has changed; the capitalists find themselves in a situation where they have no way out except war. When you seize revolutionary power, you will have a revolutionary road to peace: you will turn to the peoples with a revolutionary appeal, you will make your tactics understood by your example. By following the revolutionary method of achieving peace, you will forestall the destruction of hundreds of thousands of human lives. Then, you may rest assured that the German and the French people will back you up. And the English, American, and Japanese capitalists, even if they wanted to wage war upon the revolutionary working class which, with the capitalists curbed and removed and with the reins of government in its own hands, would grow ten times as strong,—even if the American, English, and Japanese capitalists wanted war, there are ninety-nine chances in a hundred that they could not do it. All you would have to do is to declare that you were no pacifists, and that you intended to defend your republic, your workingmen's proletarian democracy, against the onslaughts of the German, French, and other capitalists—and this would suffice to make your peace secure.

This is why we consider our declaration on the offensive to be of fundamental significance. The time for a break in the entire history of the Russian Revolution has come. The Russian Revolution began with the aid of the English imperialist bourgeoisie, the latter having thought that Russia was something like China or India. What happened, however, was that by the side of the government composed of a majority of landowners and capitalists there sprang up the Soviets, an unusual representative institution of unprecedented strength which you are now destroying by your participation in the coalition cabinet of the bourgeoisie. What happened, however, was that, in all countries, revolutionary struggle from below against the capitalist governments began to meet with much greater sympathy. To go ahead, or to retreat? this is the question. In times of revolution it is impossible to remain in one place. This is why the offensive is a break in the entire Russian Revolution, not in the strategic meaning of the offensive, but in its political and economic meaning. Objectively, irrespective of the will and consciousness of one particular Minister, an offensive now means the continuation of the imperialist slaughter for the sake of crushing Persia and other weak peoples. The passing of power to the revolutionary proletariat supported by the poorest peasants means passing to as safe and painless a form of revolutionary struggle for peace as the world has ever known, passing to a situation where the power and the victory of the revolutionary workers will be made secure in Russia and throughout the whole world. (*Applause from a part of the audience.*)

Pravda, Nos. 82 and 83, June 28 and 29, 1917.

II

COMRADES! Allow me, by way of introduction to the analysis of the war question, to recall to your minds two points in the proclamation to all peoples issued on March 27 by the Petrograd Soviet of Workers' and Soldiers' Deputies. "The time has come," the proclamation reads, "to begin a resolute struggle with the predatory aspirations of the governments of all countries, the time has come for the peoples to take the matter of war and peace into their own hands." Another place in the proclamation addressed to the workers of the Austro-German coalition reads: "Refuse to serve as tools of depredation and violence in the hands of kings, landowners, and bankers." These are the two points that are reiterated in tens, in hundreds, I think in thousands, of resolutions passed by the workers and peasants of Russia.

To my mind, these two points best reveal that contradiction, that hopelessly entangled situation into which the workers and peasants have fallen owing to the present policy of the Mensheviks and the Narodniks. On the one hand, they are for supporting the war, on the other, they are the representatives of classes that are not interested in the predatory aspirations of the governments of all countries, and they cannot help but say so. This psychology and ideology, however vague, is uncommonly deep-seated in every worker and peasant. It is a realisation of the fact that the war is being waged as a result of the predatory aspirations of the governments of all countries. But together with this, there is only a very hazy understanding, indeed, no understanding at all, of the fact that every government, whatever its form, is an expression of the interests of certain classes, and that, therefore, to contrast the government with the people, as it is done in the first passage I have quoted, is to be guilty of grave theoretical confusion and utter political helplessness, is to condemn oneself and one's entire policy to a wavering, unstable situation and conduct. The same applies to the concluding words of the second passage I have quoted. The excellent admonition: "Refuse to serve as tools of depredation and violence in the hands of kings, landowners, and bankers," is splendid, except that here are omitted the words: "and our own"; for when you, Russian workers and peasants, turn to the workers

and peasants of Austria and Germany where the governments and
ruling classes are conducting the same kind of a predatory brigand
war as that conducted by the Russian, the English, and the French
capitalists and bankers, when you say: " Refuse to serve as tools
in the hands of your bankers," while at the same time you let your
own bankers into the cabinet and seat them together with the
Socialist Ministers, you are reducing your declarations to zero, you
are by your actions negating your whole policy.   It appears as if
you have never had those excellent aspirations and wishes, for you
are helping Russia carry on exactly the same sort of imperialist
war, the same sort of predatory war.   You are pitting yourselves
against the masses whom you represent, for those masses will never
take the capitalist standpoint so frankly expressed by Miliukov,
Maklakov, and others, who say: "There is no idea more criminal
than that the war is being waged in the interests of capital."

I do not know whether this idea be criminal, but I have no doubt
that in the opinion of those who half-exist to-day and who will
perhaps disappear to-morrow, it is criminal; yet this is a perfectly
sound idea.   It is the only one that expresses our conception of
the war; it is the only one that shows that it is in the interests of
the oppressed classes to struggle against the oppressors.   And when
we say that the war is a capitalist war, a predatory war, and that
we must not create illusions, we do not in the least suggest that
such a war could have been brought on by the crimes of individual
persons, individual kings.

Imperialism is a distinct stage in the development of world capital.
Capitalism, after decades of growth, has reached a point where
a small group of overwhelmingly rich countries—there being no
more than four of them: England, France, Germany, and America—
has accumulated such fabulous wealth, reaching up to hundreds
of billions, has accumulated such colossal power concentrated in
the hands of a few big bankers and a few capitalists—there being
half a dozen of them, at most, in each of these countries—has
accumulated such colossal power, that it has the world in its grip,
that it has, literally, partitioned the whole globe as far as territories and colonies are concerned.   The colonies of these Powers
are found adjacent to each other in every country in the world.
Economically too these Powers have divided the globe among themselves; there is not a bit of territory in any part of the world
where they have not got concessions, or where they have not pene-

trated with their finance capital. This is the basis of annexations. Annexations are not mere inventions, and they have come about not because freedom-loving people suddenly turned into reactionaries. Annexations are nothing else but the political expression and the political form of that domination by giant banks that is the inevitable consequence of capitalism. It is no one's fault. Shares—these are the basis of banks; accumulation of shares—this is the basis of imperialism. Great banks ruling the whole world by means of hundreds of billions of capital, uniting entire branches of industry by means of capitalist and monopolist combines—this is your imperialism that has split the whole world into three groups of overwhelmingly rich brigands!

At the head of one, the main group that is nearer to us in Europe, is England; at the head of the other two are Germany and America; the rest are accomplices who are forced to help the others as long as capitalist relations exist. That is why, if you visualise clearly the core of the matter, a thing instinctively felt by every oppressed human being, instinctively realised by the vast majority of Russian workers and peasants,—if you visualise it clearly, you will understand how ridiculous is the thought of struggling against war with words, manifestos, proclamations, and Socialist congresses. They are ridiculous because, no matter how many declarations are issued, no matter how many political overturns are made, the banks remain all-powerful, despite the overthrow of Nicholas Romanov in Russia. Russia has made a giant step forward; it has perhaps caught up with France which, under different circumstances, has accomplished the same thing in one hundred years, but has remained a capitalist country nevertheless. The capitalists are still here. If they are somewhat pressed, so were they in 1905; but has this undermined their power? Though it seems new to the Russians, in Europe every revolution has proved that with each rise of the revolutionary wave the workers gain a little more, but that the capitalists retain power. It is impossible to carry on a struggle against the imperialist war in any way other than by a world-wide struggle of the revolutionary classes against the ruling classes. It is not the landowners, though there are landowners in Russia and though they are playing there a more important rôle than in any other country, but it is not they who have created imperialism. It is the capitalist class headed by the greatest financial magnates and banks; and while this class, lording it over the oppressed proletarians, is not overthrown, there is no escape from this war. To hold on to the illusion that you can, by means of proclamations and appeals to other peoples, unite the toilers of all the countries, is possible only from the limited Russian point of view, which is not cognisant of the manner in which the press of Western Europe, where the workers and peasants are used to political upheavals and have seen them dozens of times, is laughing at such phrases and appeals. In Europe one does not know that the proletarian masses of Russia, honestly believing and condemning the predatory aspirations of the capitalists of the world and wishing for the liberation of the peoples from the bankers, have actually risen. They, the Europeans, do not understand why you, who have organisations, not found in any other country in the world, such as the Soviets of Workers', Peasants', and Soldiers' Deputies, why you, having weapons, are sending your Socialists into the cabinet, why you, in spite of everything, are giving the government over to the bankers. Abroad you are being accused not merely of naïveté, that would not be so bad, but also of hypocrisy: the Europeans have forgotten how to understand naïveté in politics, they have forgotten to understand that in Russia there are tens of millions of people who for the first time have been stirred into life, that in Russia they do not know the connection between classes and the government, the connection between the government and war.

The war is a continuation of bourgeois politics, and nothing else. The ruling class is also the one to determine the policy in time of war. War is all politics, and it realises the same capitalist ends but by different means. This is why your appeal, "Overthrow your bankers," addressed to the workers and peasants, calls forth in a class-conscious European worker either mirth, or bitter tears; for he says to himself: "What can we do, if over there they have overthrown a half-savage, idiotic and beastly monarch, the kind we have removed long ago, and are now—together with their 'near-Socialist' Ministers—supporting the Russian bankers?"

The bankers remain in power, they are conducting their foreign policy by way of an imperialist war, supporting *in toto* all the treaties concluded for Russia by Nicholas II. In this country it is particularly glaring. The principles of Russia's imperialist foreign policy have been determined not now but by the former government with the now deposed Nicholas Romanov at the head. It was he who concluded these treaties, and these treaties are still secret; the capitalists cannot publish them, for capitalists are capitalists. But a worker or a peasant cannot understand this tangle; for he reasons that if we urge the overthrow of the capitalists in other countries, then we ought first of all to overthrow our own bankers. Otherwise no one will believe us or take us seriously; they will say: "You Russians are naïve savages, you write words that in themselves are excellent, that, however, have no practical meaning." Worse yet, they may think that we are hypocrites. You could actually read such arguments in the foreign press, were the press of all shades allowed to enter Russia across the border, without being kept back in Torneo by the English and French authorities. From a mere collection of quotations from foreign newspapers you could realise what a glaring contradiction you find yourselves in; you could convince yourselves how incredibly ludicrous and erroneous is the idea of fighting against war by means of Socialist conferences, by agreements with Socialists at congresses. Were imperialism the fault or the crime of individuals, then Socialism could remain Socialism. Imperialism is the last stage in the evolution of capitalism, which has reached the point of having divided the whole world into bits, and of having two giant groups in a life and death struggle. You must either serve one, or serve the other, or overthrow both; there is no other way out! When you oppose a separate peace on the ground that you do not wish to serve German imperialism, you are right; this is precisely why we too are against a separate peace. As a matter of fact, however, and regardless of your wishes, you go on serving Anglo-French imperialism and its aims, as predatory and annexationist as those which the Russian capitalists had, with the help of Nicholas Romanov, embodied into treaties. We do not know the text of those treaties, but any one who has followed political literature, who has read at least one book in economics or diplomacy, knows the content of those treaties. And if my memory serves me right, has not Miliukov in his books written that those treaties and promises would rob Galicia, rob the Straits, Armenia, preserve the old annexations and get a heap of new ones? This is known to every one, yet the treaties are kept secret, and we are told that any attempt at rejecting them means a break with the Allies.

As regards separate peace, I have already stated that there can be no separate peace for us; the resolution of our party proves beyond a shadow of a doubt that we reject this as we reject any

agreement with the capitalists. To us separate peace means entering
into an agreement with the German robbers, who are quite as predatory as the others.   But an agreement with Russian capital in the
Russian Provisional Government is also a separate peace.   The
Tsar's treaties are still in force, and they also rob and stifle other
peoples.   When I hear, "peace without annexations or indemnities"
—words every Russian worker and peasant ought to say, because
life is teaching them to say so, because they are not interested in
banking profits, because they want to live—I must say that the
Narodnik and Menshevik leaders of the present Soviet of Workers'
and Soldiers' Deputies are in utter confusion with regard to this
slogan.   In their *Izvestia* they have explained it to mean a *status quo*,
i. e., the pre-war situation, a return to what existed before the beginning of the war.   Would that not be a capitalist peace?   And
what a capitalist peace!   If you advance such a slogan, remember
that the course of events may place your parties in power.   In revolutionary times this is possible, you will have to do what you
promise, and if you now offer peace without annexations, it may
be accepted by the Germans but not by the English, for the English
capitalists have not lost one inch of ground; on the contrary, they
have grabbed land all over the world.   The Germans have grabbed
much, but they have also lost much, and not only have they lost
much, but they are facing now the intervention of America, a most
formidable foe.   If you, who are proposing peace without annexations, understand by it the *status quo*, you sink to a position where
your proposal means a separate peace with the capitalists, for if
you propose the *status quo*, then the German capitalists, confronted
with America and Italy, with whom they had once made treaties,
will say: "Yes, we accept this peace without annexations; to us it
is not defeat, but victory over America and Italy."   Viewed objectively, it is you who are slipping into a separate peace with the
capitalists for which you blame us, for you break neither in principle, nor in policy, nor in deeds, in your practical steps, with the
bankers, who are the expression of capitalist world domination, and
whom you and your "Socialist" Ministers in the Provisional Government are supporting.

You are thus placing yourselves in such a contradictory and
shaky position, that the masses fail to understand you. The masses,
not interested in annexations, declare: "We do not wish to fight
for any capitalists."   When we are told that such a policy can be

stopped by congresses and agreements among the Socialists of all countries, we say: "Perhaps, if imperialism were the fault of individual criminals; but imperialism is the culmination of world capitalism, and the working class movement is connected with it."

The victory of imperialism is the beginning of an inevitable, unavoidable division of the Socialists of the world into two camps. He who persists in referring to the Socialists as to an entity, as to something that can be an entity, deceives himself and others. The whole course of the war, two and a half years of war, have led to this schism. The Basel Manifesto, which declared that war is a product of imperialist capitalism, was unanimously signed. Not a word about "national defence" is contained in that Manifesto. No other manifesto could have been written before the war,—just as at present no Socialist would propose to write a manifesto on "national defence" in case of a war between America and Japan, where neither his own skin nor that of his capitalists and Ministers would be involved. Just try. Write a resolution for international congresses! You know that war between Japan and America is imminent, it has been prepared for decades, it is not accidental, and it does not matter who will be the one to fire the first shot. It is ridiculous! You know full well that both American and Japanese capitalists are equally predatory. Still, there would be talk about "national defence" on either side; it would be either a crime or a terrible weakness, a "defence" of the interests of our capitalist enemies. This is why we say that the schism among the Socialists is irreparable. The Socialists have completely deserted Socialism, they have gone over to the side of their governments, their bankers, their capitalists, this they have done in spite of their verbal renunciation and condemnation of the latter. It is not a matter of condemnation. By condemning the Germans for supporting their capitalists, we are covering up the fact that we are defending the same "sin" committed by the Russians! Once you condemn the German social-chauvinists, *i. e.*, those who are Socialists in words—perhaps many of them are Socialists at heart—but chauvinists in deeds, who in deeds defend not the German people but the filthy, greedy, predatory German capitalists, then do not defend the English, French, or Russian capitalists! The German social-chauvinists are not worse than those who, in our cabinet, are perpetuating the same policy of secret treaties and pillage, and

who are covering it up with good innocent wishes. Those wishes
may have much good in them, they may, on the part of the masses,
be absolutely sincere, but I do not and cannot discern one word
of political truth in them. These are only your wishes; the war,
however, is the same old imperialist war, with the same old secret
treaties! You call upon other peoples to throw off their bankers,
yet you support your own bankers! Speaking of peace, you have
not said what kind of peace! When we pointed out the glaring contradiction underlying the conception of peace on the basis of
status quo, we received no answer. In your resolution which deals
with peace without annexations, you will not be able to say that
it is not a *status quo*. You will not be able to say that *status quo*
means the restoration of pre-war conditions. What, then? To
deprive England of the German colonies? Just try to do it by
peaceful agreements! The whole world will laugh at you. Just try
to take away from Japan, without a revolution, the stolen Kiaochow
and the islands in the Pacific! [243]

You have become entangled in inextricable contradictions. When
we, however, say: "Without annexations," we mean that this slogan
is only a subordinate part of the struggle against world imperialism.
We declare that we want to free all peoples, and that we mean
to begin with our own. You talk of fighting against annexations,
of a peace without annexations, yet within Russia you persist in
conducting an annexationist policy. This is monstrous! In the
case of Finland and the Ukraine, you, and your government, and
your new Ministers, are carrying out an annexationist policy. You
are picking flaws in the Ukrainian Congress, through your Ministers
you are prohibiting its sessions. What is this if not annexation?
Such a policy means mocking at the rights of a nationality that suffered tortures under the Tsars because its children wanted to use
their native tongue. Such a policy shows fear of independent republics, which, from the point of view of workers and peasants,
are not in the least terrifying. Let Russia be a union of free
republics. The worker and peasant masses will not fight to prevent
this. Let every people be liberated, let first of all those nationalities
be liberated with whom you are making the revolution in Russia.
Unless you do this, you are doomed to be "revolutionary democracy"
in words, while in practice your whole policy spells counter-
revolution.

Your foreign policy is anti-democratic and counter-revolutionary, and a revolutionary policy may place you in a position where a revolutionary war is indispensable. However, this may not happen, either. Of late this point has been stressed by speakers and the press. I would like to dwell on it at some length.

What practical way out of this war do we see? We say: the only way out of this war is revolution. Support the revolution of the classes oppressed by the capitalists, overthrow the class of capitalists in your own country, and thus set an example for other countries. This is Socialism. This is the only way to fight the war. Everything else is promises, or phrases, or innocent, well-meaning wishes. Socialism has been rent asunder in all the countries of the world. You make confusion more confounded when you associate with those Socialists who are supporting their own governments; you forget that in England and Germany the real Socialists, those who express the Socialism of the masses, have been left isolated, and are in prisons. Yet they alone stand for the interests of the proletarian movement. Suppose in Russia the oppressed class finds itself in power? People ask: "How will you alone tear yourselves free from the war?" We say: "To tear ourselves free from the war alone is impossible." Every resolution of our party, every speech of our orators at meetings says that it is absurd to imagine we could tear ourselves free from the war all alone. Hundreds of millions of people, hundreds of billions of capital are involved in this war. There is no way out of it, except by the passing of power to the revolutionary class that is actually bound to destroy imperialism, i. e., to break all the financial, banking, and annexationist fetters. While this is still not done, nothing is done. The overturn reduces itself to this, that instead of tsarism and imperialism you now have received a thoroughly imperialist near-republic which, even on the part of the revolutionary workers and peasants, cannot treat Finland and the Ukraine democratically, i. e., without fearing a split.

When they say that we want a separate peace, it is untrue. We say: no separate peace with any capitalists, and first of all with the Russian capitalists! The Provisional Government, however, has a separate peace with the Russian capitalists. Down with this separate peace! While we do not recognise any separate peace with the German capitalists, and do not enter into any negotiations with them, we are at the same time opposed to a separate peace with the English and French imperialists. We are told that a break with the latter means entering into an agreement with the German imperialists. Untrue. We must break with them forthwith, for this is a predatory alliance. We are told that we must not publish the treaties. Indeed, this would heap disgrace upon our entire government, upon our whole policy before the eyes of every worker and every peasant. If we published these treaties, if we clearly said at meetings to the Russian workers and the Russian peasants everywhere, even in each remote little village: "This is what you are fighting for; for the Straits, for the retention of Armenia," then they would all reply: "We do not want such a war." (*Chairman:* Your time is up. *Voices:* Please.' Ten more minutes. (*Voices:* Please.)

I say that this alternative: either with the English or with the German imperialists, that peace with the Germans means war against the English, and vice versa—is absurd. Such an alternative is of service to those who do not break with their capitalists and bankers, who allow for every possible alliance with them. It is of no service to us. We speak of defending our alliance with the oppressed classes, with the oppressed nationalities. Stay faithful to such an alliance, and you shall be a revolutionary democracy. This is not an easy task. This task does not allow us to forget that under certain circumstances we may not be able to avoid a revolutionary war. No revolutionary class can forswear fighting a revolutionary war without being doomed to ludicrous pacifism. We are not Tolstoians! If the revolutionary class seizes power, if there are no more annexations in its state, if banks and big capital cease to wield power, a thing rather difficult in Russia, it will mean that the revolutionary class is waging a revolutionary war in deeds, not in words. We cannot forswear waging such a war. This would mean falling into Tolstoiism, into philistinism, into forgetting the whole science of Marxism and the experience of all European revolutions.

Russia cannot be stricken out of the war all alone. But Russia has mighty allies who keep on growing. They do not as yet have faith in you, because your position has been so contradictory and naïve, because you have been advising other peoples to renounce annexations while you are introducing them in your own country. To other peoples you say: "Overthrow the bankers," yet you do not overthrow your own bankers. Try a different policy. Publish the treaties and expose them to the contempt of every worker and peasant. Say: "No peace with the German capitalists, and a complete break with the Anglo-French capitalists! Let the English get out of Turkey, and let them not fight for Bagdad! Let them get out of India and Egypt! We do not want to fight to save the accumulated loot, just as we refuse to spend one atom of our energy to help the German brigands save their loot." If you do the things you have talked about—and in politics words are not given much credence, and for good reason—if you not only say but actually do these things, then the allies that are now potential allies will show what they can do. Look at the sentiment of all the oppressed workers and peasants—they sympathise with you, they regret that you are so weak, that, having arms, you let the bankers stay. Your allies are the oppressed workers in all countries. You will have the same thing that the revolution of 1905 revealed. At the outset it was terribly weak. But what were its results internationally? What foreign policy did the history of 1905 determine for the Russian Revolution? At present you conduct the foreign policy of the Russian Revolution in full accord with the capitalists. But 1905 has shown what the foreign policy of the Russian Revolution ought to be. The fact is indisputable, that immediately after October 30, 1905, mass disturbances began in the streets of Vienna and Prague and barricades were built. Following 1905, there came 1908 in Turkey, 1909 in Persia, and 1910 in China.[244] If you call the real revolutionary democracy, the working class, the oppressed, instead of making agreements with the capitalists, then your allies shall not be the oppressing but the oppressed classes, not nationalities where now the oppressing classes are temporarily in power, but nationalities that are now being torn to pieces.

We are reminded here of the German front concerning which not one of us has suggested any change, except the free distribution of our proclamations, which have the Russian text printed on one side and the German on the other, and which say: "The capitalists of both countries are robbers; their removal is only a step toward peace." But there are other fronts. There is a Russian army at the Turkish front; its size I do not know. If this army, now kept in Armenia and perpetrating annexations which you, while preaching peace without annexations to other peoples, tolerate though you have authority and strength; if that army carried out this programme, if it turned Armenia into an independent Armenian republic, if it gave that republic the money that we give to the French

and English financiers, things would be much better! It is said
that we cannot get on without financial support from England and
France. But this support "supports" as a rope supports a hanged
man. Let the revolutionary class of Russia say: "Down with
such support, we do not recognise the debts contracted with the
French and English capitalists, we call upon all to rise against the
capitalists! No peace with the German capitalists, and no alliance
with the English and French capitalists!" If we actually carry on
such a policy, our Turkish army will be free to turn to other fronts,
for all the peoples of Asia would see that it is not only in words
that the Russian people proclaims peace without annexations on
the basis of self-determination of nations, but that the Russian
workers and peasants actually place themselves at the head of all
oppressed nationalities, and that their struggle against imperialism
is to them of grave revolutionary importance and not an empty wish
or a glittering ministerial phrase.

Our situation is such that the danger of a revolutionary war,
though possible, is not inevitable, for the English imperialists will
scarcely be able to wage war upon us, if we turn to the peoples
surrounding Russia with our example of action. Prove that you
are setting free the republic of Armenia; enter into agreements
with councils of workers' and soldiers' deputies in all countries;
prove that you are for a free republic, and the foreign policy of the
Russian Revolution will become really revolutionary, really democratic. It is such now only in words; in point of fact, however, it
is counter-revolutionary, for you are bound up with Anglo-French
imperialism, but you do not wish to say so openly, you are afraid
to admit it. Instead of calling upon others to "overthrow their
bankers," it would be better were you frankly to say to the Russian
people, to the workers and peasants: "We are too weak, we cannot
throw off the yoke of the Anglo-French imperialists, we are their
slaves, that is why we are in the war." This would be the bitter
truth, but it would have revolutionary significance, it would actually
bring nearer the end of this predatory war. This would mean a
thousand times more than the agreement with the French and English social-chauvinists, than the convocation of congresses, than the
continuation of a policy where you are actually afraid to break
with the imperialists of one country and are the allies of the
imperialists of another. You may rely on the oppressed classes
in the European countries, on the oppressed peoples of weaker

countries who had been crushed by Russia under the Tsars, who are still being crushed, as is Armenia now; basing yourselves on them, you can give freedom by helping their workers' and peasants' committees; you can become the leaders of all oppressed classes, of all oppressed peoples in their war against German and English imperialism, who cannot unite against you, for they themselves are in a life and death struggle against each other, for they find themselves in a helplessly difficult situation whenever the foreign policy of the Russian Revolution, a sincere union with the oppressed classes and oppressed peoples, is likely to be successful; and there are ninety-nine chances in one hundred that it will be successful!

In the Moscow paper of our party, we recently came across a letter from a peasant who speaks of our programme.[245] I take the liberty to conclude my speech with a quotation from the letter showing how the peasant understands our programme. The letter appeared in No. 59 of the *Social-Democrat*, the Moscow paper of our party, and was reprinted in No. 68 of the *Pravda*:

We must press the bourgeoisie harder, let it burst at all the seams. Then the war will be ended. But if we do not press the bourgeoisie hard enough, things will be bad.

Pravda, Nos. 95, 96 and 97, July 13, 14 and 15, 1917.

ON THE EVE OF THE JULY DAYS

Россійская Соціалъ-Демократическая Рабочая Партія.

ПРАВДА

ОРГАНЪ
Центральнаго Комитета
•
Петербургскаго Комитета
Р. С.-Д. Р. П.
1917

Суббота, 23-го Іюня (10 Іюня ст. ст.) 1917 г.   ЕЖЕДНЕВНАЯ ГАЗЕТА   Цѣна № 8 коп.   № 82.

Ко всѣмъ трудящимся, ко всѣмъ рабочимъ и солдатамъ Петрограда.

Въ виду того, что Съѣздъ Совѣтовъ Рабочихъ и Солдатскихъ Депутатовъ, къ которому присоединился Исполнительный Комитетъ Совѣта Крестьянскихъ Депут., постановилъ, признавши обстоятельства совершенно исключительными, запретить всякія, даже мирныя, демонстраціи на три дня,

Центр. Комитетъ Росс. С.-Д. Рабочей Партіи

ПОСТАНОВЛЯЕТЪ

ОТМѢНИТЬ назначенную имъ на 2 часа дня, въ субботу, демонстрацію.

Центральный Комитетъ призываетъ всѣхъ членовъ партіи и всѣхъ сочувствующихъ ей провести это постановленіе въ жизнь.

Front Page of *Pravda,* June 23, 1917, Devoted to the Bolshevik Proclamation Calling Off the Street Demonstration Announced for That Day (see pp. 238-240)

THE WILD BULLS OF JUNE 16 WANT AN IMMEDIATE OFFENSIVE

THE gentlemen of June 16 * who, after 1905, helped Nicholas Romanov drown our country in blood, crush the revolutionists, restore the omnipotence of the landowners and the capitalists, have held conferences simultaneously with the Congress of Soviets.[246]

While Tsereteli, finding himself in bourgeois captivity, resorted to a thousand subterfuges to hush up the importance, the imminence, the urgency of the political question bearing on an immediate offensive, our wild bulls of June 16, companions-in-arms of Nicholas the Bloody and Stolypin the Hangman, landowners and capitalists, did not hesitate to state the question frankly and straightforwardly.   Here is their latest, most essential, and *unanimous* resolution concerning the offensive:

> The Imperial Duma (??) affirms that only an immediate offensive, only close co-operation with the Allies, will insure a speedy termination of the war, and secure the liberties won by the people.[247]

This at least is clear.

These people are real politicians, men of action, faithful servants of *their* class, the landowners and the capitalists.

But how do Tsereteli, Chernov and Co. serve their class?   They are trying to get off with expressing good wishes in words, but supporting the capitalists in deeds.

Tsereteli repeatedly asserted that the question of an *immediate* offensive should not even be brought up, for, were he, Minister Tsereteli, to know anything about such an offensive, he, Minister Tsereteli, would say nothing about it to any one.   Speaking thus, Tsereteli never suspected (O innocence!) that he was being *refuted* by the wild bulls of June 16, refuted in *deeds*, for the latter were not in the least afraid to speak openly, in a resolution, about an offensive, not an offensive in general, but an *immediate* offensive. And they were right.   For this is a political question, a question involving the destiny of our entire revolution.

* On June 16, 1907, the Second Duma was dissolved and a new electoral law promulgated which insured the control of the Duma to the feudal and industrial interests.—*Ed.*

221

There is no middle ground here: one must be either for or against an "immediate offensive"; one cannot refrain from expressing an opinion; to evade the question by referring to or hinting at military secrets is not worthy of a responsible politician.

To be for an immediate offensive means to be for the prolongation of the imperialist war, for slaughtering Russian workers and peasants with the aim of stifling Persia, Greece, Galicia, the Balkans, etc., for reviving and strengthening the counter-revolution, for reducing to naught all the phrases about "peace without annexations," for waging war to obtain annexations.

To be opposed to an immediate offensive means to stand for all power passing into the hands of the Soviets, for the awakening of the revolutionary initiative of the oppressed classes, for an immediate offer to the oppressed classes of all countries of "peace without annexations," peace based on the very clear condition of overthrowing the yoke of capital, of liberating *all* the colonies without exception, *all* the oppressed and subject nationalities without exception.

The former road is together with the capitalists, in the interests of the capitalists, for attaining the aims of the capitalists,—a road of confidence in the capitalists who for almost three years have been promising everything under the sun, and more, provided we "carry" the war to a "victory."

The latter road is one of breaking with the capitalists, of distrusting them, of curbing their vile greed, of putting a limit to their making millions of profits on contracts,—a road of confidence in the oppressed classes, and first of all in the workers of all countries, a road of confidence in an international workers' revolution against capital, a road of supporting it with all possible means.

One must choose either one way or the other. Tsereteli, Chernov and Co. prefer the middle road. But in this case there is no middle road; and should they vacillate or try to get off with phrases, they, *i. e.*, Tsereteli, Chernov and Co., would irretrievably degrade themselves to the extent of becoming tools in the hands of the counter-revolutionary bourgeoisie.

Pravda, No. 74, June 19, 1917.

GRATITUDE

WE are very grateful to the chauvinist paper, the *Volia Naroda*, for its having reprinted (in its issue of June 17) our documents relating to our passage through Germany. From these documents it is evident that even then we recognised Grimm's behaviour as "ambiguous" and rejected his services.

This is a fact and facts cannot be denied.

To the vague insinuations of the *Volia Naroda*, we answer: Do not be cowards, gentlemen, accuse us openly of a definite crime or misdemeanour! Try it! Is it really hard to understand that to indulge in vague insinuations, and yet be afraid to make a definite accusation over one's signature, is dishonest?

Pravda, No. 74, June 19, 1917.

IS THERE A ROAD TO A JUST PEACE?

Is there a road to peace without an exchange of annexations (seized territories), without the division of spoils among the capitalist bandits?

There is: through a proletarian revolution against the capitalists of all countries.

Russia is at the present moment nearer than any other country to the beginning of such a revolution.

Only in Russia can power be transferred to already existing institutions, to the Soviets, immediately, peacefully, without turmoil, for the capitalists are not in a position to resist the Soviets of Workers', Soldiers' and Peasants' Deputies.

With such a transfer of power, it would be possible to curb the capitalists who are making billions of rubles on war contracts, to expose all their tricks, to arrest the millionaire treasury-looters, to break their absolute power.

Only after the transfer of power to the oppressed classes, could Russia appeal to the oppressed classes of the other countries not with empty words, not with idle proclamations, but by calling their attention to its experience, by making concrete *proposals for a general and immediate peace.*

"Comrades, workers and toilers of all the countries!" we would say in that appeal for an immediate peace. "Enough of blood! Peace is possible. A just peace means a peace without annexations, without seizures of territory. Let the German capitalist bandits together with their crowned murderer Wilhelm know that we will enter into no negotiations with them, that we regard as annexations not only their seizures made since the war, but Alsace-Lorraine, too, as well as the Danish and Polish districts of Prussia.

"We also regard Poland, Finland, the Ukraine, and other lands not inhabited by Great-Russians, as annexed by the Russian Tsars and capitalists.

"We regard all the colonies, Ireland and so on, as annexed by English, French and other capitalists.

"We, Russian workers and peasants, shall not hold any of the non-Great-Russian lands and colonies (such as Turkestan, Mongolia, Persia) against their will.   Down with war for the division of colonies, for the division of annexations (seized lands), for the division of capitalist spoils!"

The example set by the Russians will be followed inevitably,— perhaps not to-morrow (revolutions are not made to order), but undoubtedly some day in the future—by the workers and toilers of at least two great countries: Germany and France.

For both are perishing, the first of hunger, the second of de-population.   Both will conclude peace on our just terms, *despite their capitalist governments*.

The road to peace lies straight before us.

Should the capitalists of England, America, and Japan try to resist *such* a peace, then the oppressed classes of Russia and of other countries would not hesitate to start a revolutionary war *against the capitalists*.   In *such* a war they would defeat the capitalists not only of the three countries that are remote from Russia and that are preoccupied with their own rivalries,—they would defeat the capitalists *of the whole world*.

The road to a just peace lies straight before us.   Let us not be afraid to enter upon it. . . .

Pravda, No. 75, June 20, 1917.

THE ENEMIES OF THE PEOPLE

PLEKHANOV's *Yedinstvo* (justly called even by the Socialist-Revolutionist *Dielo Naroda,* a paper united with the liberal bourgeoisie) has recently recalled the law of the French Republic of 1793 relating to the enemies of the people.

This reminder is very timely.

The Jacobins of 1793 were the representatives of the most revolutionary class of the eighteenth century, the city and the country poor. Against this class that had actually (not merely in words) done away with their monarch, with their landowners, with their moderate bourgeoisie by means of the most revolutionary measures, including the guillotine, against this truly revolutionary class of the eighteenth century the combined monarchs of Europe were waging war.

The Jacobins proclaimed as enemies of the people those "aiding the allied tyrants in their plots against the Republic." The example of the Jacobins is instructive. It has not yet become obsolete, except that it should be applied to the revolutionary class of the twentieth century, to the proletarians and semi-proletarians. For to this class, in the present twentieth century, the enemies of the people are not the monarchs, but the landowners and the capitalists as a class.

If the "Jacobins" of the twentieth century, the proletarians and semi-proletarians, assumed power, they would proclaim as enemies of the people the capitalists who are making billions in the imperialist war, *i.e.,* the war for the division of capitalist spoils and profits.

The "Jacobins" of the twentieth century would not guillotine the capitalist; following a good example does not necessarily require imitating it. It would be sufficient to arrest from fifty to one hundred magnates and bank leaders, the chief perpetrators of treasury robbing and bank thieving; it would be sufficient to arrest them for a few weeks, in order to expose their methods and to show to all the exploited "who needs the war." Upon exposing the methods of the banking kings, we could release them, but we would first place the banks, the capitalist syndicates as well as the contractors "working" for the government under the control of the workers.

226

The Jacobins of 1793 went down into history as the great exemplars of fighters in a truly revolutionary struggle waged against the class of the exploiters by the class of the toilers and the oppressed who had taken the power of the state into their own hands.

The deplorable *Yedinstvo* (of a bloc with whom the Menshevik defencists became ashamed) wants to take over the letter of Jacobinism, but not its spirit,—its external manifestations, but not the content of its policy. Essentially, this is equivalent to a betrayal of the revolution of the twentieth century, a betrayal concealed under lying references to the revolutionists of the eighteenth century.

Pravda, No. 75, June 20, 1917.

NOTE

FROM the *Novoie Vremia* of June 19:

Whence and how has in these days of freedom appeared this black hand that is moving the marionettes of Russian democracy? Lenin! . . . But his name is legion. At every cross road another Lenin pops up. And it becomes obvious that the impelling force here lies not in Lenin himself but in the receptiveness of the soil to the seeds of anarchy and madness.

Anarchy, in our opinion, is the reaping of scandalous profits on war contracts by the capitalists. Madness, in our opinion, is the carrying on of a war for the division of spoils, for the division of capitalist profit. And if it is these views that find sympathy "at every cross road," it is because these views give correct expression to the interests of the proletariat, the interests of the toilers and the exploited.

Pravda, No. 75, June 20, 1917.

"THE GREAT WITHDRAWAL"

"THE great withdrawal of the bourgeoisie from the government"—this is what one speaker, in a report to the Executive Committee last Sunday, has called the forming of the coalition government, the entrance of the former Socialists into the cabinet.[248]

Only the first three words in this phrase are correct. "The great withdrawal" does indeed characterise and explain May 19 (the forming of the coalition government). Indeed, on that date, "the great withdrawal" did begin, or, to be more correct, did most clearly manifest itself. But instead of it being the great withdrawal of the bourgeoisie from the government, it was the great withdrawal of the Menshevik and Narodnik leaders from the revolution.

The present Congress of the Soviets of Workers' and Soldiers' Deputies is significant just in so far as it has thrown this fact into bold relief.

May 19 was a victory day for the bourgeoisie. The bourgeois government was then on the verge of disaster. The masses were definitely, indubitably, ardently, and irreconcilably against the government. One word from the Narodnik or Menshevik leaders of the Soviets would have sufficed to induce the government to relinquish its power; at the meeting in the Mariinsky Palace, Lvov frankly had to admit this.

The bourgeoisie executed a skilful manœuvre that was new to the Russian petty bourgeoisie and to the large Russian masses in general, that has intoxicated the Menshevik and Narodnik leaders hailing from the intelligentsia, and that has correctly revealed the Louis Blanc nature of the last-mentioned group. Let us remind the reader that Louis Blanc was a notorious petty-bourgeois Socialist who entered the government in 1848 and again attained dubious fame in 1871. Louis Blanc considered himself *the leader* of "labour democracy" or of "Socialist democracy" (this latter word was used in the France of 1848 as frequently as in the Socialist-Revolutionist and Menshevik literature of 1917), but in reality he was a tail-end of the bourgeoisie, a plaything in their hands.

During the almost seventy years that have elapsed since then, this manœuvre, so novel in Russia, has been executed many a time by the bourgeoisie in the West. The purpose of this manœuvre is to place the leaders of "Socialist democracy" who are "withdrawing" from Socialism and from the revolution in the innocuous position of an *appendage* to the bourgeois government, to screen the government from the people by means of the near-Socialist Ministers, to cover up the counter-revolutionary character of the bourgeoisie by a glittering, effective sign of "Socialist" ministerialism.

This method of the bourgeoisie has been especially well worked out in France; it has also been repeatedly tried in the Anglo-Saxon, Scandinavian, and various Latin countries. It is precisely such a manœuvre that was executed in Russia on May 19, 1917.

"Our" near-Socialist Ministers have found themselves in just such a situation. The bourgeoisie has begun to use them as its cat's paw; it has started doing such things *through them* as it could never have done without them.

Through Guchkov it was impossible to lure the masses into continuing the *imperialist,* annexationist war, the war for a general redistribution of colonies and annexations. Through Kerensky (and Tsereteli, who has been busier defending Tereshchenko than fighting for the postal and telegraph toilers) the bourgeoisie has found it possible, as correctly admitted by Miliukov and Maklakov, to do it; it has found it possible to "organise" for the continuation of just such a war.

Through Shingarev it was not possible to secure the retention of the land by the landowners even until the convocation of the Constituent Assembly (if an offensive takes place, it will "completely rehabilitate Russia," said Maklakov; this means that the Constituent Assembly, too, would be "rehabilitated"). Through Chernov this will become possible. The peasants have been told, although they have not readily subscribed to this idea, that to rent the lands from the rich landowners on the basis of arrangements entered into with individual owners is "order," but that to abolish the landownership at one stroke and to rent from the people, pending the convocation of the Constituent Assembly, the land which formerly belonged to the rich landowners is "anarchy." Without Chernov, this idea of the landowners and the counter-revolutionists could have never been carried out.

Through Konovalov it would have been impossible to secure the protection (*and the increase*; see the ministerial newspaper, *Rabo-*

chaia Gazeta, concerning the coal operators) of the outrageous profits on war contracts. Through Skobelev, or with his participation, this protection can be secured in the form of preserving the old, in the form of a near-"Marxist" denial of the possibility of "introducing" Socialism.

It is impossible to introduce Socialism, *therefore,* it is possible to hide from the people and to retain the outrageously high profits made by the capitalists not in their purely capitalist enterprises but on contracts for the army and the government. This is the excellent Struveist reasoning pursued jointly by Tereshchenko, Lvov and the "Marxist" Skobelev.

Through Lvov, Miliukov, Tereshchenko, Shingarev and Co. it was impossible to exert any influence on popular meetings and on the Soviets. Through Tsereteli, Chernov and Co. it is possible to exert an influence in the old bourgeois direction, it is possible, by means of especially effective, especially "well" sounding phrases, to pursue the old bourgeois-imperialist policy, to the point even of abrogating the people's elementary, democratic right of electing their own local administrations, to the point even of having such local administrations appointed or confirmed from above.

By abrogating this right, Tsereteli, Chernov and Co., without realising it, turned from ex-Socialists into ex-democrats.

"A great withdrawal," to be sure!

Pravda, No. 76, June 21, 1917.

AN EPIDEMIC OF CREDULITY

"COMRADES, the resistance of the capitalists has apparently been broken."

We glean this pleasant news from a speech by Minister Peshekhonov. This news is a "knock-out"! "The resistance of the capitalists has apparently been broken. . . ." [249]

And such ministerial speeches are being listened to and applauded! What is this but an epidemic of credulity?

On the one hand, they use the bugbear of the "dictatorship of the proletariat" to scare themselves and to frighten others. Yet, on the other hand, they speak of breaking the resistance of the capitalists. But in what does the idea of the "dictatorship of the proletariat" differ from the idea of breaking the resistance of the capitalists? In nothing at all. The dictatorship of the proletariat is a scientific term, indicating the class which is to play the leading rôle in it, and designating the special form that the power of the state is to assume, i. e., power based not on law, nor on elections, but on the direct and armed force of this or that section of the population.

What is the purpose and significance of the dictatorship of the proletariat? It is to break the resistance of the capitalists! And if in Russia "the resistance of the capitalists has apparently been broken," then we may as well say that in Russia "the dictatorship of the proletariat has apparently been realised."

The "only" trouble is that we have before us nothing but a ministerial phrase. Something in the nature of Skobelev's brave exclamation: "I will take 100 per cent profit!" It is one of the flowers of that "revolutionary-democratic" eloquence, that is now swamping Russia, intoxicating the petty bourgeoisie, befogging and corrupting the masses, scattering by the handful the germs of the present epidemic of credulity.

A scene in a certain French comedy—the Frenchmen, it seems, have excelled all other peoples in the game of Socialist ministries—has a phonograph that repeats before audiences of voters in every section of France a speech containing promises made by a "Socialist" Minister. We suggest that citizen Peshekhonov have his historic phrase: "Comrades, the resistance of the capitalists has apparently been broken," utilised by a company making phonograph records. It would be very convenient and useful (for the capitalists) to make this phrase popular in all the languages of the globe. Behold, they would say, the splendid successes of the Russian experiment in having the bourgeoisie and the Socialists form a coalition cabinet.

Still, it would not be amiss if citizen-Minister Peshekhonov,—whom both the Mensheviks and the Socialists-Revolutionists (who in 1906 shunned him in their press, because they regarded him as a petty bourgeois who had gone too far toward the right) now call Socialist,—after he has entered the cabinet together with Tsereteli and Chernov,—it would not be amiss if citizen Peshekhonov answered the following simple and modest question:

Is it not too much to try to break the resistance of the capitalists? Should we not try to disclose before the labour unions and the major parties the unheard-of profits made by the capitalists? Should we not try to abolish commercial secrets?

Is it not too much to speak of the "dictatorship of the proletariat" ("breaking the resistance of the capitalists")? Should we not rather *expose the looting of the treasury?*

When the price of coal is raised by the revolutionary government, as reported by the ministerial *Rabochaia Gazeta*, does it not look like looting the treasury? Hadn't we better make public at least once a week the "lists of securities" of the banks and other documents relating to war contracts and the prices paid according to those contracts, rather than deliver orations about "the resistance of the capitalists having been broken"?

Pravda, No. 76, June 21, 1917.

THE VALUE OF ARGUING TO THE POINT

DEAR comrades, writers of the *Novaia Zhizn!* you are dissatisfied with our criticism, you call it angry.[250] We shall endeavour to be mild and pleasant.

To begin with, we are going to take up the two questions propounded by you.

Can one seriously consider the control, to say nothing of the regulation, of industry without destroying the "inviolability of commercial secrets"?

We have been maintaining that the *Novaia Zhizn* has not answered this "practical" question. The *Novaia Zhizn* objects, claiming that the reply to it can be "found" "even" in the *Rabochaia Gazeta*.

But we fail to find it, dear comrades! And you will never find it either. Try as carefully as you may, you will not find it.

You will pardon us for saying it, but the *Novaia Zhizn* has sinned chiefly in that it has been only declaiming about "control," without really tackling the practical question concerning the "inviolability of commercial secrets" in a practical way.

Second question: Are we to confuse the immediate introduction of Socialism (something which the *Novaia Zhizn* has been arguing against, but which we have never suggested) with the immediate assumption of business control over banks and syndicates? When, in answer to that, we pointed out that we had no intentions to expropriate, regulate, or exercise control over petty economy, the *Novaia Zhizn* replied that ours was a "valuable confession," a "legitimate" one, but "too hastily" made.

Good heavens, dear comrades, how can you call it hasty when it is just a brief paraphrase of the lengthy and painstaking resolution passed by our conference? Is it possible that you have not been interested enough to read our resolution?

In polemics it is advisable to stick to the point. Equivocation in such cases is harmful.

Pravda, No. 76, June 21, 1917.

234

A BIRD IN THE HAND OR TWO IN THE BUSH

MINISTER PESHEKHONOV has said many beautiful and high sounding things in his speech: That "we should divide all we have equitably," and that the "resistance of the capitalists has apparently been broken," etc.

But he has cited only one exact figure. Only one exact fact has he pointed out in his speech, and out of eight columns only six lines have been devoted to this fact. Here is the fact: Nails are shipped from the factory at twenty kopecks per pound, they reach the consumer at two rubles per pound.

Is it not possible, now since "the resistance of the capitalists has been broken," to pass a law requiring the publication of: 1. All the documents pertaining to prices of the war contracts? 2. All the actual prices of war contracts in general? 3. The producer's cost of articles supplied to the government? 4. Is it not possible to give the workers' organisations an opportunity to verify all the facts bearing on the above?

Pravda, No. 76, June 21, 1917.

INTRODUCTION OF SOCIALISM OR EXPOSURE OF TREASURY LOOTING?

IT has been definitely settled that Socialism cannot be introduced in Russia. This has been established—in an almost Marxist fashion—by Mr. Miliukov at the conference of the "wild bulls" of June 16.[251] In this, Miliukov followed the ministerial Menshevik *Rabochaia Gazeta*. It was also subscribed to by the largest party in Russia in general, and in the Congress of Soviets, in particular,—the party of the Socialists-Revolutionists, which is not only the largest party, but is also the party that manifests the greatest ideological (disinterested) fear of seeing the revolution continued in the direction of Socialism.

Strictly speaking, a simple perusal of the resolution passed by the Bolshevik Conference on May 7-12, 1917, reveals that the Bolsheviks too recognise the impossibility of immediately "introducing" Socialism in Russia.

Why then the quarrel? Why the noise?

Because by shouting against the "introduction" of Socialism in Russia, they are sustaining (many of them without realising it) the efforts of those who are opposed *to the exposure of treasury looting.*

Let us not quibble over words, citizens! It is not only unworthy of "revolutionary democrats," but of grown-ups in general. Let us not talk of the "introduction of Socialism," which everybody rejects. Let us talk of the exposure of treasury looting.

When capitalists work for the defence, *i. e.,* for the government, it is obviously no more "pure" capitalism, it is a special form of national economy. Pure capitalism means commodity production. Commodity production means work for an *uncertain* and free market. But the capitalist "working" for the defence does not work for the market at all, he fills the orders of the government, and money is invariably advanced to him by the treasury.

In our opinion, to hide the extent of the profits made on this unique operation and to appropriate the profit in excess of what is necessary to cover the living expenses of a man actually participating in production is treasury looting.

If you do not share our opinion, then, clearly, you disagree with the overwhelming majority of the population. There is not a shadow of a doubt that the workers and peasants of Russia, in their enormous mass, share our opinion, and that they would express it directly, were the question put to them without evasions and excuses, without diplomatic subterfuges.

And if you do share our opinion, then let us fight together against evasions and subterfuges.

In order to yield most in such a *common* undertaking, in order to show a maximum of conciliation, we permit ourselves to propose to the Congress of the Soviets the following draft resolution:

The first step towards regulation, or even simple control, of production and distribution (remark not to be included in the text of the resolution: even Minister Peshekhonov has promised to try to "divide all we have equitably") —the first step in any serious struggle with the economic crisis and approaching catastrophe must be a decree concerning the abolition of commercial (and bank) secrets in all transactions connected with deliveries to the government or with defence in general. Such a decree to be supplemented immediately by a law punishing as criminal offences all direct and indirect attempts to conceal pertinent documents and facts from people and groups who have mandates from: (a) any Soviet of Workers' and Peasants' Deputies; (b) any union of workers, employés, etc.; (c) any of the major political parties (the word "major" should be defined on the basis of membership).

Everybody is agreed that the immediate introduction of Socialism in Russia is impossible.

Does everybody agree that the exposure of treasury looting is an immediate necessity?

Pravda, No. 77, June 22, 1917.

PERPLEXED AND FRIGHTENED

An atmosphere of fear and perplexity reigns over **Petrograd**. It has reached unheard-of intensity.

A small incident illustrated this before the coming of the grave event—the ban on the demonstration planned by our party for Saturday.[252]

The small incident involved the seizure of Durnovo's country home. Minister Pereverzev first determined to clear Durnovo's country home of its invaders, but later, at the congress, he declared that he would leave to the people even the orchard surrounding the country home and that the trade unions were not being forced to evacuate Durnovo's place at all! All that was necessary, he claimed, was to arrest a few Anarchists.[253]

If the seizure of Durnovo's country home was illegal, then it was not right to leave the orchard to the people, and to let the trade unions remain on the premises. If there were legitimate grounds for arresting individuals, then their arrest had no bearing on the house at all, for the arrest would have taken place irrespective of whether the persons had been on the premises or not. As it happens, neither the house has been vacated nor the arrest made. The government has found itself in the position of people perplexed and frightened at the same time. Had these people not been nervous, there would have been no "incident," for in reality everything has remained as of old.

The grave event is the one involving the demonstration. The Central Committee of our party together with a great number of other organisations, the bureau of trade unions among them, decided to arrange a peaceful demonstration, a march along the streets of the capital. In any constitutional country such demonstrations are regarded as the inalienable right of the citizens. No government of a free country sees anything illegal in a peaceful street demonstration, the slogan of which is the demand for a change in the constitution or for a change in the composition of the government.

But now perplexed and frightened people, among them the majority of the Congress of Soviets in particular, decided to make an unheard-of political "affair" out of this contemplated demonstra-

238

tion. The majority of the Congress of Soviets passes a thundering resolution, full of desperate and sharp words against our party, opposing the demonstration and prohibiting all demonstrations, including peaceful ones, for three days.

When this formal resolution was passed, the Central Committee of our party as late as Friday, 2 A.M., decided to call off the demonstration. On Saturday morning, at a hastily called conference with representatives of the boroughs, this decision was carried out.

The question is: How does our other "government," the Congress of Soviets, explain this prohibition? In a free country every party, of course, has a right to call demonstrations, every government may, by declaring a state of emergency, prohibit such demonstrations. The political question however remains: Why has this demonstration been prohibited?

Here is the only political reason clearly indicated in the resolution of the Congress of Soviets:

" . . . We know that the hidden counter-revolutionaries are making ready to take advantage of your demonstration" (*i. e.*, the demonstration arranged by our party).

This is the cause of prohibiting our peaceful demonstration. The Congress of Soviets happens to "know" that there are "hidden counter-revolutionaries" and that they wanted "to take advantage" of the demonstration planned by our party.

This statement of the Congress of Soviets is extremely important. And we have to emphasise over and over again this statement of fact, which stands out by virtue of its substantial character above the stream of abusive words hurled at us. What measures does our other government undertake against these "hidden counter-revolutionaries"? Just what is it that this government happens to "know"? Just how did the counter-revolutionaries want to utilise this or that pretext?

The people cannot and will not wait, patiently and passively, for this hidden counter-revolution to come out in the open.

If our other government does not wish to find itself in the position of people who, by resorting to floods of abuse, are trying to hide the fact that they are perplexed and that they have permitted themselves to be frightened by the Rights, it will have to tell the people a great deal about the "hidden counter-revolutionaries," it will have to do a great deal of earnest fighting against them.

INNUENDOES

THOSE who rage, storm, fulminate, gnash their teeth, pour a ceaseless stream of abusive and pogrom-provoking words upon our party, do not accuse us of anything directly, they only "insinuate."

Insinuate what?

There is only one thing they can insinuate: The Bolsheviks want to overthrow the government, they are Catilines, and for that reason are monsters and outcasts deserving of being torn to pieces.

Our enemies do not dare to make this foolish statement openly, that is why they resort to "insinuations," that is why they thunder "rhetorically." For this accusation is exceedingly stupid. A *coup d'état* by means of a peaceful demonstration, decided upon on Thursday, planned for Saturday and announced on Saturday morning. Well, gentlemen, whom do you really want to astound with your nonsensical insinuations?

"A demand for the overthrow of the Provisional Government,"— says the resolution of the Congress of Soviets. "The removal of a number of Ministers from the Provisional Government" (one of the inscriptions on the contemplated banners was to read: Down with the bourgeois members of the government!) "is tantamount to a *coup d'état.*"

Why, then, has no one tried or even threatened to arrest those who have repeatedly appeared in the streets of Petrograd carrying the banner: "All power to the Soviet"?

These frantic persons have been frightened by their own shadow.

A government conscious of the fact that it represents the will of the majority of the people should have no reason to fear demonstrations announced in advance.

A government of that kind would not prohibit such demonstrations.

Only one who realises that he has no majority back of him, that he has not the support of the masses, is likely to be so savagely angry, is likely to make such insinuations in malicious articles.

Pravda, No. 79, June 24, 1917.

"DISQUIETING RUMOURS"

THE Provisional Government is calling upon the "population" to-day to preserve its calm in view of "the rumours that are being spread throughout the city and that are disquieting to the population."

Does not the Provisional Government think that one sentence in the resolution passed by the Congress of the Soviets is and should be a thousand more times more disquieting to the people than any "rumours"? That sentence is:

"We know that the hidden counter-revolutionaries are making ready to take advantage of your (Bolshevik) demonstration."

This is more than *"rumours."* How can they fail to alarm the population?

Pravda, No. 79, June 24, 1917.

A RIDDLE

WHAT is the difference between an ordinary bourgeois government and a government which is extraordinary, revolutionary, and which does not regard itself as bourgeois?

The answer is the following:

The ordinary bourgeois government can prohibit demonstrations only on constitutional grounds or after declaring martial law.

The extraordinary and almost Socialist government can prohibit demonstrations without any grounds and for reasons of circumstances known only to itself.

Pravda, No. 79, June 24, 1917.

DRAFT OF AN ARTICLE ON THE SOVIETS OF WORKERS', SOLDIERS', AND PEASANTS' DEPUTIES

WE hold that the unique institution known as the Soviets of Workers', Soldiers', and Peasants' Deputies is the nearest approach to an all-people's organ for the expression of the will of the majority of the people, a revolutionary parliament.

On principle we always have been, and are, in favour of having all the power pass into the hands of such an organ, despite the fact that at present this organ is in the hands of the defencist Mensheviks and Socialists-Revolutionists, who are hostile to the party of the proletariat.

The inner contradiction, the weak, unstable, powerless position of the Soviets with regard to the counter-revolution is the result of the fact that they permit the existence of a nest of counter-revolution, represented by the ten bourgeois Ministers, and that they do not break with Anglo-French imperialist capital. This shakiness of their position causes the nervousness of the present majority of the Soviets and their peevishness against those who point out this weakness of their stand.

We refuse to co-ordinate, to bring into harmony our struggle against the counter-revolution with the "struggle" of the defencist and the ministerialist parties.

We cannot recognise the decisions of the Soviets as the proper decisions of a proper government while there remain ten counter-revolutionary Ministers, part and parcel of the Miliukov spirit and the Miliukov class. But even if the Soviets should seize the entire power (something we wish and always would support), even if the Soviets should become the supreme revolutionary parliament, we would *not* submit to those of its decisions which restrained our freedom of agitation, for instance, by prohibiting proclamations at the front or in the rear, or by prohibiting peaceful demonstrations, etc. In that event we would prefer to become an illegal, officially persecuted party, rather than give up our Marxist, internationalist principles. We shall act similarly if the congress of the Soviets should find it necessary to brand us officially before the entire population of Russia, as "enemies of the people" or as "enemies of the revolution."

Of the reasons given for prohibiting demonstrations for three days, we regard as conditionally sound only one, namely, that the hidden counter-revolutionists, who had been quietly waiting for an opportunity, wanted to take advantage of this demonstration. If the facts on the strength of which this reason is advanced are correct, if the names of the counter-revolutionists are known to the entire Soviet (as they are known to us privately from the oral information given to us by Liber and others of the Executive Committee), then these counter-revolutionists should be immediately proclaimed enemies of the people, they should be arrested and their followers and aides questioned by the courts.

The fact that the Soviet does not take any such measures makes even this correct motive only conditionally correct, or altogether incorrect.

Written June 23 or 24, 1917. First published in 1924, in Byloie, No. 24.

SPEECH DELIVERED AT THE SESSION OF THE PETROGRAD COMMITTEE OF THE R. S.-D. L. P., JUNE 24, 1917, ON THE PROHIBITED DEMONSTRATION [254]

THE dissatisfaction of the majority of the comrades with the calling off of the demonstration is quite legitimate, but the Central Committee could not act otherwise for two reasons: First, we received a formal prohibition of all demonstrations from our semi-official government; second, a plausible reason was given for this prohibition, namely: "We know that the hidden counter-revolutionaries are making ready to take advantage of your demonstration." In support of this, certain names were mentioned, for instance, a certain general, who, it was promised, would be arrested within three days, and others; we were informed that there had been arranged a demonstration of the Black Hundreds for the 23rd of June,—they were to break into our procession and cause a general slaughter.

Even in simple warfare it sometimes happens that for strategic reasons it is necessary to postpone an offensive fixed for a certain date; it is all the more likely to happen in the case of the class struggle, depending upon the degree of vacillation shown by the moderate petty-bourgeois groups. One must know how to gauge the situation and to be daring in one's decisions.

It was absolutely necessary for us to cancel our arrangements. This has been proved by subsequent events. To-day Tsereteli has delivered his historical and hysterical speech.[255] To-day the revolution has entered upon a new phase of its development. They began by enjoining our peaceful demonstration for three days, they now wish to prohibit it for the entire duration of the congress; they demand of us submission to the decisions of the congress; they threaten us with expulsion from the congress. But we have declared that we prefer to be arrested rather than give up our freedom to agitate.

Tsereteli, who in his speech has revealed himself as an out-and-out counter-revolutionist, has made the statement that one must fight the Bolsheviks not with words nor resolutions, but by depriving them of all the technical means at their disposal,—which constitutes the sum total of all bourgeois revolutions; namely, first, the arming of the proletariat, then the disarming of it, so that it may not go further. The situation must indeed be very serious if it calls for a ban on a peaceful demonstration.

Tsereteli, who came to the congress from the bosom of the Provisional Government, expressed an unmistakable desire to disarm the workers. He disclosed a savage temper, he demanded that the Bolsheviks as a party should be outlawed by revolutionary democracy. The workers must now realise that there cannot be any more talk of a "peaceful demonstration." The situation is much more serious than we thought it was. We had decided on a peaceful demonstration, in order to exert the maximum of influence upon the decisions of the congress—this is our right,—but now we are being accused of having formed a conspiracy to arrest the government.

Tsereteli says that besides the Bolsheviks there are no counter-revolutionists. The assembly that sat in judgment over us was organised with a special solemnity and consisted of the Presidium of the Congress, of the Executive Committee of the Soviet of Workers' and Soldiers' Deputies in a body, of the bureau of the fractions of all the parties at the congress. At their session to-day they have blurted out to us the whole truth, they have declared an offensive against us.

The reply of the proletariat should be a maximum of calm, care, discipline, organisation, and realisation that peaceful demonstrations are a thing of the past.

We must offer them no pretext for an attack, let them attack first, and then the workers will realise that those people are making an attempt on the very existence of the proletariat. But the forces of life are with us and it is uncertain how successful their attack will turn out to be; there are armies at the front, the spirit of discontent is rife among them, in the rear high prices, economic disintegration, etc., prevail everywhere.

The Central Committee does not wish to influence your decision. Your right to protest against the actions of the Central Committee is legitimate, and your decision should be a free decision.

First printed in 1925 in *Krasnaia Lietopis*, No. 9, from the minutes of the session of the Petrograd Committee of the R. S.-D. L. P.

A LETTER TO THE EDITOR

I AM being asked the cause of my absence at yesterday's, Sunday's, conference of the Executive Committee, the Presidium of the Congress and the bureau of all the fractions. The reason is that I advocated the refusal of the Bolsheviks as a matter of principle, to participate in this conference and urged that they send a written declaration that they refuse to participate in any conferences dealing with the question mentioned (the prohibition of demonstrations).

N. LENIN.

Pravda, No. 80, June 26, 1917.

AT THE BREAKING POINT

THE Russian Revolution, in the first stage of its development, gave power to the imperialist bourgeoisie and created alongside of that power the Soviets of Deputies, in which the majority belonged to the petty-bourgeois democracy. The second stage of the revolution (May 19) formally removed from power the cynically candid representatives of imperialism, Miliukov and Guchkov, and actually transformed the majority parties in the Soviets into government parties. Our party remained, before and after May 19, a minority opposition party. This was inevitable, for we are the party of the Socialist proletariat, and are of a definitely international orientation. When an imperialist war is waged, a Socialist proletariat whose outlook is international cannot help being in opposition to any power carrying on such a war, be that power monarchical, republican, or that of the "Socialists"-defencists. And the party of the Socialist proletariat is bound to attract larger and larger masses of the population that is being ruined by the protracted war and that is growing distrustful of the "Socialists" serving imperialism, just as before it grew distrustful of the genuine imperialists. The struggle against our party, therefore, began in the very first days of the revolution. And however base and loathsome a character the struggle carried on by the Cadets and the Plekhanovites against the party of the proletariat may assume, the meaning of the struggle is quite clear. It is the same struggle that the imperialists and the Scheidemannites were carrying on against Liebknecht and F. Adler (both of whom were declared "insane" by the central organ of the German "Socialists," to say nothing of the bourgeois press which denounced these comrades as simply "traitors" working for England). This is the struggle of the *whole* of bourgeois society, *including petty-bourgeois democracy* regardless of how r-r-revolutionary that democracy may be, against the Socialist, international proletariat.

In Russia this struggle has reached the stage where the imperialists are endeavouring—with the aid of the leaders of the petty-bourgeois democracy, the Tseretelis, the Chernovs and Co.—to destroy the growing power of the proletarian party with a single blow, sharp

248

and decisive. As a pretext for such a decisive blow, Minister Tsereteli has struck upon a method usually resorted to by counter-revolutionists: *he charges us with conspiracy*. This charge is a mere pretext. The fact of the matter is that it is necessary for petty-bourgeois democracy, directed by the Russian and the Allied imperialists, to destroy the Socialist-internationalists. They think that the moment is ripe for such a blow. They are agitated, they are frightened, and under the whip of their masters they have made up their mind: now or never.

The Socialist proletariat and our party must be cool and collected, must show the maximum of persistence and vigilance; let the coming Cavaignacs begin first. Our conference had already anticipated their arrival. The proletariat of Petrograd will give them no opportunity to disclaim responsibility. The proletariat will adhere to its policy of watchful waiting, it will gather its forces and prepare to resist whenever those gentlemen decide to turn from words to action.

Pravda, No. 80, June 26, 1917.

AN INCONSISTENT STAND

THE resolution of the Congress condemning our party,[256] as printed in to-day's papers, will no doubt be compared by every class-conscious worker and soldier with our party declaration directed to the All-Russian Congress of Soviets,—a declaration made public on the 24th, and printed in to-day's *Pravda.*

The inconsistency in the stand of the leaders of the Congress has been revealed by their resolution and particularly by our declaration.

"The basis for the success and the strength of the Russian Revolution is the unity of the entire revolutionary democracy—the workers, the soldiers, and the peasants," reads the first and cardinal point of the resolution passed by the Congress. And, of course, this point is incontrovertibly correct if we understand by "unity" *the unity in the struggle against counter-revolution.* But what if a certain number of the "workers, soldiers, and peasants," through their leaders, enter into a bloc and unite with the counter-revolution? Is it not clear that it is precisely *this* part of "democracy" that ceases to be "revolutionary" in fact?

The Narodniks (Socialists-Revolutionists) and the Mensheviks will probably become indignant at our mere admission of the thought that it is possible, that it is conceivable, that any part of the "workers, soldiers, and peasants" will unite with the counter-revolution.

Those who might attempt to gloss over our arguments and evade the issue by indignation, we would refer to the third point of that same resolution: ". . . *the resistance* of the counter-revolutionary forces of the *propertied classes is growing.*" This is a sound statement. It would be more correct to say: of the bourgeoisie, or of the capitalists and landowners (instead of the "propertied classes" which include also the wealthy groups of the petty bourgeoisie).

No doubt, the resistance of the bourgeoisie is growing.

But it is the bourgeoisie that controls the majority of the Provisional Government, with which the leaders of the Socialists-Revolutionists and the Mensheviks have united, not only politically, but also organisationally, in one institution,—the cabinet.

This is the basis of the inconsistent stand taken by the leaders of the Soviet, this is the fundamental cause of the instability of their entire policy.   On the one hand they are united with the bourgeoisie through the cabinet, where they are under the sway of the bourgeois majority, the bourgeois Ministers; on the other hand, they are forced to admit that "the resistance of the counter-revolutionary forces of the propertied classes is growing!!'"

It is obvious that, under such conditions, the party of the revolutionary proletariat can admit "unity" with the "revolutionary" democracy (revolutionary in words, not in deeds), only "so long as" . . . We are for "unity" with it, so long as it fights counter-revolution.   We are against "unity" with it, so long as it joins hands with the counter-revolution.

The imperative question confronting us now is the "growing" resistance of the counter-revolutionary bourgeoisie.   To evade this main and fundamental question by resorting to general phrases about "the unity and the concerted action of revolutionary democracy," to ignore the fact that a section of revolutionary democracy is at one and in harmony with the counter-revolution, would be illogical and foolish.

It follows, therefore, that in point of principle all the arguments in the resolution of the Congress condemning our demonstration as "secret," and maintaining that all manifestations and demonstrations are to be only made with the knowledge and the consent of the Soviets, fall to the ground. These arguments mean nothing. The proletarian party, in accordance with its declaration to the All-Russian Congress, will never subscribe to such ideas. For any demonstration, as long as it is peaceful, is a means of agitation; and they can neither stop us from agitating nor can they impose on us joint agitation.

On the formal side, the resolution is even weaker. To prohibit or to proscribe, one must be a power in the state. First become a power, gentlemen, leaders of the present Soviet,—we are in favour of it, although you are our opponents—then only will you have the right to forbid or to proscribe. So long as you are not yet in possession of state power, so long as you suffer the domination of ten bourgeois Ministers, you are still the victims of your own weakness and indecision.

Phrases about a "clearly expressed will," etc., will not help you. A will, if it is the will of the state, must be expressed in the form of a law, must be executed by the government, otherwise the word "will" is a mere perturbation in the air, an empty sound. Had you only for a moment, gentlemen, thought of *law*, you would not have failed to recall that the constitution of a free republic cannot prohibit any peaceful manifestations or mass demonstrations arranged by any party or group.

The inconsistent stand has generated extremely queer revolutionary ideas; ideas as to the methods of fighting counter-revolution, ideas of state (constitution), ideas of jurisprudence. When we discount the savage vilification of our party, nothing is left.

Despite this savage vilification of our proposed manifestation,— the manifestation is to be held . . . a week later.

Pravda, No. 81, June 27, 1917.

THE UKRAINE

THE failure of the policy of the new coalition Provisional Government appears more and more obvious. The "Universal Act" relating to the organisation of the Ukraine, issued by the Ukrainian Central Rada and adopted on June 24, 1917, by the All-Ukrainian Army Congress, is an eloquent exposure of that policy and documentary proof of its failure.[257]

Without separating from Russia, without breaking with the Russian State, reads the act, let the Ukrainian people have the right to determine its own life on its own land . . . All laws pertaining to the establishment of order here, in the Ukraine, are to be made only by the Ukrainian Assembly; but those laws which are to help establish order throughout the entire Russian State shall be made by the All-Russian Parliament.

These are perfectly clear words. It is made evident that at the present moment the Ukrainian people does not wish to separate from Russia. It demands autonomy without denying the necessity of a supreme power such as the "All-Russian Parliament." No Socialist, and even no democrat, would venture to deny the legitimacy of the Ukrainian demands. No democrat can deny the *right* of the Ukraine freely to separate from Russia. It is precisely this unqualified recognition of the above right that makes possible the advocacy of a free union of the Ukrainians and the Great-Russians, of a *voluntary* combination of the two peoples into one state. It is precisely this unqualified recognition of the above right that makes possible an actual break, conclusive, irreparable, with the accursed tsarist past, when *everything* in the government's power was done to bring about a *mutual estrangement* of peoples so closely related linguistically, geographically, historically, and temperamentally. The accursed tsarism transformed the Great-Russians into executioners of the Ukrainian people, and bred in the latter a hatred for all those who forbade Ukrainian children to speak, even to learn, their native tongue.

Revolutionary democracy of Russia, if it really wants to be revolutionary and democratic, must break with this past, must regain for the workers and peasants of Russia the brotherly faith of the workers and peasants of the Ukraine. This cannot be accomplished without the complete recognition of the rights of the Ukraine, the right of separation included.

We are opposed to petty states. We stand for the closest ties among the workers of all countries against the capitalists of "their" countries and of the world generally. But in order that these ties be voluntary, the Russian worker, having no faith either in the Russian or in the Ukrainian bourgeoisie, stands for the right of the Ukraine to a separate existence, without imposing his friendship on the country, but merely wishing to win it over by treating it as an equal, as an ally and brother in the struggle for Socialism.

The *Riech*, the paper of the indignant bourgeois counter-revolutionists, half crazed with anger, madly attacks the Ukrainians for their "arbitrary" decision. "This action of the Ukrainians," it says, "constitutes a direct violation of the law, and calls for the immediate application of severe legal punishment." [258] There is nothing to add to this outbreak of the brutalised bourgeois counter-revolutionists. Down with the counter-revolutionary bourgeoisie! Long live the free union of the free peasants and workers of a free Ukraine with the workers and peasants of revolutionary Russia!

Pravda, No. 82, June 28, 1917.

THE CLASS ORIGINS OF PRESENT AND "FUTURE" CAVAIGNACS

"WHEN the real Cavaignac comes, we shall fight together with you in the same ranks," we were told in No. 80 of the *Rabochaia Gazeta*,[259] organ of that same Menshevik Party to which belongs Minister Tsereteli, the gentleman who in his deplorably famous speech threatened to disarm the Petrograd workers.

The above-quoted remark of the *Rabochaia Gazeta* brings out in bold relief the fundamental errors of the two ruling parties in Russia, the Menshevik and the Socialist-Revolutionist parties, and therefore deserves attention. You seek Cavaignacs at the wrong time and in the wrong place, seems to be the burden of the arguments of the ministerial organ.

Let us recall the class rôle played by Cavaignac. In February, 1848, the French monarchy was overthrown. The bourgeois republicans came into power. They, too, like our Cadets, wanted "order," meaning by that the restoration and the strengthening of the instruments for oppressing the masses developed by the monarchy: the police, the standing army, and the privileged bureaucracy. They, too, like our Cadets, wanted to put an end to the revolution, for they hated the revolutionary proletariat with its then very hazy "social" (*i. e.*, Socialist) aspirations. They, too, like our Cadets, were implacably hostile to the idea of extending the French Revolution to the rest of Europe, the idea of changing it into a world proletarian revolution. They, too, like our Cadets, artfully utilised the petty-bourgeois "Socialism" of Louis Blanc, by making him a member of the Cabinet and thus transforming him from a leader of the Socialist workers, which he wanted to be, into a mere appendage, hanger on of the bourgeoisie.

Such were the class interests, the position and the policy of the ruling class.

Another basic social power was the petty bourgeoisie, vacillating, frightened by the red spectre, carried away by the outcries against the "Anarchists." In its aspirations dreamily and loquaciously "Socialistic," gladly calling itself a "Socialist democracy" (even this very name has now been adopted by the Socialists-Revolutionists

255

and the Mensheviks!), the petty bourgeoisie was afraid to entrust itself to the leadership of the revolutionary proletariat, failing to realise that this fear condemned it to entrusting itself to the bourgeoisie. For while in a society with a keen class struggle between the bourgeoisie and the proletariat, particularly when this struggle is inevitably made more acute by a revolution, there can be no "middle" course, the whole essence of the class position and aspirations of the petty bourgeoisie consists in wanting the impossible, in aspiring towards the impossible, i. e., towards just such a "middle course."

The third determining class force was the proletariat which aspired not towards a "conciliation" with the bourgeoisie, but towards a victory over it, towards a fearless development of the revolution onward, and, what is more, on an international scale.

This was the objective historical soil from which sprang Cavaignac. The vacillations of the petty bourgeoisie "pushed it aside" from active rôles, and the French Cadet, General Cavaignac, taking advantage of the fear of the petty bourgeoisie to entrust itself to the proletariat, decided to disarm the Paris workers, to shoot them down in large numbers.

The revolution was terminated by this historical shooting; the petty bourgeoisie, numerically preponderant, had been and remained the politically impotent tail of the bourgeoisie, and three years later France again saw the restoration of a particularly vile form of Cæsarist monarchy.

The historic speech of Tsereteli on June 24 was obviously inspired by the Cadet Cavaignacs (perhaps directly inspired by the bourgeois Ministers, or, maybe, indirectly prompted by the bourgeois press and bourgeois public opinion,—the difference does not matter), Tsereteli's historic speech is remarkable and is historic for the reason that Tsereteli has blurted out with inimitable naïveté the "secret malady" of the entire Socialist-Revolutionist and Menshevik petty bourgeoisie. This "secret malady" consists in the following: first, the complete inability of the petty bourgeoisie to carry out an independent policy; second, its fear to entrust itself to the revolutionary proletariat and to support whole-heartedly the latter's independent policy; third, its inevitable surrender to the Cadets or to the bourgeoisie in general (i. e., its surrender to the Cavaignacs).

This is the crux of the matter. Neither Tsereteli nor Chernov, nor even Kerensky has been personally called upon to play the rôle of a Cavaignac. Other people will be found who, at the proper moment, will tell the Russian Louis Blancs: "Step aside." But the Tseretelis and the Chernovs are leaders pursuing the very petty-bourgeois policy that makes the appearance of Cavaignacs possible and inevitable.

"When the real Cavaignac comes we shall fight together with you"—an excellent promise, a splendid intention! Only it is a pity that it reveals a lack of understanding the class struggle, typical of the sentimental and cowardly petty bourgeoisie. For Cavaignac is not a mere incident, his "coming" is not a casual occurrence. Cavaignac is a representative of a class (of the counter-revolutionary bourgeoisie), and carries out the policies of that class. And you, gentlemen, Socialists-Revolutionists and Mensheviks, are supporting that very class and those very policies. It is to this class and its policies that you, who are admittedly in control of the majority in the country at the present moment, are giving predominance in the government, and thus furnish it with an excellent foundation upon which to work.

Indeed, at the All-Russian Peasant Congress the Socialists-Revolutionists dominated almost everything. At the All-Russian Congress of Workers' and Soldiers' Delegates, the bloc of the Socialists-Revolutionists and the Mensheviks constituted an overwhelming majority. The same thing happened in the elections for the Borough Councils of Petrograd. The fact stares one in the face: The Socialists-Revolutionists and the Mensheviks are now the dominant party. And this dominant party voluntarily abdicates its power (the majority in the government) to the party of the Cavaignacs!!

Once there is a swamp there is sure to be the devil.* Once there is a shaky, vacillating petty bourgeoisie, afraid of the development of the revolution, the Cavaignacs are sure to come.

In Russia there are many things now that make our revolution different from the French Revolution of 1848: The imperialist war, the proximity of more advanced (and not, as was in the case of France at that time, more backward) countries, an agrarian and a national movement. But all this may affect only the manner of Cavaignac's appearance, the moment, the external pretexts, etc. It cannot affect the essence of the matter, because the essence lies in class relationships.

* A Russian saying.—*Ed.*

In words Louis Blanc too was as remote from Cavaignac as heaven from earth.   Louis Blanc too had made countless promises "to fight in the same ranks" together with the revolutionary workers against the bourgeois counter-revolutionists.   Nevertheless no Marxist historian, no Socialist, would dare to doubt that it was the weakness, the instability, the gullibility of the Louis Blancs in their relation to the bourgeoisie that called forth a Cavaignac and assured his success.

It is only on the steadfastness and vigilance or the lack of these, it is on the strength or weakness of the revolutionary workers of Russia that the victory or the defeat of the Russian Cavaignacs depends.   For Cavaignacs are inevitably created by the counter-revolutionary spirit of the Russian bourgeoisie with the Cadets at their head, by the shakiness, cowardice, and vacillations of the petty-bourgeois parties of the Socialists-Revolutionists and the Mensheviks.

Pravda, No. 83, June 29, 1917.

THE UKRAINE AND THE DEFEAT OF THE RULING
PARTIES IN RUSSIA

THE ruling parties of Russia, *i. e.*, the Cadets, who have a majority in the government and the power of capital on their side,
and the Socialists-Revolutionists and the Mensheviks who have the
recognised majority in the country (but who are powerless in the
government and in the economic life of the capitalist country), have
all suffered an obvious defeat on the Ukrainian question, and what's
more, a defeat on a national scale and on a question of utmost
importance.

The Socialists-Revolutionists and the Mensheviks have been willing to tolerate the fact that the Provisional Government of the
Cadets, *i. e.*, of the counter-revolutionary bourgeoisie, has not been
fulfilling its elementary democratic obligations, has not declared
itself in favour of the right of the Ukraine to autonomy and to
freedom of separation. The Ukrainians, as Minister Chernov informs us in to-day's *Dielo Naroda*, have demanded incomparably
less than that. All they have asked was "that the Provisional Government should formally declare that it is not opposed to Ukrainian
autonomy." This is a most modest and legitimate demand. The
other two demands are just as modest: (1) That the Ukraine
through its local population elect one representative to the Central
Russian Government; the reasonableness of this demand can be
judged from the fact that in 1897 the number of Great-Russians
in the Empire was 43 per cent and that of the Ukrainians 17 per
cent of the population. The Ukrainians therefore would be justified in demanding not one, but six Ministers out of the sixteen!!
(2) In the Ukraine "there ought to be one representative of the Central Russian Government, elected by the local population." What
could be more legitimate than this? What right has a democrat
to set aside the principle, proved in theory and confirmed by the
experience of democratic revolutions, that "no officials for the local
population should be appointed from above"??

The Provisional Government's rejection of these most modest and
most legitimate demands is a manifestation of the unheard-of shamelessness, of the savage brazenness of the counter-revolutionists,

is a true example of the "bullying" policy pursued by the Great-Russians. And the Socialists-Revolutionists and the Mensheviks are making a mockery of their own party programmes, are tolerating it in the government, and are defending it now in their own papers!! How disgracefully the Socialists-Revolutionists and the Mensheviks have fallen! How pitiful to-day are the subterfuges of their organs, the *Dielo Naroda* and the *Rabochaia Gazeta.*

Chaos, confusion, "Leninism in the national question," anarchy—these outcries of an enraged landowner are hurled by the newspapers at the Ukrainians.

Ignoring their outcries, what is the substance of their argument?

Not until the Constituent Assembly is convoked will it be possible to settle in a "regular" manner the boundaries of the Ukraine, her freedom, her right to collect taxes, etc., etc.—this is their only argument. They demand a "guarantee of regularity." And it is this expression used in the editorial of the *Rabochaia Gazeta* that constitutes the whole essence of their argument.

But this is an obvious lie, gentlemen, this is the glaring shamelessness of the counter-revolutionists. To advance such an argument means actually to help the real traitors to the revolution!!

"Guarantees of regularity" . . . think of it, for just a moment at least. Nowhere in Russia, neither in the central government, nor in any local department (except in the very small institution: the Borough Councils of Petrograd) are there any guarantees of regularity; in fact, there is no regularity at all. There is clearly no regularity in the existence of the Duma or of the Imperial Council. There is clearly no regularity in the composition of the Provisional Government, for its composition is a travesty upon the will and the intelligence of the workers, soldiers and peasants of Russia. There is clearly no regularity in the composition of the Soviets (of Workers', Soldiers', and Peasants' Deputies), for these institutions have not as yet worked out any laws assuring complete and strictly democratic elections. Still, this does not prevent our party, as well as the worker and peasant masses, from regarding the Soviets at present as the best expression of the will of the majority of the population. Nowhere in Russia have there been, or could there possibly have been, such "guarantees of regularity." Such "guarantees" have never existed in revolutionary periods like the present. Everybody knows it, nobody demands it, everybody realises the inevitability of this.

It is only for the Ukraine that "we" demand "guarantees of regularity"!

You have become mad with fear, gentlemen, Socialists-Revolutionists and Mensheviks.   You have surrendered to the counter-revolutionary howls of the Great-Russian landowners and capitalists and their leaders, Rodzianko and Miliukov, Lvov and Tereshchenko, Nekrasov and Shingarev and Co.   You are already the perfect picture of people overawed by the rising Cavaignacs (who are as yet in "hiding").

There is absolutely nothing terrible, there is not a suggestion of anarchy or chaos in either the resolutions or the demands of the Ukrainians.   Accede to their most legitimate and most modest demands, and authority will be just as effective in the Ukraine as it is everywhere in Russia, where the Soviets (which possess no "guarantees of regularity") are the *sole* authority.   You and all the peoples of Russia will be given these "guarantees of regularity" by the future Diets, by the coming Constituent Assembly, not only with regard to the Ukraine, but with regard to all questions.   For at the present moment there is clearly no "regularity" in Russia about any question.   Accede to the Ukrainians, reason dictates it. Otherwise, it will be worse.   Force will not hold the Ukrainians, it will only anger them.   Accede to the Ukrainians—you will thus open the path leading to the mutual confidence and brotherly union of the two nations on a basis of equality.

The Socialists-Revolutionists and the Mensheviks, the ruling parties, have suffered a defeat on the Ukrainian question; they have surrendered to the counter-revolutionary Cadet Cavaignacs.

Pravda, No. 84, June 30, 1917.

HOW TO FIGHT COUNTER-REVOLUTION

ONLY a few days ago Minister Tsereteli in his "historic" speech declared that there was no counter-revolution. To-day the ministerial *Rabochaia Gazeta* strikes an entirely different note in its article "Formidable Symptoms."

"There are clear indications that the counter-revolution is mobilising."

We are grateful for this; finally they have come to recognise the fact at least.

But the ministerial organ goes on as follows: "We do not know its (the counter-revolution's) staff, we do not know to what extent it is organised."

Is that so? You do not know the staff of the counter-revolution! Permit us to help you out of your ignorance. The staff of the forming counter-revolution is in the Provisional Government, in that very coalition cabinet in which you, gentlemen, have six of your comrades! The staff of the counter-revolution is located within the walls of the conference rooms of the Fourth Duma, where rule Miliukov, Rodzianko, Shulgin, Guchkov, A. Shingarev, Manuilov and Co.—for Cadet members of the coalition cabinet are the right hand of Miliukov and Co. The staff of the counter-revolution is recruited from among reactionary generals. The staff of the counter-revolution contains some of the retired high officers.

If, besides crying about the counter-revolution, you really wish to fight it, then you must say, together with us: Down with the ten capitalist Ministers. . . .

The *Rabochaia Gazeta* points out, further, that the chief tool in the hands of the counter-revolution is the press which is inciting to anti-Semitism and Jew-baiting. That is correct. But what is the logical conclusion? Are you not, gentlemen, the government party? What have you done to bridle the vile counter-revolutionary press? How can you, who call yourselves "revolutionary democracy," afford not to take revolutionary measures against the unbridled, frankly counter-revolutionary press? Moreover, why should you not establish a government organ with a monopoly on all the advertisements? This would deprive the vile counter-revolutionary press of its chief source of income, therefore of its chief possibility of lying to the people. We do not at all see why we should have thousands upon thousands of people, capable of productive labour, drawn into such work as the publication of the *Novoie Vremia*, the *Malenkaia Gazeta*, the *Russkaia Volia* and similar reptile papers.

What have you done to fight the counter-revolutionary press that is making every effort to arouse the people against our party? Nothing! You yourselves have supplied that press with material for their baiting. You have been busy fighting the Left peril.

You are reaping what you have sown, gentlemen.

So it was, so it shall be—as long as you continue to vacillate between the position of the bourgeoisie and the position of the revolutionary proletariat.

Pravda, No. 84, June 30, 1917.

A QUEER DISTORTION OF QUOTATIONS

The newspapers *Dien* and *Novaia Zhizn*, which have published a more detailed report of the conclusions of the investigating commission,[260] have quoted a part of my testimony not mentioned by the *Birzhevka* which in certain respects has published an even more complete report of the conclusions.

In both of the first-mentioned papers there is a quotation from my testimony which begins with the words: "I do not believe that work of provocateurs is involved here." There is no interpunction before the quotation. The result is sheer nonsense, for it gives the impression that it is at the present moment that "I do not believe."

Only an extremely queer distortion of the quotation by both papers could result in such nonsense. In fact, what I testified was the following: "I personally on numerous occasions (up to the discovery that Malinovsky was a provocateur) reasoned thus: after the Azef case nothing can surprise me. But I do not believe that work of provocateurs is involved here, not only because I do not see any evidence, any proof, but also because" (and further, the quotation is the same as in the *Dien:* if Malinovsky were a provocateur, the secret police would not gain as much as it has counted on, for we have conducted everything through two legal agencies, etc.).

Thus, in my testimony I was speaking of the past. The *Dien* and *Novaia Zhizn* * by a queer distortion of the quotation have attributed to me the absurdity, as though I spoke of the present.

The result is something entirely contradictory to what I actually said.

N. Lenin.

Pravda, No. 84, June 30, 1917.

---

* Both papers contain another misprint: "The Bolsheviks will *not* organise an armed insurrection." The word *not* should be omitted.

264

PROSECUTE RODZIANKO AND DZHUNKOVSKY FOR CONCEALING A PROVOCATEUR!

FROM the conclusions reached by the investigating commission in the case of the provocateur Malinovsky, it is obvious that the following has been established to be the fact:

Both Dzhunkovsky and Rodzianko had discovered as early as May 20, 1914, that Malinovsky was a provocateur.[261]

Neither one of these political leaders warned any of the political parties represented in the Duma, and chiefly the Bolsheviks, of the fact that there was a provocateur in their midst!

Is this not a crime?

After this, can Dzhunkovsky and Rodzianko be tolerated among blameless citizens?

Let every political party think of it, express itself about it!

Pravda, No. 84, June 30, 1917.

ANOTHER COMMISSION

ECONOMIC disintegration has begun. The bourgeoisie is carrying on an offensive along the entire front. Decisive measures are
imperative.

What does the Provisional Government intend to do?

In order to save Russia, in order to carry on the struggle against
economic disintegration, in order to build up our economic life,
the government has worked out a project for a new organisation,
a detailed plan for the struggle against economic ruin.

At the head of this business of "organising the nation's economy
and labour" it places an Economic Council.

At last measures are being taken, and from words we are passing
to deeds. Excellent, it should have been done long ago!

But what is the composition of this Economic Council?

Who is going to conduct the fight against economic ruin, who is
going to carry on the struggle against the economic policy of the
capitalists, the employers, the shop and factory owners?

It appears that the overwhelming majority in this Council will
consist of capitalists. Is this not a mockery?

Here is the composition of this worthy institution:

Bourgeois Ministers	6
Representatives of the capitalists (bank council, stock exchange, agri-culture, etc.)	9
TOTAL	15
From the workers (Soviet of Workers' and Soldiers' Deputies)	3
From trade unions	3
From the Peasant Deputies	3
TOTAL	9

The membership further includes the Ministers of War and of
Labour, and three representatives of the co-operatives.

As will be seen, it is the capitalists who will decide matters.

Another institution is to be created which under the best of circumstances will be absolutely useless.

266

Furthermore, in accordance with the usual practice, there will be created countless commissions, subcommissions, committees, etc.

This is the way they intend to carry on the struggle against economic disintegration.

The shark has been thrown into the river. . . .

Pravda, No. 85, July 1, 1917.

THE FIRST OF JULY

REGARDLESS of anything, the first of July will be written in the annals of the Russian Revolution as one of the critical days.[262]

The relative position of the classes, their relation towards each other in the struggle, their strength, particularly as compared with the strength of the party,—all this was revealed so distinctly, so strikingly, so convincingly by the Sunday demonstration, that whatever the pace, whatever the tempo of the further development of the revolution, the gain in clarity and understanding is tremendous.

The demonstration has in a few hours scattered like a handful of dust the vapid talk about Bolshevik conspirators and has shown with incontestable obviousness that the vanguard of the toiling masses of Russia, the industrial proletariat and the army in the capital, stands in an overwhelming majority for the slogans that have always been defended by our party.

The measured step of the workers' and soldiers' battalions. Some half million participants in the demonstration. The unity of the forceful offensive, the unity around the slogans, among which "All Power to the Soviets," "Down with the Ten Capitalist Ministers," "Neither Separate Peace with the Germans, nor Secret Treaties with the Anglo-French Capitalists," etc., were predominant. No one who saw the demonstration has any doubt that these slogans have gained the upper hand among the organised vanguard of the worker and soldier masses of Russia.

The demonstration of July first became a demonstration of the strength and the policies of the revolutionary proletariat which is giving direction to the revolution, and is showing the way out of the blind alley. Therein lies the colossal historical significance of the Sunday demonstration, and therein does it differ in principle from the demonstrations which took place on the day of the funeral of the victims of the revolution, or from those held on the first of May. Then it was a universal tribute to the first victory of the revolution and its heroes, a glance backward, cast by the people over the first lap of the road to freedom and passed by them most quickly and most successfully. The first of May was a *holiday* of good wishes and hopes bound up with the history of the labour movement of the world, with its ideal of peace and Socialism.

Neither of the demonstrations aimed at pointing out the direction of the further advance of the revolution. Neither could point out that direction. Neither the first nor the second demonstration had placed before the masses, and in the name of the masses, any concrete and definite questions of the hour, questions as to whither and how the revolution must proceed.

In this sense the first of July was the first political demonstration of *action*; it was an exposition of issues not in a book nor in a newspaper, but in the street; not through leaders, but through the masses. It showed how the various classes act, wish to act, and should act, to further the revolution.

The bourgeoisie had hidden itself. The bourgeoisie refused to participate in a peaceful demonstration arranged by an admitted majority of the people, with freedom for all party slogans, with combating counter-revolution as the chief aim. This can be easily understood. The bourgeoisie is the counter-revolution. It hides from the people; it organises actual counter-revolutionary conspiracies against the people. The parties which are ruling Russia at the present moment, the Socialist-Revolutionist and Menshevik parties, clearly showed themselves on the historic day of July first to be parties of indecision. Their slogans were expressive of vacillation, and their slogans proved—clearly and obviously to all— to be a minority. To remain where they are, to leave everything unchanged,—this is what they advised the people with their slogans and their hesitation. And the people felt, as they themselves felt, that that was impossible.

Enough of hesitation—said the vanguard of the proletariat, the vanguard of the worker and soldier masses of Russia. Enough of hesitation. The policy of faith in the capitalists, in *their* government, in *their* reformist exertions, in *their* war, in *their* offensive,— this policy is hopeless. Its collapse is near. Its collapse is inevitable. It will be the collapse of the ruling parties, the Socialists-Revolutionists and the Mensheviks as well. Economic ruin is imminent. There is no escape from it except by revolutionary measures undertaken by a revolutionary class standing at the helm.

Let the people break with the policy of confidence in the capitalists, let it show confidence in the revolutionary class—the proletariat. It alone is the source of power. It alone is sure to serve the interests of the *majority*, the interests of the toilers and the exploited, of those crushed by war and capital, of those capable of winning a victory over war and capital!

A crisis of unheard-of dimensions is descending upon Russia and the whole of humanity. The only escape is in placing confidence in the most organised vanguard of the toilers and the exploited, in the support of its policy.

Whether the people will soon realise this, and how well they will apply this knowledge in actual life, we do not know. But what we do know is that outside of this there is no escape from the blind alley, that possible hesitations or brutality will avail the counter-revolutionists nothing.

There is no way out except in the complete faith of the masses of the people in their leader, the proletariat.

Pravda, No. 86, July 3, 1917.

THE REVOLUTION, THE OFFENSIVE, AND OUR PARTY

TSERETELI, in informing the Congress of the Soviets of the beginning of the offensive,[263] said: "The turning point of the Russian
Revolution has been reached." Indeed, the turning point not only
of the Russian Revolution, but also of the whole development of
the World War, has been reached. The Russian Government, after
three months of hesitation, has actually come to the decision which
the "Allied" governments have been demanding.

The offensive has been declared in the name of peace. But it is
"in the name of peace" that the imperialists of all countries are
throwing armies into battle; at each offensive, in each of the warring countries, the generals try to raise the spirit of the soldiers
by holding out the refreshing hope that that offensive will most
speedily bring peace.

This usual method of the imperialists has been embellished by
the Russian "Socialist" Ministers with high sounding phrases, in
which words about Socialism, democracy, and revolution sound like
rattles in the hands of an adroit juggler. No crackling phrases can
hide the fact that the revolutionary armies of Russia are sent into
battle to achieve the imperialist aims of England, France, Italy,
Japan, and America. No sophisms of the former Zimmerwaldist
and present partner of Lloyd George, Chernov, can hide the fact
that even though the Russian army and the Russian proletariat do
not actually have any annexationist aims, the imperialist predatory
character of the struggle between two world trusts is not in the
least changed by this. So long as the secret treaties binding Russia
to the imperialists of other countries have not been revised, so long
as Ribot, Lloyd George and Sonnino, allies of Russia, continue to
talk about the annexationist aims of their foreign policy, the offensive of the Russian armies is and remains an aid to the imperialists.

But, object Tsereteli and Chernov, we have repeatedly declared
that we renounce any sort of annexation. So much the worse, say
we; this means that your deeds do not square with your words, for
in your deeds you serve Russian, as well as foreign, imperialism.
And when you begin to co-operate actively with "Allied" imperial-

ism, you render splendid service to the Russian counter-revolution. The joy of all the Black Hundreds and all the counter-revolutionists over the decisive turn in your policy, is the best corroboration of this fact. Indeed, the Russian Revolution is passing through the turning point. The Russian Government, through its "Socialist" Ministers, has done something which the imperialist Ministers, Guchkov and Miliukov, could not do. It has placed the Russian army at the disposal of the general staffs and the diplomats who act in the name and on the basis of the unabrogated secret treaties, to gain the objectives frankly proclaimed by Ribot and Lloyd George. The government has been able to fulfill its task only because the army has trusted and followed it. The army has marched to death, believing that it is making sacrifices for the sake of freedom, for the sake of the revolution, for the sake of an early peace. But the army has done it only because it is a part of the people, which at this stage of the revolution is following the parties of the Socialists-Revolutionists and the Mensheviks. This general and basic fact—the confidence of the majority in the petty-bourgeois policy of the Mensheviks and the Socialists-Revolutionists which is dependent upon the capitalists,—determines the stand and the conduct of our party.

With unflagging energy we shall continue to expose the policy of the government, resolutely warning the workers and the soldiers, as in the past, against their absurd faith in uncoordinated and disorganised action.

It is a phase of the people's revolution that we are now passing. The Tseretelis and the Chernovs, having become dependent upon imperialism, are carrying into effect a phase of petty-bourgeois illusions, of petty-bourgeois phrases, under which is hidden the same cynical imperialism.

This phase must be brought to an end. Let us help bring it to an end as speedily and as painlessly as possible. This will rid the people of the last petty-bourgeois illusions and bring about the transfer of power to the revolutionary class.

Pravda, No. 87, July 4, 1917.

WHEREIN DO YOU DIFFER FROM PLEKHANOV, MESSRS. SOCIALISTS-REVOLUTIONISTS AND MENSHEVIKS?

THE *Dielo Naroda* has repeatedly declared the *Yedinstvo* to be social-imperialist. The *Rabochaia Gazeta* has officially condemned the election bloc with the *Yedinstvo* (after the elections had taken place to almost all the Borough Councils).

The offensive now begun dissipates the mist of phrases and shows the people the unadorned truth. Every one sees that in the earnest and practical question of the offensive, Plekhanov and the Menshevik and Socialist-Revolutionist leaders *are as one*.

It means then that you are all "social-imperialists" (using the expression of the *Dielo Naroda*), all of you—the *Yedinstvo*, Kerensky and Chernov, Tsereteli and Skobelev.

Pravda, No. 87, July 4, 1917.

WHITHER HAVE THE SOCIALISTS-REVOLUTIONISTS AND THE MENSHEVIKS BROUGHT THE REVOLUTION?

THEY have brought it to surrender to the imperialists.

The offensive is a renewal of the imperialist war. Nothing has essentially changed in the mutual relations of the two gigantic capitalist combines, now at war with each other. Even after the revolution of March 12, Russia has remained under the powerful sway of the capitalists who are bound by an alliance and by the former tsarist secret treaties with Anglo-French imperialist capital. The economics and the politics of the continued war are the same as before: the same imperialist bank capital reigns in economic life; the same secret treaties, the same foreign policy of one group of imperialists combined against another group of imperialists.

The phrases of the Mensheviks and the Socialists-Revolutionists remain phrases which in point of fact only place a sugar coating over the bitter pill of renewed imperialist warfare that most naturally meets with an ecstatic howl of approval on the part of all the counter-revolutionists, the entire bourgeoisie, and Plekhanov who "like a little rooster hops after the bourgeois press," to use an expression of the Menshevik *Rabochaia Gazeta* which, itself, hops after the motley crew of social-chauvinists.

One must not forget, however, the peculiar distinctive features of the present resumption of the imperialist war. The resumption has been made after three months of hesitation, during which months the worker and peasant masses expressed a thousand times their condemnation of a war of annexations (but all the while continuing to support the government of the annexationist and predatory Russian bourgeoisie). The masses were hesitating, as if making ready to carry out *at home* the advice given to foreign peoples in the proclamation of March 27, addressed to all the peoples of the world: "Refuse to serve as tools of annexation and violence in the hands of the bankers." But what happened is that here at home in "revolutionary and democratic" Russia, the masses have themselves remained tools of annexation and violence "in the hands of the bankers."

274

The uniqueness of this situation lies in the fact that it has been created by the parties of the Socialists-Revolutionists and Mensheviks themselves under conditions of comparatively great freedom for the organisation of the masses. It is these parties that at the present time command a majority. The All-Russian Congress of Soviets and the All-Russian Peasant Soviet have proved it beyond doubt.

It is these parties that are now responsible for the policy of Russia.

It is these parties that are responsible for the renewal of the imperialist war, for the new hundreds of thousands of victims actually sacrificed in order that one group of capitalists may overcome another group of capitalists, and for the new sharpening of the economic crisis which inevitably will follow the offensive.

We have here a classic example of the self-deception of the petty-bourgeois masses, and their deception by the bourgeoisie with the aid of the Socialists-Revolutionists and the Mensheviks. In words both these parties are "revolutionary democracy." In reality, it is precisely they who have entrusted the destinies of the people to the counter-revolutionary bourgeoisie, the Cadets; it is precisely they who have deserted the revolution, and joined the ranks of those who stand for the continuation of the imperialist war; have deserted democracy and made "concessions" to the Cadets in the question of power (take for instance the "confirmation" from above of officials elected by the local population); in the question of land (renunciation by the Mensheviks and the Socialists-Revolutionists of their own programme, which promises support to the revolutionary actions of the peasants, including the confiscation of landowners' estates); in the question of nationalities (defence of the undemocratic attitude of the Cadets towards the Ukraine and Finland).

The petty-bourgeois masses cannot but vacillate between the bourgeoisie and the proletariat. So it was in all countries, particularly in the years 1789-1871. So it is now in Russia. The Mensheviks and the Socialists-Revolutionists have led the masses to adopt the policy of the counter-revolutionary bourgeoisie.

This is the essence of the situation. Herein lies the significance of the offensive. Herein is its uniqueness: not force but confidence in the Socialists-Revolutionists and the Mensheviks has led the people astray.

For how long?

Not for long. The masses will learn by their own experience. The sad experience with the new (just now begun) phase of the war, with the new crisis, made more acute by the offensive, will inevitably lead to a political downfall of the Socialist-Revolutionist and the Menshevik parties. The immediate task confronting the proletarian party is to help the masses realise and make proper use of this experience, to prepare properly for this great crash, which will reveal to the masses their real leader—the organised city proletariat.

Pravda, No. 88, July 5, 1917.

CAN "JACOBINISM" FRIGHTEN THE WORKING CLASS?

THE organ of "Socialist thought" (no jesting!), the bourgeois and chauvinist *Dien*, returns to the really interesting editorial of the *Riech* for July 1.²⁶⁴ The *Dien* has completely failed to understand that editorial, in which the historian alongside of the angered counter-revolutionary bourgeois takes the floor. The *Dien* reads into the editorial the "firm" and settled determination of the Cadets to withdraw from the "coalition government."

That is nonsense. The Cadets threaten in order to frighten the Tseretelis and the Chernovs. That is not serious.

What is serious and interesting is how the editorial writer of the *Riech* on July 1 approached the question of power from an historian's standpoint.

If, he writes, under the former composition of the government it was possible at least to some extent to direct the course of the Russian Revolution, now, apparently, it is destined to develop in accordance with the elemental laws of all revolutions. . . . The question of the uselessness of the further existence of a government combination that has not justified itself is already being advanced not only by the Bolsheviks (note this: *not* only by the Bolsheviks!) . . . and not only by the majority in the Soviet. . . . The question must be taken up also by the capitalist Ministers themselves.

It is a true admission by an historian that not only the Bolsheviks, but the entire interrelation of classes, the life of society as a whole, has brought to the fore the question of "the uselessness of the further existence of a government combination that has not justified itself." What we have now is vacillation. The offensive is a possible road to victory by the imperialist bourgeoisie. Is there any other possible road?

The historian on the *Riech* thus answers this question:

If they seize "all power," the Soviets will soon learn that they have very little power. And they will have to make up for the lack of power by resorting to the historically well-known methods of the Young Turks and the Jacobins. . . . Will they, having raised the whole issue anew, be willing to sink to Jacobinism and terror, or will they make an effort to wash their hands of the whole matter? This is the question of the hour that must be settled in a few days.

277

The historian is right. Whether in a few days or not, it is indeed very soon that this question will be settled. *Either* the offensive, a turn to counter-revolution, a success (for how long?) of the imperialist bourgeoisie, "washing of hands" by the Chernovs and the Tseretelis, or—"Jacobinism." The bourgeois historians see in Jacobinism a downfall (to "sink"). The proletarian historians regard Jacobinism as the greatest expression of an oppressed class in its struggle for liberation. The Jacobins gave France the best models of a democratic revolution; they repelled in an exemplary fashion the coalition of monarchs formed against the republic. The Jacobins were not destined to win a complete victory, chiefly because eighteenth century France was surrounded on the continent by countries that were too backward, and also because France itself was not possessed of the material requisites for Socialism, since there were no banks, no capitalist syndicates, no machine industry, no railroads.

"Jacobinism" in Europe or on the boundary line between Europe and Asia in the twentieth century would be the rule of the revolutionary class, of the proletariat, which, supported by the poorest peasants and relying on the presence of the material requisites for an advance towards Socialism, could not only achieve the same great, ineradicable, unforgettable things that were achieved by the Jacobins of the eighteenth century, but could also lead to a permanent triumph of the toilers on a universal scale.

It is natural for the bourgeoisie to hate Jacobinism. It is natural for the petty bourgeoisie to fear it. The class-conscious workers and toilers have faith in the transfer of power to the revolutionary oppressed class, for *that* is the essence of Jacobinism, and it is the only escape from the present crisis, the only way of stopping economic disintegration and the war.

Pravda, No. 90, July 7, 1917.

ON THE NEED OF ESTABLISHING A UNION OF AGRICULTURAL WORKERS IN RUSSIA

I

THERE is one exceedingly important question that must be put before the present All-Russian Conference of Trade Unions in Petrograd.[265]   It is the question of establishing an All-Russian Union of Agricultural Workers.

Every class in Russia is organising.   Yet the class that is exploited more than any other class, that is poorer, more divided, and more crushed than any other—the class of agricultural wage workers—has, it seems, been overlooked.   In some outlying non-Russian regions, in the Lettish region, for instance, they do have organisations of agricultural wage workers.   In the great majority of Great-Russian and Ukrainian provinces there are no such class organisations of the village proletariat.

It is the bounden duty of the vanguard of the Russian proletariat, the trade unions of industrial workers, to come to the aid of their brothers, the village workers.   The difficulties in organising the village workers are enormous—this is obvious; it is also confirmed by the experience of all the capitalist countries.

All the more necessary is it for us, therefore, to avail ourselves of the political freedom now existing in Russia, and to begin, directly, most speedily and energetically, to organise an all-Russian union of village workers.   The Conference of trade unions is the body that can and must do it.   The most experienced, the most educated, the most class-conscious representatives of the proletariat, now attending the Conference, are the ones who can and must issue a call to the agricultural workers in the villages inviting them to join the ranks of the independently organised proletariat, the ranks of their trade unions.   The factory wage workers are the ones to take the initiative in utilising the nuclei, groups, and branches of trade unions, scattered all over Russia, for the awakening of the agricultural worker to an independent life, to an active participation in the struggle for the betterment of his condition, and to the defence of his class interests.

279

Many will think, perhaps, and this may even be the prevailing opinion at the present moment, that just now, when the peasants are organising all over Russia, proclaiming the abolition of private ownership of land, and the "equalising" of its use, the forming of a trade union of agricultural workers is untimely.

On the contrary. It is precisely during such a period that an organisation of this sort is particularly timely and absolutely necessary. Those who hold to the class position of the proletariat cannot doubt the soundness of the proposition introduced by the Bolsheviks and adopted also by the Mensheviks at the Stockholm Congress of the Russian Social-Democratic Labour Party, in 1906, and incorporated since then in the programme of the Russian Social-Democratic Labour Party. That proposition reads:

> Under all circumstances, and under whatever conditions the democratic agrarian reform may occur, the party will unswervingly strive for an independent class organisation of the rural proletariat, it will endeavour to disclose to it the irreconcilable conflict between its interests and those of the peasant-bourgeoisie, to warn it against the seduction of the petty economy system which, as long as commodity-production exists, can never eliminate the poverty of the masses, and, finally, to reveal to it the need for a complete Socialist overturn, as the only way of abolishing all poverty and all exploitation.

There is not a class-conscious worker, not a member of a trade union, who would not admit the soundness of these propositions. Their practical realisation, in so far as the *independent class organisation of the village proletariat* is concerned—is the proper business of the trade unions.

We feel that it is precisely in revolutionary times, when among the toiling masses generally, and among the workers particularly, the tendency to assert oneself, to make a way for oneself, is so powerful, when the workers are so determined not to permit the establishment of a new order of life unless they themselves, independently, settle all questions involving labour,—that it is precisely at such a time that the trade unions will not limit themselves to their narrow craft interests, will not forget their weaker brothers, the agricultural labourers, and will make every effort to come to the latter's aid by organising the Union of Agricultural Workers of Russia.

In the following article we shall endeavour to indicate a few practical steps in this direction.

II

In the previous article we dwelt on the principle involved in the question of a union of agricultural workers in Russia. We shall now touch upon some practical aspects of this question.

The union of agricultural workers in Russia comprises every one who is exclusively, or mainly, or even partly, engaged as a hired worker in any agricultural enterprise.

Experience will show whether or not such unions must be subdivided into parallel organisations such as unions of pure agricultural workers and unions of workers who are only partly engaged in wage labour. This is, after all, not so essential. The essential thing is that the fundamental class interests of everybody who sells his labour power are alike; and that the welding together of all those who earn even a part of their livelihood by hiring themselves out to others is absolutely necessary.

The wage workers in the city, in the shops and the factories, are bound by thousands and millions of ties with the wage workers in the village. The call of the former to the latter cannot but find a response. The mere issuance of a call, however, is not enough. The urban worker is possessed of much more experience, knowledge, ability, and strength. A part of this strength must be directly devoted to helping and elevating the agricultural worker.

A day must be set, the earnings of which the organised workers will contribute toward developing and strengthening the cause of uniting the urban and rural workers. Let a certain part of this sum be given as the contribution of the city workers to the cause of unionising the rural worker. Let a part of this fund be used to cover the expense of publishing a series of very popular leaflets, of starting at least one weekly agricultural workers' paper, of sending at least a small number of agitators and organisers into the village for the immediate establishment of unions of agricultural wage workers in various localities.

Only experience will indicate to such unions the true path of further development. The first task of every such union must be to better the living conditions, to obtain higher wages, better housing, better food, etc., for all those who sell their labour power to agricultural enterprises.

We must start a determined struggle against the wrong idea that the impending abolition of private property in land is likely to "give" land to every agricultural worker and farm-hand, and is thus likely to undermine the very foundation of hired labour in agriculture. This is a wrong and extremely harmful idea. The abolition of private property in land is an enormous and unquestionably progressive reform, a reform absolutely conducive to economic development and to the enhancement of proletarian interests, a reform which every wage worker will support with all his might and main, yet a reform that does not in the least eliminate hired labour.

You cannot eat land. You cannot cultivate land without live stock, implements and seeds, without a reserve of goods and money. To rely on "promises," whatever their source, that the hired workers in the villages will be helped in obtaining live stock, implements, etc.,—would be the worst kind of a delusion, unpardonable naïveté.

The basic rule, the first commandment of any trade-union movement must be: Do not rely on the "state," rely only on the *strength of your class.* The state is the organisation of the ruling class.

Do not rely on promises; rely only on the unifying power and on the class-consciousness of the workers.

The immediate task of the trade union of agricultural workers must therefore be not only to struggle for the general improvement of the lot of the workers, but also, and mainly, to defend their *interests,* their *class interests,* when the great land reform is being instituted.

"Farm-hands must be subject to the management of the Volost Committees," is often heard from the peasants and the Socialists-Revolutionists. The point of view of the class of agricultural wage workers is just the opposite: the Volost Committees must be subject to the management of the "hands"! By calling attention to this contrast, we can clearly see the difference between the employer's and the employé's positions.

"The land must belong to the entire people." This is correct. But the people is divided into classes. Every worker knows, sees, feels, experiences this truth, a truth deliberately covered up by the bourgeoisie, and *perpetually forgotten by the petty bourgeoisie.*

No one will help the poor men as individuals. No "state" will help the village wage worker, the farm-hand, the day labourer, the poorest peasant, the semi-proletarian, unless he helps himself. And his first step must be an independent class organisation of the village proletariat.

NEED OF A UNION OF AGRICULTURAL WORKERS 283

Let us hope that the All-Russian Conference of Trade Unions will most energetically devote itself to this cause, will issue its call throughout Russia, will extend a helping hand, the mighty hand of the organised vanguard of the proletarians, to the proletarians in the village.

N. LENIN.

Pravda, Nos. 90 and 91, July 7 and 8, 1917.

A FLOUNDERING REVOLUTION

"THE Bolsheviks are responsible for everything"—this is agreed upon both by the Cadets who direct the counter-revolution, and by the Socialists-Revolutionists and the Mensheviks who call themselves "revolutionary democracy," probably because of the daily departures by this worthy bloc from principles of democracy and revolution.

"The Bolsheviks are responsible for everything"—for the growing disorganisation to check which nothing is being done, for the bad state of affairs in the matter of supplies, and for the "failure" of the Provisional Government with regard to the Ukraine and Finland. Really, one might imagine that a malicious Bolshevik had wormed his way into the midst of the modest, moderate, cautious Finns and "confused" the whole people!

The universal howl of anger and fury against the Bolsheviks, the odious campaign of vilification carried on by the odious gentlemen, the Zaslavskys and the anonymous writers in the *Riech* and the *Rabochaia Gazeta,*—all this is inevitable with representatives of a floundering revolution who, because of their many failures, seek to vent their anger on some one.

The Cadets are the party of the counter-revolutionary bourgeoisie. This has been admitted by the bloc of the Socialists-Revolutionists and the Mensheviks which is ruling Russia and which has declared in a resolution passed by the Congress of Soviets that the resistance of the propertied class grows and constitutes the basis of the counter-revolution. Yet at the same time, this bloc, daily accused by the *Riech* of lack of character, is in its turn combined in a bloc with the Cadets, in a most original bloc at that, as fixed by the composition of the Provisional Government!

Russia is ruled by two blocs: the bloc of the Socialists-Revolutionists with the Mensheviks, and the bloc of that bloc with the Cadets, who in their turn are in a bloc with all those political parties who are to the Right of them. A floundering revolution is the inevitable result. For all the parts of this ruling "bloc of blocs" are floundering.

The Cadets themselves have no faith in their own republicanism, not to speak of the Octobrists and the monarchists of the other colours that are hiding behind the Cadets and voting for them. The Cadets have no faith in the "social-blocists," though willingly using their Ministers as errand boys for all kinds of "pacification,"—at the same time they hiss in anger and indignation at the "excessive demands" of that mass of peasants and party of workers which has now entrusted itself to the Socialists-Revolutionists and Mensheviks in response to their glorious promises ("to satisfy the toilers without offending the capitalists"), but which has the impudence to expect and demand the actual fulfillment of these promises!

The social-blocists have no faith in each other: The Socialists-Revolutionists have no faith in the Mensheviks, and conversely. So far not one "better half" has dared to come out officially and to declare clearly and frankly, how, why, in the name of what principle, and to what extent the followers of Struve-construed "Marxism" and the followers of the "right to the land" doctrine have combined. The unity, even within each of the two "better halves," is ripping at the seams: the Congress of the Socialists-Revolutionists voted down Kerensky by a vote of 136 to 134, which event caused the withdrawal of the "Grandmother" * herself from the Central Committee, and the issuance of a statement by the Central Committee that Kerensky was not elected only because he is overburdened (unlike Chernov) with ministerial duties.[266] The "Right" Socialists-Revolutionists in the *Volia Naroda* denounce their party and its congress, the Lefts are finding refuge in the *Zemlia i Volia*, and dare to maintain that the masses do not want war and continue to regard it as imperialistic.

The Right Mensheviks have migrated to the *Dien*, headed by Potresov, at whom "love's caressing glances" are cast by the *Yedinstvo* itself (which only recently, during the Petrograd elections, was in bloc with the whole Menshevik party). The Left wing is in sympathy with internationalism and is founding its own paper. A bloc of the banks and the Potresovs in the *Dien*, a bloc of all the Mensheviks, including Potresov and Martov, in a "united" Menshevik party.

Floundering of the worst kind, indeed.

"Defencism" ill-conceals this floundering state of the revolution,

* Catherine Breshkovsky.—*Ed.*

for even now, even after the resumption of the imperialist war, even in the midst of the present ecstasy called forth by the offensive, the "offensive" of Potresov's followers upon his opponents belonging to the same bloc, the attacks of Kerensky's followers upon his opponents within the other bloc have become more savage than ever.

"Revolutionary democracy" no longer has any faith in the revolution; it is afraid of democracy, it fears more than anything else a breach with Anglo-French capitalists, and it fears the displeasure of the Russian capitalists. ("Our revolution is a bourgeois revolution,"—Minister Chernov "himself" has come to believe in this "truth" so amusingly distorted by Dan, Tsereteli, and Skobelev.) The Cadets hate the revolution and democracy.

A floundering revolution, indeed.

The universal savage howl of anger and fury against the Bolsheviks is really the common complaint of the Cadets, the Socialists-Revolutionists and the Mensheviks about their own lack of cohesion and strength.

They are in the majority. They are in power. They are in alliance with one another. And they see that nothing comes of their efforts!! How can they help raging against the Bolsheviks?

The revolution has brought to the fore problems of unusual difficulty, of colossal importance, of world-wide scope. It is impossible to check the spreading economic disintegration, or to free ourselves from the horrible claws of the imperialist war, unless one resorts to most resolute revolutionary measures, calculated to arouse the unbounded heroism of the oppressed and the exploited masses,—unless the masses give their confidence and support to its organised vanguard, the proletariat.

Until now the masses have been trying out an "easier" escape: namely, the bloc of the Cadets with the bloc of the Socialists-Revolutionists and the Mensheviks.

But no escape has been found.   •

Pravda, No. 91, July 8, 1917.

WHY WE MUST CONTROL PRODUCTION

CONCERNING CAPITALISTS' INCOMES AND WORKERS' EARNINGS

NOWADAYS one hears everywhere complaints from the manufacturers, the industrialists, the professors, the former Cadet Ministers, the Kutlers, and generally from all those "high class" people who reside in the rich sections of the city, that the workers have become spoiled, that they are earning more than their employers, that they are demanding the impossible, that owing to the excessive demands of the workers, the manufacturers are forced to shut down their shops and factories, and so on, without end. In short, they are trying to prove that the ones responsible for the industrial crisis and for the disorganisation of supplies that is bound to follow that crisis, are not the employers, not those who either hand-in-hand and in full agreement with the old Romanov gang, or independently, have until now been lording it over the land, but rather those who until now could neither do anything, nor even say anything without receiving for it imprisonment or other punishments. This is why I wish to present a few facts, or rather figures, from which the reader can see for himself how our capitalists are being ruined and how the workers are growing rich.

We have before us the 1916 report of the Kolomna Machine Construction Company, published in the *Riech* of May 31. On an invested capital of 15 million rubles, together with 482,500 rubles of borrowed capital (*i. e.,* capital secured from other capitalists and bankers) a total profit of 7,482,832.35 rubles, *i. e.,* about 50 per cent (48.33 per cent) has been made within one year. This means that the capitalists, without as much as lifting a finger, have been making a profit of fifty kopecks on each invested ruble.

To grasp the enormity of this profit, we must remember that the banks pay no more than from 4 to 6 kopecks on the ruble per year, that state loans (when the state treasury borrows money from domestic or foreign capitalists) yielding 5.5 kopecks on the ruble per year are considered most profitable, and the capitalists gladly put their money into such loans.

True, the capitalists of the Kolomna Machine Construction Com-

287

pany have not divided the entire profit among themselves; they have taken for themselves about sixteen kopecks (15.6) per ruble. But even this interest is three times as large as that paid by banks or governments on state loans. What, then, have they done with the rest of the money? Have they, perchance, distributed it among the factory employés in view of the rise in the cost of living? No, not at all! They put aside 3,104,195.36 rubles for the amortisation fund, 900,000 rubles for improvements in the plant, 515,138.50 rubles for compensation to the members of the board, to the half-dozen capitalists who are running the business, etc., etc.

True, property is subject to wear: with time machines do become dilapidated and finally have to be replaced by new ones. This certainly must be taken into account; but let us see how the capitalists do their accounting.

The original capital invested in this plant was 15,000,000 rubles plus 482,500 rubles in bonds sold to other capitalists. Altogether, we have 15,482,500 rubles. This capital has not been increased any more, the capitalist proprietors of the plant have not taken any money from their pockets to add to this capital. Yet, the amortisation fund which is formed through yearly deductions from the profits, already amounts, without the 1916 addition, to 15,017,-158.39 rubles. But there is other capital also accumulated through yearly deductions from the profits. There is a reserve capital of 3,882,952.97 rubles; there is a special fund of 360,000 rubles at the disposal of the shareholders; there is surplus capital amounting to 508,870.06 rubles. If we add all these sums, the total will be 19,768,981.42 rubles. Add to this the sum put aside in 1916,—4,004,195.36 rubles, and the total will be 23,772,176.78 rubles.

Thus capital formed from yearly deductions from the profits is over one and one-half times (154 per cent) larger than the original capital invested by the capitalists in their enterprise. This means that, besides the large profits they have been making yearly, every ruble of their original investment was increased by an additional 1.54 ruble. The shares of each capitalist have become two and a half times greater than their original value. If the present shareholders determine to increase the invested capital, and issue new shares, they will, as is usually done in such cases, set a price of 250 rubles on each 100-ruble share.

But one may think that this is an exceptional case, that this is a metal plant working for the "defence," having government orders;

and government orders are profitable to such plants. That our manufacturers wax rich on the "defence" of the country is true; but neither do the other capitalists prosper any less than our capitalist-"defencists": they are all "saving the country" quite efficiently and are all pressing their "victory to the end."

We have before us another 1916 report, that of the Volga Insurance Company. Original capital, 1,000,000 rubles; profit, 1,657,161.55 rubles which makes about 1.66 rubles (165.7 per cent) of profit on every ruble invested. After all the deductions have been taken care of, the shareholders divided amongst themselves (received as dividends) 400,000 rubles, i. e., 40 kopecks (40 per cent) on each ruble of the original investment, while the remainder of 28,735.26 rubles was kept to be accounted in the next year's profits.

This company has no property that can be depreciated and has to be replaced. That is why it has no amortisation fund. But it has a reserve capital composed of yearly deductions from the profits. Up to this year the reserve capital was 365,533.92 rubles; adding to this this year's quota of 281,672.06 rubles, we have 647,225.93 rubles. And when we add to the above the surplus capital of 106,156.18 rubles plus the remainder of the profits left for the next year, we have 782,117.37 rubles, which constitutes 78.21 per cent of the original capital. Thus we see in this report, too, a case where the capitalists, in addition to their large (40 per cent) yearly profits, have their original capital almost doubled, in various forms.

Such reports can be cited without end from various branches of industry, insurance, steamship, transportation, and other companies, banking, etc. But there is another indicator whereby we can judge how good or bad is the business of our manufacturers and bankers.

When business is bad and profits on various enterprises are not large, the capitalists try not to put more money into these enterprises; they look for more profitable places where to invest their money. Do they behave so now?

On April 11, at the general meeting of the shareholders of the same Volga Insurance Company, it was decided to "work for a permission" to raise the capital stock of the company to 4,000,000 rubles, i. e., to quadruple it. The same is taking place in many other corporations: the cement company Asserin is issuing 50,000 new shares valued at 5,000,000 rubles; the machine and pipe plant Promet—

20,000 new shares, 2,000,000 rubles; the chemical products plant Dembor—15,000 shares, 1,500,000 rubles; the Bokov Crystal Anthracite Mines—60,000 new shares, 6,000,000 rubles; the Northern Mechanical Plants of Petrograd—40,000 shares, 4,000,000 rubles; the Petrograd railway car works—140,000 new shares, 14,000,000 rubles; the rubber plant Bogatyr—75,000 shares with a face value of 100 rubles each, 7,500,000 rubles in total, while the price per share is 180 rubles, meaning that the actual total would be not 7,500,000 but 13,500,000 rubles; the Moscow Industrial Bank—40,000 shares at 250 rubles each, face value 10,000,00 rubles, market price per share 405 rubles, actual increase in capital, 16,200,000 rubles.

Thus nine different stock companies are increasing their total capital stock by 54,000,000 rubles (in reality this increase is much greater). By the size of the profits, as well as by the colossal increase in invested capital, we may see how our capitalists "are going to ruin."

Let us see now how the workers are "waxing rich." [207]

Pravda, No. 91, July 8, 1917.

MARVELS OF REVOLUTIONARY ENERGY

OUR near-Socialist Ministers are developing almost unusual energy. Peshekhonov has declared that "the resistance of the capitalists has apparently been broken" and that in Holy Russia everything we possess will be "equitably" divided. Skobelev has declared that the capitalists will have to give up one hundred per cent of their profits. Tsereteli has declared that the offensive in this imperialist war is the most righteous thing from the standpoint of democracy and Socialism.

But the record of all these manifestations of marvelous energy has been beaten, no doubt, by Minister Chernov. At the last meeting of the Provisional Government Chernov made the Cadets listen to his report on the general policy of the department entrusted to him, and declared that he intended to introduce as many as ten bills! [268]

Aren't these marvels of revolutionary energy? Six weeks have passed since the nineteenth of May, and during this short period there have been promised as many as ten bills! And what bills! The ministerial *Dielo Naroda* announces that these bills "in their totality will embrace all the fundamental aspects of the economic life of the village."

"All aspects" . . . neither more nor less. Where do they get the energy to promise so much?

There is only one thing suspicious about it: the ministerial paper devotes more than one hundred lines to an enumeration of *some* of these splendid bills, without saying anything definite about any one of them. It refers to "stopping the enforcement of certain decrees relating to the peasants" . . . but which decrees we are not told. The bill concerning the "chambers of conciliation" is the most interesting. Who shall settle differences with whom, nobody knows. On "the regulation of rent relations" we are kept in utter darkness; we do not even know whether it refers to renting the estates of the large landowners which, according to promises, were to be expropriated without compensation.

"Reform to insure the greater democratisation of the local land

291

committees." . . . Would it not be better, if you, gentlemen, au-
thors of eloquent and sweeping promises, mentioned, say, ten local
land committees and pointed out exactly their present, though post-
revolutionary, still, according to your own admission, not fully
democratic composition?

This is just the point. The seething activity of Minister Chernov,
as well as of the other above-mentioned Ministers, offers the best
illustration as to the difference between a liberal bureaucrat and
a revolutionary democrat.

The liberal bureaucrat submits to his "superiors," i. e., Messrs.
Lvov, Shingarev and Co., extensive reports concerning hundreds
of bills designed to benefit humanity and the people . . . while to
the people he serves up mere talk, glorious promises, Nozdrev *
phrases (such as 100 per cent profit, or a "Socialist" offensive at
the front, etc.)

The revolutionary democrat, simultaneously with the presentation of his report to his "superiors," or even before presenting it,
uncovers, exposes every evil, every fault before the people, thus
appealing to the active interest of the people.

Peasants, expose the landowners, expose how much they are
collecting from you in the form of "rentals," how much delay they
have caused in the "chambers of conciliation" or in the local land
committees, how much cavilling and interfering they have been
guilty of in the matter of cultivating the entire land, in the matter
of using the landowners' farm implements in order to meet the needs
of the people, particularly the poorest sections of it! You, peasants,
expose it yourselves, while I, "the Minister of revolutionary Russia,"
"the Minister of revolutionary democracy," will help you publish
all such revelations, will help remove all forms of oppression by
your pressure from the bottom and mine from the top!!! This
is how a "revolutionary democrat" would speak and act!

Nothing of the kind. Nothing of the kind. This is the language
used by the ministerial paper respecting Chernov's "report" to
Messrs. Lvov and Co. "Though he does not deny the existence of a
number of agrarian excesses in some provinces, V. M. Chernov
thinks that on the whole rural Russia has proved much more
balanced than could be expected." . . .

With regard, however, to the only clearly stated bill, "Stopping

* Nozdrev is a character in Gogol's novel, Dead Souls, notorious for gross
exaggerations.—Ed.

the sale and purchase of land," not a word is uttered as to why this bill has been held up. For the peasants have long since been promised the immediate cessation of the sale and purchase of lands. This was promised in May; still, on the eighth of July we are told in the papers that Chernov has presented a "report," and that the Provisional Government "has not yet arrived at a definite decision"!!!

Pravda, No. 92, July 10, 1917.

A SHIFTING OF CLASS POSITIONS

EVERY revolution, if it is a real revolution, reduces itself to a shifting of class positions. That is why the best method of setting the masses straight as well as of fighting those who deceive the masses by swearing in the name of the revolution, is to analyse what class positions have shifted and are shifting in the present revolution.

In 1904-1916, the relative positions of the classes in Russia in the last years of tsarism became especially clear. A handful of semi-feudal landowners, headed by Nicholas II, was in power and was closely associated with the magnates of finance capital who were reaping profits that were unheard-of in Europe and for whose benefit predatory treaties were concluded in the field of foreign relations.

The liberal bourgeoisie, headed by the Cadets, constituted the opposition. Fearing the people more than reaction, it moved closer to power by compromising with the monarchy.

The people, *i. e.*, the workers and the peasants, their leaders driven underground, were revolutionary; they constituted "revolutionary democracy," proletarian and petty-bourgeois.

The revolution of March 12, 1917, swept away the monarchy and placed the liberal bourgeoisie in power. The latter, working in direct agreement with the Anglo-French imperialists, had wished only a court revolution. Under no circumstances would it go beyond a constitutional monarchy with property qualifications for voting. And when the revolution actually advanced further, toward the complete abolition of the monarchy and the creation of Soviets (of Workers', Peasants', and Soldiers' Deputies), the liberal bourgeoisie all turned counter-revolutionary.

Now, four months after the overturn, the counter-revolutionary character of the Cadets, the main party of the liberal bourgeoisie, is as clear as day. Everybody sees this. Everybody is forced to admit it. But not nearly everybody is ready to face this truth and to ponder its meaning.

We have now in Russia a democratic republic governed by a free agreement of political parties which are freely advocating their views among the people. The four months since March 12 completely solidified and gave a definite shape to *all* more or less significant parties which appeared at the elections (to the Soviets and to local institutions) and have revealed their connections with the respective classes.

In Russia the counter-revolutionary bourgeoisie is in power now, while petty-bourgeois democracy, namely, the Socialists-Revolutionists and Mensheviks, play the rôle of "His Majesty's Opposition." In its essence the policy of these petty-bourgeois parties consists in compromising with the counter-revolutionary bourgeoisie. The petty-bourgeois democracy is rising to power by filling, first of all, the local institutions (as did the liberals in the time of tsarism by winning places in the zemstvos). This petty-bourgeois democracy wants to share power with the bourgeoisie, but not to overthrow it, exactly as the Cadets wanted to share power with the monarchy without overthrowing it. And the accord between the petty-bourgeois democracy (the Socialists-Revolutionists and the Mensheviks) and the Cadets is due to the close class-ties between the petty and the upper bourgeoisie, just as the accord between the capitalist and the landowner who were embracing each other at the feet of the "adored" monarch, in our twentieth century setting, was based on close class-ties.

Only the form of the accord has changed: During the Tsar's régime it was crude; the Tsar allowed a Cadet no further than to the backyard of the Duma. In a democratic republic the accord has become more refined in the European sense; the petty bourgeois are permitted, in a harmless minority, to occupy a few harmless (for capital) posts in the cabinet.

The Cadets have taken the place of the monarchy. The Tseretelis and the Chernovs have taken the place of the Cadets. Proletarian democracy has become real revolutionary democracy.

The imperialist war has hastened this development to an extraordinary degree. Without this war the Socialists-Revolutionists and the Mensheviks would have been sighing for decades for ministerial posts. The same war, however, is hastening the further development of the revolution. For it brings to the fore problems, not in a reformist but in a revolutionary manner.

The parties of the Socialists-Revolutionists and the Mensheviks, in agreement with the bourgeoisie, could have given Russia a great many reforms, had it not been for the fact that the objective forces in world politics are revolutionary, and that mere reforms will not answer the purpose.

The imperialist war is crushing and will destroy the peoples. Petty-bourgeois democracy can perhaps temporarily avert ruin. But it is only the revolutionary proletariat that can save us from ruin.

Pravda, No. 92, July 10, 1917.

HOW THE CAPITALISTS HIDE THEIR PROFITS

ON THE PROBLEM OF CONTROL

WHAT a great deal of talk about control, yet how little all this talk means. . . . How they circumvent what is essential by resorting to general phrases, grandiloquent turns of speech, solemn "projects" doomed forever to remain mere projects.

Yet the point is that unless the commercial and bank secrets are done away with, unless a law making the books of commercial firms accessible to the trade unions is passed, all phrases and projects concerning control are sheer rhetoric.

To take a small but instructive illustration. A certain comrade, a bank employé, has communicated to us the following information demonstrating the manner in which profits are being concealed in official financial statements.

The *Vestnik Finansov* [Financial Messenger], No. 18, May 20, 1917, has published the report of the Petrograd Discount and Loan Bank. According to that report, the net profits of the bank amount to 13,000,000 rubles (the exact amount is 12,960,000; in the text we shall use round numbers; in parentheses, the exact amount).

On closer scrutiny the informed person will immediately see that the statement does not show the entire net profit, and that a considerable part of the profit is cleverly concealed under other items, so that, unless the commercial and bank secrets are completely done away with, no "law," no "forced loan," and, in general, no financial measure will ever enable us to lay our hands on that part of the profit. Indeed, in the statement we find the separate item of 5,500,000 rubles of reserve capital. It is precisely under this item of reserve capital that profits are always and everywhere being concealed. If I, a millionaire, upon making a profit of 17,000,-000 rubles, decide to set aside 5,000,000 as a special reserve fund, all I have to do is simply to list the 5,000,000 rubles as "reserve capital," and all the various laws concerning "state control" and "state taxation of profits" are circumvented!!

Again. There is a separate item of moneys made in interest and commissions—almost 1,000,000 rubles (825,000). "The question is," writes the bank employé, "what sums do generally constitute the profits of a bank, if money made in interest is not listed under profits??"

Moreover, a sum of 300,000 rubles is listed under previous profits, and is not included in the total of profits!! Together, then, with the foregoing item, we have another mere million of profits hidden away. Similarly, the sum of 224,000 rubles of "unpaid dividends" to shareholders is also not included in the total of profits, though everybody knows that dividends are paid out of net profits.

Furthermore. The statement contains also another item of 3,800,000 rubles—suspense account. "What this suspense account is," the comrade writes, "is difficult to explain to one who is not directly in touch with this business. Suffice it to say that in preparing a financial statement it is easy to conceal under this item a part of the profit, then to be transferred 'where needed.'"

To summarise. The profit has been listed as 13,000,000 rubles; yet, in point of fact, it is most likely somewhere between 19 and 24 millions—almost 80 per cent profit on an invested capital of 30 millions.

Is it not obvious that the government's threats to the capitalists, the government's promises to the workers, the government's laws and projects to take 90 per cent of the profits of the richest capitalists are mere sound and fury signifying nothing, so long as the commercial and bank secrets are not abolished?

Pravda, No. 94, July 12, 1917.

PHRASES AND FACTS

MINISTER SKOBELEV published an appeal to all the workers of Russia. In the name of "our" (so it says: our) Socialist ideal, in the name of the revolution, in the name of revolutionary democracy, and so on, and so forth—the workers are urged to accept "chambers of conciliation" while all "arbitrary" actions are harshly condemned.

Here is how well the near-Socialist, the Menshevik Minister Skobelev sings his part:

> You (workers) are fully justified in your indignation against the enrichment of the propertied classes during the war. The Tsar's government wasted billions of the people's money. The revolutionary government must turn these billions back into the people's treasury.[269]

He sings well . . . he will land somewhere! Mr. Skobelev's appeal was published on July 11. The coalition cabinet was formed on May 19. And during all this time, while economic ruin and a catastrophe of unheard-of gravity were approaching with seven league boots, the government took not one earnest step against the capitalists who have accumulated "billions." In order to "turn these billions back into the people's treasury," a decree should have been issued on May 20 abolishing all commercial and bank secrets and establishing immediate control over banks and capitalist syndicates, for otherwise it is *impossible* even to find, let alone "turn back," these billions.

Does the Menshevik Minister Skobelev really think that the workers are little children whom he can feed with promises of the impossible (to return billions is impossible, may God help us to put a stop to treasury looting and to return at least one hundred or so millions) without doing for weeks and weeks the possible and the necessary?

And here, on the very day when the Menshevik Minister Skobelev was handing out another basketful of most effective republican, revolutionary and "Socialist" phrases, Comrade Avilov, who tries to "unite" the defencists (*i. e.*, the chauvinists) with the workers, conceived the unusually happy idea of writing an article in the *Novaia Zhizn,* containing not deductions but facts.[270]

There is nothing in the world so eloquent as these simple facts. On May 19 the coalition cabinet is formed. In a solemn declaration it promises . . . *control* and even "organisation of production." On May 29 the Executive Committee of the Petrograd Soviet adopts "instructions" for its Ministers, demanding "the immediate (hear! hear!) and most energetic realisation (upon my word, this is what it says!) of government control of production" and so on, and so forth.

Now, energetic realisation begins.

On the first of June, Konovalov retires and makes a very "energetic" declaration against "the extreme Socialists"! On June 14 the All-Russian conference of the representatives of industry and commerce takes place. The conference declares itself resolutely against control. The three associate Ministers remaining after Konovalov's resignation begin an "energetic realisation." The First Assistant Minister Stepanov, in the conflict of the Donetz mine owners (who resort to sabotage to impede production) supports . . . the employers. After this the employers reject all the conciliatory proposals made by Skobelev.

The Second Assistant Minister Palchinsky sabotages the fuel conference.

The Third Assistant Minister Savvin establishes "a crude and even silly caricature" of regulation in the form of some sort of "inter-departmental conference."

On June 23 the First Assistant Minister Stepanov presented to the Provisional Government a "report" . . . in which he took issue with the programme of the Executive Committee.

On July 4 the Congress of Soviets passed another resolution. . . .

Committees of supplies are being organised by the people on their own initiative, from below. From above a chief "economic council" is promised. The Second Assistant Minister Palchinsky explains: "It is difficult to say when it (the economic council) will begin to function."

This sounds like mockery, but these are the facts.

The capitalists make sport of the workers and the people, continuing the policy of secret lock-outs and of hiding their outrageous profits, while the Skobelevs, the Tseretelis, the Chernovs are being sent to "pacify" the workers with phrases.

Pravda, No. 94. July 12, 1917.

THE CRISIS IS APPROACHING, CHAOS IS SPREADING

THE alarm has to be sounded daily. All kinds of foolish little people have been reproaching us for being "too much in a hurry" to transfer all state power to the Soviets of Workers', Soldiers', and Peasants' Deputies; it would be, they felt, more "moderate and well behaved," if we maintained our dignity and "waited" for the dignified Constituent Assembly.

But now even the most foolish of petty-bourgeois fools can see that *life does not wait*, and that it is not we but the approaching chaos and disaster that are "in a hurry."

Petty-bourgeois faint-heartedness, as typified by the Socialist-Revolutionist and Menshevik parties, has resolved: Let us leave the conduct of all affairs to the capitalists; perhaps the chaos will "wait" until the convocation of the Constituent Assembly!

Day after day facts prove that the chaos will most likely not wait until the convocation of the Constituent Assembly, and that disaster is upon us.

Take, for example, the facts published to-day. The Economic Department of the Executive Commitee of the Petrograd Soviet of Workers' and Soldiers' Deputies has resolved "to bring to the attention of the Provisional Government" the fact that "the metal industry of the Moscow region (fifteen provinces) is in a terribly critical condition," that "the management of the Goujon plant is obviously disorganising production, and deliberately leading to the shutting down of the plant," and that "the state power" (left by the Socialists-Revolutionists and the Mensheviks in the hands of the party of the Goujons, the party of counter-revolutionaries and lock-out capitalists), therefore, "must take the management of the plant into its own hands . . . and must supply means." [271]

Current expenses, amounting to five million rubles, must be paid immediately.

The Conference (the Economic Department and a delegation from the Supplies Department of the Moscow Soviet of Workers' Deputies) "brings to the attention of the Provisional Government" (poor, innocent, childishly-uninformed Provisional Government! It knew

301

nothing about it! It is without guilt! It will learn; it will be convinced, its conscience will be stirred by the Dans and the Cherevanins, the Avksentievs and the Chernovs!) "the fact that the Moscow Factory Conference and the Temporary Bureau of the Supplies Committee of the Moscow Region have already had occasion to prevent the shutting down of the Kolomna Locomotive plant as well as the Sormovo and Briansk plants in Bezhetsk. Still, the Sormovo plant is now at a standstill as a result of a strike, while the other plants are liable to stop work at any moment. . . ."

Disaster does not wait, it is advancing with terrific speed. As to the Donetz region, this is what A. Sandomirsky, who is, no doubt, well posted on the facts, writes in to-day's *Novaia Zhizn:*

> The vicious circle—lack of coal, lack of metals, lack of locomotives and rolling stock, cessation of production—is spreading ever wider. Yet while coal is being burned and metal piled up, these things cannot be obtained when and where they are needed.[272]

The government, supported by the Socialists-Revolutionists and Mensheviks, simply hampers the struggle against ruin. A. Sandomirsky cites the case of Palchinsky, Assistant Minister of Commerce and, in point of fact, colleague of the Tseretelis and Chernovs, who, on the complaint of the manufacturers, has prohibited (! !) "arbitrary" (! !) control commissions from acting on the inquiry instituted by the Donetz committee to determine the quantity of metal on hand.

Just think what a madhouse it is: the country is perishing, the people are on the verge of hunger and disaster, there is a lack of coal and iron despite the fact that these products are obtainable, the Donetz committee is conducting an inquiry concerning the quantity of metal, *i. e.,* it is in search of iron for the people, and at the same time the servant of the manufacturers, the servant of the capitalists, Minister Palchinsky, in union with Tsereteli and Chernov, puts a stop to this inquiry. And the crisis is becoming more acute, and disaster is upon us.

How and where is money to be obtained? Clearly, it is easy enough to "demand" five millions for one factory; but we must realise that much more is needed, if we consider all the factories.

Is it not self-evident that unless the measure we have demanded and advocated ever since the beginning of April is adopted, unless all the banks are consolidated into one bank, unless control is exercised over that bank, unless the commercial secrets are abolished, no money can be obtained?

The Goujons and the other capitalists, with the co-operation of the Palchinskys, are "deliberately" (this word belongs to the Economic Department) leading us toward the cessation of production. The government is on their side. The Tseretelis and the Chernovs are mere ornaments, or mere pawns.

Is it not high time for you, gentlemen, to realise that the Socialist-Revolutionist and Menshevik parties will, as parties, be responsible to the people for this disaster?

Pravda, No. 95, July 13, 1917.

BUT HOW IS IT TO BE DONE?

THE *Rabochaia Gazeta* is disturbed over the political significance of the offensive. One of its contributors even reproaches another with the fact that the latter's evasive phrases may, in their final analysis, be reduced to an admission that the Russian revolutionary army is, objectively, shedding its blood not for peace without annexations but for the annexationist plans of the Allied bourgeoisie (*Rabochaia Gazeta*, No. 93, page 2, column 1).[273]

This "objective" significance of the offensive cannot but disturb the working masses who are still in part following the Mensheviks. And this is reflected also in the pages of the *Rabochaia Gazeta*. Not wishing to venture upon an open break with the workers, the paper makes an effort to tie up somehow the "offensive" with the revolutionary proletarian struggle for peace. The misfortune of the cunning and clever editors is that it is impossible to establish here any connection at all, except a negative one.

And it is difficult to imagine people more pitiful and more confused than these esteemed editors, who are frightened by those very spirits which they, together with the Socialists-Revolutionists, have conjured up.

On the one hand the *Rabochaia Gazeta* reports that "in Europe the significance of the Russian offensive is now seen in an entirely wrong light. The English and the French bourgeois newspapers see in it the renunciation of the 'Utopian' plans of the Soviet. Chauvinist resolutions are being passed under the pretext of hailing Kerensky and the advancing revolutionary army. And while the military drums are thundering in honour of the Russian offensive, the persecution of those who agree with the Russian democracy, who accept the same peace platform, is growing."

A very valuable admission! Particularly since it comes from the pages of the ministerial paper which only yesterday regarded our prophecies concerning the inevitable consequences of the offensive as expressions of Bolshevik malice. It turns out that it is not a question of Bolshevik "malice" at all, but that the policy adopted by the leaders of the Soviet has its own logic and that this logic leads towards the strengthening of anti-revolutionary forces inside and outside of Russia.

Now this unpleasant fact the *Rabochaia Gazeta* would somehow like to gloss over. And to achieve that the editors propose a very simple method: "It is urgently necessary that the Central Executive Committee of the Congress of Soviets of Workers' and Soldiers' Deputies, together with the Soviet of Peasants' Deputies, should come out with a definite and categorical declaration that, as far as Russian democracy is concerned, the aims of the war remain the same as before," and so on, and so forth. You see how resolutely the Mensheviks fight against war: They are ready to make one more immediate and categorical declaration. How many such "urgent," most "categorical," most "passionate" declarations have already been made! And how many more times will it be necessary to repeat the same categorical declarations in the quickest order to whitewash somewhat the acts of the government which the ministerial *Rabochaia Gazeta* supports whole-heartedly.

No, gentlemen, even your most "categorical" words, declarations, and notes will not diminish the facts which you yourselves report. These facts could be counteracted only by deeds, deeds that would actually mean a break with the policy of continuing the imperialist war. The government of Lvov-Tereshchenko-Shingarev-Kerensky-Tsereteli cannot do this. All it can do is to prove, by its cowardly and pitiful policy towards Finland and the Ukraine, its utter inability to carry out its most "categorical" declarations about "no annexations" and about the "right" of self-determination. But under existing conditions all these promised declarations will serve merely as means of confusing the masses. To confuse the masses with the high-sounding declarations, and not at all to carry on a "proletarian struggle for peace"—this is the programme of the *Rabochaia Gazeta*, this is its actual answer to the growth of anti-revolutionary forces in connection with the offensive.

Pravda, No. 95, July 13, 1917.

HOW AND WHY THE PEASANTS HAVE BEEN DECEIVED

IT is well known that when the peasant deputies of Russia came together in Petrograd to the All-Russian Soviet of Peasants' Deputies they were promised—promised by the Socialists-Revolutionists, promised by the government—that the sale and purchase of land would be immediately prohibited.

At first, Minister Pereverzev really wanted to carry out the promise and stopped by telegraph all deals involving the sale and purchase of land. But later some one's invisible hand interfered and Minister Pereverzev withdrew his telegram sent to notaries, i. e., he again permitted the sale and purchase of land.

The peasants grew uneasy. If we are not mistaken, they even sent a special delegation to the Ministry.

There, assurances were given to the peasants, soothing persuasion was used, the way one does with children. They were assured that a *law* prohibiting the sale and purchase of land would be issued immediately and that Pereverzev's temporary order was "set aside" "only" for the purpose of issuing such a law.

The Socialists-Revolutionists pacified the peasants, fed them with promises. The peasants believed them. The peasants felt reassured. The peasants left for their villages.

Weeks and weeks passed.

On July 7 (not before then) the news appeared in the papers that Minister Chernov, leader of the Party of Socialists-Revolutionists, proposed to the government a bill (it is only a bill so far) concerning the prohibition of the sale and purchase of land.

On July 12 the papers published the report of a "private conference" of the Imperial Duma, that had taken place on July 11. At this conference, Mr. Rodzianko, according to the report in the *Riech* (a paper belonging to the party that has a majority in the Provisional Government), "in his concluding remarks dwelt on the question of deals in land in connection with the new" (O yes, exceedingly new! strikingly new!) "measures of the government. He maintained that if deals in land are prohibited, the land will lose its value" (for whom? for the landowners, obviously!! But it is from these very landowners that the peasants want to take away the land!), "all securities will become worthless, and the landowners" (the former landowners, Mr. Rodzianko) "will be deprived of all credit. From what sources,"—queries M. V. Rodzianko,—"will the owners of estates pay their debts to the banks? In most cases the debts are overdue already, and such a bill will lead to the immediate liquidation of all land holdings in a legitimate way, without bids."

In view of this, Mr. Rodzianko proposed to the conference that the Provisional Committee be instructed to consider this question in an attempt *to forestall the introduction of a law* that would prove ruinous to private ownership of land, as well as to the state.[274]

This is when the "invisible hand" came to light! Here it is, this "clever mechanism" of the coalition government, with near-Socialist Ministers, exposed by what this gentleman blurted out—this former president of the former Imperial Duma, this former landowner, this former confidant of Stolypin the Hangman, this former protector of the provocateur Malinovsky—Mr. Rodzianko!

Let us assume, now that Mr. Rodzianko has so awkwardly blurted out the truth, that the law prohibiting the sale and purchase of land will finally be passed. Finally!

That, however, is not the only point involved. The point is that this striking example should help us, as well as the peasant masses, to see and understand just *how and why the peasants have been deceived.* For the fact, the incontrovertible and indubitable fact remains: the peasants have been deceived; what they were promised at the All-Russian Soviet of Peasants' Deputies as something that would be carried out immediately has not yet been carried out.

How have the peasants been deceived? They have been fed on promises. This is precisely the "clever mechanism" of all the coalition cabinets in the world, i. e., of all the bourgeois cabinets where traitors to Socialism participate.

Former Socialists serve in these cabinets, regardless of whether they know it or not, as tools with which the capitalists deceive the masses.

Why have the peasants been deceived? Because the tools used for deception, the Socialists-Revolutionists—making an assumption most favourable to them—themselves failed to understand the clever machinations of class rule and class policy in the present administration of Russia. The Socialists-Revolutionists allowed themselves to be carried away by phrases. As a matter of fact, however, and as the "incident" with Rodzianko proves beyond a shadow of a doubt, Russia is actually ruled by a bloc of two blocs, by an alliance of two alliances.

One bloc is the bloc of the Cadets with the monarchist-land-owners, among whom Mr. Rodzianko occupies the first place. The existence of this bloc as a political fact was established before the whole of Russia at the Petrograd elections, when all the Black-Hundred papers, all the papers to the right of the Cadets supported the Cadets. This bloc has a majority in the government, thanks to the Socialists-Revolutionists and the Mensheviks. This bloc caused the delay in prohibiting deals involving the purchase and sale of land, this bloc supports the landowners and the lock-out capitalists.

The second bloc is the bloc of the Socialists-Revolutionists and the Mensheviks. This bloc has deceived the people with empty promises. Skobelev and Tsereteli, Peshekhonov and Chernov have handed out no end of promises. It is easy to make promises. This method of the "Socialist" Ministers of feeding the people with promises has been tried in all the advanced countries of the world and has everywhere led to catastrophe. What makes the situation in Russia unique is the fact that the downfall of the Socialist-Revolutionist and Menshevik parties will be more precipitous and will come sooner than usual because of the revolutionary state of the country.

Let every worker and every soldier use this very instructive example to explain to the peasants how and why they have been deceived!

Not by forming a bloc (alliance) with the capitalists, but only by allying themselves with the workers will the peasants be able to achieve their ends.

Pravda, No. 96, July 14, 1917.

WHO IS RESPONSIBLE?

MR. N. ROSTOV quotes in the ministerial *Rabochaia Gazeta* a number of excerpts from soldiers' letters which prove the extreme lack of information in the village. All letters, says the author, who, according to his own words, has at his disposal a bulky package of letters mailed to the Agitation Department of the Executive Committee of the Soviet of Workers' and Soldiers' Deputies from the remotest parts of the country, contain one universal cry: Newspapers, send us newspapers!

Here the Menshevik writer suddenly becomes startled and exclaims in fear: "If the revolution does not appear to them (the peasants) as a clear fact of great usefulness, they may rise against the revolution". . . . The peasants are "as benighted as ever before."

The Menshevik and ministerial official woke up with his package of letters a little too late. More than seven weeks have passed since the Mensheviks became the servants of the capitalists on May 19, and during all this time the bourgeois, counter-revolutionary slander and vilification of the revolution has been freely circulated in the village by means of the bourgeois papers that gained predominance, and by means of the direct and indirect servants and adherents of the capitalist government supported by the Mensheviks.

Had not the Mensheviks and the Socialists-Revolutionists been betraying the revolution, supporting the counter-revolutionary Cadets, power would have been in the hands of the Executive Committee even as early as the middle of May. The Executive Committee could immediately have established a state monopoly on private advertisements in the newspapers, and thus it could have obtained tens of millions of copies of newspapers for *free* distribution in the village. The huge printing presses and the reserve of paper would have been used by the Executive Committee for the purpose of educating the village and not for the purpose of stupefying it with some dozen or so of bourgeois, counter-revolutionary newspapers which have actually become dominant in the newspaper field.

The Executive Committee could have then disbanded the Imperial Duma and, thus saving the people's money on this and on many other things, it could have used that money for sending a thousand agitators, if not thousands of them, into the village.

In times of revolution, procrastination is often equivalent to a complete betrayal of the revolution. The responsibility for the delay in the transfer of power to the workers soldiers and peasants, for the delay in carrying out revolutionary measures calculated to educate the benighted villages, rests wholly on the Socialists-Revolutionists and on the Mensheviks.

In this they have betrayed the revolution. They bear the blame for the fact that in the mattter of fighting against the counter-revolutionary bourgeois press and agitation, the workers and soldiers are forced to confine themselves to limited primitive means, when for this work they could and should have had general state means at their disposal.

Pravda, No. 96, July 14, 1917.

APPENDICES

Ich bestätige,

1) dass die eingegangenen Bedingungen, die von Platten mit der deutschen Gesandtschaft getroffen wurden, mir bekannt gemacht worden sind;

2) dass ich mich den Anordnungen des Reiseführers Platten unterwerfe;

3) dass mir eine Mitteilung des "Petit Parisien" bekanntgegeben worden ist, wonach die russische provisorische Regierung die durch Deutschland Reisenden als Hochverräter zu behandeln drohe;

4) dass ich die ganze politische Verantwortlichkeit für diese Reise ausschliesslich auf mich nehme;

5) dass mir von Platten die Reise zur bis Stockholm garantiert worden ist.

Bern - Zürich, 9. April 1917.

Facsimile of Signatures of the Russian Bolsheviks Who Journeyed with Lenin from Switzerland to Russia after the March Revolution (see Appendices, Document IV)

WRITINGS OF V. I. LENIN FROM MARCH TO JULY, 1917, WHICH HAVE NOT BEEN FOUND

DRAFT RESOLUTIONS FOR THE ALL-RUSSIAN APRIL (MAY) CONFERENCE OF THE R.S.-D.L.P.

At the sessions of the Conference, the delegates received drafts of most of the resolutions to be discussed. The drafts had been written by Lenin; they served as material for the work of the Conference, and were made the basis of the resolutions adopted by the commission under Lenin's guidance and passed by the Conference. The drafts had been set up in the press of the *Soldatskaia Pravda*, and 20 to 30 proof-sheets had been prepared. In his speeches at the April Conference Lenin often refers to those drafts. (See *p. 271 ff*, Book I of this volume.)

NOTES OF A LECTURE ENTITLED, "WAR AND REVOLUTION," MAY 28, 1917

In the case prepared by the Investigator of the Petrograd Judicial Chamber, Alexandrov, in the Minutes of Inspection of Corpus Delicti found in searching Kshesinskaia's house (Headquarters of the Central Committee) in the July Days, there is a brief description of a manuscript containing 15 loose sheets; also the following about its contents:

In this lecture Lenin refers to the development of capitalism in all countries saying that there is not a spot on the globe where capital has not reached out its heavy hand. As the cause of the present war, Lenin points to the capitalists who aim at widening their sphere of activities at the expense of others; he points out that all governments in all countries are predatory, that they deceive the people and wish to seize other peoples' lands, to enslave the people. In Lenin's opinion, the war conducted by the capitalists of all countries cannot be ended without a workers' revolution against those capitalists. Lenin considers it necessary that all power should be given over to the Soviets of Workers', Peasants', and Soldiers' Deputies. In conclusion Lenin says: "When power will have passed into the hands of Soviets of Workers', Soldiers', and Peasants' Deputies, then the capitalists will express themselves against us; Japan against, France against, England against, all governments of all countries will express themselves against us; the capitalists will be against you; the workers will be for you; then there will be an end to the war begun by the capitalists. Here is the answer to the question on how to end the war."

The "case" contains no indication as to when and before what audience the lecture was delivered, neither does it disclose whether the notes were made by Lenin himself or by one of the audience.

It is possible that a series of unsigned popular articles in the *Soldatskaia Pravda* was written by Lenin.

EXPLANATORY NOTES

182. The "Special Session of the Deputies of all Four Imperial Dumas" was convened on May 10, 1917, by the Duma Committee in connection with the government crisis which arose as a result of the events of May 3-5. Tsereteli, who was present as a Deputy of the Second Imperial Duma, delivered an important political speech in reply to the speeches of the monarchists Shulgin and Rodzianko, dissociating himself from the counter-revolution "from the Right and from the Left."

The people did not overthrow the Tsar in order to place twelve new ones in his place [i. e., twelve autocratic Ministers.—Ed.] The people do not consider them infallible. [The speaker referred to the statement of Minister Nekrasov who greeted the control of the social organisations, and continued.—Ed.] In a democratic country it cannot be otherwise. A union of all is necessary who are capable of logically standing on the ground of democratising the country in its internal and foreign policy. . . . The chief danger consists in the fact that our bourgeoisie will follow not Nekrasov but Shulgin, that it is proving faithless to the agreement [with the revolutionary democracy.—Ed.] That would be the signal for civil war in which the Revolution and the country would be ruined.

The speaker sees indications of this threat in the speeches of Shulgin as well as of Rodzianko who speak of complete victory. No one can be fooled now by the catchword of the destruction of German militarism. The people recognise that the armed destruction of foreign militarism is the best means of placing the most burdensome yoke of militarism on the necks of the people at home. That is why the people are disturbed by phrases like Rodzianko's and notes like those of May 1. This can only be avoided by continuing logically and unswervingly along the path of the programme announced in the agreement of March 15 and in the Declaration of March 27. The speaker believes that the Russian bourgeoisie will muster enough political sense to follow this path. Did he not believe it, he would have been the first to go with those who speak of the dictatorship of the proletariat and the revolutionary peasantry, although he knows what danger this signifies. . . . [See *Rabochaia Gazeta*, Number 42, May 11, 1917.]—p. 19.

183. Petrogradskaia Storona—the home of the ballet dancer Kshesinskaia, which the Bolsheviks appropriated for their central headquarters, was located in that part of the city.—p. 20.

184. Under the pressure of the street demonstration, the Provisional Government tried to dissipate the impression which Miliukov's note had evoked. On May 5, 1917, the government published the following communiqué:

In view of the doubt which arose concerning the interpretation of the Note of the Minister of Foreign Affairs on the occasion of the transmission of the declaration of the Provisional Government concerning the tasks of the war (of March 27) to the Allied Governments, the Provisional Government considers it necessary to declare:

1. The Note of the Minister of Foreign Affairs was the object of careful and extended considerations on the part of the Provisional Government after which the text of the Note was unanimously adopted.

2. It is self-evident that this Note, where it speaks of decisive victory over

314

the enemy, has in mind the achievements of those tasks which were set up in the Declaration of March 27 and expressed in the following words: "The Provisional Government views it as its right and its duty to declare this very day that the aim of free Russia is not the domination of other peoples, not the confiscation of their national property, not the forcible conquest of foreign territories, but the setting up of a permanent peace on the basis of the self-determination of peoples. The Russian people do not seek to strengthen their external position of power at the expense of foreign peoples, they do not seek the enslavement and the humiliation of any one. In the name of the highest principles of justice they have broken the chains which weighed upon the Polish people. But the Russian people will not permit their native land to come out of the great struggle humiliated and sapped of its vital energies."

3. By the "sanctions" and "guarantees" of a permanent peace mentioned in the Note, the Provisional Government understands the limitation of armaments, international courts, etc.

This declaration will be communicated to the ambassadors of the Allied Powers by the Minister of Foreign Affairs.—p. 23.

185. Paragraph 9 of the Programme of the Russian Social-Democratic Labour Party adopted in 1903 reads: "The right of self-determination for all nations belonging to the empire." In May, 1917, Lenin proposed to replace this point by the following:

The right of all nationalities which are now part of the Russian state freely to separate and to form independent states. The republic of the Russian people should draw to itself other peoples or nationalities not through violence, but through voluntary and mutual agreement to build a common state. The common aims and brotherly union of the workers of all countries are incompatible with either direct or indirect violence practiced upon other nationalities. [See p. 338, Book I of this volume.]—p. 26.

186. The appeal of the Executive Committee of the Petrograd Soviet of Workers' and Soldiers' Deputies, "To the Socialists of All Countries" (May 15, 1917), as well as the simultaneous proclamation "To the Army" (see note 187) were written under the impression of the revolutionary mass actions during the April Days and were intended to justify the social-patriotic policy and to prepare the offensive at the front under the cover of a revolutionary phraseology. The Socialist compromisers stated:

The war is a monstrous crime. It is the imperialists of all countries who prepared the world conflagration and rendered it inevitable by their greed for conquest, by their insane armament race. . . . In this war, the imperialists of all countries are all victors alike . . . the toilers of all countries all the defeated alike. . . . The Russian Revolution is the uprising against the horrors of the world carnage; it is not only a national revolution, it is the first stage of the international revolution that will put an end to the war. . . . The revolutionary democracy of Russia does not want any separate peace which would only permit the Austro-German coalition full freedom of action. . . . Russian democracy wants a general peace on a basis which is acceptable to the toilers of all countries who do not want conquests, do not strive for plunder and are equally interested in the free expression of the will of all peoples and in the destruction of the power of international imperialism. . . . Peace without annexations and indemnities. The Provisional Government of revolutionary Russia has appropriated this programme. And the revolutionary democracy of Russia appeals to you, Socialists of all countries: you must not permit the voice of the Russian Provisional Government to be the only voice in the coalition of the Entente Powers. . . . You must force your governments to state unequivocally and definitely that the programme of peace without annexations

and indemnities on the basis of the self-determination of peoples is their programme.
Thereby you will lend weight and strength to the advance of the Russian Government. You will give our revolutionary army . . . the certainty that its sacrifices of blood are not misused. You will give it the possibility . . . of fulfilling its war tasks. The revolutionary democracy of Russia appeals to you, Socialists of the Austro-German coalition: you cannot permit the troops of your governments to become the executioners of Russian freedom. . . . Revolutionary and democratic Russia turns to the Socialists of the belligerent and neutral countries with the appeal to prevent the triumph of imperialism. . . . The Petrograd Soviet of Workers' and Soldiers' Deputies has decided to take the initiative in calling an international conference of all Socialist parties and fractions of all countries. . . . Not a single fraction of the proletariat must fail to participate in the common struggle for peace. . . . Proletarians . of all countries, unite!—p. 30.

187. The Proclamation of the Petrograd Soviet of Workers' and Soldiers' Deputies "To the Army" of May 15, 1917, aimed to restore discipline, fight fraternisation, and prepare the contemplated offensive at the front. The Socialist compromisers tried to replace the antiquated patriotic ideals of tsarist times by the new-baked "revolutionary" ideology of the war and the offensive. In this appeal to the soldiers in the trenches, they said:
The toiling masses did not need the war. They did not begin it. It was started by the tsars and the capitalists of all countries. . . . The Soviet of Workers' and Soldiers' Deputies has appealed to all peoples with a proclamation for the cessation of the carnage. . . . Russia is awaiting the reply to this call. But, comrade-soldiers, remember: Our proclamations will have no value if Wilhelm's regiments trample down revolutionary Russia. What will happen if the Russian army to-day thrusts its bayonets in the ground and says that it will not fight any more, that it doesn't care what happens in the world! The German Kaiser, the German Junker and capitalist will place their heavy boots upon our necks, occupy our cities, villages and provinces, and make the Russian people pay tribute. Have we overthrown Nicholas to kneel before Wilhelm? . . . The Soviet of Soldiers' and Workers' Deputies leads you to peace by calling the workers and peasants of Germany and Austria-Hungary to rise and revolt; it leads you to peace by having gotten our Government to renounce the policy of conquest, by demanding the same renunciation from the Allied Powers, by convening an international congress of the Socialists of the whole world. . . . We need time, comrade-soldiers. Remember that at the front, in the trenches you are now standing guard over Russian freedom. . . . You are defending with your bodies not the Tsars, nor the Protopopovs and the Rasputins, not the rich landowners and capitalists. . . . You are defending your brothers, the workers and peasants. The front cannot be defended if you decide under all circumstances not to lift a finger in the trenches. . . . Only by taking the offensive can one save himself or his brothers on the other sectors of the front from destruction. . . . Do not reject the offensive. . . . Beware of provocations, beware of traps! The fraternisation developing at the front may easily be transformed into such a trap. . . . There is no revolution there yet; the troops there are still with Wilhelm and Karl. . . . Not by fraternisation will you achieve peace, not by a silent agreement made at the front by isolated companies, battalions, regiments! Those who assure you that fraternisation is the road to peace are leading you to your ruin, to the ruin of Russian freedom. Do not believe them! Push everything aside that weakens your fighting force, that carries disintegration and discouragement into the army. Your fighting force is serving the cause of peace. . . . —p. 32.

188. The instructions for the election of delegates in the factories and regiments were probably written by Lenin after the middle of May, 1917. The

official party draft of the "Instructions for the Election of Delegates to the Soviet of Workers' and Soldiers' Deputies" was published in Number 51 of the *Pravda* of May 20, 1917. The wording of this draft is altogether different from that of Lenin's unfinished manuscript and was written by another person.— p. 43.

189. This refers to the session of Deputies of the Duma on May 17, 1917, in which "enduring faithfulness to our glorious allies" was decided upon. —p. 49.

190. *Vecherneie Vremia* (*Evening Times*)—Petrograd evening paper published from 1911 to 1917, close to the political tendency of the *Novoie Vremia* (see note 89). The publisher of the paper was Suvorin, Jr., a son of the owner of the *Novoie Vremia.*—p. 53.

191. All-Russian Union of Zemstvos—an organisation which united the Zemstvos (provincial assemblies) of the different governments and districts for the purpose of the better organisation of sanitation and provisions for the army. The city administrations had their own organisations. City and district organisations were organised in the *Zemgor* or Zemstvo and City League. The bourgeoisie had a twofold aim in creating these organisations: First, the organisation of the social forces for victory over the external enemy, and secondly a gradual permeation of the tsarist state apparatus by the organisations of the bourgeoisie. During the war this organisation developed into a big factor of power. During the civil war, it worked for the White Guards. There are still units of the Zemstvo League abroad, in the centres of counter-revolutionary émigrés, their function being to supply help to émigrés.—p. 54.

192. The War Industries Committees were organised by the Russian manufacturers in the fall of 1915. Their purpose was to maintain orders for goods for the army, distribute them among the separate plants and to eliminate competition among themselves. Officially, of course, they announced their purpose to be the "supplying of the army" and the furthering of the cause of "national defence." Representatives of the industrial workers were also drawn into the committees; in most cases, however, the workers, under the leadership of the Bolsheviks, boycotted the committees.

The central War Industries Committee was located at Petrograd and guided the activity of the local committees. Its chairman was Guchkov. The purpose of drawing the workers into these organisations was to establish class "peace" and handicap strikes.—p. 54.

193. Free Economic Society—one of the oldest scientific societies in Petrograd. In the nineties as well as in the first decade of the present century it served as the centre of the liberal and radical intelligentsia.—p. 55.

194. The first All-Russian Peasant Congress met at the People's House in Petrograd from May 17 to June 11, 1917. Delegates from the front as well as from the provinces were present. Altogether there were 1115 delegates, 537 of whom were Socialists-Revolutionists, 465 non-partisan, 103 Social-Democrats, 6 Trudoviks (see note 32), 4 People's Socialists (see note 29).

Avksentiev was elected chairman. Breshko-Breshkovskaia was elected honorary chairman, together with Chernov and Vera Figner. The Congress was greeted by the "Socialist Ministers" Chernov, Peshekhonov, Kerensky and Skobelev. Reports were delivered by: Chernov (on the political situation and the Provisional Government), Kondratiev (on the administration of food and supplies), Nekrasov (on the condition of transport), Bunakov-Fundaminsky and Kochetov (on the war), Kilchevsky (on the Soviets of Peasant Deputies), Oganovsky, Chernov, Peshekhonov, Vikhlaiev, Bykovsky and S. L. Maslov (on the agrarian question). Tsereteli reported to the Congress on the events at Cronstadt (see note 224), but was powerfully rebutted by Trotsky. The Congress elected an executive committee of thirty, predominantly Socialists-Revolutionists (including Chernov, Breshko-Breshkovskaia, Kerensky, Avksentiev, Rubanovich, Vera Figner, Chaikovsky, Gotz, Maslov, etc.). The Congress, which was entirely under the influence of the Right Wing of the Socialists-Revolutionists, expressed itself unanimously in favour of turning the land over to the people. With all votes except those of a small number of Bolsheviks, the Congress adopted the Socialist-Revolutionist plan of the so-called "socialisation of the soil," but put off the execution of the programme until the "convocation of the Constituent Assembly" and forbade the peasants to occupy the landowners' estates on their own initiative. The resolution proposed by Lenin on the agrarian question did not meet with the approval of the Congress and won only a small number of votes. The Congress declared for the complete support of the Provisional Government (in contrast to the reservation of the Executive Committee of the Petrograd Soviet: "To the extent that . . ."), accepted the coalition with the bourgeoisie and the participation of the Socialists in the Provisional Government, sanctioned the "Liberty Loan," and zealously supported the preparations for the offensive at the front by all the social-chauvinist resolutions of the Socialists-Revolutionists.—p. 56.

195. This article by Lenin is a reply to an article entitled "Secrets of Foreign Policy" in the *Riech*, Number 107, of May 22, 1917. The following is the essence of this last article: The acceptance of the point regarding the renunciation of annexations by the Provisional Government has caused Russia's allies to take a stand again on the question of war aims. The author has information that England is ready to compromise in order to bring about peace. England can renounce the solution of the Alsace-Lorraine, Czech, Polish, etc., questions. It will gladly give up the Russian demands in reference to Constantinople and the Straits, but never Mesopotamia and Palestine, which have been conquered by force. Such a formulation of the question, however, is extremely disadvantageous to Russia, and shows the senselessness of the slogan set up by the Socialists of renouncing annexations. Finally, it is necessary to lead the Russian army into an offensive, whereby it is necessary to tell it that it is not fighting for the interests of the Allies but above all for Russian interests.—p. 64.

196. This refers to an article in the *Riech*, Number 107, of May 22, 1917, entitled "On the Edge of the Abyss." The author of the article protested against fraternisation at the front, citing the letter of an artilleryman named

Veselovsky who saw salvation only in a Napoleon and demanded the introduction of iron discipline in the army.—p. 69.

197. The second Provisional Government (first coalition government) was formed on May 18, 1917. It was composed as follows:

Minister President and Minister of the Interior—Prince G. E. Lvov
Minister of War and Marine—A. F. Kerensky
Minister of Agriculture—V. M. Chernov
Minister of Justice—N. P. Pereverzev
Minister of Foreign Affairs—M. I. Tereshchenko
Minister of Finance—A. I. Shingarev
Minister of Communications—N. V. Nekrasov
Minister of Commerce—A. I. Konovalov
Minister of Supplies—A. V. Peshekhonov
Minister of Education—A. A. Manuilov
Minister of Labour—M. I. Skobelev
Minister of Posts and Telegraph—I. G. Tsereteli
State Comptroller—I. V. Godniev
Supreme Procurator of the Holy Synod—V. N. Lvov

The "Socialist Ministers" in the government delegated by the Petrograd Soviet were: Tsereteli and Skobelev of the Mensheviks; Kerensky and Chernov of the Socialists-Revolutionists; Peshekhonov and Pereverzev of the People's Socialists. To do justice to the conditions laid down by the Amsterdam Socialist Congress of 1904 concerning participation in bourgeois coalition governments, the Congress having decided that Socialists could participate in bourgeois governments only in exceptional cases, under the control of the party and on the basis of a definite programme, the Executive Committee of the Petrograd Soviet set up the following as conditions for participation: 1. Active work in the interest of peace on the basis of the Manifesto of the Petrograd Soviet of March 27 (see note 85) ; 2. Regulation of industry and reform of finances; 3. Preparatory measures for the solution of the agrarian and labour questions; and 4. The speediest convocation of the Constituent Assembly. Not a single one of these obligations was fulfilled. The first coalition government ended with the bankruptcy of July 15, when the Cadets left the government. Their pretext was the agreement concluded by Tsereteli and Tereshchenko with the Ukrainian Rada. The worker and soldier masses replied to this with the demonstrations of July 16-18 and with the demands of the transfer of power to the Soviets (July Events).—p. 70.

198. The Petrograd Soviet had elected a commission for convoking an international conference, consisting of the following persons: the former Bolshevik and zealous defender of the fatherland, Goldenberg, the Right Mensheviks Smirnov and Ehrlich and the Socialist-Revolutionist Russanov. They were delegated to go abroad. The contemplated conference did not materialise.—p. 73.

199. The article "What Does the Provisional Government Want?", published in Number 63 of the *Izvestia* of May 24, 1917, constituted the continuation of a series of articles dealing with the declaration of the Provisional Government of May 19, and took up questions of the economic life of the

country. The author affirmed the extraordinarily serious economic condition of the country. The article stated, among other things:

The economic forces of the country are greatly undermined. . . . In agriculture, which constitutes the basis of the entire economic life of the country, a violent crisis has broken out, threatening Russia with starvation. . . . The result of the planlessness of coal production is that a large part of the coal mines are finding themselves in a condition of complete collapse. . . . The metal industry is disorganised. . . . The machines are used up more and more each day, but they cannot be replaced. . . . Fewer products are being produced than is necessary to cover current needs. . . . It is still worse with trade and commerce; here complete chaos reigns. . . . Prices are rising with unrestrainable speed. . . . The workers are hungry; the peasants are being ruined. But beside this, enormous quantities of wealth are accumulating in the hands of the capitalists.

The Provisional Government, according to the writer, however, has the power and the will to master these difficulties, as is proved by paragraph 3 of the Declaration of the Provisional Government (see note 201) and its promise of state and social control of production and exchange. But to carry this out, "the support of the entire democracy, which has promised its support to the government, is necessary."—p. 78.

200. The resolution of the economic department of the Petrograd Soviet, published in the *Izvestia*, Number 63, May 24, 1917, confirms the disorganisation of the country's economy and considers the situation catastrophic, particularly "with the present attitude of the state power." The fulfillment of the task of normalising economy must proceed along two parallel lines:

(a) The creation of organs which will ascertain the economic situation in its totality, and (b) the creation of executive organs which will carry out the planned regulation of the economic life. . . . The time has arrived when we must pass from anarchic production and private syndicates to the labour of the economic organism of the nation as a whole under the leadership of the state. . . . The task of the respective organisations must be the greatest possible utilisation of the existing productive forces in the most important branches of industry and their further development. . . . The country is already in a state of catastrophe, and the only thing that will save it is the creative effort of the entire people under the guidance of the government which has voluntarily assumed the grandiose task of salvaging a country ruined by war and the Tsar's régime.—p. 79.

201. The Declaration of the Coalition Government of May 19, 1917, proclaimed the "ideas of freedom, equality and fraternity," promised the "most rapid conclusion of a general peace without annexations and indemnities on the basis of the right of self-determination of peoples with the full agreement of the Allies." For this purpose it placed to the forefront the "fortification of the principles of the democratisation of the army, the organisation and the strengthening of its fighting force in defensive as well as in offensive actions." With reference to the internal economic tasks and the struggle against economic disorganisation the declaration proclaimed: "§ 3. The Provisional Government will fight unswervingly and determinedly against the economic disorganisation of the country by further planfully carrying out a state and social control of production, transport, exchange and distribution of products, and if necessary, it will take the organisation of production into its own hands."—p. 79.

202. The resolution mentioned here read as follows:

The Conference of Front Delegates declares that the report of the session of May 25 in the *Riech* and other bourgeois papers in no way corresponds with the facts.

The attitude of the Conference towards Comrade Zinoviev's speech was altogether different from that described in the *Riech* and the Conference is indignant at the distortion of the facts.

The consideration of the questions bound up with Comrade Zinoviev's report and Comrade Anisimov's reply is continued, and the Conference thanks them for the explanation.—p. 81.

203. The report appeared in the *Riech*, Number 112, May 27, 1917.—p. 83.

204. This refers to the article by V. Bazarov published in the *Novaia Zhizn*, May 29, 1917, entitled "The Conflict in the Donetz Basin." The article stated:

According to the revelations of the members of a workers' delegation, the capitalists of the Donetz Basin are practicing systematic passive resistance; they are deliberately neglecting and disorganising production. At the mines, no carpentry has been done in the shafts since the revolution; the miners must work under frightful conditions and are exposed at every moment to the danger of being buried alive. . . . The machinery everywhere has been entirely worn out. There are pits that work only four hours, during the other eight hours "steam is gathered." . . . Repairs are nowhere undertaken. . . . In spite of the terrible metal and coal famine, the delegates succeeded in discovering large stores of metal, coal and coke which lay around for months without being sent to the place of consumption, although there was rolling stock. The administration of one mine allowed the pits to be flooded by pretending that it was impossible to replace a worn-out valve, in spite of the fact that the administration had a valve in store. It was found by the workers and put in the place of the damaged one against the order of the manager.

All this occurred with the knowledge and with the silent condonement of the Provisional Government, a condonement which later on was not even concealed. Lenin, who raised the demand for workers' control, returned repeatedly to the condition of the industry in the Donetz Basin and to the protracted conflict created there between workers and employers.—p. 86.

205. This refers to the resolution of the April Conference "On the Union of the Internationalists against the Petty-Bourgeois Defencist Bloc." The text of the resolution will be found among the appendices in this book.—p. 89.

206. "Interborough Organisation of the United Social-Democrats," (*Mezhraiontsy*)—the organisation arose in Petrograd during the war and existed up to the sixth congress of the Bolsheviks in July, 1917, when it merged with the Bolshevik Party. Up to the March Revolution it numbered about 200 organised workers; it distributed leaflets and published two numbers of an illegal paper *Vperiod* (*Forward*). It represented an internationalist standpoint in its attitude toward the war and was close to the Bolsheviks in its tactics. Trotsky, Lunacharsky, Volodarsky, Uritsky and others belonged to the *Mezhraiontsy* in the summer of 1917. The Conference of the *Mezhraiontsy* at which the unity question was discussed took place on May 23, 1917. The Bolshevik Central Committee was represented at the Conference by Lenin, Zinoviev and Kamenev. The Conference rejected the resolution introduced by Lenin and adopted Trotsky's resolution.—p. 89.

207. Legal Bolshevik publishing house which existed even before the revolution. In 1917 it renewed its activity. Later it was renamed *Communist*. *Prosveshcheniïe (Education)*—legal Bolshevik semi-monthly journal which appeared in Petrograd between 1911-1914 in place of the prohibited *Mysl (Thought)*. It was renewed in 1917, but only one number appeared.—p. 89.

208. This refers to the article in the *Izvestia*, Number 67, May 29, 1917, entitled "Without Annexations." The author defined the meaning of annexations as follows: "Annexations—that means the forceful seizure of territory that is a part of the domain of another state on the day when war is declared." The author does not admit that Courland, Lettland and the other national territories which belonged to the former Russian empire were annexations. —p. 91.

209. The resolution of the Executive Committee of the Petrograd Soviet "On Measures against Disorganisation" of May 29, 1917, read as follows:

1. The Economic Department of the Executive Committee of the Soviet of Workers' and Soldiers' Deputies is transformed into a department for the organisation of national economy and includes the following sub-departments: Industry, fuels, supplies, transport, finance and general; 2. A close organisational connection is established between the Economic Department and the existing Labour Department; 3. The duty of the Department is to work out the programmatic and organisational principles for the regulation of economic life and establish the basic elements of a plan of regulation; 4. The representatives of the Soviet of Workers' and Soldiers' Deputies in the government, the Ministers and their alternates maintain a close organisational connection with the Department by actively participating in the elaboration of the principles and in the construction of the plan; 5. The Government sets up commissions to work out drafts of laws for the organisation of a supply committee with sub-departments in place of the functioning organs which were inherited from the old régime and unsystematically reformed by the first Provisional Government; 6. The Economic Department must proceed at once to work out the principles for the draft laws in order to carry into practice that economic and financial plan which was established in the resolution of the Economic Division: (1) on the organs for ascertaining the general economic situation; (2) on the creation of an organisation in the most important industrial branches; (3) on the control of the activity of the banks; (4) on financial measures; (5) on the distribution of the labour power of the country.

The resolution was published in the *Izvestia*, Number 68, May 30, 1917.— p. 93.

210. This article is Lenin's reply to an article published in the *Izvestia*, Number 68, May 30, 1917, entitled "The Re-elections to the Soviet of Workers' and Soldiers' Deputies." The Menshevik author, dissatisfied with the growing influence of the Bolsheviks in the factories and the success of their campaign for re-election to the Soviet, wrote:

In some factories the elections are taking place entirely without speeches, without resolutions, the old delegates being deposed and new ones elected. . . . To be able to work successfully, the deputies must be elected for a definite term, for two or three months, for instance; but under no circumstances are they to be elected for a week or for the interval of time between meetings. . . . The elections to the Soviet are no child's play, but a serious, responsible affair which must be fulfilled in all seriousness. . . .—p. 94.

211. The question of the sabotage of the mine owners of the Donetz Basin was taken up in the session of the Executive Committee of the Petrograd Soviet on May 16, 1917. The *Izvestia*, Number 68, of May 30, 1917, reports the following concerning this matter:

The delegates of the Donetz Basin workers, Sandomirsky and others, pictured the sad condition of all the branches of the Donetz Basin industries, which is obviously a danger to the existence of the country. In the opinion of the delegation, the only way out of the situation is for the state to immediately interfere. After discussing the matter, the following resolution was adopted: 1. Setting maximum prices for all products of the mining and steel industries at the present level; 2. Regulation of profits; 3. Establishment of minimum wages and further planned regulation of these wages in connection with supplying the workers with necessities at fixed prices, in order to guarantee an adequate standard of life; 4. The formation of state-regulated trusts is to be undertaken; 5. All measures are to be carried out by the central and local institutions of the Donetz-Krivoirog Basin (for example, the Donetz Committee). These institutions must be of a democratic character and must be formed with the participation of workers' representatives, employers, the government, and democratic revolutionary organisations.—p. 100.

212. In the same number are printed the theses of S. L. Maslov's report at the first Peasant Congress. They may be summarised as follows:

The whole land becomes the common property of the people with the right of use by the toiling inhabitants. The final decision rests with the Constituent Assembly. All trading in land is immediately forbidden. All arbitrary seizure of the land must be rigidly forbidden. The land committees and the arbitration commissions are to decide upon the land disputes between the landowners and the peasants, to regulate conditions of tenancy, to take care that prohibition of the purchase and sale of land as well as its arbitrary seizure is observed, and to further the extension of the cultivated area. The land committees are government organs on which representatives of the Soviets of Peasants' Deputies must co-operate.—p. 103.

213. The resolution of the April Conference of the Bolsheviks on the agrarian question demanded the immediate and complete confiscation of all private, church, crown and landowners' estates and urged the peasants to take immediate possession of the land for the purpose of nationalisation of all the land later on. The complete text of the resolution will be found among the appendices in this book.—p. 106.

214. The draft resolution on the agrarian question was introduced by Lenin at the first All-Russian Congress of Peasant Deputies, and received only a few votes. For further details on the first Peasant Congress see note 194. —p. 109.

215. This refers to the session of the Main Land Committee of June 2, 1917. At this session, a declaration on the agrarian question was adopted which stated in part:

. . . At the basis of future agrarian reforms there must be the principle that all lands of economic importance must be put to the use of the labouring, agricultural population. . . . Until the Constituent Assembly is convened there can be no final solution of the agrarian question and surely it cannot be carried out. . . . The attempts of the people to alleviate their land-hunger by seizing the lands of others on their own initiative constitute a serious danger for the state and instead of bringing a solution of the agrarian problem, will

create a mass of new problems which cannot be solved without the most
violent uprooting of the whole life of the people. . . .
For the purpose of a better preparation for the agrarian reform, the declaration proposes to guide the organisation of land committees in the paths "which
must not go beyond the limits set by the law." Smilga's motion to come out
for the immediate organised seizure of the large landed estates by the
peasantry was rejected by the Socialist-Revolutionist majority.—p. 111.

216. The American Civil War (1861-1865) was essentially a war between
the bourgeoisie of the North and the slave oligarchy of the South for the control of state power; a war between two irreconcilable economic systems which
ended in the destruction of slavery. The plantation economy of the South
rested on slave labour. The development of industry in the North, resting
upon the exploitation of "free" labour-power, could not permit the Southern
policy of the expansion of slavery into the territories of the West. By 1861,
the class struggle of the capitalist bourgeoisie and the slave oligarchy finally
broke out into open civil war, after having been carried on for decades on the
political and ideological fronts. Although the war at first favoured the South,
the industrial and numerical superiority of the North soon told against it, and
ultimately resulted in the utter collapse of the Confederacy. On September
22, 1862, President Lincoln issued a proclamation of emancipation, declaring
all slaves in the Southern states free on and after January 1, 1863. Following
the close of the Civil War in 1865, a constitutional amendment was adopted
abolishing slavery once for all. The historical significance of the American
Civil War was three-fold: It destroyed American slavery; it cleared the ground
for the "free" development of American capitalism; and laid the basis for the
development of a labour movement on a national scale.—p. 126.

217. *Viedomosti Obshchestvenovo Gradonachalstva (Bulletin of the Public
City Administration)*—official Petrograd paper which published the government
regulations and official announcements. The word "public" was added to the
title after the March Revolution.—p. 131.

218. The resolution on the economic measures to overcome disorganisation
was written by Lenin for the conference of factory committees and published
as the resolution of the Central Committee of the Bolsheviks in the Moscow
Social-Democrat, Number 64, June 7, 1917. The resolution appeared in the
Pravda eight days later (*Pravda*, Number 71, June 15), not as the resolution
of the Central Committee but as a draft resolution of the Organisation Bureau
for the convocation of the Conference of Factory Committees.
    From June 12-16, 1917, the Conference of Factory Committees met at
Petrograd and was dominated by a Bolshevik majority. The Bolsheviks also
occupied the leading rôle in the Organisation Bureau for the convocation of
this conference. The Organisation Bureau appointed Zinoviev as the reporter
on the chief point on the agenda ("Condition of Industry, Control of Production and Regulation of Labour in Petrograd"). The resolution on Zinoviev's
report presented by the Organisation Bureau and dealing with economic
measures to fight disorganisation was the draft prepared by Lenin and ap-

proved by the Central Committee (the Organisation Bureau had only made a few slight changes in Lenin's text). This resolution was then adopted by 290 out of 421 votes, all other resolutions being rejected. The resolution adopted by the Conference as a basis was referred to a commission for final editing; the text as confirmed by the Commission was then adopted at the closing session of the conference on June 16, by 297 against 21 votes with 44 abstaining. —p. 135.

219. The resolution of the First All-Russian Peasant Congress on the war, which was adopted May 28, 1917, announced as its aim peace without annexations and war indemnities on the basis of the self-determination of peoples by popular referendum. The means of securing such a peace was to be the pressure of the toiling masses of all belligerent countries upon their governments, following the example of the Russian Revolution which had secured the "recognition from the Provisional Government of the principles of a democratic peace," as well as the convocation of an international Socialist Conference. The All-Russian Soviet of Peasant Deputies, the resolution stated, "indignantly rejects any thought of a separate peace as an overt violation of the honour of revolutionary and liberated Russia. . . . The basic duty of the toiling people of revolutionary Russia is to carry on the most active defence of the country, not hesitating before any sacrifices, and to take the most determined measures to raise the fighting force of the army for offensive and defensive purposes. As long as the revolutionary army must fight against armies which are led by emperors, it is fighting for the security of the great possession of the Russian people. . . ."

The position of the Petrograd Soviet of Workers' and Soldiers' Deputies on the war is contained in the two proclamations of the Soviet of May 15, 1917, "To the Socialists of All Countries" and "To the Army" (see notes 186 and 187).—p. 138.

220. This refers to the article by V. Bazarov entitled "The Present Anarchy and the Coming Napoleon" in the *Novaia Zhizn*, Number 30, June 6, 1917. —p. 141.

221. From the appeal of the Labour Department of the Petrograd Soviet "To All Labour Departments of the Soviets of Workers' and Soldiers' Deputies," *Izvestia*, Number 70, June 1, 1917.—p. 143.

222. From the article, "The Struggle Between Capital and Labour," *Izvestia*, Number 70, June 1, 1917.—p. 143.

223. In an extraordinary session on May 29, 1917, the Executive Committee of the Petrograd Soviet took up the general economic situation. Cherevanin, Avilov, Bazarov, Shuba, Kukovetsky and Gromann reported in the name of the Economic Department of the Executive Committee. The reports dealt with the separate aspects of the economic life of the country: production, consumption, supplies, finances, etc. All of the reporters indicated the extremely critical condition of the country and pointed to the necessity of taking immediate and decisive measures.—p. 143.

224. Cronstadt was one of the most important revolutionary centres in 1917. The sailors of the Baltic Fleet, the garrison of Cronstadt and the factory workers manifested a revolutionary spirit and organised solidly around their Soviet. The Bolsheviks exerted a great influence upon the masses. Due to a conflict between the Soviet and the Cronstadt Government Commissar, Pepelaiev, the Cronstadt Soviet passed a resolution on May 30, 1917, insisting upon the abolition of the office of Government Commissar and the transfer of all power to the Cronstadt Soviet. The resolution stated:

The sole power in Cronstadt is the Soviet of Workers' and Soldiers' Deputies which maintains direct communication with the Petrograd Soviet of Workers' and Soldiers' Deputies on all governmental matters.

The resolution was introduced by non-partisans and adopted by the non-partisan majority of the Soviet with the support of the Bolsheviks and the Left Socialists-Revolutionists. Thereupon, the Provisional Government issued a trumpet blast about the "defection" of Cronstadt from the Russian Empire. The bourgeois Menshevik-Socialist-Revolutionist press raised a howl about the establishment of a "Cronstadt Republic." To smooth over the difficulty, the representatives of the Petrograd Soviet, Chkheidze, Gotz and others, came to Cronstadt. They were later followed by Ministers Tsereteli and Skobelev who succeeded in effecting a compromise with the Cronstadt Soviet. It was agreed that the Cronstadt Soviet should name a candidate for the Cronstadt Government Commissar's post who would be confirmed by the Provisional Government. In addition, the following resolution of a general, political nature was adopted:

In reply to the question of the representatives of the Provisional Government, I. G. Tsereteli and M. I. Skobelev, concerning our attitude toward the central power, the Cronstadt Soviet of Workers' and Soldiers' Deputies declares: "We recognise this power completely. Recognition, naturally, does not exclude criticism and the wish that the revolutionary democracy create a new organisation of the central power by placing all power in the hands of the Soviets of Workers' and Soldiers' Deputies. By means of an ideological influence upon the views of the majority of the democracy, we hope to succeed in directing this majority into the path which we consider the only correct one. Nevertheless, as long as this is not achieved, as long as the majority does not agree with us and supports the present Provisional Government, we recognize this Government and consider its laws and regulations just as valid for Cronstadt as for all other parts of Russia. . . ." (*Izvestia,* Number 74, June 7, 1917.)

Lenin disapproved of the premature action of the Cronstadters, and the further work of the Bolshevik fraction in the Cronstadt Soviet as well as the negotiations concerning the allaying of the conflict took place under his direct supervision.—p. 148.

225. Erfurt Programme—see note 162 in Book I. The programme was sent to Engels for criticism, and he subjected it to a detailed analysis. This criticism of 1891 was published ten years later under the title "In Criticism of the Social-Democratic Draft Programme" in the *Neue Zeit* (Vol. I, 1901-1902). See also V. I. Lenin: *The State and Revolution,* Chap. IV (*Collected Works,* Vol. XXI).—p. 152.

226. On June 12, 1917, an extraordinary session of the Petrograd Committee of the Bolsheviks took place, occupying itself primarily with the establishment

of a popular Petrograd paper. Before that the Executive Committee of the Petrograd Committee had expressed itself unanimously in favour of establishing a special Petrograd organ. In the discussion, the majority of the local party functionaries stood for an independent organ. Lenin opposed this plan. His speech is reproduced as recorded in the minutes. It is, of course, incomplete and inaccurate, and only gives Lenin's train of thought.

Both of the resolutions which Lenin proposed, the second of which bore the character of a compromise, were rejected by a majority. The vote on the first resolution resulted as follows: 12 for, 16 against, 2 abstaining; the vote for the second resolution is not reported in the minutes. The resolution of the Petrograd Committee for creating their own organ was likewise rejected by a tie vote—14 to 14—leaving the question unsettled. The next day, Lenin, who attributed fundamental importance to this question, addressed a "Letter to the Borough Committees" (see p. 170 of this book), in which he called upon the party membership to express its opinion upon this question. The letter was read at the session of the Petrograd Committee, June 19, 1917.—p. 161.

227. *Russkaia Gazeta* (*Russian Gazette*)—popular paper published by Parvus and Trotsky, which appeared in Petersburg in 1905.—p. 162.

228. The notes of the English and French Governments to the Russian Foreign Minister were in reply to his note of May 1, 1917, and to the Declaration of the Provisional Government of April 9 (see notes 145 and 118 in Book I). The English Ambassador's note stated among other things:

The British Government heartily shares the feelings . . . of free Russia. It did not begin this war as a war of conquest and is not continuing it for any such end. Its aim at the beginning was to defend the existence of its own country and to establish respect for international obligations. To these tasks, to-day, has been added the task of liberating the peoples that are being oppressed by a foreign tyranny. The British Government is therefore sincerely happy that free Russia has announced its intention of freeing Poland, and not only the Poland which was dominated by the old Russian absolutism, but also those parts of Poland which belong to the German and Austrian Empire. . . . The British Government is of the opinion that the treaties which it has concluded from time to time with the Allies, are, in their general features, in accord with the above-mentioned limitations [*i. e.*, with the declaration of the Provisional Government.—*Ed.*]; but if the Russian Government wishes, the British Government is quite ready to examine these treaties with its allies and if necessary revise them.

The French note contained the following resolution of the Chamber of Deputies of June 4:

The Chamber of Deputies expects from the war forced upon Europe by the attack of imperialist Germany not only the liberation of the occupied territories, but also the return of Alsace-Lorraine to the lap of the motherland and a just reparation of the damages. While rejecting every thought of conquering and enslaving foreign peoples, it considers that the efforts of the armies of the Republic and the Allies will permit, after the defeat of Prussian militarism, the achievement of substantial guarantees of peace and independence for the big and small peoples in one league of nations. . . .—p. 164.

229. This refers to the article "The Notes of the French and English Governments" in the *Rabochaia Gazeta*, Number 67, June 10, 1917.—p. 164.

230. The conference of the representatives of the mining industrialists and the workers of South Russia which met in Petrograd in May, 1917, and occupied itself with questions of wages and other demands of the workers, proved fruitless since the capitalists refused to make any concessions. The workers' delegation asserted that an increase of wages "to a considerable extent or even entirely at the expense of the employers' profits" was possible, hence without making it necessary to increase the price of coal. The representatives of the capitalists, on the other hand, demanded an immediate increase in the fixed price of coal. It was decided to form a Government Commission with representatives of both parties in order to investigate on the spot the conditions of work and the cost of production. The workers published the following declaration:

The workers' delegation affirms that the only practical result of the conference in Petrograd is the appointment of a special commission to determine the conditions of work and the cost of production, and that the industrialists did not consider it possible to agree to the provisional fixation of wages proposed by the representative of the Ministry of Labour; it declares that it rejects the responsibility for any possible complications in the mining region of the South, and that the workers' delegation, on its part, will make every effort to see that the peaceful progress of work in the factories and mines is not disturbed.

The delegation of the industrialists replied with a counter-declaration:

An increase of wages to the extent demanded by the labour conference will lead to such a catastrophic increase in the cost of producing mineral fuels, iron ore, cast iron and other industrial wares and therewith also all other industrial and consumers' articles for the masses, that this question, in its extent and significance, acquires the character of a general state and national question. Consequently, the industrialists are not only not in a position, but consider themselves not justified to decide upon the question raised in the demands of the labour conference; they cannot assume the responsibility for the consequences of an unavoidable increase in the cost of production and the shattering of the economic life of the country which might develop.—p. 167.

231. The quotation is from the article "The Country Is in Danger" in the *Rabochaia Gazeta*, Number 56, May 27, 1917.—p. 167.

232. The reproduction of this speech which Lenin delivered at the first Petrograd Conference of Factory-Shop Committees, as has already been indicated in the text, is based upon a brief newspaper report. In the personal notes of A. Kaktyn, a few more exact formulations have been preserved:

Control has now become a real vital necessity, no longer a phrase, but a generally recognised fact. The capitalists and their supporters are exerting themselves to reduce this measure to an empty sound. . . . A bacchanal of marauders reigns in the country. The new government has increased prices for the marauders—the coal industrialists of the South. . . . Must not serve as the errand boy of the capitalists. Control must not look like that. We need a real control, the control of the workers. . . . Through the control of the Junkers and capitalists, Germany has created a hard-labour régime for the workers. . . .—p. 173.

233. B. V. Avilov's resolution which he had proposed at the Conference of Factory-Shop Committees, was rejected by all against 13 votes. The resolution read as follows:

The present economic ruin which is a result of the war and the anarchic robber-economy of the capitalists and the government can only be overcome by the planned regulation of the entire economy by the state and public power, by an increased taxation of the propertied classes and by the substitution of state loans for the issue of paper money. The state must create in the shortest time, with the co-operation of the revolutionary democracy, central organs for providing the country with all of the most important products which are to be distributed at fixed prices in a planful manner. All branches of big industry must be united under the control of the state and revolutionary democracy in the form of compulsory trusts, in order to carry out the orders of the central supply organs. The prices of raw materials for the separate industrial branches must be fixed and the distribution of their products regulated. All trade and all banks are to be placed under the control of the state. Definite minimum wages must be fixed and the supply of the most urgent necessities for the inhabitants secured. The task of the factory committees in this connection is to co-operate in the control of the operations of the factories in reference to their supply of raw materials, fuels and equipment, the correct pace of production, the norms of manufacturing costs and the distribution of the products as well as the determination of the conditions for transferring the work in the factories to a peace basis. The factory committees must try to unite according to industrial branches in order to be able to exercise the same functions of control for whole branches of industry with the co-operation of organs of state power and the employers. The local and district unions of the factory committees of the different industrial branches must set as their task the union of the factory committees of similar enterprises according to districts, in order to unite these district unions into an all-Russian union. Besides, the local and district unions must ascertain the general situation in all factories of their respective districts from the point of view of partially supplying them with material within the limits of the district as well as supplying them with means of transportation.—p. 173.

234. The communication of the Department of International Relations of the Executive Committee of the Petrograd Soviet of Workers' and Soldiers' Deputies to the secretary of the International Socialist Bureau, Huysmans, reads:

In view of the various interpretations which the entrance of the representatives of the Soviet of Workers' and Soldiers' Deputies into the Provisional Government has called forth—many wanted to compare this entrance to the participation in the government under entirely different conditions—the Department for International Relations of the Soviet of Workers' Deputies considers it necessary to state the following: 1. The Socialist Ministers were sent into the revolutionary Provisional Government by the Soviet with the definite order to arrive at a general peace by way of the agreement of nations and not to drag out the imperialist war in the name of the liberation of peoples by means of arms. 2. The reason for the participation of the Socialists in the revolutionary government was not the cessation of the class struggle but its continuation with the aid of political power. That is also the reason why the entrance of the Socialists into the government for the purpose of working together with those representatives of the bourgeois parties who have expressed themselves openly for the policy of democracy and peace has become possible only after part of the enemies of the proletariat found themselves in the Peter-Paul Fortress and the rest deprived of their power by the movement of the revolutionary masses on May 3-5. 3. The participation of the Socialists in the government followed the existence of complete freedom for the proletariat and the army. State of siege, political censorship, limitation of the right to strike, of assembly and speech do not reduce this freedom in the least. In addition, the Russian proletariat possesses means for the complete control of those elected by it. 4. The entrance of the representatives of the Russian Socialist proletariat into the government in no way signifies the loosening of the ties which bind it with the Socialists of all lands who carry on the struggle against imperialism, but, on the contrary, signifies the strengthening of these ties in the common struggle for general peace. (*Izvestia*, Number 78, June 12, 1917).—p. 175.

235. *Vorwärts* (*Forward*)—the central organ of the German Social-Democracy founded in 1876. It adopted a social-chauvinist attitude at the very outset of the war.—p. 192.

236. The leading editorial of *Riech*, Number 128, June 16, 1917.—p. 192.

237. The First All-Russian Congress of Soviets met on June 16, 1917, at Petrograd. Altogether there were 790 delegates, for the most part Mensheviks, a smaller part belonging to the Socialists-Revolutionists. Only 103 delegates or 13 per cent of the total number of delegates were Bolsheviks. The sessions of the Congress were entirely under the control of the Mensheviks (Tsereteli, Dan) and the Socialists-Revolutionists. The Congress expressed itself for participation of the Socialists in the bourgeois Provisional Government, for the "defence of the fatherland," for the "Liberty Loan," and for the support of the offensive at the front demanded by the Entente. The Congress forbade the Bolshevik demonstration on June 23 in Petrograd, but the demonstration which the Congress itself had fixed for July 1 and intended as a manifestation of confidence in the Provisional Government, proceeded entirely under Bolshevik slogans. The Congress elected a central executive committee consisting of Mensheviks and Socialists-Revolutionists which existed until the Second Soviet Congress. Lenin's double appearance at the Congress naturally found no response from the compromising majority of the delegates. Lenin delivered his first speech on June 17 during the discussion on the report of F. Dan: "The Provisional Government and the Revolutionary Democracy." The speaking time was limited by the order of business; Lenin's speech was repeatedly interrupted by heckling from the majority and the applause of the minority. This speech on the attitude towards the Provisional Government is reproduced according to the stenographic report which Lenin personally corrected. The second speech (on the war) was delivered on June 22 and is reprinted according to the text published in the *Pravda*. It is possible that the *Pravda* text was also looked over by Lenin.—p. 193.

238. Minister of Posts and Telegraphs—Tsereteli.—p. 198.

239. Liakhov's policy in Persia—that is, the policy of tsarism which was directed towards the suppression of every popular movement in neighbouring Persia. The first Russian Revolution of 1905 was the starting point for a revolutionary mass movement in Persia which forced the Shah to grant a constitution and a parliament. The Russian colonel Liakhov, who commanded the Persian Cossack brigade which was under the guidance of Russian instructors, dispersed the parliament in 1908 and helped to suppress the revolutionary movement. During the imperialist war a Russian Division occupied northern Persia under the pretext of preventing a threatening Turkish attack, and devastated and plundered the country. Liakhov who had a command on the Turkish front committed many atrocities against the inhabitants of that part of Turkish Armenia occupied by the tsarist troops.—p. 199.

240. The question of granting passports to the Socialists of the Entente powers for the contemplated International Socialist Conference in Stockholm kept the Menshevik and Socialist-Revolutionary Soviet leaders, the initiators of the Conference, in suspense the whole summer of 1917. The Entente governments changed their decisions repeatedly, now declaring themselves ready to grant the passports, now absolutely denying the request.—p. 202.

241. Albania, which declared itself independent during the Balkan War of 1912, constituted from that time on the object of dispute of the neighbouring states. In the secret treaty concluded by the Entente with Italy, by which Italy obligated herself to join the Entente in the war, Middle Albania, together with Valona, among other things, was promised the Italians as booty. See also the article "One of the Secret Treaties," p. 66 of this book.

Greece was forced into the war by England and the other Entente powers in 1917 against the will of the people by means of a regular coup d'état (King Constantine was forced to abdicate) with the co-operation of the former Greek Prime Minister Venizelos, an agent of England.

Persia was occupied by England and Russia during the war under the pretext of fighting Turkish bands; Russian troops occupied the northern part of Persia, and English troops who came up from the Persian Gulf, the southern part.—p. 203.

242. This refers to the declaration of the Bolsheviks and the Social-Democratic Internationalists at the First Soviet Congress concerning the question of the offensive. The text will be found among the appendices in this book. —p. 203.

243. Kiaochow—a city in the Chinese province of Shantung; seaport. The territory of Kiaochow with its fruitful hinterland was "leased" to Germany in 1898 by China with all sovereign rights for 99 years. During the imperialist war Japan seized this colony from Germany; it promised to return the territory to the rightful owner, China, but did not keep its promise. The islands in the Pacific Ocean: the Marianas and Carolinas together with the Palow Islands belonged to Germany before the war. During the war Japan seized them for herself. To-day they are Japanese mandatory territories.—p. 213.

244. The Russian Revolution of 1905 exercised a lasting influence upon the countries of the East. In 1908, a revolution broke out in Turkey. The Sultan Abdul Hamid was overthrown and the Young Turks took over power. In 1909, a revolutionary movement of the people in Persia forced the abdication of the Shah Muhammed Ali and the re-establishment of the constitution forcibly abolished in 1908 with the help of the Tsar (see also note 239); the Medshlis was re-convoked. In 1910 a revolutionary movement under the leadership of Sun Yat-sen began in China, which in the course of its development led to the overthrow of the monarchy and the establishment of a republic (declaration of independence of the southern provinces with Sun Yat-sen as president in 1911; abdication of the Manchu Dynasty and proclamation of the Chinese Republic in 1912).—p. 216.

245. The letter of the peasant, G. Andreiev, to which this refers, stated among other things:

I am a muzhik, a peasant. In the summer I live in the village; even before I worked at the factory, I lived in the village and now I visit it two or three times a year. . . . Since 1905 I have been a Socialist-Revolutionist, but when they began to say that we should not take the land away from the landlords, my thoughts began to turn away from them; and when they gave their consent to the liberty loan, I ran away and entered the party of the Bolsheviks, but not of the Mensheviks, because I understand, if not much, at least what I am about. . . . I shall present my opinion of the various parties in the village for the village meeting. I view the village meeting this way: the zemsky nachalnik [under tsarism, the zemstvo representative in the village.—Ed.], the starshina [the senior volost official elected by the peasants in pre-revolutionary times. —Ed.], the village elder, the rich peasant and the poor peasant, just like myself. I compare the nachalnik with the cadets who defend capital and the whole bourgeoisie. . . . The starshina I compare with the learned professors who want one side to be well off, but that the other be not hurt, the matter being postponed for about a thousand years, and that for the time being everybody calm down. . . . The village elder I compare with the Mensheviks. . . . The rich peasants I compare with the Socialists-Revolutionists. . . . Then I take the poor peasant. I compare him with the Bolshevik Social-Democrats. . . . They do not think about the war like the village elder or the rich peasant. Since the people do not need the war, the people must stop it at once, not any old way, and should not put out its head to catch bullets. . . . Fraternisation at the front, but not to sleep in the hinterland; work untiringly for the holy truth. We must not stop and wait until some one drops out from the sky, and puts an end to the war. We must press the bourgeoisie harder, let it burst at all the seams. Then the war will be ended. But if we do not press the bourgeoisie hard enough, things will be bad. . . .—p. 218.

246. The Gentlemen of June 16—on June 16, 1907, the Second Imperial Duma was dispersed and a new electoral law proclaimed. This electoral law gave the feudal and commercial-industrial interests in the Duma a powerful preponderance. After this, these elements of the Imperial Duma used to be called "The Gentlemen of June 16" (the Cadets, Octobrists, the Rights) who owed their predominance to the Stolypin electoral law of June 16, 1907.— p. 221.

247. The resolution demanding the immediate offensive of the Russian Army was adopted by the conference of the members of the Imperial Duma on June 16, 1917.—p. 221.

248. The phrase about "the great withdrawal of the bourgeoisie" was used by Liber on June 17, 1917, in his report at the First Soviet Congress. In this report he viewed the retirement of the Minister of War Guchkov as the "beginning of the great withdrawal of the bourgeoisie from the government." —p. 229.

249. This refers to the report of A. Peshekhonov, the Minister of Food Supplies, given at the June 18, 1917, session of the Soviet Congress on the food question.—p. 232.

250. This refers to the article: "Press Review. An Angry Criticism," in the Novaia Zhizn, Number 41, June 19, 1917.—p. 234.

251. The conference of the "wild bulls" of June 16—this is what Lenin called the conference of the members of the Imperial Duma (see also the article "The Wild Bulls of June 16 Want an Immediate Offensive," p. 221, of this book). At this conference of June 16, 1917, Miliukov delivered a big speech on the international and internal policy, which was directed against the Bolsheviks and the Soviet.—p. 236.

252. The Central Committee of the Bolsheviks had announced a demonstration in Petrograd for June 23, 1917, under the slogans: "Down with the Capitalist Ministers," "All Power to the Soviets." The proletarian and soldier masses of Petrograd were highly indignant against the Provisional Government, which was dragging the war out and refused to alleviate the most urgent needs of the masses. The Mensheviks and Socialists-Revolutionists who belonged to the government and had the majority at the Soviet Congress, saw that the sentiment of the masses was beginning to turn in favour of the Bolsheviks and issued an order, under the pretext of threatened counterrevolutionary action, prohibiting the demonstration; in addition, they sent to the factories on the night of June 23 delegates of the Congress to agitate against the demonstration. The appearance of the delegates, however, found no response among the workers and they were hostilely received by them. The Central Committee, after it had been informed of the order prohibiting the demonstration, decided to call it off and announced its decision in the Pravda (see note 254).—p. 238.

253. The villa of the former tsarist Minister Durnovo was occupied by Anarchists and a few workers' organisations during the March Days as had been done with the palace of Kshesinskaia by the Bolsheviks. The owners fought to have the villa vacated. Minister of Justice Pereverzev made several futile attempts to drive out the "usurpers" with military force. Under the pretext that there were criminals among the Anarchists, the Minister of Justice undertook a new attack upon the villa on the night of July 2; as a result two Anarchists were killed, the rooms demolished and the house destroyed. The attack of the government aroused the entire Petrograd proletariat.—p. 238.

254. The calling off of the demonstration of June 23, 1917, by the Bolshevik Central Committee at the request of the Soviet Congress caused dissatisfaction among the workers, who nevertheless submitted to the decision of the Central Committee, as well as among some party functionaries in the districts. In an extraordinary session of the Petrograd Committee Lenin delivered a speech in which he backed up the decision of the Central Committee. The Petrograd Committee then approved the action of the Central Committee. The speech reproduced in the text is not a stenographic report but a brief account recorded in the minutes.—p. 245.

255. On June 24, 1917, there took place a united session of the Executive Committee of the Petrograd Soviet, the presidium of the Soviet Congress and all fraction committees of the parties represented at the Congress. After a

report by Dan and a reply by Kamenev, Tsereteli delivered a speech in which
he declared that the demonstration planned by the Bolsheviks for June 23
was a "conspiracy for overthrowing the government and the seizure of power
by the Bolsheviks," that the Bolsheviks who in reality were then the only
counter-revolutionary party would have to be put beyond the pale of "revolutionary democracy" and the Soviet parties and that the arms in the hands
of the workers would have to be taken away from them. The representatives
of the Bolshevik fraction left the meeting as a protest. Lenin did not participate in the conference, having been against participation from the beginning.
—p. 245.

256. The resolution of the First Soviet Congress on the events of June 22
and 23, 1917, which was proposed by the presidium and adopted at the session
of June 24, stated after a long introduction which emphasised the need of
unity on the part of the revolutionary democracy for the struggle against
counter-revolution:

The All-Russian Soviet Congress of Workers' and Soldiers' Deputies decidedly
condemns the attempt to organise a demonstration in Petrograd behind the
back of the Soviet, without some effective measures having been taken against
the demonstration becoming an armed one and leading to bloody conflicts,
ruinous for the revolution, and decides: 1. Groups and parties which belong
to the Soviets of Workers' and Soldiers' Deputies have no right to undertake mass actions against the clearly expressed will of the Soviets as the
appointed organs of the revolutionary democracy; 2. Peaceful, unarmed demonstrations may be organised by these groups and parties only with the consent of the Soviets; 3. All armed actions, including demonstrations with armed
participants, may only be organised by the decision of the Soviets as the
sole organs which represent the will of the entire revolutionary democracy.
The Congress calls upon all comrades, workers, soldiers and peasants to submit to this decision and not to follow arbitrary calls which are strictly contradictory to the above-mentioned decisions, no matter from what side these
calls come. Every breach of this decision adds water to the counter-revolutionary mill and threatens to unleash a civil war. At the same time, the
Congress decides to form a commission for the purpose of thoroughly clarifying all the circumstances which led to the preparation of the demonstration of
June 22 and 23, the representatives of all the parties belonging to the Soviet
to participate in it, and directs this commission to pay special attention to
what extent and in what forms dubious and counter-revolutionary elements
participated in this movement which strove to utilise it for their own ends.

The Bolshevik fraction presented a special declaration to the Congress on
this matter. (For the text of the declaration see appendices in this book.)—
p. 250.

257. The Universal Act of the Ukrainian Central Rada stated among other
things:

Without separating from Russia, without breaking with the Russian State,
let the Ukrainian people have the right to determine its own life on its own
land, a Ukrainian National Assembly—a Seim—elected by universal, equal,
direct and secret ballot shall establish the state order in the Ukraine. All
laws pertaining to the establishment of order here, in the Ukraine, are to
be made only by the Ukrainian Assembly; but those laws which are to help
establish order throughout the entire Russian State shall be made by the
All-Russian Parliament. . . . We thought that the Central Government of
Russia would help us in this work; that we, the Ukrainian Central Rada,

would be able to establish a system of law in our country in agreement with it, but the Provisional Government has rejected all of our demands. . . . Wherever the administrative power, for whatever reason, has remained in hands hostile to the Ukraine, we instruct our citizens to launch a comprehensive, powerful organisation and upon informing the population, elect a new administration. In the cities and in those places where the Ukrainian people are living together with other nationalities, we instruct all citizens to come to an immediate agreement with the democracies of all nationalities and to proceed with them to prepare a new correct life. . . . After we have accomplished this preliminary organisational work, we shall permit the representatives of all the peoples of the Ukraine to meet and establish the laws for the country, those laws which we shall prepare and which the All-Russian Constituent Assembly will have to confirm. . . . We, the Ukrainian Central Rada, order all organised citizens of the cities and villages and all Ukrainian public offices, to levy a tax on the population from July 1 on for the people's cause. . . . Ukrainian people, your fate is in your hands. . . .—p. 253.

258. From the leading editorial of the *Riech*, Number 137, June 27, 1917. —p. 254.

259. In the *Rabochaia Gazeta*, Number 80, June 27, there appeared an article entitled: "Call to Order." The Menshevik author of the article attacks the Bolsheviks and recommends that they "separate from the agitators who are everywhere preaching the forcing of civil war; to draw away from those who believe that 'the Socialist Ministers have sold themselves to the bourgeoisie'; even the Soviet Congress has been bribed by the landowners and capitalists. . . ." The author of the article sees no danger of counter-revolution from the Right; there are no Cavaignacs to be seen anywhere; nevertheless, "when the real Cavaignac comes, we shall fight together with you in the same ranks. . . ."—p. 255.

260. The Extraordinary Investigating Commission established by the Provisional Government for the investigation of the crimes of the old régime, under the chairmanship of the attorney N. K. Muraviov, examined Lenin concerning the case of the provacateur Malinovsky. The Mensheviks and together with them the entire bourgeois press tried to play up the Malinovsky case especially big for factional reasons.—p. 264.

261. Dzhunkovsky who was appointed Vice-Minister of the Interior in 1914, learned upon looking through the documents of the police department that Malinovsky, the Duma Deputy, was also a police spy. The presence of spies in the Imperial Duma was too much even for Dzhunkovsky and he informed Rodzianko, the President of the Duma, of Malinovsky's activities as a spy. Rodzianko thereupon called Malinovsky to him and advised him to disappear, which Malinovsky did: he resigned his mandate and went abroad. Rodzianko informed neither the Social-Democratic fraction, to which Malinovsky belonged, of the latter's activity as a spy, nor any other Deputy. Rodzianko thereby revealed himself as shielding a spy. (For Malinovsky see Biographical Notes.) —p. 265.

262. On July 1, 1917, a grand demonstration took place in Petrograd. The Soviet Congress which had forbidden the Bolshevik demonstration planned

for June 23 and in addition prohibited all street demonstrations "for three days," had itself been forced by the pressure of the masses to arrange a demonstration for Sunday, July 1, which, to the surprise of the compromising Soviet Congress, turned into a complete triumph for the Bolsheviks. About 400,000 workers and soldiers demonstrated on that day. Ninety per cent of the banners bore the slogans of the Central Committee of the Bolsheviks: "Down with the Ten Capitalist Ministers," and "All Power to the Soviets." The slogan "Confidence in the Provisional Government" which the Menshevik-Socialist-Revolutionist Soviet Congress set up was to be seen only on three banners and these belonged to a Cossack regiment, the *Yedinstvo* group, and the Petrograd organisation of the Bund, respectively. Similar demonstrations took place in Moscow, in the Moscow Province and in other cities. The first of July had shown that the masses were united for the revolution and had no use for the compromisers.—p. 268.

263. The offensive at the front long prepared by the Provisional Government and the Menshevik-Socialist-Revolutionist Bloc at the demand of the Entente powers began on July 1, 1917. After Kerensky had visited the front and had persuaded the troops in hundreds of meetings to undertake the offensive, the army on the West and Southwest front proceeded to attack. The attack brought initial results in the first two days, a few thousand Austrians being captured, but the technically feebly prepared and badly led offensive was soon transformed into a serious defeat for the Russian army and the imperialist policy of the Provisional Government. The Russian troops were not only forced to surrender the newly-won terrain, but they even had to execute a considerable retreat, losing many in dead and captured. The initial success aroused great enthusiasm among the compromisers and the bourgeoisie, but it soon gave way to a complete loss of head. On July 2, Tsereteli delivered a patriotic speech at the Soviet Congress "On the Offensive of Our Army" to which Lenin's article refers. From this time on, the Bolsheviks, who already had the leadership of the Petrograd factories and regiments, began to gain rapidly in influence upon the army. The front quickly overtook revolutionary Petrograd.—p. 271.

264. The leading editorial of the *Riech* of July 1, 1917, occupied itself with the demonstration announced for this day in Petrograd and arrived at the following conclusions, keeping in view the sentiment of the masses who were turning away from the coalition Socialists:

The aim of the Coalition Government, the creation of a strong power in which confidence is placed has not been attained. . . . The Socialist Ministers have discredited themselves among their own followers by their "Cadet" declarations at the Soviet Congress and have had to trail in the wake of the Bolsheviks in the last week. . . . Instead of a stronger power, the Coalition Cabinet presents a weaker power . . . the leadership of the Revolution must give way before the elementary laws of all revolutions. . . .

The *Riech* was of the opinion that the question of the usefulness of the further existence of the Government Coalition was not only raised by the Bolsheviks, but would also have to be raised by the capitalist Ministers. When the slogan "All Power to the Soviets" was realised, "the Soviets would convince themselves that they had very little power at their disposal and they would seek to replace this lack of power by Young-Turk or Jacobin methods." In conclusion, the *Riech* declared the decisive question of the Russian Revolu- tion to be "whether they (the Socialists—*Ed.*) would be ready, in raising the entire question anew, to sink to the level of Jacobinism and terror, or whether they would make the attempt to wash their hands of the whole thing." The article was most probably written by Miliukov. Lenin's expressions, "his- torian" and "miserable counter-revolutionary bourgeois," refer to him.—p. 277.

265. The First All-Russian Conferenec of Trade Unions met at Petrograd from July 4 to July 11, 1917.—p. 279.

266. At the Third Congress of the Socialists-Revolutionists which met at Moscow on June 7, 1917, Kerensky was not elected to the Central Committee. The Lefts (the Kamkov group) and a part of the Centre (the Kogan-Bern- stein group) voted against him. Breshko-Breshkovskaia, whom the Socialists- Revolutionists called the "Grandmother of the Russian Revolution" and who occupied an extreme Right position, refused to accept her election to the Central Committee as a protest against the failure to elect Kerensky to the committee.—p. 285.

267. The article "Why We Must Control Production" was not continued. Lenin most likely was prevented from completing it by the July events.—p. 290.

268. The *Izvestia* of the All-Russian Soviet of Peasant Deputies says con- cerning the report of Minister of Agriculture Chernov made at the session of the Provisional Government and the bills introduced by him:

. . . The basic thought of the report is that the urgent need of the moment is the promulgation of a whole series of laws which, in their totality, em- brace all basic phenomena of the economic life of the village. The Ministry of Agriculture therefore lays before the Provisional Government ten bills which are of immediate importance for the regulation of social relations in the sphere of agriculture, and in addition, two supplementary bills on the reform of the committee of experts of the Ministry. of Agriculture in order to adapt it to the need of placing science in the service of agrarian reform, and furthermore on the organisation of a Department for Economics and Politics in the Ministry.

The *Izvestia* of the Soviet of Workers' and Soldiers' Deputies wrote on June 25, 1917:

The Ministry is presenting ten bills to the Provisional Government on stop- ping the sale, purchase and mortgaging of the land, on interference in the economic life of the village, etc. The worst would be for the legislation to come too late. . . .

Of the ten, or more correctly twelve, bills, not a single one became law during the existence of the Provisional Government, not until November, 1917. —p. 291.

269. The appeal of the Minister of Labour to the workers was published in the *Novaia Zhizn*, Number 60, July 11, 1917. Minister of Labour Skobelev tells the workers in this appeal that the Provisional Government has set itself

the task of fighting against economic disorganisation with all its might and will control and regulate national economy through the authority of the revolutionary power. The leading and controlling organs are to be transformed on the basis of extensive representation of the workers. Therefore the workers should give up any arbitrary deeds and keep from interfering in the matter of production.—p. 299.

270. This refers to the article by Avilov "The Chaos in the Ministry of Commerce" in the *Novaia Zhizn*, Number 60, July 11, 1917. The author shows how the Ministry of Commerce, with Palchinsky and Stepanov at the head, is sabotaging the promises of the government concerning control and regulation of industry as announced in the Declaration of the Coalition Government of May 18, 1917.—p. 299.

271. The resolution of the Economic Department of the Executive Committee of the Petrograd Soviet of Workers' and Soldiers' Deputies "On the Metal Industry of the Moscow District" reads:

The following is to be brought to the attention of the Provisional Government: The metal industry of the Moscow region (15 provinces) is in a terribly critical condition which is dangerous for the entire economy and for the political stability of the state. The Goujon-Works which supply 85 per cent of the metal for the whole region have posted an announcement that from July 1 on the works will be closed. Bari, Dynamo, Bromley and other works are threatening to close down. The state cannot permit the closing down of these plants under any circumstances. In view of the fact that the management of the Goujon plant is obviously disorganising production and deliberately leading to the shutting down of the plant on the pretext of lacking means of production in spite of its ability to secure credit, the state must take the management of the plant into its own hands by creating a management on the pattern of that of the Putilov-Works and the Society of 1886 and must supply means of production. It must be kept in mind, however, that this indispensable measure will unavoidably result in the necessity of a regulation of the entire metal industry in the direction indicated by the resolution of the All-Russian Soviet Congress (fixation of prices, regulation of profits and wages, compulsory syndication and trustification etc.); this requires that the Economic Council and the Economic Committee become active at once and official district supply committees be formed. In this case the Conference of Moscow Factories must be urgently granted the right to establish a management in the Goujon-Works and the Conference must be supplied with means of production to the amount of five million rubles.—p. 301.

272. A. Sandomirsky's article "The Struggle for the Organisation of Industry" in the *Novaia Zhizn*, Number 61, July 12, 1917, gives a clear picture of the results of the sabotage of the mining industrialists in the South of Russia which they had begun as early as April-May. He states among other things:

The chaos in the Donetz Basin is increasing from day to day. The Provisional Donetz Committee and the District Committee of the Soviets are receiving telegram upon telegram on the closing of shafts and mines, on the closing down of factories because of lack of raw material, on the excitement among the workers who are not being granted any increase in wages or are not being paid at all because there is no money. . . . The vicious circle—lack of coal, lack of metals, lack of locomotives and rolling stock, cessation of production—is spreading ever wider. Yet while coal is being burned, metal piled up, these things cannot be obtained when and where they are needed. The Workers' Soviet of the Marievka District telegraphs that at the Marievka mine of Kazakevich 300,000 poods of coal are stored up; the coal is burning; but the attempt of the workers to take the coal out has failed because the teamsters demand four kopecks just as the other mines pay, whereas the management is only willing to pay 3.8 kopecks.

The workers' attempts to take up the struggle against the chaos met with the most determined resistance of the industrialists, who were being supported by Palchinsky, the Vice Minister of Commerce.

In view of the lack of exact data, the Donetz Committee [an official commission on a parity basis for arbitrating conflicts between labour and capital. —*Ed.*] decided to institute an inquiry on the metal supplies through the Soviets of Workers' and Soldiers' Deputies as well as through the factory committees. When they proceeded to the work of controlling the metal, Palchinsky issued an order: "Any kind of arbitrary control commissions must not be admitted."

When the Donetz Committee demanded 500,000 poods of metal from Pankin for repairing the locomotives, the colonel was insulted because they had not begged it but demanded it of him. And only after an exchange of letters with Petrograd did they receive 328,000 instead of 500,000 poods, not in May but in June. Palchinsky had forbidden the removal of the Donetz Committee from Yekaterinoslav to Kharkov and failed to confirm the unanimous election of Professor Rubin as chairman of the Conference for Fuels, "because it is impermissible that one person occupy two posts."—302.

273. Due to the offensive, a polemic developed in the *Rabochaia Gazeta* among the Mensheviks Potresov, Cherevanin and Ivanovich. Ivanovich reproached Cherevanin in an article "Shall We Fear Peace?" (*Rabochaia Gazeta*, Number 93, July 12, 1917) to the effect that his position on the offensive and a possible victory at the front led to the recognition of the correctness of the Bolshevik assertions that the Russian army was objectively fighting for the imperialist interests of the Allies. Against this Ivanovich insisted that the victory of the Russian army over Hindenburg was simultaneously a victory over Entente imperialism.—p. 304.

274. The private conference of members of the Imperial Duma in Petrograd took place July 11, 1917, in the Tauride Palace and occupied itself with the financial and economic condition of the country and the condition of industry. Bublikov reported; Prince Lvov, Shidlovsky and Kuzmin also spoke. Rodzianko concluded, developing the train of thought cited by Lenin. —p. 307.

BIOGRAPHICAL NOTES

A.

ADLER, FRIEDRICH (born 1879)—Son of Victor Adler. From 1907 to 1911 assistant professor of theoretical physics in the University of Zürich, simultaneously editing the *Volksrecht*, organ of Swiss Social-Democracy; later elected Secretary of the Austrian Social-Democratic Party. On October 22, 1916, he assassinated the Austrian Prime Minister, Count Stuergkh, and was sentenced to death. Sentence commuted to eighteen years' hard labour. In 1916 and 1917 Lenin considered the imprisoned Adler as one of the future builders of the Third International. The most popular slogan of the May Day demonstrations of 1917 in Russia was the demand for Adler's liberation. Freed after the Austrian Revolution of 1918, Adler, however, returned to Social-Democracy and conducted a struggle against the Communists. Attempted to build a "centrist" Two-and-one-half International, which, in 1922, under his initiative, combined with the Second International, whose General Secretary Adler is at present. Politically Adler is an eclectic, full of inconsistencies and contradictions; in the realm of philosophy he is a follower of the empirio-monist anti-Marxist Ernst Mach, who denies the objectivity of the material world, and whom Lenin subjected to a thoroughgoing criticism in his *Materialism and Empirio-Criticism*, Vol. XIII of the *Collected Works* of V. I. Lenin.—I 150; II 248.

ADLER, VICTOR (1852-1918)—Founder and leader of Austrian Social-Democracy. In 1886 founded the Social-Democratic paper *Gleichheit*, laying the basis for unity between the "moderates" and the "radicals" which was finally achieved at the Unity Congress of the Austrian Social-Democracy in Hainfeld in 1889. With the help of the *Arbeiterzeitung*, Adler initiated the struggle for universal suffrage which was the axis of the Austrian labour movement from its origin to 1907. Adler devoted himself entirely to parliamentary struggles, hoping to utilise the division of the bourgeoisie into small national fractions in the interest of the working class. In the course of the struggle, however, Adler proved that he was no revolutionary Socialist. He elevated opportunism to a political art, thereby becoming the father of Austro-Marxism or Kautskyism. During the war he remained a social-patriot with a pacifist bent. After the revolution (1918), he became Secretary of State for Foreign Affairs, but died shortly afterwards. Very active in the Second International since its foundation in 1889. Adler was one of the clearest minds in the reformist, centrist camp. His tactics were directed not towards clarifying but towards covering up the contradictions within the International. —I 147.

ALEXANDER I (1777-1825)—Russian Tsar from 1801 to 1825.—I 313.

AMFITEATROV, A. V. (1862-1923)—Well-known Russian political satirist.

Contributed to newspapers of widely different political views. Gained popularity in 1902 by publishing a sketch in the paper *Rossia*, entitled "The Obmanov Family," a slightly veiled satire on the House of Romanov (*Obman* in Russian means fraud, swindle). For this he was banished. In 1905 published a magazine, *Krasnoie Znamia* (*Red Banner*) abroad. Returned to Russia in 1917, where he wrote for bourgeois publications, lying about and calumniating Lenin and the Bolsheviks. Later emigrated abroad.—I 188.

ANDRONNIKOV—Menshevik. Member of the Committee for the Return of the Russian Political Emigrés (in Switzerland).—I 222.

ANGARSKY, N. S. (pseudonym of Klestov; born 1873)—Narodnik in his youth; Marxist in the early twentieth century; Bolshevik. Was active abroad, participating in the Paris group of the *Iskra* (*Spark*). In Russia, worked in a number of southern committees and in the Moscow Committee of the Russian Social-Democratic Labour Party. Arrested many times; sentenced to Siberia; escaped. In 1917 a member of the Moscow Committee and delegate to the April Conference. Later active in the Moscow Soviet. Writer.—I 307, 308.

AVILOV, B. V. (born 1874)—Russian Social-Democrat; originally a Bolshevik. Participated in the Third Congress of the Russian Social-Democratic Labour Party (1905). Was banished to Siberia. After the March Revolution of 1917, member of the Petrograd Committee of Bolsheviks; in April, 1917, however, joined the staff of the *Novaia Zhizn* (*New Life*). Later a member of the Central Committee of Social-Democrats Internationalists, which he quit in 1918, abandoning political activity altogether.—II 144, 173, 174, 179, 189, 191, 299.

AVKSENTIEV, N. D. (born 1878)—One of the oldest leaders of the Socialist-Revolutionary Party. Member Executive Committee of the Petersburg Soviet of Workers' Deputies in 1905; member Central Committee of the Socialist-Revolutionary Party in 1907. Since then in the Right Wing of his party, which defended legality and the abolition of terrorism. During the war, extreme chauvinist, participant in defencist Socialist-Revolutionary organs, *Za Rubezhom* (*Beyond the Border*) and *Novosti* (*News*) and co-editor of the social-chauvinist magazine, *Prizyv* (*Call*) appearing in Paris (other participants being Plekhanov, Alexei Lubimov, Argunov, Volsky, and Bunakov). Member of one of the coalition cabinets under Kerensky. After the November Revolution, one of the organisers of the civil war on the Czechoslovakian front. Member of the Ufa Directory (1918), early dispersed by Kolchak. At present lives abroad and is engaged in work against the Soviet government.—II 302.

AXELROD, P. B. (1850-1928)—Well-known Russian Menshevik leader. In the seventies a follower of Bakunin, participant in the Narodnik movement. Arrested in a village, where he was engaged in propaganda work; escaped and emigrated abroad, where, together with Plekhanov, founded the Liberation of Labour Group in 1883. In 1900, member of the editorial staff of *Iskra*. At the Second Party Congress in 1903, he joined the Mensheviks. Subsequently initiated the idea of a "workers' congress," i. e., of dissolving the Social-Democratic Party into non-partisan labour organisations. One of the leaders of Liquidators. Member of the Zimmerwald Conference, centre group.

Active in attempts at organising Two-and-one-half International; conducted
an active campaign against Communism. Member of the International Socialist Bureau of the Second International. Died in Berlin in April, 1928.—
I 83, 147, 222, 242.

AZEF, E. F. (1870-1918)—Famous provocateur, one of the founders of the
Socialist-Revolutionary Party, leader of its terrorist organisation, and peren-
nial member of the Central Committee until 1908, when, exposed by Burtzev
and the ex-chief of the police department, Lopukhin, fled party trial. During
the war, lived in hiding in Germany.—II 157, 264.

B

BADAIEV, A. E. (born 1883)—Member of the Fourth Imperial Duma elected
by the Workers' Electoral College of Petersburg Province. Bolshevik.
Worker. Tried during the war, together with the Bolshevik Duma fraction,
and banished to Siberia. After the revolution, active in supply and co-
operative organisations.—I 74.

BALBANOVA, ANGELICA—Born in Ukraine. First a Menshevik; later emigrated abroad, where she became active in the Italian Socialist Party. During the war was an internationalist and, as member of the Central Committee of the Italian Socialist Party, was active in founding the Zimmerwald
Union; member of the International Socialist Commission. In 1917, moved
from Switzerland to Stockholm to support the Russian Revolution. Returned
to Russia in 1919, where she joined the Russian Communist Party and the
Comintern. In 1924, expelled from the Comintern for collaboration with
"centrists."—I 222.

BAUER, OTTO (born 1882)—Leader of Austrian Social-Democracy, prior to
the war an adherent of its Left Wing. During the war was called to colours,
made war prisoner in Russia, and sent to Siberia, where he was released by
the Kerensky government at the demand of the Petrograd Soviet. During
his brief stay in Petrograd, being himself in favour of defending his Austrian
fatherland, he supported the policy of the Russian defencists. After the
November (1918), Revolution in Austria, Secretary of State for Foreign
Affairs in coalition government. As opponent of the Third International,
published several books against Communism and the Soviet system. One
of the organisers of the Two-and-one-half International. Head of "Austro-
Marxian School." In July, 1927, utilised all his influence as head of Austrian Social-Democracy to suppress uprising of Vienna workers. Bauer is
the perfect type of centrist politician, in practice constantly capitulating before the bourgeoisie.—I 92.

BAZAROV, V. (pseudonym for V. A. Rudnev; born 1874)—Russian economist
and philosophical essayist. Belonged to the Bolshevik Party after the Congress of 1903. In 1905, member of the Petersburg Committee of Bolsheviks.
Contributed to the legal and illegal Bolshevik press; co-editor of the central
Bolshevik organ and member of the Bolshevik central organisation. In the
period of reaction which followed 1907, he deviated from Bolshevism.
Remained internationalist during the war, contributing to the magazines, *Sovre-*

mennik (*Contemporary*) and *Lietopis* (*Annals*), and in 1917 to the paper, *Novaia Zhizn.* In 1919, during Denikin's rule in the South, contributed, together with the Mensheviks, to the magazine, *Mysl* (*Thought*) published in Kharkov. Together with Stepanov, undertook a new Russian translation of *Capital.* Machist in philosophy. At present works in the State Planning Commission.—II, 141, 144, 189-191, 201.

BEBEL, AUGUST (1840-1913)—One of the founders of the German Social-Democratic Party and its leader. Son of a Prussian soldier, and an orphan since the age of twelve, he entered a wood-turning shop at the age of fourteen. As a journeyman, he travelled for two years through Germany, Austria, and Switzerland. Met Wilhelm Liebknecht in 1865, and joined the First International. In the elections of 1867, first held after the introduction of universal suffrage, was elected to the Reichstag. At the Eisenach Congress of 1869 founded, together with Wilhelm Liebknecht, the German Social-Democratic Party. During the Franco-Prussian War refrained, together with Liebknecht, from voting military appropriations, and after the September upheaval in France and the promulgation of a republic, voted against a loan and protested against the annexation of Alsace and Lorraine. Consistently fought against every attempt at transforming Social-Democracy into a demo-cratic-reformist party (Dühring, Bernstein, Vollmar). Considering himself a disciple of Marx and Engels, he defended both the immediate workers' demands and the general, ultimate aims of the movement. Counteracting Right Wing tendencies in Social-Democracy, Bebel put the formal unity of the party above everything else. Therefore, he was often compelled to compromise with the Right Wingers, drawing a line of demarcation between himself and the Left radical movement growing up under Rosa Luxemburg's leadership in the last years before the war. Leader of the Second International prior to the war.—I 161.

BERGER, VICTOR L. (born 1860)—Head of the American Socialist Party, a revisionist and advocate of fusion with bourgeois reformist political groups for which he was fought in former years, to-day is the ideological leader of the party. First Socialist to be elected to Congress (1910). Teacher by profession. Editor of the Socialist paper, *The Milwaukee Leader,* since 1911. During the war was an extreme German chauvinist and his opposition to America's entrance into the war was dictated by his pro-German attitude and the consideration of the Milwaukee German voters to whom he was responsible for his successive elections. In 1919, Berger was instrumental in the expulsion of the Left Wing from the Socialist Party which later organised itself as the Communist Party. In Congress as well as in his party work and in his writings he aims to impress the bourgeoisie with the loyalty of the Socialists to American institutions. At present, chairman of the National Executive Committee of the Socialist Party and member of the Masons. During the elections of 1928, Berger, the only Socialist member of Congress, was defeated in the district which he represented for many years.—I 146.

BETHMANN-HOLLWEG, THEOBALD (1856-1921)—Chancellor of the German Empire and Prime Minister of Prussia since 1909, also during the war. Representative of the Junker and banking interests. Close collaborator of Wilhelm in the preparation and organisation of the imperialist war. Held Chancellorship when the Empire broke down.—I 92, 189; II 30.

BIEDNY, DEMIAN (pseudonym of E. A. Pridvozov; born 1883)—Satirical poet, author of numerous political satires in verse. One of the most popular Russian writers. During the civil war his verses were a source of inspiration to Red Army. Decorated with order of the Red Flag. Communist.—II 93.

BISMARCK, OTTO VON (1815-1898)—Chancellor at the time the German Empire was formed. Accomplished unification of Germany, with Prussian Kingdom and Hohenzollern dynasty as foundation, by means of wars with Denmark, Austria and France. Annexed Silesia that belonged to Denmark and Alsace-Lorraine that belonged to France. Introduced universal suffrage in Germany with the aim of winning over the working class and playing them off against the liberal bourgeoisie. Author of the "Anti-Socialist" laws which were abolished in 1891 after his resignation. Was known as the "Iron Chancellor."—I 174.

BISSOLATI, L. (1857-1919)—One of the founders of the Italian Socialist Party and many times editor of its central organ, *Avanti*. In 1911 supported the war against Turkey, undertaken with the purpose of acquiring colonies in Africa (Tripoli), for which he was expelled from the party. Formed a separate reformist group. From the beginning of the imperialist war advocated Italy's joining it on the side of the Entente. After war was declared enlisted voluntarily and was wounded. In 1916-1918 was a member of the cabinet without a portfolio.—I 146; II 192.

BLANC, LOUIS (1811-1882)—French Utopian Socialist, publicist, and historian. In his book, *Organisation of Labour* (1840), he advanced the theory of the gradual introduction of Socialism by means of organising industrial and agricultural associations which, supported by the State, successfully compete with and drive out private enterprises. Proceeding from the idea of solidarity of interests within society, Blanc categorically rejected the class struggle and the method of revolutionary force. "If the bourgeoisie once becomes animated with noble aspirations, it will do everything to rejuvenate the country. . . . Let it merge with the people and take the initiative in passing from competition to association." During the 1848 Revolution, Blanc entered the Provisional Government as a workers' representative; futilely demanded the organisation of a Ministry of Labour. By way of concession, the Provisional Government organised a totally powerless commission under his chairmanship to study the situation of the workers (Luxembourg Commission), whose moderate suggestions, however, were rejected. In persuading the workers to wait and let their representatives act, Louis Blanc dreamt of creating a "social republic" which would accomplish class co-operation by doing away with class contradictions. In the words of Marx, this proved to be a "social enslavement of the workers by the Republic." In attempting to reconcile the irreconcilable, Blanc was a plaything in the hands of the bourgeoisie. After the suppression of the June uprising of the Paris workers he was compelled to emigrate. Returned to France after the fall of the second monarchy, and was elected to the National Assembly. In 1871, when the

Paris Commune was organised, he remained with the Versailles crew that crushed the Commune. Was more important as an historian than as a political leader.—I 42, 43, 46, 111-113, 123, 138, 251, 252; II 21, 22, 93, 191, 229, 255, 257, 258.

BORGBJERG, FREDERIK (born 1866)—Outstanding Danish Social-Democrat; opportunist. Came to Russia in 1917 with the proposal of calling an International Socialist Conference on termination of war and possible conditions of peace. Member of Stauning's Social-Democratic cabinet in 1924. Represented Denmark in the League of Nations.—I 288-291, 300, 314.

BOSH, EUGENIE (1879-1925)—Old member of Bolshevik Party. During the war was very active, together with Piatakov, in publishing the magazine, *Communist*, abroad. After her return to Russia in 1917, worked in the Ukraine; was a member of the first Ukrainian Soviet Government; later was active at civil-war fronts.—I 21.

BOURDERON, A. (born 1858)—Member of the French Socialist Party. Workingman. Secretary Coopers' Union. Participated in the Zimmerwald Conference.—I 149, 151.

BRANTING, HJALMAR (1860-1925)—Leader of the Swedish Socialist Party. One of the leaders of the Second International. Right Wing reformist, favouring Franco-British orientation during the war. Prime Minister of the Royal Swedish Government after the war and member of the Council of the League of Nations.—I 146.

BRESHKO-BRESHKOVSKAIA, E. K. (born 1847)—Called by the Socialists-Revolutionists "The Grandmother of the Revolution." Started revolutionary activities in 1873. Was tried in 1878 and convicted to five years of hard labour. Having returned from Siberia in 1896, was active in creating the Workers' Party for the Political Liberation of Russia, which in 1902 joined the newly organised Socialist-Revolutionary Party. Adhered to the policy of political terror; devoted her major energy to working among the peasants. Member of the Central Committee of the Socialist-Revolutionary Party. In 1907, arrested and banished to Siberia; she was liberated by the March Revolution. Joined the Right Wing of the party (*Volia Naroda*); favoured the war and the coalition government. After the November Revolution a vicious opponent of the Soviet power; while living abroad is conducting a veritable crusade of lies and calumny against the Soviet government.—II 285.

BRONSKI, M. G. (born 1882)—Old Polish Social-Democrat. Bolshevik. Represented Polish Social-Democracy at Kienthal Conference. Now member of Collegium of the People's Commisariat for Finances in U.S.S.R.—I 92, 188.

BUCHANAN, GEORGE WILLIAM (1854-1924)—British ambassador to Russia, 1910-1918. Exercised great influence over Russian politics, actually dictating the will of British imperialists. The Octobrist and Cadet bourgeoisie besought him for aid and protection. In the March Days, 1917, Guchkov and Miliukov acted on an understanding with him. When Kornilov advanced against Petrograd in 1917, there were British armoured cars in his "Wild Division." Buchanan's demands were law for Kerensky, who upon his insistence established severe punishment for abusing the Allied powers or their representatives in the press. Under this law the *Social-Democrat*, organ of the Moscow Committee of the Russian Social-Democratic Labour Party (Bolsheviks), was dragged to court for disclosing Buchanan's assistance to Kornilov. The ill-fated military advance undertaken by Kerensky in 1917 was due to the pressure of Buchanan and other Allied ambassadors.—I 31.

BYKOVSKY—Narodnik. Active in co-operatives.—I 219.

C

CARLSON, C. N. (born 1865)—One of the pioneers of the Swedish labour movement. Internationalist during the war. Member of the Left Wing Socialist Party which in 1919-1922 was a section of the Communist International. Later returned to the Second International.—I 92, 149, 187.

CATILINA, LUCIUS SERGIUS (108-62 B.C.)—Led a movement in 63 B.C. aiming at introducing democratic agrarian reform. To fight the "conspiracy," the frightened patrician Senate clothed Cicero with unlimited authority. Catilina suffered defeat at consular elections, fled from Rome, and induced a number of legions to start an insurrection, but was defeated and fell in battle. Catilina's "conspiracy" was the last link in a long series of attempts at introducing agrarian reform, starting with the attempt of the Gracchus brothers.—II 240.

CAVAIGNAC, EUGÈNE LOUIS (1802-1857)—French general, Minister of War in Provisional Government of French Republic after Revolution of February, 1848; clothed with dictatorial powers, during the June days, he crushed the uprising of Paris workers. Member of the Constitutional Convention and President of Council of Ministers in 1849. Was Republican candidate for President of the Second Republic, but was defeated by Prince Louis-Napoleon (Napoleon III). Cavaignac has become synonymous with "butcher of the working class."—II 249, 255, 256, 258, 261.

CHEREVANIN, F. A.—Menshevik-Liquidator and defencist. Writer. Started Social-Democratic activities towards the end of the nineties. Contributed to all Menshevik publications in 1906-1907. Delegate to Stockholm and London Congresses of the party. In 1917, one of the editors of the Menshevik organ *Rabochaia Gazeta* (*Worker's Gazette*). Member Menshevik united Central Committee after the August, 1917, congress of the Menshevik Party.—I 178, 180; II 143, 147, 302.

CHERNOMAZOV, M. S. (known as Miron; born 1882)—Was active in the Bolshevik Party and was night editor of the Bolshevik paper, the *Pravda*. Under suspicion of being a provocateur, he was removed from party activities in the fall of 1912; all party connections with him were severed. After the March Revolution it became evident from the Police Department archives that the suspicion against Chernomazov was well founded. The Cadet press wrote insinuatingly about his connections with the Bolsheviks in order to discredit them.—I 73-76.

CHERNOV, V. M. (born 1876)—Started political activities in the nineties; theoretician and leader of the Socialist-Revolutionary Party since its foundation. During the war he occupied a vacillating position between internationalism and defencism; participated in the Zimmerwald Conference, but refrained from voting for its Manifesto. Rabid defencist after the March Revolution upon his return to Russia. As Minister of Agriculture in the first coalition cabinet of the Provisional Government, he fought against the peasants seizing the landowners' land. Resigned after the July events. In January, 1918, he was elected chairman of the Constituent Assembly which had a two-thirds majority of Right Socialists-Revolutionists and was dispersed by the Soviet Government. Was active in the uprising of the Czechoslovaks and Socialists-Revolutionists in the Volga region in 1918 and headed the Ufa congress of the members of the Constituent Assembly. Was arrested by Kolchak but soon released. Participated in the Paris congress of members of the Constituent Assembly in 1921. Attempted to aid the Kronstadt uprising in 1921 and went there for this purpose.—I 69, 167, 242, 248; II 33, 34, 45, 46, 48-51, 58, 61, 63, 65, 69, 80, 94, 133, 142, 146, 155, 157, 159, 160, 176, 180-182, 221, 222, 230, 231, 233, 248, 256, 257, 259, 271-273, 277, 278, 285, 286, 291-293, 295, 300, 302, 303, 306, 308.

CHKHEIDZE, N. S. (1864-1926)—Menshevik leader from the Caucasus. Participated in the Third and Fourth Imperial Dumas as leader of the Social-Democratic fraction. Maintained a confused, vacillating position in relation to the war. Chairman Petrograd Soviet of Workers' and Soldiers' Deputies, from March to the end of Summer, 1917. Defencist. Favoured coalition with the bourgeoisie. After the November Revolution he retired from political activities, still aiding from abroad the Georgian Mensheviks. Ended life by suicide.—I 19-21, 26, 36-42, 45, 46, 67, 70, 71, 73, 79, 80, 83, 84, 96, 98, 102, 107, 109, 111, 113, 116, 117, 120, 123, 126, 127, 134, 136, 145, 147, 148, 154, 174, 186, 193, 202, 206, 209, 211, 214, 227, 228, 233, 234, 248, 249, 265, 274, 277, 286, 296; II 33, 34, 76.

CHKHENKELI, A. I. (born 1874)—Menshevik; lawyer; member Third Imperial Duma.—I 19, 21, 26.

D

DAN, F. J. (born 1871)—Leader of Mensheviks, physician and writer. Participated in many revolutionary organisations and revolutionary publications prior to 1905; was banished to Siberia. The 1905 Revolution made possible his return to Russia. Participated in party congresses in 1906 and 1907. Was repeatedly elected to Organisation Committee and Central Committee of Mensheviks. In the years of reaction supported the Liquidators; during a war a pacifist and moderate internationalist ("centrist"). After the March Revolution Dan was "revolutionary" defencist and conciliationist; after the November Revolution active opponent of the Communist Party and Soviet power in the name of bourgeois democracy. At present émigré, member Second International.—II 286, 302.

DAVID, EDUARD (born 1863)—German Social-Democrat, reformist, author Socialism and Agriculture, defender of petty-bourgeois peasant interests; revisionist. During the imperialist war extreme social-chauvinist. On the eve of the November (1918) Revolution, entered ministry of Prince Maximilian of Baden, which aimed to save the Hohenzollern Empire by concessions. After the 1918 Revolution, Minister without portfolio in Scheidemann's cabinet. In 1919, elected chairman of the National Assembly.— I 30, 87, 148, 190.

DEUTSCH, L. G. (born 1855)—Joined the revolutionary movement in the seventies as Narodnik, holding Bakunin's views. Together with Stefanovich, attempted to arouse peasants in 1877; was arrested and escaped. In 1883 was one of the founders of the Liberation of Labour Group, together with Plekhanov, Zasulich, Axélrod. Emigrated abroad, but was extradited from Germany to Russia. Spent sixteen years at hard labour and in banishment; fled via America in 1901. In 1906 again arrested in Petersburg and banished to Siberia, from where he again fled abroad. During the war, held an extremely chauvinist and conciliationist position. In 1917 was a member of the *Yedinstvo* group headed by Plekhanov.—I 262; II 133.

DMITRIEV, RADKO (died 1918)—General, commanding the joint Bulgarian and Serbian army in the Balkan War, and victor over Turks in 1912. Commander of Bulgarian army in war against Serbia, Greece and Rumania, where he suffered complete débâcle. With the beginning of the World War, being an extreme enemy of Austria, entered Russian service and commanded one of the Russian armies against the Central Powers joined in by Bulgaria. "Hero of Three Wars" and favourite of Russian bourgeois press after beginning of war. Executed in Piatigorsk in 1918.—I 230.

DOBROSKOKOV, N. V.—Provocateur; was active among Mensheviks; after exposure became officer in the Petersburg military police, then Chief of Police of Petrozavodsk.—II 157.

DURNOVO, P. N. (1835-1923)—Governor-General of Moscow in 1905; member Imperial Council. After the March Revolution his suburban summer home in Petrograd was occupied by workers' organisations, which act aroused the ire of the bourgeois press as an act of "anarchy."—II 238.

DZHUNKOVSKY, V. F. (born 1855)—Governor-General of Moscow, then Assistant Minister for Internal Affairs in charge of police. Having learned that his predecessors had secured the services of the Duma member, Malinovsky, to spy upon his fellow-members, and considering secret service inadmissible among the Deputies, Dzhunkovsky secretly informed the Duma president, Rodzianko, of Malinovsky's rôle. Without informing either the Social-Democratic fraction or the Duma as a whole, Rodzianko demanded that Malinovsky quit the Duma, whereupon the provocateur resigned and left the country.—II 265.

DZIERZYNSKI, FELIX (1877-1926)—One of oldest members of Polish Social-Democracy, active since the early nineties. Many times arrested, imprisoned and sent to Siberia and to hard labour. After the April, 1917, Bolshevik Conference, was made member of the Central Committee, which he remained to his very death. Chairman of Extraordinary Commission to Combat Counter-Revolution (commonly known as Che-ka). People's Commissar for Internal Affairs, later People's Commissar for Communications, finally President Supreme Economic Council of the U.S.S.R.—I 314.

E

ENGELS, FRIEDRICH (1820-1895)—Closest friend and inseparable comrade-in-arms of Karl Marx, co-founder of scientific Socialism and dialectical material-ism. (*Cf.* a sketch of Engels' life written by V. I. Lenin in 1895—*Collected Works*, Vol. I, and D. Riazanov, *Karl Marx and Friedrich Engels.*)—I 50, 110, 119, 124, 139, 154, 156, 204, 271, 282, 316, 328; II 17, 18, 92, 94, 152, 197.

G

GAPON, G. A. (died 1906)—Priest, leader of workers' organisation created by police authorities to divert workers from politics. Politically a complete nonentity, Gapon was raised on the crest of the mass movement to the position of organiser and leader of the January 22, 1905, workers' mass march to the Winter Palace, where it was met by volleys fired by soldiers killing several hundred and wounding many more. January 22 is considered the starting-point of the 1905 Revolution. After January 22 Gapon unfrocked himself and emigrated abroad, where he joined the Socialist-Revolutionary Party, only to quit it later and to return to Russia under another name. Was exposed as keeping relations with Count Witte and the Police Department and killed by workers, his former followers, with the aid of the Socialist-Revolutionist Ruthenberg.—I 241.

GEORGE, DAVID LLOYD (born 1863)—English statesman, lawyer by pro-fession. Liberal M.P. since 1890; from 1908-1915 Chancellor of the Ex-chequer. Prior to the war advocated democratic and social reforms, like extension of suffrage, social insurance against old age, sickness, and unem-ployment; fought against the opposition of the House of Lords by limiting its veto right. During the war Minister of Munitions, Minister of War, and between 1916 and 1922 Premier and Chairman of the Military Council with dictatorial powers. His policies, both internally and abroad, were directed towards ruthlessly carrying out the dictates of British imperialism; in a bloc with the Conservatives he introduced universal military service, annihilated the achievements of the working class in their struggle against the employers, suppressed Ireland in 1916 with blood and iron. For three years, with the means of the British Treasury, supported the struggle of the Russian counter-revolution against the Soviet power. At present leader of the Liberal Party.—II 271, 272.

GOLDENBERG, I. P. (pseudonym of Meshkovsky; born 1873)—Leading Bolshevik during 1905 Revolution and member of the Central Committee; defencist and conciliationist in 1917.—I 109, 110.

GORKI, MAXIM (pseudonym of A. M. Peshkov; born 1868)—Famous Russian writer, one of the most outstanding figures in modern Russian literature. Actively participated in public life, keeping in touch with the labour move-ment and the Social-Democratic Party. Being close to Bolsheviks, variously aided the party; kept close relations with V. I. Lenin, who considered Gorki's literary activities of great value for the working class. During the war Gorki remained internationalist, taking a leading part in the publication of the inter-nationalist magazines, *Sovremennik* and *Lietopis*. In 1917 he participated in the *Novaia Zhizn*, a conciliation paper advocating unity. The November Revolution, however, confused Gorki. Refusing to accept it as a whole, he at the same time was unable to offer active opposition to it and to the proletariat that had accomplished it. Returned to Russia in 1928, closer to the Revolution and the proletarian dictatorship than before.—I 56, 57.

GORTER, HERMANN (1894-1927)—Dutch poet and Left Wing Socialist, later Communist. In 1907 founded, together with Pannekoek, Henrietta Roland-Holst, Wynkoop, and others, a radical weekly *De Tribune*. Expelled from the official party in 1909, participated in founding the Left radical Dutch Social-Democratic Party. Belonged to the Zimmerwald Left during the war supporting Lenin's policies. Marxian theoretician and head of the "Dutch Marxian school" which was the Dutch Left opposition to the Communist International.—I 149.

GOUJON—Large-scale Moscow capitalist and manufacturer. French citizen. —II 301, 303.

GREULICH, HERMANN (1842-1925)—Swiss Right Wing Social-Democrat, member of Gruetli Verein, a social-reformist organisation which up to 1915 existed as autonomous part of Swiss Social-Democratic Party.—I 151.

GRIMM, D. D. (born 1864)—Professor of Roman Law and Rector of Petersburg University; member of Imperial Council as representative of Academic Electoral College; Constitutional Democrat; later Assistant Minister of Education in Provisional Government.—I 36.

GRIMM, ROBERT (born 1881)—Secretary Swiss Social-Democratic Party during the war; internationalist of a pacifist brand; chairman Zimmerwald and Kienthal Conference; member Zimmerwald Secretariat; editor of the official organ of the Swiss Social-Democratic Party, *Berner Tagwacht*. In 1917 came to Russia and was expelled by the Kerensky Government in consequence of intercepted telegraphic correspondence between Grimm and the Swiss Minister, Hoffman, who was probing into possible conditions of peace. One of the organisers of the Two-and-one-half International.—I 83, 147, 151, 315; II 192, 223.

GROMAN, W. G. (born 1874)—Menshevik. Statistician and economist. Writer. Active in co-operative movement. Member Petersburg Soviet in 1917. At present active in the State Planning Commission of the U.S.S.R.— II 145.

GUCHKOV, A. I. (born 1862)—Large Moscow real-estate owner and industrialist. Participated as volunteer in Boer War; participated in uprising of Macedonian rebel bands. In the Russo-Japanese War was attached to the Red Cross in the Far East. Founder of the Octobrist Party in 1905. Representative of reactionary circles of the big bourgeoisie. President of the Third Imperial Duma. During the war chairman Central War Industries Committee. Minister of War and Navy in the First Provisional Government. Annexationist and advocate of "war to victory"; favoured re-establishment of rigid discipline in the army. Resigned in May, 1917. Supported all counter-revolutionary movements of 1917-1921. Emigrated to Berlin.—I 19, 21, 28, 31, 32, 34

38, 42, 43, 45, 47, 50-52, 55, 57-60, 62, 65-67, 70-73, 75-80, 83, 84, 97, 100, 113, 121, 123, 126, 134, 135-137, 155, 159, 162, 171, 181, 182, 199, 201, 208, 211, 225, 228, 230, 234, 235, 243, 246, 248, 250, 263, 273, 276, 278, 286; II 20, 21, 23, 29, 33, 53, 159, 176, 230, 248, 262, 272.

GUESDE, JULES (1845-1922)—Leader and theoretician of French orthodox Marxism. Prior to the war fought against revisionism (Millerand and Jaurès who supported Millerand) and the anarcho-syndicalists. With the declaration of the war shifted to an extremely defencist position, advocating the *union sacré*. Minister without portfolio in the bourgeois "defence of the father-land" cabinets. One of the most influential leaders of the Second International. —I 72, 87, 103, 146; II 192.

GUILBEAUX, HENRI (born 1885)—French poet and writer, member of the French Socialist Party. During the war emigrated to Switzerland, where he edited an internationalist magazine, *Demain*. Belong to the Left Wing Zimmerwaldists. At present Communist. Wrote a book on Lenin.—I 92, 149, 187; II 81.

GVOZDEV, K. A.—Menshevik-Liquidator; worker. During the war defencist; chairman labour group Central War Industries Committee. Assistant Minister of Labour in one of the coalition cabinets of the Provisional Government. At present works in the People's Commissariat for Communications.—I 21, 26, 30, 35, 39.

H

HAASE, HUGO (1863-1919)—One of the leaders of German Social-Democracy, close to its centre group; friend and supporter of Bebel. During the war occupied, together with Ledebour and Kautsky, a vacillating position, voting in the Reichstag against military appropriations (at first voting, August 4, 1914, voted for appropriations), but failed to draw the necessary conclusions from this act. In 1916 left the official party and joined the Independent Social-Democratic Party, which he founded together with Ledebour. After the November (1918) Revolution, he was a member of the cabinet composed of Independents and Scheidemannists. Was treacherously killed by a German officer in 1919.—I 82, 87, 147, 148, 289.

HANECKI, J. S. (born 1879)—One of the oldest members of Social-Democracy of Poland and Lithuania. Chairman Polish Social-Democracy at the second, fourth, and fifth congresses of the Russian Social-Democratic Labour Party. Participated in the Basel International Congress, 1912. After the March Revolution, lived in Stockholm, keeping up communications between the Bolsheviks in Russia and the revolutionary Social-Democrats abroad. At present active in the People's Commissariat for Trade. One of his under-ground pseudonyms is Kuba.—I 69, 72, 149.

HARTSTEIN. See *Levi, Paul*.

HEILMANN, ERNST (born 1881)—German Social-Democrat, Right Winger, editor of the social-patriotic paper, *Volksstimme*. Held the same views as Parvus, and contributed to his chauvinist magazine, *Die Glocke*.—I 151.

HENDERSON, ARTHUR (born 1863)—English trade unionist; one of the leaders of the British Labour Party, M.P., active in the Second International. During the war, member of the coalition (Liberal-Conservative) cabinet of Lloyd George. In 1917, however, was forced to quit, after expressing himself in favour of convoking in Stockholm a Socialist conference of the Second International with a view of preparing the beginning of peace negotiations, which idea enraged the British bourgeoisie. Home Secretary in Macdonald's Labour Cabinet in 1924.—II 178, 181-183, 192.

HERZEN, A. I. (1812-1870)—Famous Russian publicist, father of Russian Narodnik theory and liberalism. In the forties, he was a Left Wing Hegelian and fought at the head of the Russian "Westerners" (those advocating the acquisition of Western European culture and institutions) against the Slavophiles (those advocating national seclusion and autocracy as a peculiar national characteristic). Having emigrated abroad, published in London and Geneva the magazines, *Poliarnaia Zvezda* (*The Polar Star*) and *Kolokol* (*The Bell*), in which he fought against tsarism and demanded the liberation of the peasants.—II 184.

HILLQUIT, MORRIS (born 1870)—Wealthy corporation lawyer, leader and theoretician of the American Socialist Party. Came to the United States from Riga in 1886. Member of the National Executive Committee of the Socialist Party for many years. Represented his party at various international Socialist congresses of the Second International; author of a number of books popularising Socialism. During the war he occupied a centrist position and in 1920 he was even in favour of the American Socialist Party joining the Communist International "with reservations." Later he moved more to the Right, becoming an open enemy of Communism and Soviet Russia. At present he is an advocate of the League of Nations, class collaboration and fusion with bourgeois political groups. Fathered the proposal of the Socialist Party abandoning the class struggle provision in the platform and basing the party organisation on loosely formed clubs of Socialist voters, which was carried into effect at the 1928 convention of the party. Was instrumental in the attack of the official trade union leaders against the Left Wing, particularly of the needle workers' unions.—I 147.

HOBSON, JOHN ATKINSON (born 1858)—Outstanding English economist, author of a series of books dealing with modern capitalism; first of the modern bourgeois economists to point out the transition of capitalism into a new phase, imperialism. Professor of Oxford University.—I 320.

HÖGLUND, ZETH (born 1884)—Leader of Swedish Left Socialist Party. During the war joined the Zimmerwald Left. Parliamentary Deputy. Since 1922 Communist and editor of the Communist paper, *Stormklockan.* Expelled from Communist Party for opportunism in 1924. At present a member of the Second International and editor of the collected works of the revisionist Branting.—I 149.

HUYSMANS, CAMILLE (born 1871)—Belgian Socialist, Secretary International Socialist Bureau of the Second International prior to the war.

Professor of philosophy. Was a member of one of the bourgeois Belgian cabinets.—I 151, 315; II 175.

HYNDMAN, HENRY MAYERS (1842-1922)—Organiser and leader of British Socialist Party, which had little influence over the British labour movement. Swerved to social-chauvinism with the beginning of the war, for which he was expelled from the party.—I 146.

J

JORDANIA, NOE (pseudonym of Kostrov; born 1869)—Georgian Social-Democrat; many times arrested. One of the founders of Georgian Social-Democracy and influential among the Russian Mensheviks. Member of the first Imperial Duma and leader of the Duma fraction. Head of the Menshevik Government of Georgia after the November Revolution. At present plotting abroad against the U.S.S.R.—I 303.

K

KALININ, M. I. (born 1875)—Tver Province peasant, later Petersburg worker; joined the Socialist Party in 1898. First arrested for belonging to the Petersburg Union of Struggle. Active in party work in Petersburg, Reval and Moscow. Participated in the Stockholm Congress of the Russian Social-Democratic Labour Party (1906). In the years of reaction following 1907, continued party activity and was repeatedly arrested and banished to Siberia. Was freed from prison by the March Revolution. Member of the Bolshevik committee in Petrograd (1917). In 1919 elected Chairman All-Russian Central Executive Committee of Soviets. Since 1924 chairman Central Executive Committee of the U.S.S.R. Member Central Committee of the Communist Party of the Soviet Union and its Political Bureau.—I 205, 214.

KAMENEV, L. B. (born 1883)—Social-Democrat since 1901; joined Bolsheviks in 1903; worked in Moscow, Tiflis, and Petersburg; participated in third and fifth party congresses. After 1908 worked abroad in Bolshevik organs. Early in 1914 was sent by the Central Committee to Russia to direct activities of Social-Democratic Duma fraction and the editorial staff of the *Pravda*. Arrested and banished to Siberia together with five Bolshevik Duma Deputies. Was freed by the March Revolution. At the All-Russian April Conference of the Bolsheviks, where he opposed Lenin's theses, was elected a member of the Central Committee. Arrested by Kerensky Government after the July events. In the fall of 1917, opposed uprising, fighting against Lenin for the idea of a "democratic" development of the Russian Revolution. After the victory of the November Revolution was in favour of a coalition government composed of all Socialist parties, including Bolsheviks; disagreeing with the majority he resigned from the Central Committee. At the second Soviet Congress Kamenev was elected chairman of the All-Russian Central Executive Committee of Soviets, but within a few days was replaced by J. N. Sverdlov. From 1918 to 1926, Chairman of the Moscow Soviet. Later Acting Chairman of the Council of People's Commissars and Chairman of the Council of Labour and Defence. In 1923-24 fought energetically against

the Trotsky Opposition, joining, however, in 1925 the "New Opposition";
in 1926 formed a bloc with Trotsky and became one of the leaders of the
Trotsky Opposition. Was expelled from the party in 1927, but later dis-
avowed his errors and was readmitted.—I 72, 73, 75, 125, 127, 128, 209, 285-
287, 290.

KAMKOV, B. D.—Member of the Socialist-Revolutionary Party; inter-
nationalist. After the return to Russia in 1917 opposed the official S.R. Party.
After the November Revolution, he was leader of the Left Wing Socialists-
Revolutionists which split away from the official party and joined the Council
of People's Commissars. In July, 1918, being a member of the Central
Committee of his party, he was instrumental in organising the assassination
of the German ambassador, Count Mirbach, and the insurrection of the Left
Wing Socialists-Revolutionists in Moscow. After the failure of the attempt
to provoke war with Germany, Kamkov kept in hiding, but was soon
arrested.—II 177.

KARL HAPSBURG (1887-1922)—Austrian Emperor and King of Hungary,
1916-1918 (under the name of Karl IV). Dethroned by the November
Revolution. Died in exile.—I 262.

KAUTSKY, KARL (born 1854)—Theoretician of German Social-Democracy
and of the Second International, economist and historian. In 1880, living in
Zürich, contributed to the Socialist press together with Eduard Bernstein, at
that time still a Marxist. Having started scientific work under the direct
supervision of Engels and having taken over the literary inheritance and
the unfinished works of Marx and Engels, Kautsky continued their theoretical
work. Editor since 1887 of the theoretical Marxian magazine, *Neue Zeit*.
When Bernstein attempted to revise Marx, Kautsky unreservedly criticised
his revisionism. With the beginning of the war, Kautsky took a centrist
position, making every effort theoretically to combine internationalism with
defencism. After the November Revolution he wrote a number of books
criticising the Soviet system and defending bourgeois democracy and parlia-
mentarism. After the war was very active in attempting to unite the Independent Socialist Party and the Social-Democratic Party. Once the celebrated
revolutionary theoretician of international fame, a man considered the
greatest Marxian since Marx and Engels, he sank to open counter-revolution
following the war.—I 20, 50, 63, 71, 82, 87, 99, 102, 109, 111, 116, 140, 141,
147, 148, 151, 154, 176, 204, 289, 315, 317, 320.

KERENSKY, A. F. (born 1881)—First became known as defence counsel in
political trials. As a Socialist-Revolutionist, joined the Trudovik fraction
when he became a member of the Fourth Imperial Duma. Social-patriot
from the very beginning of the war. After the March Revolution, being
Assistant Chairman of the Petrograd Soviet, accepted the post of Minister
of Justice in the Provisional Government, despite the decision of Soviet to
the contrary. After Guchkov's resignation, became Minister of War and
Navy. At the insistence of the Entente Powers, led the Russian army which
was tired of war and unwilling to fight, into the June offensive, which turned
into a débâcle. Having suppressed the July movement of the Petrograd

workers by military force, became Premier in a number of coalition cabinets that followed one another with kaleidoscopic change. After Kornilov's abortive march on Petrograd in August, Kerensky became Commander-in-Chief, but without real power. Conducted a conciliationist policy, sinking from reformism to counter-revolutionism and Bonapartism. After the November Revolution had swept away the last coalition government, Kerensky fled from Petrograd after being defeated in an attempt to lead the army against the revolution. Emigrated abroad, where he sank into total insignificance.—I 19, 21, 23, 26, 36-42, 46, 62, 63, 65, 66, 69-71, 79, 84, 131, 134, 145, 180, 182, 188, 205, 210, 243, 276; II 69, 146, 155, 159, 181, 182, 184-186, 196, 230, 257, 273, 285, 286, 304, 305.

KOKOVTSEV, V. N., COUNT (1853-1928)—Finance Minister in Stolypin's Cabinet and Premier after Stolypin. Later devoted himself to banking. During the civil war was active in counter-revolution of the South. Monarchist. Died in Paris.—I 181.

KOLLONTAI, A. M. (born 1872)—First worked with the Mensheviks; was active in the women's movement. Took an internationalist position from the very beginning of the war. Went to America, where she conducted internationalist propaganda. Upon her return to Russia after the events of July, 1917, was arrested by the Kerensky Government together with other Bolsheviks whom she had joined abroad. In 1921, during the discussion on the rôle of the trade unions, she belonged to the so-called Workers' Opposition. At present Soviet representative in Norway.—I 19.

KON, F. J. (born 1864)—Communist. First belonged to the Polish Proletarian Party; sentenced by court-martial to many years of hard labour in Siberia. Returned to Poland in 1904, where he joined the opposition to the Polish Socialist Party, and fought Pilsudski and his faction. Was a member of the Zimmerwald Conference. Joined the Communist Party of Poland after its formation. During the Polish war against Russia in 1920, Kon was a member of the Military Revolutionary Committee of Poland. In 1922-23 was one of secretaries of the Communist International.—I 222.

KONOVALOV, A. I. (born 1875)—One of the largest textile manufacturers of Russia; member of the Fourth Imperial Duma; outstanding member of the progressive bloc. Minister of Commerce and Industry in Kerensky's cabinet. Arrested on November 7 in the Winter Palace during the revolutionary uprising, but soon released. Lives abroad; made efforts to unite the former manufacturers.—I 19, 181, 234; II 48, 80, 186, 230, 300.

KOSSOVSKY (M. J. Levinson; born 1867)—One of the oldest participants of the Jewish Social-Democratic movement; founder and member of the Central Committee of the Bund. Menshevik.—I 91.

KOSTROV.—See Jordania.

KOVALEVSKY, M. M. (1851-1916)—Outstanding Russian political scientist, professor, member Imperial Council. Deprived of professorship 1887, because of liberal views; lived abroad since then. Early in the twentieth century founded the Higher Russian School in Paris. Returned to Russia in 1905.

356 APPENDICES

During the first Russian Revolution organised the Democratic Reforms Party, more moderate than the Cadet Party. Member First Imperial Duma.— I 183, 187.

KRUPSKAIA, N. K. (born 1869)—Lenin's wife. One of the oldest Bolsheviks. Became imbued with revolutionary sentiments in childhood under the influence of her family. In the early nineties joined the Marxists; worked in the Petersburg Union of Struggle for Liberation of the Working Class; was arrested in 1896 after the great textile strike and banished to Siberia, where she married Lenin; was his closest collaborator and assistant up to his last days. Emigrated abroad with him, where she continued party activities energetically. Secretary of *Iskra*. In 1905-1907, Secretary Central Committee, Bolshevik Party. Since the November Revolution unremittingly active in the field of education.—I 325.

KRUSSER.—Lieutenant, arrested by the Provisional Government for anti-war propaganda at the front.—II 148, 149.

KRUTOVSKY.—Commissar of the Provisional Government in Yeniseisk Province, Siberia.—II 16.

KRYLENKO, N. V. (born 1885)—In 1905-1908 leader of revolutionary student movement; simultaneously active in the Petersburg Bolshevik organisation. The March Revolution found him at the front as lieutenant. Participated in the First Congress of Soviets, June, 1917; arrested at front for Bolshevik propaganda. In November, 1917, when Commander-in-Chief Dukhonin refused to follow the order about starting peace negotiations, Krylenko was appointed Chief Commander. Effected liquidation of White Guard activities at the front and election of new commanders. At present acting People's Commissar of Justice and Senior Assistant Attorney General for the R.S.F.S.R.—II 188.

KSHESINSKAIA, M. F. (born 1872)—Well-known ballet dancer in Petrograd opera. Former mistress of Nicholas II and Grand Dukes. Now living abroad. —I 178, 186.

KUBA.—See *Hanecki*.

KUKOVETSKY.—Member Executive Committee First Petrograd Soviet of Workers' and Soldiers' Deputies.—II 145.

KUTLER, N. N. (1859-1924)—Liberal bureaucrat, Assistant Minister of the Interior in 1904, then Assistant Minister of Finance and later Minister of Agriculture in Witte's cabinet. Presented a liberal plan for land reform, whereby part of the land was to be forcibly taken from the landowners with due compensation and turned over to peasantry; for this plan he was compelled to resign, after which he joined the Cadet Party and was elected as its representative to the Second and Third Imperial Duma. Being closely connected with banking and industrial circles, Kutler in 1917 participated in various parity commissions organised by the Ministry of Commerce as a representative of the interests of the Southern Russian industrialists. Member of the Board of the State Bank in 1922-24 where he was employed as a specialist.—II 78, 167, 287.

L

LARIN, J. (M. A. Lurie; born 1883)—Writer and publicist; old party functionary; originally Menshevik and Liquidator, author of the most Right Wing plan of convening a "general labour congress" to take the place of the party (1907). During the war followed the section of the Mensheviks headed by Martov. After the March Revolution took the most Left position among the Mensheviks-Internationalists. In July, 1917, joined the Bolshevik Party. Works in economic organisations.—I 215.

LAW, BONAR (1858-1923)—Conservative British statesman. State Secretary for the Colonies, 1915; Chancellor of the Exchequer and Leader of the House of Commons, 1916-19; Premier, 1922.—I 20.

LAZZARI, CONSTANTINO (died 1927)—Member of the Italian Socialist Party and its Secretary; participated in the Zimmerwald Conference; signed its Manifesto; centrist; belonged to the same orientation as Serrati; sympathised with the Communist movement, but never mustered up enough courage to break with the Socialist Party. Suffered from brutal Fascist persecution in the last years of his life.—I 149.

LEDEBOUR, GEORG (born 1850)—Old Marxist, collaborator of Bebel and Haase; during the war took an internationalist position; signed the Zimmerwald Manifesto; notwithstanding revolutionary temperament, opposed the Zimmerwald Left. Belonged to the Independent Socialist Party of Germany; when the latter split in Halle in 1920, he refused to join the Communist International. When the Independent Socialist Party decided to join the Social-Democratic Party of Germany, however, he quit the former. Since then has been the leader of the Socialist Alliance, which in most questions of political action collaborates with the Communist Party of Germany.—I 147, 148, 289.

LEGIEN, KARL (1861-1920)—President General Commission German Trade Unions since 1890. Acknowledged leader of reformist trade unionism. With persistence and skill Legien utilised the upward trend of economic development of imperialism favourable to the union bureaucracy, in order to secure commanding positions for union leaders within the German labour movement. Since 1906 greatly influenced Central Committee of Social-Democratic Party; after Bebel's death became, together with Ebert, actual leader of the party, though not belonging to the Central Committee. With the outbreak of the World War secured full support of the Social-Democracy for the government. Participated actively in maintaining social truce and suppressing strikes during the war. In 1918 created, together with Stinnes, a Central Labour Association consisting of employers and trade-unionists. One of the outstanding social-chauvinists and counter-revolutionists, using all the power of trade union bureaucracy to save capitalism in Germany.—I 87, 148.

LEVI, PAUL (pseudonym of Paul Hartstein; born 1883)—Lawyer; member of the Spartacus League; later member Central Committee Communist Party of Germany; member presidium Second Congress of Communist International. In 1920-21 supported the Italian Serrati, who disobeyed the Comintern's demand to break with the reformists; together with Serrati attempted to organise Right Wing within Comintern. At the same time publicly criticised the tactics of the Communist Party of Germany during the uprising of 1921 in an uncommunist manner. Expelled from Comintern, he returned to the German Social-Democratic Party and the Second International, where he conducts an anti-Bolshevik policy adorned with "revolutionary" phrases.— I 92, 152, 188.

LIBER (M. I. Goldmann; born 1880)—Leader of the Bund and member of its Central Committee. Exiled several times; escaped from exile for the last time in 1910. Represented the Central Committee of the Bund at general Russian conferences; member Central Committee of party after London Congress (1907); Menshevik-Liquidator; defencist during war; favoured coalition with bourgeoisie during Revolution. Influential member of First Central Executive Committee of Soviets.—II 244.

LIEBKNECHT, KARL (1871-1919)—Son of Wilhelm Liebknecht. Belonged to Left Wing of German Social-Democracy from beginning of his career; devoted much time to work among the youth. On August 4, 1914, as member of Reichstag, refused to vote military appropriations, while the entire Social-Democratic fraction, numbering 110 Deputies, voted for them. Carried his struggle for the International into the street, appealing to the workers to demonstrate against war and to fight for the Socialist revolution. One of the founders of the revolutionary Social-Democratic Spartacus League. At the May First demonstration of 1916 in Berlin Liebknecht, then drafted into the army, was arrested and sentenced to two-and-one-half years of hard labour, from which he was released by the November (1918) Revolution. After the Bolshevik victory in Russia, Liebknecht, then in prison, was one of the first to appeal to the workers to organise Soviets after the Russian example; in November, 1918, he actually organised Soviets. Was at the head of the uprising of the Berlin workers in January, 1919; when the movement was suppressed, Liebknecht, a member of the Revolutionary Committee, together with Rosa Luxemburg, was arrested by Scheidemann's government and treacherously assassinated by German officers. Liebknecht's name during the war became a synonym of Socialist revolution and a battle-cry for the Communist International, for which he helped lay the ideological foundation.— I 20, 87, 98, 102, 103, 148, 153, 166, 184, 188-191, 280, 282, 283; II 81, 192, 202, 248.

LIEBKNECHT, WILHELM (1826-1900)—One of the founders of German Social-Democracy. Participated in the Revolution of 1848 and was compelled to emigrate to London, where he came close to Marx and Engels. After the amnesty of 1860 he returned to Germany, where he fought first the influence of Lassalle, then of Schweitzer, Lassalle's successor and follower. At the elections of 1867, first held on the basis of universal suffrage, he was elected to Parliament. During the Franco-Prussian War, he, together with Bebel, abstained from voting military appropriations; after the overthrow of Napoleon III he voted against military appropriations. In 1872 he was accused of high treason and sentenced to two years' imprisonment. Having served his sentence, he continued activities both in Parliament and among the masses of workers; under the impediments of the anti-Socialist Law, he fought for the principles of revolutionary Social-Democracy against every attempt to deviate from them (by Vollmar, Bernstein, etc.).—II 172.

LINDHAGEN, CARL (born 1860)—Originally a Swedish Liberal; later Socialist and Mayor of the City of Stockholm. During the war an Internationalist and a member of the Left Wing Socialist Party, which joined the Comintern in 1919. In 1922 left the Comintern to go back to the Second International.— I 92, 149, 187.

LIUDMILA (party name for L. N. Stahl; born 1872)—Old member of Bolshevik party; repeatedly arrested and exiled to Siberia. The March Revolution found her abroad as political émigré.—I 20, 21.

LONGUET, JEAN (born 1876)—French Socialist, grandson of Karl Marx. Was "pacifist" during the war, though continually voted for military appropriations. Was leader of minority opposition within the party. When at the Congress of Strassburg in 1918, the minority became a majority, Longuet became leader of the party and editor-in-chief of L'Humanité. After the Tours Congress of 1920, at which the Communists gained the upper hand, Longuet with his adherents quit the party. He joined the Two-and-one-half International, and, together with it, went back into the Second International in 1922.—I 82, 102, 109, 111, 147, 315.

LORIOT, FERNAND—Teacher by profession; during the war revolutionary Socialist and adherent of the Zimmerwald Left. One of the founders of the French Communist Party, where he fought against the Right Wing (Frossard and others). Later he turned to the Right, and in 1927 quit the Communist Party of France.—I 92, 149, 187; II 81.

LUNACHARSKY, A. V. (party name Voinov; born 1875)—Active in the revolutionary movement since school days. Beginning with 1904, did editorial work in Bolshevik central organs. In 1905 was close collaborator in editing open Bolshevik organ, the Novaia Zhizn. Participated in various party congresses, also in international Socialist Congress in Stuttgart (1907). In the years of reaction he, together with Bogdanov and others, formed the centre of a group disagreeing with the Bolsheviks both in relation to Duma activities and in philosophical problems. (See V. I. Lenin, Materialism and Empirio-Criticism, Collected Works, Vol. XIII.) During the war belonged to the internationalists. After the March Revolution Lunacharsky returned to Petrograd, where he joined the Bolshevik Party. People's Commissar of Education of the R.S.F.S.R. since the November Revolution. Writer and playwright.—I 222.

LUXEMBURG, ROSA (1871–1919)—Participated in German, Polish and Russian labour movements. Author of many works on economics and other problems. In 1893 participated in founding the Social-Democracy of Poland and wrote a number of works giving a theoretical foundation to the Polish Social-Democratic movement. Since 1897 she participated actively in the German Social-Democratic movement, where she occupied a Left position and fought against Bernsteinism and its French counterpart Millerandism. Participated at the London Congress of the R.S.-D.L.P. in 1907, where she worked jointly with the Bolsheviks. From the very beginning of the World War she occupied an internationalist position, publishing, together with Mehring and Zetkin, one copy of the magazine, *International*. Together with Karl Liebknecht formed the Spartacus League and wrote (in prison), under the pseudonym Junius, a pamphlet entitled *The Crisis of Social-Democracy*, where she pointed out the collapse of the Second International and the necessity of forming the Third International. After the November (1918) Revolution in Germany, she conducted a widespread Communist propaganda, but was soon assassinated, together with Karl Liebknecht, by German officers. Lenin, who always valued Luxemburg highly, wrote a number of articles directed against some of her errors, particularly those related to the national question.—I 110, 149, 312.

LVOV, G. J., PRINCE (1861-1925)—An outstanding public figure and Zemstvo leader. Member of Imperial Duma, President Zemstvo Union during the war. Prime Minister in the Provisional Government from March to July, 1917. Large landowner.—I 35, 37, 43, 58, 62, 65-67, 72, 84, 94, 97, 106, 113, 121, 123, 132, 133, 141, 177, 210, 225, 228, 248, 260, 261, 276; II 16, 22, 34, 61, 65, 142, 176, 184, 229, 231, 261, 292, 305.

M

MACDONALD, JAMES RAMSAY (born 1866)—Leader of Independent Labour Party and of the Labour Party of England, M.P. and advocate of class collaboration and gradual transition to Socialism (the so-called "constructive Socialism"). Pacifist during the war. Participated in 1921 in the Vienna Conference of the Two-and-one-half International. At present one of the leaders of the Second International, where he occupies an extreme Right position. In 1924 head of the Labour Cabinet, which pursued a moderate liberal policy.—I 82, 102, 109, 147; II 202.

MACLEAN, JOHN (1879-1923)—English Socialist; school teacher in Scotland, where he exercised a great influence over the labour movement, leading its Left Wing. During the war was imprisoned for internationalist propaganda. Belonged to the Comintern in the first years of its existence.—I 149, 190; II 202.

MAKLAKOV, V. A. (born 1869)—Well-known Moscow attorney; member of the Second, Third and Fourth Imperial Dumas; member of the Cadet Party, where he belonged to the Right Wing. Kerensky's ambassador in Paris in 1917.—II 50, 51, 200, 207, 230.

MALINOVSKY, R. V. (1878-1918)—Member of Fourth Imperial Duma, elected by the workers of Moscow Province; at the same time employed in the secret service of the Police Department. Due to oratorical talent, became a figure among the Deputies. In the summer of 1913, fearing exposure, was compelled to resign from the Duma and go abroad. In 1918 he returned to Petrograd, gave himself up voluntarily; was shot by decree of the Supreme Tribunal.—I 74; II 155-157, 264, 265, 307.

MANDELBERG, V. J. (born 1870)—Member of Second Imperial Duma from

Siberia, where he was in exile during elections. Menshevik. Physician.—
I 222.

MANUILOV, A. A. (born 1861)—Professor of Political Economy and Rector
of Moscow University, also one of the editors of the *Russkie Viedomosti*. In
1910 forced to resign for not fighting the student movement with sufficient
energy. Member Imperial Council, elected by the academic Electoral College.
Minister of Education in Provisional Government. Prepared reform of
Russian orthography, which was put into effect by the Soviet Government in
1918. Member Central Committee Constitutional-Democratic Party. In 1924
appointed member of the Board of the State Bank.—I 65, 146; II 262.

MARKOV, N. J. (born 1866)—Member of reactionary Union of Russian
People; member of Third and Fourth Imperial Dumas and leader of the
extreme Right. Large landowner in Kursk Province.—II 122, 123.

MARTOV, L. (1873-1923)—Leader of Mensheviks. Participated in Petersburg Union of Struggle for the Liberation of the Working Class. Contributed
to *Iskra*. At Second Congress of R.S.-D.L.P. in 1903 headed the minority.
During the war he was a Menshevik-Internationalist. Participated in the
Zimmerwald Conference (Centre) and edited the pacifist *Nashe Slovo* (*Our
Word*), which appeared in Paris. After the March Revolution he, together
with a group of like-minded Mensheviks, returned to Russia through Germany. During the first period of the revolution, he occupied an internationalist position, disagreeing with the majority of his party, which adhered
to a social-defencist policy. At the Second Soviet Congress he advocated
the formation of a government consisting of representatives of all Socialist
parties; when the Mensheviks and the Right Socialist-Revolutionists left the
Congress, he stayed. Soon, however, he succumbed to the Menshevik influence, and later passed into the camp of the enemies of the Soviet Government.
In 1920 he emigrated to Berlin, where he edited the *Sozialistichesky Vestnik*
(*Socialist Messenger*), central organ of the Mensheviks.—I 69, 83, 91, 147,
153, 184, 187, 222, 242, 265; II 89, 177, 285.

MARX, KARL (1818-1883)—One of the foremost thinkers of the 19th century;
founder of scientific Socialism and dialectical materialism. "Marx continued
and completed, genius-fashion, the three main spiritual tendencies of the
nineteenth century represented by the three foremost countries of humanity:
classical German philosophy, classical English political economy, and French
Socialism" (Lenin). *Cf.* V. I. Lenin, *Collected Works*, Vol. XVIII; also D.
Riazanov, *Karl Marx and Friedrich Engels*, and *Marx: Man, Thinker and
Revolutionist*, a collection of essays edited by Riazanov.—I 50, 54, 80, 101, 110,
119, 124, 140, 154, 156, 204, 230, 231, 237, 271, 281, 287, 300, 309; II 92, 94, 197.

MASLOV, P. P. (born 1867)—Well-known Menshevik economist, specialist
in agrarian questions. At the Stockholm Congress of the R.S.-D.L.P. in 1906,
he advanced an opportunist agrarian programme ("municipalisation" of the
land), which was adopted with Plekhanov's amendment as against Lenin's
programme of "nationalisation." In 1907 he worked in the Social-Democratic
fraction of the Second Duma as an "expert." During the years of reaction
he was in the extreme Right Wing of the Liquidators. During the war he

occupied an imperialist position, adducing queer Marxist arguments to prove the necessity for the Russian proletariat of complete victory over Germany. His book, *The Agrarian Question*, clearly reveals a revisionist tendency. At present professor in the Moscow University.—I 303.

MASLOV, S. L.—Right Wing Socialist-Revolutionist; writer; active in the co-operative movement. Minister of Agriculture under Kerensky. Social-patriot and advocate of coalition with the bourgeoisie.—II 103-106.

MERRHEIM, ARTHUR—Leader of the French trade union movement; Secretary Metal Workers' Union. Right Wing Zimmerwaldist. Since 1917 an enemy of the Russian Revolution and Communism.—I 149, 151.

MICHAEL ALEXANDROVICH, GRAND DUKE (1878-1918)—Brother of Nicholas II, who in March, 1917, abdicated in his favour; Michael, however, refrained from declaring himself Emperor, and stated that he would receive the crown only from the Constituent Assembly. Was shot in 1918.—I 64, 66, 67.

MIKHELSON—Large coal operator of South Russia.—II 97.

MILIUKOV, P. N. (born 1859)—Leader of Constitutional-Democratic Party and of Russian liberalism in general; assistant professor of Moscow University. In the epoch of the First Duma he was singled out by the Cadets to be Prime Minister of a proposed cabinet responsible to the Duma. During the war he was the ideologist of the Russian imperialists, advocating the annexation of the Dardanelles, Galicia, East Prussia, and Armenia, and fighting internationalism severely. During the March Revolution he defended a Romanov monarchy with Michael as Tsar. His speech at the Cossack Congress during the first period of the Revolution, his speeches against Zimmerwald and Kienthal, and his newspaper articles are full of hatred for the revolution. As Foreign Minister in the First Provisional Government, on May 1, 1917, he sent a note to the Allied Powers confirming the adherence of the Provisional Government to the treaties concluded between Nicholas II and his allies, which note called forth a protest on the part of the workers (the May Crisis) that forced Miliukov to resign. Was ideological initiator of the Kornilov movement of August, 1917. After the November Revolution he inspired counter-revolutionary activities against Soviet Russia. Is in favour of overthrowing the Soviet power with the aid of foreign bayonets. When the Germans occupied the Ukraine, he rapidly changed his orientation from the Entente to the Germans, and appealed to the Kaiser for aid; the German Revolution, however, frustrated his plans. After the Soviet armies became victorious in the civil war, he made his residence in Paris. He is editor of a Left Wing Cadet paper, *Poslednie Novosti* (*The Latest News*), and heads the "Democratic Group" of the Cadet Party.—I 19, 20, 27, 28, 31, 32, 34-39, 46, 47, 50-52, 55, 57-60, 62, 63, 65-67, 69-73, 75-80, 83, 84, 92, 104, 113, 126, 136, 137, 152, 153, 162, 172-175, 179, 180, 182-184, 187, 188, 199, 200, 210, 225, 226, 228, 234, 235, 237, 240, 243, 246, 248, 249, 256, 263, 276, 278, 286, 287, 294, 314; II 20, 21, 24, 29, 33, 49, 64-66, 69, 70, 82, 149, 176, 177, 200, 204, 207, 210, 230, 231, 236, 243, 248, 261, 262, 272.

MIRON—See *Chernomazov, M. J.*

MODIGLIANI, EMANUELE—One of the oldest members of the Italian Socialist Party; social-reformist.—I 147.

MSTISLAVSKY, S. D.—Socialist-Revolutionist, to the Left of the Chernov "centre", contributed to the *Dielo Naroda* (*The People's Cause*); later Left Socialist-Revolutionist.—II 146.

MUELLER, GUSTAV (1860-1921)—Swiss Right Wing Social-Democrat. Member of the National and Berne City Council. Artillery Colonel in the Swiss army during the war.—I 151.

MÜNZENBERG, WILLI (born 1889)—One of the founders of the Communist youth movement in Germany; worker in a shoe factory. In 1914-1921 Secretary International Socialist Youth League; later Secretary International Communist Youth League. Since 1924 Reichstag Deputy. Head of the International Workers' Aid.—I 151.

MURANOV, M. K. (born 1873)—Bolshevik. Member Fourth Imperial Duma, elected by the workers of Kharkov Province. In 1914 arrested, together with the Bolshevik Duma fraction, and exiled to Siberia. After March Revolution returned to Petrograd. At present member of Central Control Commission of the Communist Party of the Soviet Union and member of the Supreme Court of the R.S.F.S.R.—I 70, 72, 74.

MUZHIK VREDNY—See *Biedny, Demian.*

N

NAPOLEON I, BONAPARTE (1769-1821)—Emperor of the French (1804-1814). —I 313; II 69, 71.

NATANSON, H. A. (Bobrov; 1850-1919)—One of the founders of the Land and Freedom Party in 1872. Repeatedly exiled to Siberia for revolutionary activities. Member of Party of Socialists-Revolutionists and of its Central Committee since its formation in the nineties. During the war occupied an internationalist position, participating, together with Chernov, at the Zimmerwald and Kienthal conferences. In August and September, 1917, he broke with Chernov, and headed the Left Socialists-Revolutionists, who then followed the Bolsheviks. After the November Revolution he represented the Left Socialists-Revolutionists in the Central Executive Committee of the Soviets. Later he joined the Group of Revolutionary Communists, which subsequently fused with the Communists. Natanson, being a Narodnik, unconditionally joined the proletarian revolution and the Soviet power, thus representing the best traditions of the revolutionary intelligentsia, which started a struggle against absolutism and for Socialism in the seventies, and which remained faithful to this task to the very end.—I 69, 91, 222, 242.

NEKRASOV, N. V. (born 1879)—Minister of Communications in Prince Lvov's cabinet and in the coalition cabinets under Kerensky; Left Constitutional-Democrat; in the summer of 1917 made an unsuccessful attempt to organise a radical democratic party somewhat to the Left of the discredited Cadets. As Minister of Communications he accentuated the conflict with the railroad workers by refusing to satisfy their just demand for an increase in wages.

At present he works in the central organisation of the co-operatives.—I 171, 172; II 261.

NEPENIN—Russian Admiral commanding the Baltic Fleet during the World War; became notorious for his cruel treatment of the marines. Killed by the marines in Helsingfors, March 17, 1917.—I 50, 80.

NERMAN, TURE (born 1886)—Left Swedish Socialist; adhered to the Zimmerwald Left during the World War; founder of Swedish Communist Party, and editor of the Communist *Folkets Dagblad Politiken*. Gifted proletarian poet.—I 92, 149, 187.

NICHOLAS I (1796-1855)—Russian Emperor 1825-1855.—I 135.

NICHOLAS NIKOLAIEVICH, GRAND DUKE (1856-1929)—Uncle of Nicholas II; Commander-in-Chief of the Russian army from July, 1914, to August, 1915. Lived abroad as pretender to Russian throne.—I 67.

NICHOLAS II (1868-1918)—Russian Emperor 1894-1917, called "Nicholas the Bloody." Executed together with his family in Ekaterinburg in 1918.— I 23-25, 28, 31, 37, 42, 50, 55-58, 60, 65, 77, 84, 119, 130, 135, 159, 174, 175, 177, 190, 205, 210-212, 225, 246, 262, 276, 277, 298, 313; II 33, 43, 58, 66, 70, 95, 114, 122, 126, 199, 208-210, 221, 287, 294.

NOGIN, V. P. (Makar; 1878-1924)—One of the oldest Bolshevik workers engaged in underground activities all the time between arrests and exile. As worker in a Petersburg factory, he participated in the Workers' Banner Group. Later participated in many more revolutionary workers' organisations. Repeatedly arrested and escaped, either from prison or from exile. In 1917, when the majority of the Moscow Soviet became Bolshevik, he was elected Chairman of the Soviet. Later he managed the Soviet textile industry.—I 287, 315.

O

OTSOV—See *Zhitomirsky, J. A.*

P

PALCHINSKY, P.—Organiser of the Coal Syndicate, which was closely connected with banking circles; Assistant Minister of Commerce and Industry in Kerensky's cabinet. Inspired sabotage of industrialists. Assistant to Kishkin, the Cadet Governor of Petrograd; head of the defence of the Winter Palace on November 7, 1917. During the Civil War he was arrested for counter-revolutionary activities. Lenin in a letter requested his release on the ground that his special knowledge might prove useful for the Soviet State. Works at present in Soviet institutions.—II 300, 302, 303.

PANNEKOEK, ANTON—Dutch Left Socialist; expelled from the party in 1907, together with a group of like-minded (Wynkoop, Gorter, etc.), he organised a Left Socialist paper, *De Tribune* ("Tribunists"), in 1909. Joined the Comintern after its formation, but later left it, giving up political activities. Professor of astronomy.—I 50, 149.

PARVUS (A. L. Helphand, 1869-1924)—Russian political emigrant who by the end of the nineties began work in the German Social-Democracy as a Left Winger. Well-known Marxian theoretician, author of a number of works dealing with world economy. Participated in the 1905 Revolution in Russia; developed the theory of "permanent revolution." During the war he was an extreme social chauvinist and agent of German imperialism; published a magazine, *Die Glocke.*—I 151.

PASHICH, NIKOLA (1846-1926)—Serbian Prime Minister during the war and one of its leading spirits. Leader of the old Radical Party and of the Serbian Nationalists. After the war became known for his cruel suppression of the revolutionary movement.—II 66.

PEREVERZEV, P. N.—Petersburg attorney; Trudovik. Widely known by his defence in political trials; Minister of Justice in the first Coalition Cabinet of 1917. Published documents forged by Alexinsky to discredit the Bolsheviks, although the Provisional Government was undecided about their publication. This episode put an end to his political career.—II 238, 306.

PESHEKHONOV, A. V. (born 1867)—Narodnik; statistician and publicist. Leader of the People's Socialists, who occupied an intermediary position between the Constitutional-Democrats and the Socialists-Revolutionists without any influence among the masses. Minister of Supplies in the First Coalition Cabinet of the Provisional Government.—II 45, 46, 142, 176, 232, 233, 235, 237, 291, 309.

PETROVSKY, G. I. (born 1879)—Workingman; old Bolshevik; member Fourth Duma. Was arrested in November, 1914, and exiled to Siberia, together with entire Bolshevik Duma fraction. Returned to Petrograd after March Revolution. Chairman of the All-Ukrainian Central Executive Committee of Soviets and of the Central Executive Committee of the Soviet Union.—I 74.

PFLUEGER, PAUL (born 1865)—Swiss-Social Democrat; Gruetlian. Pastor. Member of Canton Parliament.—I 151.

PIATAKOV, G. L. (born 1890)—Originally an Anarchist, joined the Bolsheviks in 1910; during the war actively collaborated on the Bolshevik magazine, *Communist,* published abroad. At the All-Russian May Conference of the Bolsheviks in 1917 defended his own stand on the national question. President first Ukrainian Soviet Government in 1918. Member Central Committee Communist Party of Soviet Union for a few years and Acting Chairman of the Supreme Economic Council of the U.S.S.R. One of the leaders of the Trotsky Opposition in 1923; expelled from the party, but later readmitted after disavowing his errors.—I 21, 312, 314.

PLATTEN, FRITZ (born 1883)—Secretary Swiss Socialist Party; internationalist; Zimmerwaldist. Was in Russia during the 1905 Revolution where he was imprisoned and released on bail. Accompanied Lenin and a group of Russian emigrants through Germany on their way to Russia. After the March Revolution wished to enter Russia, but was barred by the Provisional Government. Participated in first Congress of Comintern as one of its chairmen and reporters.—I 92, 152, 183, 187.

PLEKHANOV, G. V. (1856-1918)—Founder of Russian Marxism and one of the main theoreticians of the Second International. With the beginning of the World War he took an extreme social chauvinist position, advocating class truce; together with Alexinsky and the Right Socialists-Revolutionists he published a magazine, *Prizyv*, in Paris, counselling the Russian workers to refrain from strikes and to give up their struggle against tsarism in order to win a victory over Germany. After the March Revolution he published a paper, *Yedinstvo* in Petrograd, advocating war to victory and abstention from class-struggle. After the November Revolution the Plekhanovists fought bitterly against the Soviet Government. Plekhanov himself was undecided in the last few months of his life, and while an opponent of the Soviet Government he stated that "one must not take up arms against the working class even if it is mistaken." The Marx-Engels Institute in Moscow is now publishing his collected works which will make up twenty-odd volumes.—I 30, 35, 40, 84, 88, 103, 109, 110, 116, 124, 125, 140, 141, 145, 146, 148, 152, 154, 166, 176-180, 188-190, 204, 223, 227, 236-239, 243, 244, 249, 262, 265, 280, 282, 288, 289, 301, 311, 317; II 15, 21, 31, 32, 76, 134, 146, 147, 149, 155, 156, 176, 183, 192, 226, 273, 274.

POINCARÉ, RAYMOND (born 1860)—French statesman, lawyer by profession; Minister in various French cabinets; in 1912-13 Premier and Foreign Minister, energetically working for the preparation of war. Since 1913 and during the war President French Republic; as such visited Nicholas II in Petersburg a few days prior to the war. In 1920 Chairman of Reparations Commission; in 1922 again Premier; undertook Ruhr occupation in 1923. Staunch fighter for French imperialism; has connections with the Paris Bourse; a bitter enemy of the Russian Revolution.—II 176.

POKROVSKY, N. N. (born 1865)—Last Foreign Minister of Nicholas II before the March Revolution; former Assistant Finance Minister and State Comptroller.—I 181.

POTRESOV, A. N. (Starover; born 1869)—Social-Democrat. One of the participants of the Petersburg Union of Struggle for the Liberation of the Working Class. Banished in 1898 to Northern Russia; afterwards emigrated and became member editorial staff of *Iskra*. Participated in the second Congress R.S.-D.L.P. in 1903. After the split he became one of the Menshevik leaders. Subsequently led the extremist Right Wing of the Mensheviks-Liquidators. During the war he was the most consistent representative of social-patriotism among the Mensheviks. Lives abroad at present, occupying a position to the Right of the official Mensheviks.—I 19, 20, 26, 30, 35, 84, 145, 148, 154; II 285, 286.

PRESSEMANE, ADRIEN (born 1879)—French Socialist; during the war occupied a semi-defencist, semi-pacifist position. At present in the Right Wing of the French Socialist movement.—I 82, 147.

PROTOPOPOV, A. D .(1866-1918)—Member Fourth Imperial Duma: Octobrist. In 1916, as representative of banking circles and aided by Rasputin, became Minister of the Interior. Was a careerist and a flatterer in Court circles. During the war, conferred in Sweden with the German Ambassador, seeking for the possibilities of starting peace negotiations, which action aroused the indignation of the Duma Cadets and Octobrists. In the last days of tsarism, inspired the blackest reaction. Was shot in the autumn of 1918.—I 186, II 32.

R

RADEK, KARL (born 1883)—Originally participated in the labour movement of Galicia; was active in the 1905 Revolution in Poland; edited party paper. Then emigrated to Germany, where he participated in various party publications. His investigations of the problems of imperialism and world politics were of great merit. Joined the Left Wing of German Social-Democracy grouped around Rosa Luxemburg, Franz Mehring, and Clara Zetkin. During the war belonged to the Zimmerwald Left. In 1917 the Provisional Government prohibited his entrance into Russia, and up to the November Revolution he lived in Stockholm keeping up connections with the Bolsheviks and the revolutionary Socialists of the other countries. Immediately after the establishment of the Soviet Government he came to Russia, where he joined the Communist Party. As representative of the Russian Communists he went to Germany in December, 1918, participated in the formation of the Communist Party of Germany and, after the defeat of the so-called Spartacus uprising, he was arrested. Being in prison, he greatly influenced the policies of the German Communist Party through his writings. After his release in the winter of 1919 he returned to Russia. From 1919 to 1924, member Executive Committee Communist International and member Central Committee Soviet Union Communist Party; later Director Sun Yat-Sen University in Moscow. One of the leaders of the Trotsky Opposition bloc for which he was expelled from the party at the XV Congress at the end of 1927.—I 149, 152; II 81.

RAKOVSKY, CHRISTIAN (born 1873)—Communist; originally Rumanian Socialist. Participated in Zimmerwald Conference (Centre). Was imprisoned by Rumanian Government for internationalist propaganda. In 1917 he was freed by the Russian Revolutionary Army that approached the Rumanian frontier. Since then he has worked in Russia among the Communists. Became Chairman of the Council of People's Commissars of the Ukrainian Soviet Republic. Represented the U.S.S.R. in England and France. One of the leaders of the Trotsky Opposition, expelled from the Communist Party.— II 192.

RASPUTIN-NOVYKH, GREGORY (1872-1916)—Siberian peasant; horse thief in youth; later became imbued with religious sentiments and turned into a "miracle-maker." Found his way to Court circles and, aided by the superstitions and the degeneracy of the Petersburg aristocracy, he exploited the mystic moods of the Empress Alexandra to gain a decisive influence on Nicholas II. Was killed in December, 1916, by a Russian prince with the aid of a Grand Duke and others, who thus hoped to save the dynasty.—I 28, 37, 234; II 32.

REICHESBERG, JULIAN (born 1867)—Professor University of Zürich; member Swiss Socialist Party; reformist; Russian emigrant; member Committee on Return of Russian Immigrants in 1917.—I 222.

RENAUDEL, PAUL (born 1871)—One of the leaders of the Right Wing in

French Socialist Party. In 1914-18 editor central organ, *L'Humanité*. Social-patriot.—I 87, 146.

RIAZANOV, D. B. (born 1870)—One of the oldest Russian Social-Democrats. In the nineties organised workmen's circles in Odessa. After five years of imprisonment he emigrated abroad. During the 1905 Revolution editor in Odessa; later organiser and leader of the union movement in Petersburg. Again emigrating abroad, he devoted himself to publishing the works of Marx and Engels as well as works on the history of the Internationals. From the beginning of the war occupied internationalist position. After March Revolution returned to Russia, where conducted propaganda that helped prepare November Revolution. Organised Communist Academy and Marx-Engels Institute in Moscow, whose Director he is at present. Under Riazanov's editorship the Institute has begun the publication of the Collected Works of Marx and Engels and writings of other Marxian thinkers.—I 222.

RIBOT, ALEXANDRE (1842-1923)—French statesman, one of the creators of the Russian-French Alliance. Minister and Premier in various cabinets. During the war, Minister of Finance in the coalition cabinets of Viviani and Briand. In 1917 Premier and Minister of Foreign Affairs.—II 271, 272.

RIVET, CHARLES—Petrograd correspondent of the Paris paper, *Le Temps*. —I 66.

RODICHEV, F. I. (born 1856)—Landowner, leader liberal opposition in Zemstvos. One of the founders and leaders of Cadet Party. Deputy to all Dumas. In 1917 Provisional Government's Commissar in Finland.—I 55, 312-314; II 28.

RODZIANKO, M. V., (1859-1924)—Very large landowner in many provinces, Chairman Fourth Imperial Duma; Octobrist. After March Revolution Chairman Provisional Committee Imperial Duma. Very active organiser of bourgeois reaction under Kerensky. Emigrated after November Revolution.—I 36.

ROLAND-HOLST, HENRIETTA (born 1869)—Dutch writer and Marxian Socialist; organiser women's unions. In 1916 she quit the official Socialist Party and joined the Left Socialist Party. For a time member of the Communist Party, withdrawing later from political activities. Belonged to the Zimmerwald Left during the war.—I 149.

ROLLAND, ROMAIN (born 1866)—Well-known French writer; received Nobel Prize for literature in 1916. Attempted to create a revolutionary repertory for the theatre; clashed with the bourgeoisie, whose order and culture he severely criticised in his monumental novel, *Jean Cristophe*. After the beginning of the war he wrote an anti-war book entitled *Au-dessus de la Mêlée*, whereby he aroused the enmity of all "patriotic" France. Conducted an active propaganda in favour of an international organisation of the intelligentsia against bourgeois culture and the imperialist war. Greeted the November Revolution, expressing confidence that the proletarian revolution would win because of social and moral causes.—II 81.

ROMANOV, NICHOLAS—See *Nicholas II.*

ROMANOV, MICHAEL—See *Michael*.

ROSENFELD—See *Kamenev*.

ROSTOV, N.—Pseudonym of a writer in *Rabochaia Gazeta.*—II 309.

RÜHLE, OTTO (born 1874)—German Left Social-Democrat, Reichstag Deputy. Teacher. On August 4, 1914, together with Karl Liebknecht, refused to vote for military appropriations.—I 148.

RUSSELL, BERTRAND ARTHUR WILLIAM (born 1872)—Renowned mathematician and British Socialist; pacifist during the war; writer on social and philosophical problems; author, *Theory and Practice of Bolshevism.*—I 149.

RYKOV, A. I. (born 1881)—One of outstanding leaders of the Bolshevik Party; participant in a number of party conferences and congresses.. After the first revolution in 1905 during the years of reaction, he never interrupted his party activities. In 1910 was arrested and exiled to the North, but escaped. After the party decided to call a general conference, he went to Russia to visit local organisations and was arrested in Moscow and banished, but again escaped in 1914. The March Revolution found him in Siberian exile. After the November Revolution he was People's Commissar for Internal Affairs. Then for over three years head of the Supreme Council of National Economy; later Acting Chairman Council of People's Commissars and of Council of Labour and Defence. Since Lenin's death, Chairman Council of People's Commissars of U.S.S.R., member Central Committee (since 1906) and Political Bureau of C.P.S.U.—I 287; II 157.

S

SAMOILOV, F. N. (born 1882)—Workingman; Bolshevik; member Fourth Duma, exiled to Siberia, together with Bolshevik Duma fraction. Returned after March Revolution, 1917.—I 74.

SANDOMIRSKY, A.—Menshevik-internationalist in 1917; contributor to the *Novaia Zhizn.*—II 302.

SAVVIN—Assistant Minister of Commerce under Konovalov; representative of industrial circles.—II 300.

SCHEIDEMANN, PHILIP (born 1865)—Right Wing German Social-Democrat. In 1912 member Central Committee of his party and Vice-President of Reichstag. Prior to the war belonged to the "Marxist Centre" of the German Social-Democracy. After the beginning of the war, together with Ebert, became leading representative of Social-Democratic nationalist war policies. In October, 1918, Wilhelm II made him Chancellor in the Cabinet of Prince Max. During the November (1918) Revolution he did everything in his power to prevent the revolution from spreading and to save the monarchy; seeing, however, that the movement could not be stopped, he became "representative of the people" in the "German Socialist Republic." Together with Ebert and Noske, he organised the bloody crusade against the revolution. Was elected as Chancellor by the National Assembly in 1919, but left the cabinet in 1919, refusing to sign the Versailles Treaty. Mayor of Kassel until 1927.—I 30, 87, 103, 146, 148, 152, 166. 177, 189, 230; II 31, 32, 178, 183, 192.

Schmidt, Jacques (born 1882)—Swiss Socialist, centrist; Kautskian. At present extreme Right Winger.—I 82.

Schneider, Friedrich (born 1880)—Swiss Socialist, centrist; editor *Baseler Vorwärts* during the war.—I 82.

Sembat, Marcel (1862-1922)—Member French Socialist Party, social-chauvinist; Deputy and Minister since the beginning of the war. Mason.—I 72, 87, 146; II 192.

Serrati, G. (1872-1926)—Leader Italian Socialist Party; editor central organ *Avanti*. Internationalist during the war. Participated Second Congress Communist International; but later refused to carry out Comintern decision regarding complete breach with the reformists (Turati, Modigliani, Treves, etc.), in Socialist Party. The Centre of the party followed Serrati. The Italian Socialist Party was then expelled from Comintern and the Italian Communist Party organised. In 1924 Serrati joined the Italian Communist Party.—I 149.

Shagov, N. R. (1882-1918)—Workman; Bolshevik; member Fourth Imperial Duma. In 1914 was arrested, together with the Bolshevik Duma fraction, and exiled to Siberia. Was freed by March Revolution, and returned seriously ill.—I 74.

Shchedrin-Saltykov, M. E. (1826-1888)—Well-known Russian writer, satirist, who, using "Æsopian language," ridiculed and scorned the Tsar's bureaucracy and the manners of the monarchy. One of the editors of the radical magazine, *Otechestvennye Zapiski* (*Notes of the Fatherland*).—I 229.

Shingarev, A. I. (1869-1918)—Physician and Zemtsvo leader; member Third and Fourth Imperial Dumas and leader Cadet Duma fraction. Finance Minister in the first coalition cabinets of Provisional Government. Resigned July 15, 1917, together with other Cadets, in an attempt to create a ministerial crisis. This precipitated the July events. After November Revolution he was arrested and having been transferred from the Fortress of Peter and Paul to a hospital, was killed by a group of marines.—I 19, 65, 164, 192, 219, 250, 253, 305, 307: II 35, 48, 80, 112, 114, 115, 117, 142, 230, 231, 261, 262, 292, 305.

Shuba, G. V.—Member Executive Committee, First Petrograd Soviet.—II 144.

Shulgin, V. V. (born 1878)—Nationalist, Zemstvo functionary, member Imperial Duma; editor Black Hundred paper. After the revolution active in Denikin's army. In 1925 came to Russia illegally, visiting Kiev, Moscow and Leningrad. Lives abroad, conducting a campaign against the U.S.S.R.—II 19-21, 49, 87, 262.

Skobelev, M. I. (born 1885)—Social-Democrat; Menshevik; member Fourth Duma. Vice-President and member Executive Committee Petrograd Soviet of Workers' and Soldiers' Deputies. On May 17, 1917, joined first coalition cabinet of Provisional Government as Minister of Labour. Defencist; favoured coalition with bourgeoisie. At present active in Concessions Committee of R.S.F.S.R.—I 41-43, 46, 70, 79, 80, 83, 84, 145, 186, 193, 234; II 46, 70, 83-86

94, 142, 151-153, 168, 176, 181, 182, 186, 231, 232, 273, 286, 291, 299, 300, 308.

SMILGA, I. T. (born 1892)—Bolshevik; elected member Central Committee at May Conference, 1917. Active on various fronts during civil war; was member Revolutionary Military Council of Republic. Later active in Supreme Council National Economy and other economic organisations. An adherent of the Opposition.—II 111, 115.

SNOWDEN, PHILIP (born 1864)—One of the Right Wing leaders of the British Labour Party; M.P. Chancellor of the Exchequer in the Labour Cabinet in 1924.—I 82, 147.

SONNINO, SIDNEY, BARON (1847-1922)—Italian Foreign Minister during the war. Originally adherent of the Triple Alliance (Italy, Germany, and Austria), but after the end of 1914 advocated Italy's joining the war on the side of the Entente.—II 271.

STAKHOVICH, M. A. (born 1861)—Zemstvo leader, moderate liberal, member First and Second Imperial Dumas. Organised the Octobrist Party. Member of Imperial Council.—I 36.

STAUNING, TORWALD (born 1873)—Leader Danish Social-Democracy; reformist. After beginning of the war he became Minister in bourgeois cabinet. Premier many times afterwards.—I 146, 149.

STEKLOV, J. N. (born 1873)—Began Social-Democratic activities in Odessa. Was exiled in 1894 to Eastern Siberia for ten years, fled abroad in 1899. Participated, together with Riazanov, in the organisation of a publishing group "Borba" (Struggle). After the 1905 amnesty he returned to Russia, was arrested at a meeting of the Petersburg Soviet, but soon released. Later emigrated abroad, where he contributed to Bolshevik publications. After the March Revolution, as a "revolutionary defencist," he was close to the *Novaia Zhizn*. Member Executive Committee Petrograd Soviet and its Contact Commission, created to deal with Provisional Government. At present member C.P.S.U. Was editor-in-chief of *Izvestia.*—I 73, 96-99, 107, 111, 113, 116, 117, 120, 123, 126, 127, 134, 136, 145, 173, 174, 186, 193, 202, 209, 234, 274.

STEPANOV, V. A.—Assistant Minister of Commerce in the Provisional Government; Cadet.—II 300.

STOLYPIN, P. A. (1862-1911)—Large landowner, Chairman of cabinet under Nicholas II in the years of reaction that followed the 1905 Revolution. Was instrumental in crushing the revolutionary movement and drowning it in blood. Father of the law of June 16, 1907, whereby the system of representation to the Duma was changed and an obedient Duma majority of landowner and capitalist representatives was secured. Introduced land reform, whereby individual peasants were permitted to quit the village community and secure a parcel of land as private property. This stimulated development of rich peasantry at the expense of the poor ones. According to Stolypin, tsarism was "staking on the economically strong" peasantry. Was supported by the Right Wing Russian bourgeoisie, which after June 16, 1907, formed a bloc with the landowners and nobility. Assassinated in Kiev by a provocateur.—I 51, 65, 68, 86, 130, 307; II 221, 307.

Ström, Frederik (born 1880)—Left Wing Swedish Socialist; later Communist. Left the Comintern together with Hoeglund in 1924.—I 92, 149, 187.

Struve, P. B. (born 1870)—Russian economist and publicist; Social-Democrat in the nineties, representative of the so-called "legal Marxism." Later became liberal and editor of an illegal liberal magazine abroad. After the defeat of the 1905 Revolution he became leader of the Right Wing of the Cadets. Nationalist. Fought actively against the revolution after November, 1917. Minister of the "cabinets" of Denikin and Wrangel. At present lives abroad, publishing a magazine with monarchist inclinations.—II 285.

Sukhanov, H. (born 1882)—Publicist who attempted to combine the Narodnik theory with Marxism. "Non-factional" Social-Democrat; internationalist; later Menshevik. One of the editors of the internationalist magazine, Lietopis, during the war, and member editorial staff of Gorki's Novaia Zhizn after the March Revolution. Member Committee first Petrograd Soviet; together with Steklov and Sokolov, he negotiated with the Provisional Committee of Imperial Duma concerning formation of First Provisional Government. Author of several books on agrarian problem and history of revolution. At present active in Russian economic organisations.—I 73.

T

Teodorovich, I. A. (born 1876)—Old Bolshevik, participant Second Congress R.S.-D.L.P. in 1903. Subsequently banished to Siberia. People's Commissar of Supplies in 1917. At present Acting People's Commissar of Agriculture of the R.S.F.S.R.—I 135.

Tereshchenko, M. I.—Financier and sugar king; Minister of Finance in the First Provisional Government and Foreign Minister in a number of coalition cabinets in place of Miliukov, who resigned under pressure of the workers and whose imperialist policy he continued.—I 181, 234; II 65, 70, 80, 142, 176, 177, 186, 200, 204, 230, 231, 261, 305.

Thomas, Albert (born 1878)—Member French Socialist Party; parliamentary Deputy; during the war Minister of Labour in charge of munitions. Extreme social-patriot. Came to Russia under Kerensky to arouse patriotic spirit of the Russian workers but failed. Chairman Labour Bureau of the League of Nations; member Second International.—II 64, 178, 181, 182, 192.

Tomsky, M. I. (born 1880)—Lithographer by trade; Bolshevik. Member First Soviet of Workers' Deputies, City of Reval (1905). Exiled to Siberia in 1906; escaped from there and returned to Petersburg, where he continued party activities. Was again arrested 1908; later went abroad; then worked in the Moscow organisation of the party. After a new arrest he was sentenced to five years' hard labour. The March Revolution found him in Siberia. In 1917 he worked in Petrograd and Moscow. At Sixth Conference of Trade Unions was elected to the presidium of the Central Council of Labour Unions. Member Central Committee Russian Communist Party since 1919. Member Political Bureau C.P.S.U.; chairman Central Council of Labour Unions.— II 171.

BIOGRAPHICAL NOTES

TORNIAINEN, EDVARD—Finnish Social-Democrat; writer in the Helsingfors Social-Democratic paper, *Työmies.*—I 264.

TREVES, CLAUDIO—One of the oldest members of the Italian Socialist Party; editor central organ, *Avanti,* until 1912; parliamentary Deputy; theoretician of Italian reformism; follower of Turati; nationalist during the war.—I 83, 147.

TRIER, G.—Danish revolutionary Social-Democrat; internationalist.—I 149.

TROELSTRA, PIETER (born 1860)—Leader Dutch Socialist Party and leader Socialist parliamentary fraction. Was a member of the International Socialist Bureau of Second International. Fought against the Left Wing (the "Tribunists," who were expelled from the official party in 1909). Of late abstained from political activity due to illness.—I 146.

TROTSKY, L. D. (born 1879)—Started Social-Democratic activities in Nikolaiev, was active in the South Russian Labour Union; was arrested in 1898 and banished to Siberia, from where he fled abroad in 1902. Participated in the Second Congress of R.S.-D.L.P. (1903), and after the split remained with the Mensheviks, participating very actively in the *Iskra.* During 1905 Revolution was active in Petersburg. Embraced Parvus's theory of "permanent revolution." Was member of the Executive Committee and later Chairman of Petersburg Soviet of 1905. Was arrested together with Soviet Deputies and banished to Siberia, but fled during the trip. Living in Vienna, he formed a group of Social-Democrats and published a paper, *Pravda.* In 1912 he participated in the so-called "August Bloc" created to fight Bolshevism. During the imperialist war was one of the editors of the internationalist paper, *Nashe Slovo,* published in Paris; participated in Zimmerwald Conference, where he leaned toward the centre. In 1916 was banished from France, and later from Spain, and was compelled to go to the United States. Returning to Petrograd after the March Revolution, he joined the internationalist organisation of the "Interboroughites" (Mezhraiontsy) and, together with the latter, joined the Bolshevik Party and was elected to its Central Committee. When the Bolsheviks obtained the majority in the Petrograd Soviet in September, 1917, Trotsky became its chairman. After the November Revolution, People's Commissar of Foreign Affairs. Was opposed to Brest-Litovsk peace, advocating first the policy of "neither war nor peace," then a revolutionary war. People's Commissar of Military Affairs and Chairman Revolutionary Military Council of the Republic from 1918 to 1924. During this period Trotsky occupied a leading position in the Communist Party and Communist International. Was head of a faction in the party in 1920-21 during the discussion on the rôle of the labour unions. In 1923 he started the Opposition to the party and in 1926 became leader of the "United" Opposition, which was declared by the Communist International to have degenerated into a social-democratic, counter-revolutionary tendency. At the end of 1927 expelled from the C.P.S.U., having been previously removed from all his positions in the party and the government.—I 21, 153, 184, 187, 214; II 161, 162.

TRUBETSKOY, E. N., PRINCE (born 1863)—Professor of Moscow University; member Imperial Council; close to the Cadet Party, but somewhat to the Right of it. During civil war supported Denikin.—I 36.

TSERETELI, I. G. (born 1882)—Menshevik; member Second Imperial Duma and leader of Social-Democratic fraction. After the dissolution of the Duma he, together with the entire fraction, was tried on a trumped-up charge of military conspiracy and sentenced to hard labour. Was freed from Siberia by the March Revolution. Upon returning to Petrograd, became the leader of the Mensheviks, defending the continuation of the war and a coalition with the bourgeoisie. On May 19, 1917, he joined the First Coalition Cabinet as Minister of Posts and Telegraph. Member of Executive Committee and first All-Russian Executive Committee of the Soviets. At present an émigré engaged in activity against the Soviet Government.—I 99, 106, 107, 111, 113, 116, 117, 120, 123, 126, 127, 134, 136, 145, 147, 148, 154, 167,186, 193, 211, 233, 248, 249, 265, 274, 277, 296; II 19-22, 33, 34, 45, 46, 48-51, 58, 61, 63, 65, 69, 70, 80, 142, 151-153, 159, 160, 168, 176, 180-182, 221, 222, 230, 233, 245, 246, 248, 249, 255-257, 262, 271-273, 277, 278, 286, 291, 295, 300, 302, 303, 305, 308.

TULIAKOV, I. N. (born 1877)—Worker; Menshevik; member Fourth Imperial Duma from Don Region. Died during the Civil War.—I 80.

TURATI, FILIPPO (born 1857)—Italian Socialist reformist; jurist; writer. First elected to Parliament in 1896. For participation in the so-called hunger revolts was sentenced to twelve years' imprisonment in 1898 and was freed in 1909. After the beginning of the war, was against Italian participation, and after Italy joined the war, he was for a "democratic" peace in the spirit of Wilson. After the war, he led the Right Wing at the congresses of the Socialist Party, repudiating the proletarian dictatorship and affiliation with the Comintern. Leader of Unitarian Socialist Party after the split of 1922.— I 83, 102, 109, 111, 147, 151.

TYSZKA, LEO (Jogiches; 1867-1919)—Founder of Polish Social-Democracy and member of its Central Committee since the very beginning. For leading the uprising of the Warsaw and Lodz workers in 1905, he was sentenced by the Tsar's court to eight years' hard labour, but he escaped from prison, after having converted the guards. Participated at London Congress of R.S.-D.L.P., where he was close to the Bolsheviks. In 1910 he moved to Berlin, where, together with Rosa Luxemburg, he headed the Left Wing in opposition to Kautsky's centre. During the war he, together with Karl Liebknecht, organised the first illegal Spartacus groups. The November, 1918, German Revolution found him in prison. He continued activities after the assassination of Rosa Luxemburg and Karl Liebknecht. In March, 1919, after a new attempt at uprising on the part of the Berlin workers, he was arrested by order of Scheidemann and killed in prison without trial.—I 149.

U

USTINOV, A. N.—Russian political emigrant; Socialist-Revolutionist and internationalist during the war; later Left Wing Socialist-Revolutionist; at present Bolshevik.—I 222.

V

VANDERVELDE, EMILE (born 1866)—President International Socialist Bureau prior to the war; member Belgian Socialist Party; revisionist. One of the first Socialists of Second International to enter the cabinet of his country during the war; Minister of Justice up to 1921. Author in 1914 of an appeal to the Russian workers in the name of victory to refrain from fighting tsarism. In 1917 came to Russia, together with Thomas and others, to persuade Russian workers and soldiers to continue the war. In 1922 revisited Russia as Counsel at the trial of the Socialists-Revolutionists before the Supreme Tribunal. Was for a time Foreign Minister in the Belgian Cabinet.— I 151; II 176, 181, 192.

VASSILIEV, A. V. (born 1853)—Professor of mathematics; member First Imperial Duma; since 1908 member Imperial Council; member Cadet Party; at present member Academy of Sciences.—I 36.

VERNADSKY, V. I. (born 1863)—Professor of mineralogy; member of the Academy; member of Imperial Council and of Cadet Party.—I 36.

VIKHLIAIEV, P. A. (born 1869)—Zemstvo statistician; Socialist-Revolutionist; Assistant Minister of Agriculture in First Coalition Cabinet of Provisional Government. At present Professor of Moscow University.—II 133.

VODOVOZOV, V. V. (born 1864)—Writer, economist; member People's Socialist Party; editor Left Wing papers. Contributed to the paper, *Dien (Day)*, in 1917. Now living abroad as an émigré.—II 66, 67.

W

WILHELM II (born 1859)—Last German Emperor and King of Prussia; reigned 1888-1918. Played a fateful rôle in the life of the German people. German bourgeoisie renouncing its revolution out of fear for the working class, Germany continued to be ruled by a semi-absolutist government in spite of the extraordinary development of German capitalism. Wilhelm determined the policy of the government. Parliament had only slight prerogatives, so that actual relations of class power could be realised only indirectly in governmental policy. Prior to Wilhelm, Bismarck had been the bearer of semi-absolutism. Wilhelm was his "own imperial chancellor," conducting a "personal régime" against which Parliament arose twice (1908 and 1910) without finding the power to carry its will into effect and introduce modern bourgeois conditions. The result of the contradiction between bourgeois rule and semi-absolutist, junker-bureaucratic government was a confused, uneven policy. Internally, Wilhelm tried to introduce a sort of "social empire" without effect. He then made himself the mouthpiece of the big industrialists and threatened to smash the labour movement. This only strengthened the police system. His foreign policy was characterised by bold offensives and feeble retreats, thus accentuating the contradictions between Germany and the other powers arising from the imperialist competitive struggle. The World War revealed the whole rottenness of his "personal régime." Forced to abdicate by the Revolution of November 9, 1918, he fled to Holland where he is still living. —I 31, 72, 84, 153, 162, 164, 169, 173, 176, 177, 189, 202, 212, 225, 234, 246, 262, 263, 298; II 30, 33, 58, 81, 176, 192, 224.

WILSON, ROBERT—Petrograd correspondent, London *Times.*—I 66, 172.

WYNKOOP, D. (born 1877)—Left Wing Dutch Socialist; later Communist. In 1907 he, together with a group of Left Wingers (Pannekoek, Roland-Holst, Gorter, etc.), organised a Left paper, De Tribune ("Tribunists"). In 1909 he was expelled from the official Socialist Party, and participated in the creation of a Left Social-Democratic Party. From 1918 to 1925 Deputy in Dutch parliament. In 1919 he joined the Comintern. At present he is outside the Communist movement.—I 149.

Y

YEFREMOV, I. N. (born 1866)—Large landowner. Dumas Deputy and chairman of Progressive fraction, which was more moderate than the Cadets.—I 19.

YONOV, F. M. (Koigen; 1870-1923)—One of the oldest Social-Democrats of Russia; member of the Bund and its Central Committee. Internationalist during the war. After the Bund split, became a member of the Communist Party.—II 157.

YORDANSKY, N. I. (born 1876)—Menshevik, Plekhanovist and defencist. Editor of the magazine, Sovremenny Mir (Contemporary World). Later shared the ideas of Plekhanov's Yedinstvo. After the November Revolution, shifted to the Left, closer to the Communist Party.—II 133.

YOURI.—See Piatakov.

Z

ZASLAVSKY, D. J.—Menshevik; Liquidator and defencist; member of the Bund. In 1917 one of the editors of the Dien. At present contributes to the Moscow Pravda.—II 284.

ZASULICH, VERA (1851-1919)—Famous revolutionist, who in 1878 fired a shot at the Petersburg Governor-General, Trepov, for ordering corporal punishment to be administered to the imprisoned revolutionist, Bogoliubov. Having been freed by the jury, she emigrated abroad, where she was one of the founders of the Liberation of Labour Group in 1883. In 1896 she represented the Petersburg Union of Struggle at the International Socialist Congress. After the split between the Bolsheviks and Mensheviks she joined the latter. During the war she was among the social-patriots. In 1917 she was a member of the Yedinstvo group.—I 84, 262.

ZHITOMIRSKY, J. A. (born 1889)—Provocateur; physician. Informed the Police Department about Bolshevik organisation. One of his pseudonyms was Otsov.—II 157.

ZINOVIEV, G. J. (born 1883)—Joined Social-Democracy in 1901; after the Second Congress (1903) he joined the Bolsheviks. Up to 1905 studied at Berne University while engaged in party work. During the First Russian Revolution he worked in Petersburg, where he was soon elected member of the Central Committee. Was arrested and later emigrated abroad; participated at London Party Congress. In 1908 he again attempted to work in Russia, but was again arrested and compelled to leave the country. Living abroad he participated in the Bolshevik organ, *Social-Democrat*. Participated at Zimmerwald and Kienthal Conferences. After the March Revolution returned to Petrograd together with Lenin. After November Revolution he was elected Chairman Petrograd Soviet. From 1919 to 1926 was chairman of the Executive Committee of the Communist International. During the period of preparation for the November uprising and also later, Zinoviev repeatedly manifested indecision: in the fall of 1917 he was against the uprising; after the November Revolution he was in favour of a coalition government of all the Socialist parties. In 1923-24 he energetically fought the Trotsky Opposition; in 1925 he was at the head of the New Opposition; in 1926 he entered into a bloc with Trotsky, and became one of the leaders of the United Trotsky Opposition for which he was expelled from the party at the end of 1927. Later he repudiated his errors and was reinstated.—I 21, 71, 91, 94, 104, 118, 152, 168, 176, 186, 187, 189, 193, 213, 315; II 76, 81, 82.

ZURABOV, A. G. (born 1873)—Social-Democrat; first Bolshevik, then Left Wing Menshevik; member Second Imperial Duma. During the war internationalist, for which the British Government attempted to prevent his return to Russia after the revolution. In the last years of his life he was close to the Communists.—I 104, 184, 187, 193.

DOCUMENTS AND OTHER MATERIAL

I

MANIFESTO OF THE RUSSIAN SOCIAL-DEMOCRATIC LABOUR PARTY
"TO ALL CITIZENS OF RUSSIA" *

Proletarians of all countries, unite!

CITIZENS! The fortresses of Russian tsarism have fallen. The fortune of the tsarist gang, built on the people's bones, has collapsed. The capital is in the hands of a risen people. Sections of the revolutionary troops have gone over to the side of the insurgents. The revolutionary proletariat and the revolutionary army must save the country from the utter ruin and collapse that were prepared by the tsarist government.

By tremendous efforts, at the price of blood and life, did the Russian people shake off the age-old slavery.

It is the task of the working class and the revolutionary army to create a *Provisional Revolutionary Government* which is to head the new *republican* order now in the process of birth.

The Provisional Revolutionary Government must take it upon itself to create temporary laws defending *all the rights and liberties of the people, to confiscate the lands of the monasteries and the landowners, the crown lands and the appanages, to introduce the 8-hour work-day and to convoke a Constituent Assembly* on the basis of universal, direct and equal suffrage, with no discrimination as to sex, nationality or religion, and with the secret ballot.

The Provisional Revolutionary Government must take it upon itself to secure provisions for the population and the army; for this purpose it must confiscate all the stores prepared by the former government and the municipalities.

The hydra of the reaction may still raise its head. It is the task of the people and its revolutionary government to suppress all counter-revolutionary plots against the people.

It is the immediate and urgent task of the Provisional Revolutionary Government to establish relations with the proletariat of the belligerent countries for the purpose of leading a struggle of the peoples of all the countries against their oppressors and exploiters, against royal governments and capitalist cliques, and for the purpose of terminating the bloody war carnage imposed upon the enslaved peoples against their will.

The workers of shops and factories, also the rising troops, must immediately elect their representatives to the Provisional Revolutionary Government which must be created under the protection of the rising revolutionary people and the army.

Citizens, soldiers, wives and mothers! On to the struggle, all of you! To an open struggle against the tsarist power and its satellites!

The red banner of insurrection is rising *over all of Russia!* Take the cause of liberty into your own hands everywhere, overthrowing the Tsar's henchmen, calling the soldiers to struggle.

* See page 67, Book I of this volume.

Establish in all cities and villages in Russia the government of the revolutionary people.

Citizens! By the brotherly united efforts of the insurgents have we fortified the new order of freedom that is being born on the débris of autocracy!

Forward! There is no way back! Merciless struggle!
Forward under the red banner of the revolution!
Long live the Democratic Republic!
Long live the revolutionary working class!
Long live the revolutionary people and the insurgent army!
March 11, 1917.

Central Committee, R.S.-D.L.P.

Pravda, No. 1, March 18, 1917.

II

WITHOUT SECRET DIPLOMACY *

BY L. KAMENEV

THE war continues. The great Russian Revolution has not interrupted it. And nobody cherishes any hopes that it will end to-morrow or the day after. The soldiers, the peasants and the workers of Russia who went to war obeying the call of the now overthrown Tsar and who shed blood under his banners, have freed themselves; the Tsar's banners have been replaced by the red banners of the revolution. Yet the war will continue, for the German army has not followed the example of the Russian army and still obeys its emperor who greedily strives for loot on the fields of death.

When an army faces an army, it would be the most absurd policy to propose to one of them to lay down arms and go home. This would not be a policy of peace, it would be a policy of slavery which a free people would repudiate with scorn. No, we will firmly hold our posts, we will answer a bullet by a bullet and a shell with a shell. This is beyond dispute.

A revolutionary soldier or officer, having overthrown the yoke of tsarism, will not vacate a trench to leave it to a German soldier or officer who has not mustered up courage to overthrow the yoke of his own government. We must not allow any disorganisation of the military forces of the revolution! The war must be ended in an organised fashion, by treaties among peoples who have liberated themselves, and not by submitting to the will of the neighbouring imperialist conqueror.

However, a people that has liberated itself has a right to know what it is fighting for; it has a right to define for itself its aims and tasks in a war it has not initiated. It must declare openly, not only to its friends but also to its enemies, that it strives for no conquests, for no annexations of others' lands, that it leaves it to every nationality to decide how to organise its own life.

But this is not all. A people that has liberated itself must say openly to the whole world that it is ready at any moment to enter into negotiations for the purpose of stopping the war. On conditions of giving up annexations and indemnities and recognising the right of nations to self-determination we must

* See page 73, Book I of this volume.

be ready every minute to enter into negotiations for the purpose of liquidating the war.
Russia is bound by alliances to England, France, and other countries. It can not act on the questions of peace without them. This means, however, that revolutionary Russia, freed from tsarist yoke, must directly and openly address itself to its Allies proposing to them to reconsider the question of opening peace negotiations. What the answer of the Allies will be we do not know, neither do we know what will be the answer of Germany should this proposal be made.

But one thing we know: Only then will the peoples who were drawn into the imperialist war against their will be able to make a clear account of the war aims. And when the millions of workers and soldiers on all the fronts will have made clear to themselves the real aims of the governments who drew them into the bloody war, this will be not only the end of the war but also a decisive step towards an open struggle against the system of suppression and exploitation which causes all wars.

Not a disorganisation of the revolutionary army that becomes ever more revolutionary is our slogan; neither is it the meaningless, "Down with the war!" Our slogan is—pressure on the Provisional Government with the aim of forcing it openly, before world democracy, and immediately to come forth with an attempt to induce all the belligerent countries forthwith to start negotiations concerning the means of stopping the World War.

Up to that time, however, each remains at his post.

Therefore, in greeting warmly the above published appeal of the Soviet of Workers' and Soldiers' Deputies, "To the Peoples of the Whole World," we view it only as the beginning of an extensive and energetic campaign for the triumph of peace and the cessation of world bloodshed.

Pravda, No. 9, March 28, 1917.

III

OUR DIFFERENCES *

BY L. KAMENEV

In yesterday's issue of the *Pravda* Comrade Lenin published his "theses." They represent the *personal* opinion of Comrade Lenin and by publishing them Comrade Lenin did something which is the duty of every outstanding public man—to submit to the judgment of the revolutionary democracy of Russia his understanding of current events. Comrade Lenin did it in a very concise form, but he did it *thoroughly*. Having begun with a characterisation of the World War, he came to the conclusion that it is necessary to create a new Communist Party. In his report he naturally had to criticise not only the policy of the leaders of the Soviet of Workers' and Soldiers' Deputies, but also the policy of the *Pravda* as it appeared at the time of the Soviet Congress and expressed itself in the activities of the Bolshevik delegates at the congress. This policy of the *Pravda* was clearly formulated in the resolutions on the Provisional Government and on the war, formulated and made public at the same congress after they were prepared by the Bureau of the Central Committee and approved of by the Bolshevik delegates to the congress.

Pending new decisions of the Central Committee and of the All-Russian
_____
* See page 125, Book I of this volume.

conference of our party, those resolutions remain our platform which we will defend both against the demoralising influence of "Revolutionary defencism" and against Comrade Lenin's criticism.

As regards Comrade Lenin's general line, it appears to us unacceptable inasmuch as it proceeds from the assumption that the bourgeois-democratic revolution *has been completed* and it builds on the immediate transformation of this revolution into a Socialist revolution. The tactics that follow from such analysis are greatly at variance with the tactics defended by the representatives of the *Pravda* at the All-Russian Congress both against the official leaders of the Soviet and against the Mensheviks who dragged the Soviet to the Right.

In a broad discussion we hope to carry our point of view as the only possible one for revolutionary Social-Democracy in so far as it wishes to be and must remain to the very end the one and only party of the revolutionary masses of the proletariat without turning into a group of Communist propagandists.

Pravda, No. 27, April 21, 1917.

IV

REPORT ON THE PASSAGE THROUGH GERMANY *

UPON receiving, on March 19, the first news of the beginning of the revolution in Russia, there took place, on the initiative of the International Socialist Commission (the Zimmerwald Commission), a congress of representatives of all the Russian and Polish parties that were adhering to the Zimmerwald alliance. When the congress was closing, a conference devoted to the question of political emigrants' return to Russia took place. It was participated in by Martov, Bobrov, Zinoviev and Kossovsky. Among other proposals the conference took up Martov's plan about a possibility of returning through Germany and Stockholm, on the basis of exchanging for the emigrants an equal number of Germans and Austrians interned in Russia. All conferees agreed that Martov's plan was the most feasible and acceptable. Grimm was instructed to enter into negotiations with the Swiss Government.

A few days later Comrade Grimm met Bagotsky, an agent of the committee on the return of the Russian emigrants (a committee in which all groups were represented). The meeting took place in the presence of Comrade Zinoviev. Grimm told Bagotsky that he had had a conversation with Hoffman, member of the Federal Council in charge of the political department. Hoffman, according to Grimm, had declared that the Swiss Government could not act as official mediator because this might be construed by the Entente Powers as violation of neutrality. Grimm then, so he said, privately approached the representative of the German Government with a view of learning whether he had no objection in principle. Bagotsky and Zinoviev declared that they considered that course to be promising of results, and they asked him to bring the negotiations to a fruitful conclusion.

The following day, however, representatives of some parties in Zürich declared that they did not agree with Grimm's plan. It was necessary to wait for a reply from Petrograd, they said.

The members of the Foreign Bureau of the Central Committee of the Russian Social-Democratic Labour Party then declared that they would not take upon

* See page 91, Book I of this volume.

themselves the responsibility for further delaying their return to Russia, whereupon they sent to Martov and Bobrov the following communication:

The Foreign Bureau of the Central Committee of the Russian Social-Democratic Labour Party has decided to accept Comrade Grimm's proposal concerning the return of the political emigrants to Russia via Germany. The circumstances are the following:

1. Negotiations were conducted by Comrade Grimm with the representative of a government of a neutral country, Minister Hoffman, who finds it impossible for the Swiss Government to take official steps in this matter, since it is obvious that the English Government, interested in not allowing the return of the internationalists to Russia, would construe this as a violation of neutrality on the part of Switzerland.

2. Grimm's proposals are perfectly acceptable, since they guarantee freedom of passage, and are entirely independent of any political orientation or any attitude towards the questions of national defence, continuation of the war, conclusion of peace, etc.

3. This proposal is based on an exchange of the emigrants for those interned in Russia, and the emigrants have no reason whatever to oppose propaganda in favour of such an exchange.

4. Comrade Grimm has made this proposal to all the groups of political emigrants, even stating that, under conditions as they exist at the present moment, this is the only way out and is perfectly acceptable.

5. On the other hand, everything possible has been done to convince the representatives of other groups of the necessity of accepting this proposal, as further delay is absolutely not permissible.

6. Unfortunately, the representatives of some groups have expressed themselves in favour of delay. This decision is highly deserving of condemnation and may do the greatest injury to the Russian revolutionary movement.

Taking the above into consideration, the Foreign Bureau of the Central Committee has decided to inform all party members that we have accepted the proposal to depart immediately, and that all wishing to go with us must register. A copy of the present decision will be forwarded to the representatives of all the groups.

Zürich, March 31, 1917.

N. LENIN.

G. ZINOVIEV.

When this document, with the commentaries of the opposing groups, was handed to Grimm, he made the following semi-official declaration:

Berne, April 2, 1917.

To the Central Committee Organising the
Return of Russian Emigrants in Zürich.

Dear Comrades:

I have just learned of the circular letter of the Foreign Bureau of the Central Committee of the Russian Social-Democratic Labour Party concerning the return of emigrants to Russia. I am extremely amazed at the contents of that letter, not only because it ascribes to me an entirely incorrect position, but also because of the extraordinary (one word illegible) mention of the member of the Federal Council, Hoffman, which makes further negotiations with Swiss authorities highly difficult.

In any event, I find myself constrained to state the following facts, and I leave it to your discretion to make use of the present letter in the way you deem fit.

1. Negotiations are under way, but their origin is not Comrade Grimm's proposal concerning the return of the emigrants to Russia. I have never made such a proposal, I merely served as an intermediary between Russian comrades and the Swiss authorities.

2. In accordance with the decisions of a conference of Russian comrades that met in Berne on March 19, I proposed to the Political Department of the Swiss Government to make clear whether it would not be possible to arrange something like an exchange of Russian emigrants for those interned in Russia. The proposal was rejected on the ground of the country's neutrality which does not depend on one or the other government, and without knowledge as to whether the Entente Powers, England in particular, would or would not put obstacles in the way of the emigrants' departure.

3. While the negotiations were in progress there sprang up the idea of organising in Holland a bureau for the exchange, but in view of the delays such a plan would entail, it was dropped.

4. The final results of the negotiations are the following: The Russian comrades were compelled to address themselves directly to the Provisional Government through the Minister of Justice Kerensky. It will be kept informed and will be· shown the impossibility of returning through England, so that, in view of the existing situation, it will have to approve a return through Germany. In consequence of such an agreement, the passage through Germany may take place without subsequent complications. On Friday, March 30, I notified the representatives of the Central Committee present in Berne about these facts, adding my personal opinion that this proposal, i. e., an agreement with Kerensky or Chkheidze, and the subsequent passage through Germany, were acceptable. I added that it would be up to your committee to accept or reject the proposal, and that I considered my mission ended.

5. On April 1, I received a telegram from Comrades Lenin and Zinoviev informing me that their party had decided to accept without reservations the plan of passing through Germany and of immediately organising the departure. I let them know by telephone that I would gladly help them find a mediator to conclude the negotiations between the authorities entrusted with regulating conditions for passage and the comrades who had telegraphed to me; that, personally, however, I could under no circumstances take part in those negotiations since I considered all negotiations with the Swiss authorities finished and my mission over. As the above-mentioned circular letter seems to have given rise to misunderstandings, I find it necessary to establish these points, in order to avert right now the possibility of rumours being spread. I am very sorry that our efforts were so light-heartedly made the subject of a circular letter, which was not even confidential.

With Socialist greetings,

GRIMM.

When Zinoviev afterwards demanded explanations from Grimm, he declared in the presence of Comrade Platten that he considered it his duty to make such a declaration, particularly since the exposure of Hoffman's rôle might have caused substantial injury to Swiss neutrality. At the same time Grimm declared himself ready to undertake also further steps to facilitate the departure of that group which had decided to go forthwith. However, in view of the equivocal behaviour of Grimm, the organisers of the departure deemed it more appropriate to reject his services and to ask Comrade Platten to bring negotiations to a conclusion.

On April 3 Platten informed the German Embassy in Berne that he was to continue the negotiations begun by Grimm. He proposed, in a written form, the following conditions:

Basis for Negotiations Concerning the Return to Russia of Political Emigrants Living in Switzerland.

1. I, Fritz Platten, under my own full responsibility and at my own risk, accompany the railway car with the political emigrants and refugees who return to Russia through Germany.

2. Platten alone communicates with German authorities and officials. Nobody has a right to enter the car without his permission.

3. The railway car is considered extraterritorial. There shall be no control of passports or passengers upon entering or leaving Germany.

4. Passengers will be admitted into the car irrespective of their views or their attitude towards war or peace.

5. Platten takes it upon himself to provide the passengers with railway tickets at the current rates.

6. The passage is to be made, as far as possible, without interruptions. Nobody shall leave the car, either voluntarily or by order. The car shall not be delayed during the passage unless this is technically unavoidable.

7. Passage is allowed on the basis of an exchange for German or Austrian war prisoners or for those interned in Russia.

8. The mediator and the passengers take it upon themselves personally and privately to insist among the working class that point 7 be adhered to.

9. Passage from the Swiss to the Swedish frontier should be accomplished as speedily as technical facilities permit.

Berne-Zürich, April 4, 1917.

(Signed) FRITZ PLATTEN,
Secretary, Swiss Socialist Party.

Two days later Comrade Platten made it known that the German Government had accepted those conditions.

On April 2, before the issue was brought to a conclusion, the representatives of the other groups adopted the following resolution:

Whereas, in view of the obvious impossibility of returning to Russia via England due to resistance offered by the English and French authorities, all parties have found it necessary to ask of the Provisional Government, through the Soviet of Workers' Deputies, authorisation to exchange a number of political emigrants for an equal number of German citizens;

And whereas the comrades who represent the Central Committee have decided to go to Russia through Germany without awaiting the outcome of the steps undertaken in this direction,—

Therefore we consider the decision of the comrades from the Central Committee to be a political error, as it has not been proven that it is impossible to obtain the authorisation of the Provisional Government for such an exchange.

The organisers of the trip agreed with the first part of the resolution, but they could not accept the proposition that the Provisional Government's resistance to the return of the Russian emigrants to Russia had not been proven. There is not the slightest doubt that the Provisional Government under the Entente's dictatorship will do everything in its power to halt the return of the revolutionists who fight against the predatory war of imperialism. In view of these facts the undersigned see themselves placed before an alternative of either deciding to return to Russia through Germany or remaining abroad till the end of the war. Despite the above quoted declaration of the representatives of the other groups, Platten, having obtained the consent of the German Government to his conditions, found it necessary once more to propose to the Zürich delegates to participate in the journey. While this protocol is being composed, their reply is not yet known to us.

We are informed that the paper *Petit Parisien* carried the news about Miliukov's decision to have all citizens returning through Germany tried in the courts. We therefore declare that if our trip to Russia becomes the object of such measures, we will demand that the present Russian Government, which continues the reactionary war, should be tried by the people. This government, to prove that it is against imperialist policies, continues the practices of the former government, it confiscates telegrams addressed to workers' deputies, etc.

It is our conviction that the conditions offered us for passage through Germany are perfectly acceptable to us. The Miliukovs would certainly make it easy for men like Liebknecht to return to Germany if they were in Russia. The Bethmann-Hollwegs have the same attitude towards the Russian internationalists. The internationalists of all countries have a right and a duty to utilise this gamble of the imperialist governments in the interests of the proletariat without changing their course and without making the slightest concession to the governments. Our viewpoint in relation to the war has been expounded by us in No. 47 of the *Social-Democrat* where we state that we consider admissible a revolutionary war against imperialist Germany—after the proletariat has seized political power in Russia. This viewpoint has been defended by Lenin and Zinoviev also in public speeches, as well as in an article published by Lenin at the beginning of the Russian Revolution in the paper *Volksrecht*.

Simultaneously with this we are addressing to the Swiss workers an open letter in which we express our viewpoint. From the first to the last day we have been organising our journey in full accord with the representatives of the Zimmerwald Left Wing.

From the Swiss frontier our train will be accompanied by Comrade Platten as far in the direction of Petrograd as this will be possible for him; we hope that we will be met at the Swedish frontier by the Swedish internationalists, Ström and Lindhagen.

From the very beginning our steps were perfectly open, and we are convinced that this act will be completely and absolutely approved by the workers-internationalists in Russia. This declaration is binding for all the members of our party who participate in the journey. Persons who participate in it without being members of our party, do so on their own responsibility.*

Declaration

The undersigned are appraised of the difficulties put by the Entente Governments in the way of the Russian internationalists' departure and of the conditions under which the German Government allows them to pass. The undersigned are fully aware of the fact that the German Government allows the passage of the Russian internationalists only in order thus to strengthen the anti-war movement in Russia. They declare:

The Russian internationalists who, during the war, tirelessly and with all their power have been fighting against the imperialism of all nations, particularly that of Germany, now go back to Russia to work for the revolution; by these actions they will help the proletariat of all countries and especially the proletariat of Germany to begin their struggle against their governments. The example of the heroic struggle of the Russian proletariat is the best stimulant for such a struggle. For all these reasons the ·undersigned internationalists of Switzerland, France, Germany, Poland, Sweden and Norway, consider it not only the right but also the duty of the Russian comrades to take advantage of the possibility offered them to return to Russia. At the same time we wish them the best successes in their struggle against the im-

---

* This is the end of the declaration of those participating in the journey. The rest is a declaration of representatives of other parties and their appreciation of the step taken by the Russian emigrants.—*Ed.*

perialist policy of the Russian bourgeoisie, a struggle that is part of a general struggle of the proletariat for a social revolution.

Berne, March 17, 1917.

> PAUL HARTSTEIN (Paul Levi) (Germany)
> HENRI GUILBEAUX (France)
> F. LORIOT (France)
> BRONSKI (Poland)
> FRITZ PLATTEN (Switzerland)
> LINDHAGEN, Mayor of Stockholm (Sweden)
> STRÖM, Deputy, Secretary Swedish Socialist Party (Sweden)
> CARLSON, Deputy, President Accident Compensation Fund (Sweden)
> TURE NERMAN, Editor *Politiken* (Sweden)
> KILBOM, Editor *Stormklokan* (Sweden)
> HANSEN (Norway)

Lenin Collection, II.

V

PROPOSED RESOLUTION OF THE ZIMMERWALD LEFT AT THE ZIMMERWALD CONFERENCE IN SEPTEMBER, 1915 *

The World War and the Tasks of Social-Democracy

THE World War, which has been devastating Europe for the last year, is an *imperialist war* waged for the political and economic exploitation of the world, export markets, sources of raw material, spheres of capital investment, etc. It is a product of capitalist development which connects the entire world in a world economy but at the same time permits the existence of national state capitalist groups with opposing interests.

If the bourgeoisie and the governments seek to conceal this character of the World War by asserting that it is a question of a forced struggle for *national independence*, it is only to mislead the *proletariat*, since the war is being waged for the oppression of foreign peoples and countries. Equally untruthful are the legends concerning the defence of democracy in this war, since imperialism signifies the most unscrupulous domination of big capital and political reaction.

Imperialism can only be overcome by overcoming the contradictions which produced it, that is, by the *Socialist organisation* of the sphere of capitalist civilisation for which the objective conditions are already ripe.

At the outbreak of the war, the majority of the labour leaders had not raised this only possible slogan in opposition to imperialism. Prejudiced by nationalism, rotten with opportunism, *they surrendered the proletariat to imperialism, and gave up the principles of Socialism and thereby the real struggle for the every-day interests of the proletariat.*

Social-patriotism and social-imperialism, the standpoint of the openly patriotic majority of the formerly Social-Democratic leaders *in Germany*, as well as the opposition-mannered centre of the party around Kautsky, and to

* See page 148, Book I of this volume. See also note 73 of the Explanatory Notes, Book I.

which *in France and Austria* the majority, *in England and Russia* a part of the leaders (Hyndman, the Fabians, the Trade-Unionists, Plekhanov, Rubanovich, the group *Nashe Dielo*) confess, is a more dangerous enemy to the proletariat than the bourgeois apostles of imperialism, since, misusing the banner of Socialism, it can mislead the unenlightened workers. *The ruthless struggle against social-imperialism constitutes the first condition for the revolutionary mobilisation of the proletariat and the reconstruction of the International.*

It is the task of the Socialist parties as well as of the Socialist opposition in the now social-imperialist parties, to call and lead the labouring masses to the *revolutionary struggle* against the capitalist governments for the conquest of political power for the Socialist organisation of society.

Without giving up the struggle for every foot of ground within the framework of capitalism, for every reform strengthening the proletariat, without renouncing any means of organisation and agitation, the revolutionary Social-Democrats, on the contrary, must utilise all the struggles, all the reforms demanded by our minimum programme for the purpose of sharpening this *war crisis* as well as every social and political crisis of capitalism, of extending them to an attack upon its very foundations. By waging this struggle *under the slogan of Socialism* it will render the labouring masses immune to the slogans of the oppression of one people by another as expressed in the maintenance of the domination of one nation over another, in the cry for new annexations; it will render them deaf to the temptations of national solidarity which has led the proletarians to the battlefields.

The signal for this struggle is the struggle against the World War, for the speedy termination of the slaughter of nations. This struggle demands the refusal of war credits, quitting the cabinets, the denunciation of the capitalist, anti-Socialist character of the war from the tribunes of the parliaments, in the columns of the legal, and where necessary illegal, press, the sharpest struggle against social-patriotism, and the utilisation of every movement of the people caused by the results of the war (misery, great losses, etc.) for the organisation of street demonstrations against the governments, propaganda of international solidarity in the trenches, the encouragement of economic strikes, the effort to transform them into political strikes under favourable conditions. "Civil war, not civil peace,"—that is the slogan!

As against all illusions that it is possible to bring about the basis of a lasting peace, the beginning of disarmament, by any decisions of diplomacy and the governments, the revolutionary Social-Democrats must repeatedly tell the masses of the people that only the social revolution can bring about a lasting peace as well as the emancipation of mankind.

VI

THESES OF THE CENTRAL COMMITTEE OF THE RUSSIAN SOCIAL-DEMOCRAT LABOUR PARTY (BOLSHEVIKS) PROPOSED AT THE KIENTHAL CONFERENCE, APRIL, 1916 *

1. Just as every war is only a continuation of the politics practised by belligerent states even in the preceding period of peace—with peaceful means,

* See pages 145-153, Book I of this volume. See also note 78 of the Explanatory Notes, Book I.

to be sure—so the peace concluding the war can only be a registration of the realignment of forces achieved in the course of the war.

2. As long as the pillars of present-day bourgeois social relations continue to exist, an imperialist war can only lead to an imperialist peace, that is, to the extension and augmentation of the oppression of small peoples and states by finance capital which made a gigantic upward swing not only before the war but also in the course of the war.

The objective content of that policy which was conducted by the bourgeoisie and the governments of both belligerent groups before the war and during it, leads to the increase of economic pressure, national enslavement, political reaction. Consequently, the conclusion of peace, no matter what the outcome of the war may be, can only establish the fact that the political and economic condition of the masses has become worse, since bourgeois society continues to exist.

To assume a "democratic peace" as a result of the imperialist war is to voice an empty phrase instead of studying the policy of the powers before the war and during the war; is to mislead the masses by withholding what is most important: the impossibility of a democratic peace without a series of revolutions.

3. The Socialists in no way renounce the struggle for reforms. Even now, for example, they must vote in the parliaments for every improvement in the condition of the people, small as it may be; for adequate support of the inhabitants of territories affected by the war, for mitigation of national pressure, etc. It is a bourgeois deception, however, to preach reform politics on questions which history and the whole political situation stamps as capable of solution only by revolution. These are the basic questions of imperialism, i. e., the questions of the continued existence of capitalist society as a whole, the questions of the possibility of delaying the overthrow of capitalism by attempting a new division of the earth in accord with the new alignment of forces between the great powers which had developed not only with extraordinary speed but also—which is the most important—with extraordinary unevenness. Real political activity which, without deceiving the masses, is suited to change the alignment of forces of present-day society, can only be achieved in one of the following forms: either one helps one's "own" national bourgeoisie to rob foreign countries, and calls this help "defence of the fatherland" or "saving the country"; or one helps to guide the Socialist revolution of the proletariat onto the road by augmenting the ferment already commencing among the masses, supporting strikes and demonstrations, etc., by supporting the beginnings—at present still weak—of the revolutionary mass struggle and intensifying them to a general attack of the proletariat against the bourgeoisie.

Just as all social-chauvinists now deceive the people when they speak of an "honourable" defence against a "dishonourable" attack on the part of this or that group of capitalist robber powers, so it is also pure deception and empty phrase-mongering when one speaks of a "democratic peace," as if the coming peace, which is even now being prepared by the capitalists and diplomats, could render a new "dishonourable" attack impossible and establish the former "honest" relations; as if it were not rather a continuation and sanctioning of imperialist policy, the policy of capitalist robbery, of national oppression, of political reaction, of increasing capitalist exploitation. These "Socialist" lackeys are doing good service to the capitalists and their diplomats now by confusing the people and hiding the true situation with phrases about a democratic peace, and diverting the people from a revolutionary struggle.

4. The programme of "democratic peace" which was defended to-day by the most outstanding leaders of the Second International, appears as just such deception and hypocrisy. At the Dutch Congress in Arnheim (see the *Neue Zeit*, October 2, 1915), this programme was formulated as follows by most influential official representatives of the Second International: Renunciation of revolutionary struggle until the imperialist governments have concluded peace; till then—phrases about the rejection of annexations and indemnities, recognition on paper of the right of self-determination of nations, the democratisation of foreign policy, courts of arbitration for the liquidation of political disputes, United States of Europe, etc.

Viewed objectively, this "programme of peace" leads to the increased subordination of the working class, for it reconciles the workers, who are beginning to take up a revolutionary struggle with their chauvinist leaders, by obliterating the depth of the crisis in Socialism, to return to that condition within the Socialist Party which existed before the war and which resulted in most of the leaders going over to the side of the bourgeoisie. The danger of this policy is all the greater as it is adorned with high-sounding phrases and is conducted not only in Germany but also in other countries. In England most of the leaders defend this policy. In Russia, the chauvinist idea of "defence of the fatherland" is cloaked in the phrase about "saving the fatherland." Thus Chkheidze, for example, on the one hand claims to stand on the ground of the Zimmerwald Conference, and on the other, praises, in the official fraction declaration in the Duma, the infamous speech of Huysmans (in Arnheim) and has not a single word against the voluntary participation of the workers in the tsarist, big-bourgeois war industries committees. Another leader of the Duma fraction, Deputy Chkhenkeli, delivers social-patriotic speeches in the Duma quite openly, supports the participators in the war industries committees, etc. In Italy, a similar policy is practised by Treves (see *Avanti*, March 5, 1916).

5. The most important peace questions to-day are those of annexations. And it is just this question that reveals the "Socialist" hypocrisy of to-day, and makes clear, on the other hand, the tasks of the real Socialist propaganda and agitation. It must be made clear what annexation really is, how and why Socialists must struggle against annexations. Not every acquisition of a new territory is annexation, for, in general, Socialism stands for the disappearance of boundaries between nations and, for the formation of larger states. Not every breach of the *status quo* is annexation. To believe that, would be reactionary and would contradict the basic principles of historical science. Not every acquisition of a country by the violence of war is annexation, for Socialism cannot reject in principle wars that are waged in the interest of the majority of the population. By annexations we merely understand the acquisition of a country against the will of its inhabitants. In other words: the concept of annexations is most intimately bound up with the concept of the right of self-determination of nations.

But in the present war, just because it is an imperialist war on the part of both groups of belligerent powers, we see that the bourgeois and social-chauvinist politicans come out against annexations in so far as these are practised by a hostile power. It is clear that such a "struggle" against annexations, such "unity" in the question of annexations, is nothing but hypocrisy. It is clear that the French Socialists, who are supporting the war for Alsace-Lorraine, or the German Socialists who do not demand the freedom of separation for Alsace-Lorraine or German-Poland from Germany, or the Russian

Socialists who call the war, which leads to the renewed enslavement of Poland by tsarism, "saving the fatherland"—that all these Socialists are actually annexationists.

If the struggle against annexations is to be more than an empty phrase, if it is really to educate the masses in the spirit of internationalism, then the question must be formulated in such a way as to open the eyes of the people, so that it perceives the deception in the question of annexations, and not in such a way as to cover up this deception. It is not sufficient for a Socialist to claim that he is for the equality of nations and swear that he wants to come out against all annexations. Every true Socialist, on the contrary, is obliged to demand immediately and unconditionally the freedom of separation for the colonies and nations that are oppressed by his own "fatherland."

Without this condition, even the recognition of the right of self-determination and the principles of internationalism in the Zimmerwald Manifesto is at best a still-born word.

6. An exposure of the lie of a "democratic peace," of the "peaceful" intentions of the belligerent countries, and so forth, must lie at the basis of the "peace programme" of the Socialists as well as of their struggle for the termination of the war—the lie with which demagogic Ministers, social-chauvinists and Kautskians of all countries appeal to the masses.

Every "peace programme" is hypocrisy if it does not rest upon propaganda for the necessity of the revolution and upon increasing the revolutionary ferment which is beginning everywhere among the masses (protests, fraternisation connections in the trenches, strikes, demonstrations, letters from those fighting at the front to relatives, who are called upon not to subscribe to the war loans, etc.).

The support of every mass movement in favour of terminating the war is a duty of the Socialists. In reality, however, this duty is fulfilled only by those Socialists who—like Liebknecht from the speaker's tribune in parliament—call upon the soldiers to lower their arms, and preach the revolution and the transformation of the imperialist war into a civil war for Socialism.

In order to draw the masses into the revolutionary struggle, in order to convince them of the necessity of revolutionary measures for the possibility of a "democratic peace," the slogan of "Refuse to pay the national debt" must be raised.

It is not sufficient for the Zimmerwald Manifesto to indicate the revolution by saying that the masses must make sacrifices for their own cause and not for some one else's. The people must know where it is to go and why. It is obvious that revolutionary action during the war must transform the imperialist war into a civil war for Socialism. This goal must be stated without equivocation, difficult as the achievement of this goal may be, since we are only at the beginning of the road. It is not sufficient to say with the Zimmerwald Manifesto that the capitalists are lying when they speak of a defence of the fatherland in the present war, and that the workers, in their revolutionary struggle, need not reckon with the military condition of their country. It must be stated clearly what is only indicated here: That not only the capitalists but also the social-chauvinists are misleading the masses when they apply the concept of the "defence of the fatherland" in this imperialist war; that revolutionary action during the war is impossible without threatening one's own government with defeat in the war; that every defeat of the government in a reactionary war facilitates the revolution which is alone capable of bringing about a lasting democratic peace. Finally, the masses must be told that without the establishment of an illegal organisation and an illegal press not subject to censorship, it is impossible to extend the beginning revolutionary struggle, to prepare the revolutionary struggle.

7. As for the parliamentary action of the Socialists, it must be considered that the Zimmerwald Conference not only expressed its sympathy for the five Social-Democratic Deputies of the Duma who are now pining in Siberia, but also declared itself in agreement with their tactics. One cannot recognise the revolutionary struggle of the masses and at the same time be satisfied with an exclusively legal activity.

Such tactics lead solely to the justified dissatisfaction of the masses, to their quitting the Social-Democracy and their going over to anti-parliamentary anarchism and syndicalism.

It must be clearly stated that the Social-Democratic Deputies must utilise their position not only to appear in parliament but also to develop an all-around, extra-parliamentary activity in harmony with the illegal organisations and the revolutionary struggle of the workers; that the masses themselves, through their illegal organisations, must control their leaders.

8. The question of convening the I.S.B. [International Socialist Bureau, as the leading committee of the Second International called itself.—Ed.] raises the fundamental question of principle, whether a unity of the old parties and of the Second International is possible. Each further step of the international labour movement on the road that was pointed out from Zimmerwald, shows the illogic of the position of the majority of the Zimmerwald Conference: on the one hand, the policy of the old parties and the Second International is identified with the bourgeois policy in the labour movement, with a policy which furthers the interests of the bourgeoisie and not those of the proletariat; on the other hand, the I.S.C. [International Socialist Commission—the central committee of the Zimmerwald Union.—Ed.] fears a split with the I.S.B. and promises to liquidate officially should the I.S.B. be convened again. We affirm that such a promise in Zimmerwald was not only not voted upon, but that it did not even get as far as being expressed.

The half year which has gone by since the Zimmerwald Conference has shown that the activity in the spirit of the Zimmerwald Conference—we do not speak of empty words, but of activity—in all countries is actually bound up with a deepening and extension of the split. In Germany, illegal proclamations against the decision of the official party are issued. When Otto Rühle, next to Comrade Liebknecht, openly declared that there were two parties, one that supports the bourgeoisie, and another that fights against the bourgeoisie, many, to be sure, among them Kautsky, criticised Rühle, but no one refuted him. In France, the Socialist Bourderon, an avowed opponent of the split, proposed to his party a resolution, which, if adopted, would decidedly result in a split, namely: to disavow the party committee and the parliamentary fraction (désapprouver la Comm. Adm. Perm. et le Fr. Parl.). In England, the I.L.P. member T. Russell Williams, in the moderate paper *Labour Leader*, openly recognises the unavoidability of the split and he is supported in letters from English workers. But perhaps the example of America is even more instructive, for even there, in the neutral country, there are manifested two irreconcilably hostile tendencies within the Socialist Party: on the one hand, supporters of so-called "preparedness," i.e., of the war, of militarism and navalism; on the other hand, such Socialists as Eugene Debs openly preach the civil war for Socialism and indeed in connection with the coming war.

In the whole world, the split is actually here already. There are two irreconcilable attitudes of the working class towards the war. Simply to close one's eyes will not do; it can only lead to the confusion of the labouring masses, to beclouding their consciousness, to rendering difficult that revolutionary struggle with which all Zimmerwaldists officially sympathise, and to strengthening the influence of those leaders who are accused by the I.S.C. in the circular of February 10, 1916, of misleading the masses and preparing a conspiracy ("Pact") against Socialism.

Let the bankrupt I.S.B. be restored by the social-chauvinists of all countries. The Socialists, however, have the task of enlightening the masses on the unavoidability of the split from those who carry on a policy of the bourgeoisie under the banner of Socialism.

VII

RESOLUTION ON THE CRISIS IN CONNECTION WITH THE PROVISIONAL GOVERNMENT'S NOTE, ADOPTED BY THE CENTRAL COMMITTEE OF THE RUSSIAN SOCIAL-DEMOCRATIC LABOUR PARTY, MAY 3, 1917 *

THE note of the Provisional Government has proven the perfect correctness of the stand taken by our party in the resolution of the Petrograd city conference, namely: 1. That the Provisional Government is a thoroughly imperialist government bound hand and foot by Anglo-French and Russian capital; 2. That all promises which it made or could have made (like revealing the people's will to peace," etc.) contain nothing but deceptions; 3. That the Provisional Government, no matter what persons compose it, cannot give up annexations, because in the present war, and particularly at the present moment, the class of capitalists is bound by bank capital; 4. That the policy of the petty bourgeoisie as conducted by he Narodniks, Mensheviks, the majority of the leaders of the present Soviet of Workers' Deputies, a policy consisting in nurturing illusory hopes about the possibility of "improving" the capitalists (i. e., the Provisional Government) "by means of suasion," again stands exposed by this note.

In view of the above, the Central Committee arrives at the following conclusions:

I. All changes in the personnel of the present government (Miliukov's resignation, Kerensky's recall, etc.) will be an imitation of the worst practices of bourgeois parliamentary republicanism which substitutes clique rivalries and shiftings of persons for the struggle of classes.

II. The only salvation for the mass of the petty-bourgeois population which is vacillating between the capitalists and the working class is unreservedly to join the side of the revolutionary proletariat which alone is capable of actually breaking the fetters of finance capital and annexationist policies. Only after taking over—with the aid of a majority of the people—all state power, will the revolutionary proletariat, together with the revolutionary soldiers, in the person of the Soviets of Workers' and Soldiers' Deputies, create a government that will have the confidence of the workers of all the countries and will be able speedily to end the war with a really democratic peace.

Pravda, No. 37, May 4, 1917.

* See page 245, Book I of this volume.

VIII

RESOLUTION OF THE MOSCOW REGIONAL CONFERENCE OF THE RUSSIAN SOCIAL-DEMOCRATIC LABOUR PARTY ON THE ATTITUDE TOWARDS THE PROVISIONAL GOVERNMENT *

HAVING discussed the question of our attitude towards the Provisional Government, the Regional Conference of the Central Industrial Region has come to the following conclusions:

1. The Provisional Government, being an organ of power of the bourgeosie and the landowners, is closely connected with Anglo-French imperialism and is, in its essence, counter-revolutionary.

2. Expressing the interests of these classes, the Provisional Government very slowly and reluctantly, and only under the pressure of revolutionary democracy, puts into practice the program of reforms announced by it, and offers resistance to a further expansion and a deepening of the conquests of the revolution.

3. At the same time the forces of the bourgeois and landowner counter-revolution, now in the process of organisation, are striving, with the silent permission of the Provisional Government and sometimes with its direct aid, to split the masses of revolutionary democracy and to prevent them from completing the proletarian-peasant revolution.

For this purpose the Provisional Government allows counter-revolutionary propaganda in the army, it helps organise the high commanding officers against the soldiers, it puts obstacles in the way of introducing the eight-hour workday, it delays the designating of a date for the elections to the Constitutent Assembly, it offers resistance to the passing of the whole land into the hands of the people, etc.

4. Every step of the Provisional Government, in foreign as well as in domestic politics, furnishes material that reveals the true character of this government and thereby emphasises more and more the necessity for the proletarian, semi-proletarian and revolutionary petty-bourgeois strata of city and village to concentrate all power in the organisations of these revolutionary-democratic groups of the population.

5. At the present time, the Soviets of Workers', Soldiers', and other Deputies—the organs of revolutionary power and organisation centres of the masses of revolutionary democracy—are, in a substantial majority not only devoid of sovereign power, but they do not even exert a sufficiently concentrated, organised pressure on the various local organs of the revolutionary period, namely, the Provisional Executive Committees of the provinces, the city committees of public safety, etc.; at the same time they show confidence in the Provisional Government and support its activities, sometimes even when they are clearly directed against the people (support of the "Liberty Loan").

Proceeding from these considerations the Conference states the following:

1. In order to accomplish the passing of the state power into the hands of the Soviets of Workers', Soldiers', and other Deputies or other organs that are the direct expression of the will of revolutionary democracy, it is necessary to do extensive work of clarifying proletarian class-consciousness and of uniting the city and village proletarians against petty-bourgeois vacillation, for it is only work of this nature that will assure the successful advance of the whole revolutionary people.

* See page 272, Book I of this volume.

2. In order that such work may bring results, it is necessary, first of all, to strengthen the Soviets as mass organisations and incessantly to widen their connections with the masses of revolutionary democracy, as well as to conduct many-sided activities within the Soviets of Workers' and Soldiers' Deputies tending to consolidate within them the proletarian internationalist groups of revolutionary Social-Democracy.

3. In the process of transforming themselves into sovereign organs, the revolutionary masses of the Soviets of Workers', Soldiers', and other Deputies which organise around themselves all the groups of revolutionary democracy, must exercise control over the activities of all the organs of the revolutionary period, exposing the counter-revolutionary character of the steps undertaken by the Provisional Government, by the provincial and city public committees, etc. This control, in the course of the development of a victorious proletarian-peasant revolution, will inevitably turn into control over all elements of the economic life of the state, and will appear as a forward step towards the seizure of all state power by the organised masses of the proletariat and poor peasants.

Social-Democrat, No. 45, May 15, 1917.

IX

APPEAL TO THE SOLDIERS OF ALL THE BELLIGERENT COUNTRIES *

BROTHER SOLDIERS:

We are all tired of this terrible war which has taken millions of lives, has crippled millions of people and has caused unheard-of misery, ruin, and starvation.

Day by day there grows the number of people who ask themselves. "Why was this war begun? Why is it being continued?"

Day by day it becomes clearer to us workers and soldiers, who bear the most trying burdens of the war, that the war was started and is being continued by the capitalists of all countries for the interests of the capitalists, for domination over the world, for markets to benefit the manufacturers and bankers, for the purpose of robbing weak nationalities. Colonies are being divided, territories are being seized in the Balkans and in Turkey—and this is why the European peoples must be ruined, this is why we must perish, this is why we must witness ruin, starvation, the death of our families.

The capitalist class waxes rich in all the countries on war contracts and deliveries, on concessions in the annexed countries, on high prices for goods; they gather gigantic, unheard-of, scandalous profits. Moreover, the capitalist class has saddled the peoples with a heavy burden in the form of high interest on war loans, to be borne for long decades to come. We workers and peasants face death, ruin, starvation, and still we patiently tolerate all this, we even strengthen our oppressors, the capitalists, in that the workers of the various countries exterminate each other and become imbued with hatred for each other.

Is it possible that we should continue patiently to bear our yoke, to tolerate the war between the capitalist classes? Is it possible that we should

* See page 279, Book I of this volume.

prolong this war by siding with our national government, with our national bourgeoisie, with our national capitalists, thus destroying the international unity of the workers of all countries, of the whole world?

No, brother soldiers, it is time we opened our eyes, it is time we took our fate into our own hands. In all the countries there grows, widens, and deepens the people's indignation against the capitalist class which has drawn the people into this war. Not only in Germany, but also in England, known before the war as a very free country, hundreds and hundreds of real friends and representatives of the working class are languishing in prisons for honest and truthful utterances against the war and against the capitalists. The revolution in Russia is only the first step of the first revolution after which others must and will follow.

The new government in Russia, that which has overthrown Nicholas II, a crowned bandit of the same kind as Wilhelm II, is a government of capitalists. It wages the same predatory imperialist war as do the capitalists of Germany, England, and other countries. It has confirmed the predatory secret treaties concluded by Nicholas II with the capitalists of England, France, etc.; it does not publish these treaties for public information, as the German Government does not publish its secret and no less predatory treaties with Austria, Bulgaria, etc.

On May 3, the Russian Provisional Government published a note in which it once more confirms the old predatory treaties concluded by the Tsar, and expresses its readiness to continue the war to complete victory. Thus it makes indignant even those who hitherto trusted and supported it.

The Russian Revolution, however, created, besides the government of the capitalists, revolutionary organisations established by initiative from below and representing an overwhelming majority of the workers and peasants, namely, the Soviets of Workers' and Soldiers' Deputies in Petrograd and in a majority of the cities of Russia. A majority of the soldiers and a part of the workers has hitherto followed in Russia—as do very many workers and soldiers in Germany—a policy of unconscious confidence in the government of capitalists, in their empty and false speeches on peace without annexation, on a defencive war and the like.

The workers and the poorest peasants, however, differ from the capitalists, in that they are not interested either in annexations or in conserving the profits of the capitalists. This is why every day, every step of the government of capitalists will, both in Russia and in Germany, expose the fraud of the capitalists and show that as long as the rule of the capitalists continues there can be no real democratic peace concluded without violence and based on a real renunciation of annexations, i. e., on the liberation of all colonies without exception, of all oppressed, forcibly annexed or semi-sovereign nationalities without exception, and just so long will the war in all probability be continued and accentuated.

Only where state power in two now opposing states, for instance, in Russia and Germany, will have passed entirely and completely into the hands of revolutionary Soviets of Workers' and Soldiers' Deputies capable, not in words, but in deeds, to break the whole network of relations and interests of capital;—only there will the workers of both belligerent countries become imbued with confidence in each other and will be able speedily to put an end to the war on the basis of a really democratic peace which really liberates all peoples and nationalities.

Brother soldiers!

Let us do all in our power to hasten the coming of this, to reach this goal;

let us not be afraid of sacrifices, for any sacrifice in favour of a workers' revolution will be less burdensome than the sacrifices of war.

Every victorious step of the revolution will save hundreds of thousands, even millions of people from death, ruin, and starvation.

Peace to the cottages, war to the palaces! Peace to the workers of all countries! Long live the brotherly unity of the revolutionary workers of all countries! Long live Socialism!

> Central Committee, Russian Social-Democratic Labour Party.
> Petrograd Committee, Russian Social-Democratic Labour Party.
> Editors *Pravda*.

May 4, 1917.

Pravda, No. 37, May 4, 1917.

X

RESOLUTIONS OF THE ALL-RUSSIAN APRIL (MAY) CONFERENCE OF THE R.S.-D.L.P., MAY 7-12, 1917 *

1. On the War

I.

THE present war, on the part of both belligerent groups, is an imperialist war, *i. e.*, it is waged by capitalists for the division of the benefits derived from the domination of the world, for markets, for finance (bank) capital, for the subjection of weak nationalities, etc. Each day of war enriches the financial and industrial bourgeoisie and impoverishes and saps the strength of the proletariat and the peasantry of all the belligerents, as well as of the neutral countries. In Russia, moreover, the prolongation of the war involves a grave danger to the conquests of the revolution and its further development.

The passing of state power, in Russia, into the hands of the Provisional Government, a government of the landowners and capitalists, did not and could not alter the character and meaning of Russia's participation in the war.

This fact became particularly apparent when the new government not only failed to publish the secret treaties concluded between Tsar Nicholas II and the capitalist governments of England, France, etc., but even formally and without consulting the people confirmed these secret treaties, which promised Russian capitalists freedom to rob China, Persia, Turkey, Austria, etc. The concealment of these treaties from the people completely deceived them as to the true character of the war.

For this reason a proletarian party can support neither the present war, nor the present government, nor its loans, without breaking completely with internationalism, *i. e.*, with the fraternal solidarity of the workers of all lands in their struggle against the yoke of capital.

No confidence can be placed in the promises of the present government to renounce annexations, *i. e.*, conquests of foreign countries, or in the promise to renounce forcible retention within the confines of Russia of this or that nationality. For, in the first place, the capitalists, bound by thousands of threads of bank capital, cannot renounce annexations in the present war without renouncing the profits on the billions invested in loans, in concessions, in war industries, etc. And, in the second place, the new government,

* See pages 271-319, Book I of this volume.

having renounced annexations in order to deceive the people, declared through Miliukov (Moscow, April 27, 1917) that it had no intention of renouncing annexations, and, in the note of May 1, and in the explanations of it of May 5, confirmed the annexationist character of its policies. In warning the people against the empty promises of the capitalists, the Conference therefore declares that it is necessary to distinguish sharply between a renunciation of annexations in words and a renunciation of annexations in deeds, i. e., the immediate publication and abrogation of all the secret predatory treaties and the immediate granting to all the nationalities of the right to determine by free voting whether they wish to be independent states or to be part of another state.

II.

The so-called "revolutionary defencism" which in Russia has permeated all the Narodnik parties (the People's Socialists, Trudoviks, Socialists-Revolutionists) as well as the opportunist party of the Social-Democratic Mensheviks of the Organisation Committee (Chkheidze, Tsereteli, etc.) and the majority of the unaffiliated revolutionists, represents, by its class character, on the one hand the interests and the standpoint of the wealthier peasants and a part of the small proprietors who, like the capitalists, profit by oppressing weak peoples; on the other hand "revolutionary defencism" is the outcome of the deception by the capitalists of part of the city and village proletarians, who, by their class position, have no interest in the profits of the capitalists and in the imperialist war.

The Conference declares that any concessions to "revolutionary defencism" are absolutely not permissible and would actually signify a complete break with internationalism and Socialism. As for the defencist tendencies present among the great masses, our party will struggle against these tendencies by ceaselessly emphasising the truth that any attitude of uncritical confidence in the government of the capitalists at the present moment is one of the greatest obstacles to a speedy conclusion of the war.

III.

As for the most important question of the manner of concluding as soon as possible the present capitalist war, not by an oppressive peace but by a truly democratic one, the Conference recognises and declares the following:

This war cannot be ended by a refusal of the soldiers of one side only to continue the war, by a simple cessation of war activities on the part of one side only.

The Conference reiterates its protest against the base slander circulated by the capitalists against our party to the effect that we are in favour of a separate peace with Germany. We consider the German capitalists robbers no less than the capitalists of Russia, England, France, etc., and Emperor Wilhelm just as much of a crowned bandit as Nicholas II and the monarchs of England, Italy, Rumania, and all the rest.

Our party will patiently and persistently explain to the people the truth that wars are carried on by governments, that wars are always indissolubly bound up with the policies of certain classes, that this war may be terminated by a democratic peace only if the entire state power, in at least several of the belligerent states, has passed to the class of the proletarians and semi-proletarians who are really capable of putting an end to the bondage of capitalism.

In Russia, the revolutionary class, upon having seized the state power, would

inaugurate a series of measures to undermine the economic rule of the capitalists, as well as of measures that would render the capitalists completely
harmless politically, and would immediately and frankly offer to all the
peoples a democratic peace on the basis of a complete relinquishment of every
possible form of annexation or indemnity. Such measures and such an offer
of peace would bring about an attitude of complete confidence of the workers
of the belligerent countries towards each other and would inevitably lead to
uprisings of the proletariat against such imperialist governments as might
resist the offered peace.

Until the revolutionary class in Russia shall have taken over the entire
state power, our party will, by all means, support those proletarian parties
and groups in foreign countries as are, already during the continuance of the
war, conducting a revolutionary struggle against their own imperialist governments and their own bourgeoisie. Particularly will our party support the mass
fraternisation of the soldiers of all the belligerent countries that has already
begun at the front, thereby endeavouring to transform this instinctive expression of solidarity of the oppressed into a class-conscious, well-organised movement for the taking over of all state power in all the belligerent countries by the
revolutionary proletariat.

2. ON THE ATTITUDE TOWARDS THE PROVISIONAL GOVERNMENT

The All-Russian Conference of the R.S.-D.L.P. recognises that

1. The Provisional Government, by its class character, is the organ of
landowner and bourgeois domination;

2. The Provisional Government and the classes it represents are bound
with indissoluble economic and political ties to Russian and Anglo-French
imperialism;

3. The Provisional Government does not fully carry out even the programme which it has promulgated, and when it does, it is only because of
the pressure of the revolutionary proletariat and, partly, the petty bourgeoisie;

4. The forces of the bourgeois and feudal counter-revolution, now in the
process of organisation, have already, under the cover of the Provisional
Government and with its obvious encouragement, launched an attack on
revolutionary democracy: thus the Provisional Government is postponing the
calling of elections to the Constituent Assembly, is interfering with the general arming of the people, is opposing the transfer of the land to the people
by foisting upon it the landowners' way of settling the agrarian question, is
blocking the introduction of an eight-hour workday, is condoning counter-
revolutionary propaganda in the army (Guchkov and Co.), is organising the
high commanding officers of the army against the soldiers, etc.;

5. The Provisional Government, while guarding the interests of the capitalists and landowners, is incapable of taking a number of revolutionary measures
in the economic field (supply of foodstuffs, etc.) which are absolutely and
urgently necessary in view of the impending economic catastrophe;

6. While doing this, the Provisional Government is relying at the present
moment on the confidence of, and, to a certain extent, on an actual consent
of the Petrograd Soviet of Workers' and Soldiers' Deputies which now is the
leading organisation of a majority of workers and soldiers, i. e., peasants;

7. Each step made by the Provisional Government, both in the realm of
its domestic and foreign policies, is bound to open the eyes of the city and
village proletarians and semi-proletarians and force various strata of the petty
bourgeoisie to choose between one and the other political alignment.

Proceeding from the above assumptions, the conference resolves that

1. It is necessary to do extensive work in clarifying proletarian class-consciousness and to unite the city and village proletarians against petty-bourgeois vacillation, for it is only work of this nature that will assure the successful passing of the entire state power into the hands of Soviets of Workers' and Soldiers' Deputies or other organs directly expressing the will of the majority of the people (organs of local self-government, the Constituent Assembly, etc.);

2. Such work requires comprehensive activity within the Soviets of Workers' and Soldiers' Deputies, an increase in the number of Soviets, an increase in their power, a welding together, within the Soviets, of the proletarian internationalist groups of our party;

3. In order immediately to insure and widen the conquests of the revolution, it is necessary, in basing ourselves on a solid majority of the local population, to develop, organise, and strengthen local activities springing from below and directed at introducing liberty, removing the counter-revolutionary authorities, introducing measures of an economic nature, such as control over production and distribution, etc.;

4. The political crisis of May 2-4 created by the note of the Provisional Government, has shown that the governmental party of the Constitutional-Democrats, in actually organising counter-revolutionary elements both in the army and in the streets, is already trying to fire at the workers. In view of the unstable situation which is the outcome of the existence of two powers, the repetition of such attempts is inevitable, and it is the duty of the party of the proletariat to tell the people as forcibly as possible that, in order to forestall the seriously threatening danger of such mass shooting of the proletariat as took place in Paris in the June days of 1848, it is necessary to organise and arm the proletariat, to establish a union between the proletariat and the revolutionary army, to break with the policy of confidence in the Provisional Government.

3. ON THE AGRARIAN QUESTION

The existence of landed estates in Russia is the material basis of the power of the semi-feudal landowners and augurs for the possibility of re-establishing the monarchy. This landownership inevitably dooms an overwhelming mass of the population of Russia, namely, the peasantry, to poverty, serfdom and dumbness, and the entire country to backwardness in all realms of life.

Peasant landownership in Russia, both *nadéls* * (of the village communities and of homesteads) and private lands (rented or bought), is from top to bottom and in every other direction enmeshed in old semi-feudal connections and relationships, the peasants being divided into categories inherited from the times of bondage, the land representing a maze of strips, etc., etc. The necessity of breaking all these antiquated and injurious partitions, to "un-fence" the land, to reconstruct all relationships of landownership and agriculture on a new basis, in accordance with the new conditions of Russian and world economy, forms the material basis for the peasantry's striving to nationalise all land in the state.

Whatever the petty-bourgeois utopias, in which all the Narodnik parties and groups clothe the struggle of the peasant masses against the feudal

* *Nadél* was the share which the individual peasant received of the land owned by the village community collectively. The *nadél* was held by the peasant for a number of years, pending the redistribution of the community land according to the changes in the village population.—*Ed.*

landed estates and against all feudal fetters imposed on all landownership and
land usage in Russia in general,—this struggle by itself expresses a true
bourgeois-democratic, absolutely progressive and economically necessary
tendency to break resolutely all these fetters.

Nationalisation of the land, being a bourgeois measure, signifies the very
maximum of freedom for the class struggle thinkable in capitalist society and
freedom of landownership from all non-bourgeois remnants of the past.
Nationalisation of the land as abolition of private property on land would,
besides, signify in practice such a powerful blow to private property in all
means of production in general, that the party of the proletariat must offer
every possible assistance to such a reform.

On the other hand, the well-to-do peasantry of Russia has long produced
elements of a peasant bourgeoisie, and the Stolypin agrarian reform * has
undoubtedly strengthened, multiplied, and fortified those elements. At the
other pole of the village there have equally become strengthened and multiplied
the agricultural wage-workers, the proletarians and the mass of semi-proletarian peasantry which is close to the former.

The more resolute and consistent the breaking up and elimination of noble
landownership, the more resolute and consistent the bourgeois-democratic
agrarian reform in Russia in general, the more vigorous and speedy will be
the development of the class struggle of the agricultural proletariat against
the well-to-do peasantry (the peasant bourgeoisie).

Whether the city proletariat will succeed in leading the village proletariat
and in allying with itself the mass of semi-proletarians of the village, or
whether this mass will follow the peasant bourgeoisie which gravitates towards
a union with Guchkov, Miliukov, with the capitalists, landowners and the
counter-revolution in general, the answer to this question will determine the
fate and the outcome of the Russian Revolution, provided the incipient
proletarian revolution in Europe does not exercise a direct powerful influence
on our country.

Proceeding from this class situation and relationship of forces, the Conference decides that

1. The party of the proletariat fights with all its might for a full and
immediate confiscation of all landed estates in Russia (as well as appanages,
church lands, crown lands, etc.);

2. The party is decisively in favour of immediate passing of all lands into
the hands of the peasantry organised into Soviets of Peasant Deputies or in
other organs of local self-government that are elected on a really democratic
basis and are entirely independent of the landowners and officials;

3. The party of the proletariat demands the nationalisation of all land in
the state, which means giving to the state title to all the land, with the right
of local democratic institutions to manage the land;

4. The party must wage a decisive struggle; first, against the Provisional
Government which, through Shingarev's declarations and through its own
collective actions saddles the peasants with "voluntary agreements between
peasants and landowners," i. e., in practice with a land reform after the landowners' desire, and threatens with punishment for "wilful acts," i.e., with
violent measures on the part of the minority of the population (landowners
and capitalists) against the majority; second, against the petty-bourgeois
vacillations of a majority of Narodniks and Menshevik Social-Democrats who
counsel the peasants to refrain from taking over the land pending the convocation of the Constituent Assembly;

* See note 76, Book I of this volume.

5. The party counsels the peasants to take the land in an organised way, by no means allowing the slightest damage to property and taking care to increase production;

6. All agrarian reforms generally can be successful and of abiding value only when the whole state is democratised, *i. e.*, when on the one hand the police, the standing army and the actually privileged bureaucracy have been abolished,—on the other hand there is the most comprehensive local self-government entirely free from control and tutelage from above;

7. It is necessary immediately and everywhere to start organising a separate organisation of the agricultural proletariat both in the form of Soviets of Agricultural Workers' Deputies (as well as separate Soviets of Deputies from the semi-proletarian peasantry) and in the form of proletarian groups or fractions organised within the general Soviets of Peasants' Deputies, within all the organs of local and city government, etc.) ;

8. The party must support the initiative of those peasant committees who, in a number of localities of Russia, give over the landowners' property and agricultural implements in the hands of the peasantry organised into those committees, for the purpose of cultivating all the land under social control and regulation;

9. The party of the proletariat must counsel the proletarians and semi-proletarians of the village to strive to form out of every landowner's estate a sufficiently large model farm which would be managed at public expense by the Soviets of Agricultural Workers' Deputies under the direction of agriculturists and with the application of the best technical methods.

4. ON BORGBJERG'S PROPOSAL

In connection with the arrival of the Danish "Socialist" Borgbjerg and his proposal for participation at a congress of Socialists to support the peace proposed by the German Socialists of Scheidemann's and Plekhanov's orientation on the basis of Germany's renouncing the major part of its annexations, the Conference decides:

Borgbjerg appears in the name of three Scandinavian parties, the Swedish, Danish, and Norwegian. He received his mandate from that Swedish party which is headed by Branting, a Socialist who has joined the side of "his" bourgeoisie and betrayed the revolutionary union of the workers of all countries. This Swedish party cannot be recognised as Socialist. We consider as a Socialist party in Sweden only that party of the youth which is headed by Höglund, Lindhagen, Ström, Carlson and others.

The Danish party, from which Borgbjerg had a mandate, we also fail to consider a Socialist party because it is headed by Stauning, a member of a bourgeois cabinet. Stauning's entrance into the bourgeois cabinet was the cause of a protest on the part of a group of Socialists, including Comrade Trier who left the party declaring that the Danish Socialist Party had become bourgeois.

According to his own admission, Borgbjerg acts in accord with Scheidemann and other German Socialists who have gone over to the side of the German Government and the German bourgeoisie.

There can be no doubt, therefore, that, directly or indirectly, Borgbjerg is in reality an agent of the German imperialist government.

In view of this the Conference considers participation of our party in a conference which includes Borgbjerg and Scheidemann to be inadmissible in principle, since it is our task to unite, not the direct or indirect agents of the various imperialist governments, but the workers of all countries who, already during the war, have begun to fight, and are fighting in a revolutionary way, against their imperialist governments.

Only a conference and a rapprochement with such parties and groups are capable of actually furthering the cause of peace.

We warn the workers against placing confidence in the conference which is being organised by Borgbjerg, since in reality this conference of pseudo-Socialists will be a comedy covering up the machinations of diplomats behind its back, viz., interchange of annexations, like "giving" Armenia to the Russian capitalists, "giving" the German colonies to England (after the latter had grabbed them), possibly "ceding," instead, to the German capitalists a section of the Lorraine iron ore lands which contain stupendous wealth in the form of excellent ore, etc.

The Socialists can neither directly nor indirectly participate in this filthy and covetous deal between the capitalists of the various countries made for the purpose of dividing the loot, without betraying the proletarian cause.

At the same time the Conference recognises that, even through the mouth of Borgbjerg, the German capitalists do not renounce all of their annexations, to say nothing of immediately removing the armies from all the regions that they have forcibly seized. For the Danish territories of Germany, its Polish territories, its French sections of Alsace, are just as much annexed lands in the hands of the German capitalists as Courland, Finland, Poland, the Ukraine, etc., are annexed lands in the hands of the Russian Tsars and the Russian capitalists.

As to re-establishing Poland's independence, this promise is a deception on the part of the German-Austrian capitalists, as well as on the part of the Russian Provisional Government which speaks of an alleged "free" military alliance of Poland with Russia. For, in order really to make clear the will of the peoples of all the annexed regions, it is necessary that the armies be removed and the will of the population be freely determined. Only such measures applied to the whole of Poland (i. e., not only to that part of it which was seized by the Russians, but also to that which was seized by the Germans and Austrians) and to the whole of Armenia, etc., would be a step towards transforming the government's promises into deeds.

The Conference, further, establishes the fact that the English and French Socialists who had gone over to the side of their capitalist governments have refused to join the conference that is being organised by Borgbjerg. This fact clearly proves that the Anglo-French imperialist bourgeoisie, whose agents these pseudo-Socialists are, *wish to continue and wish to prolong* this imperialist war without even wishing to discuss the question of those concessions which the German imperialist bourgeoisie is compelled to promise through Borgbjerg's mediation under the influence of growing exhaustion, starvation, economic chaos and mainly the approaching workers' revolution in Germany.

The Conference decides to make all these facts widely known, and particularly to inform the Russian soldiers at the front about them with as much detail as possible.

Let the Russian soldiers know that the Anglo-French, and with them the Russian, capitalists *are prolonging the war* not even wishing to allow such a conference on the conditions of peace as is being planned by Borgbjerg.

Let the Russian soldiers know that under the slogan, "War to victory," there are now hidden the ambitions of England to strengthen its domination in Bagdad and in the German colonies of Africa, the ambitions of the German capitalists to rob and strangle Armenia and Persia, etc., the ambitions of the Allies to bring about a complete débâcle of Germany. Let the Russian soldiers at the front vote in every military unit, in every regiment, in every company, whether they wish the war thus to be prolonged by the capitalists or whether they wish that, in order that the war be speedily terminated, all power in the state should pass, completely and fully, into the hands of Soviets of Workers' and Soldiers' Deputies.

The party of the Russian proletariat will go to a conference, and will join a brotherly union, only with such workers' parties of the other countries as are fighting in a revolutionary way within their own country for the passing of the entire state power into the hands of the proletariat.

5. On a Coalition Cabinet

All countries drawn into the war, including Russia, are moving with extraordinary rapidity towards an unheard-of catastrophe in consequence of the approaching complete economic chaos, and also in consequence of the utter exhaustion and sentiments of revolt of the soldiers.

The capitalist governments that have started or are prolonging the present war and are responsible for it, appear, therefore, particularly alarmed, and the Russian Government which, besides, has made promises incapable of fulfilment by the bourgeoisie and has bound itself by an agreement with the petty-bourgeois democratic parties of the Narodniks and Mensheviks,—an agreement which it violates daily,—is not only alarmed but publicly appeals in a manifesto issued on May 9 to the Narodniks and Mensheviks, its fellow-partners to the agreement, to help it form a coalition cabinet.

In this critical situation, one of the ways open, at least for a very short time, to the government of capitalists is to draw the leaders of the Soviet, i.e., the leaders of the Narodnik parties (Chernov, Peshekhonov, etc.) and the Menshevik party (Chkheidze, Tsereteli, etc.) into giving more active support to the imperialist war by including them in the cabinet.

The broad mass of the people, especially the soldiers, begin to feel disappointed with the Provisional Government, they begin to doubt the usefulness of an agreement with it, of a policy of confidence in it. They still cherish illusions, however, that the situation can be improved by drawing into the cabinet the leaders of petty-bourgeois democracy, an illusion which it is the duty of the party of the proletariat to dissipate with all the energy at its disposal.

The leaders of the Petrograd Soviet who are on the side of the Narodniks and Mensheviks, having entered into an agreement with the Provisional Government, having accepted the imperialist war, having supported the loan and having created for themselves by all their policies the situation of Ministers without portfolios, are now compelled to take upon themselves greater formal responsibility for the government of capitalists.

In view of all these circumstances, a coalition cabinet has become the question of the day.

The party of the proletariat declares: Every one who will enter the cabinet that conducts an imperialist war will, irrespective of his good wishes, become an accomplice to the imperialist policies of the capitalists.

On the basis of all this, the party of the proletariat expresses itself most categorically against the Soviets of Workers' and Soldiers' Deputies sending representatives into a coalition.

The party warns the people against the attempts to concentrate the attention of the population on the problem of substituting one person for another or one group of bourgeois politicians for another in the cabinet. In contrast to the unprincipled struggle of parliamentary cliques, the revolutionary Social-Democracy advances the struggle of classes; it especially raises the question of fundamentally changing the whole policy of the Soviets of Workers' and Soldiers' Deputies and of all power passing into their hands.

6. On the National Question

The policy of national oppression, being an inheritance of autocracy and monarchy, is supported by the rich landowners, the capitalists and the petty bourgeoisie in their attempt to safeguard their class privileges and to sow discord among workers of different nationalities. Present-day imperialism, by strengthening the tendency towards subjugating weak peoples, is a new factor leading to a sharpening of national oppression.

In so far as the removal of national oppression is at all possible in capitalist society, it is possible only when the state is organised and governed in a thoroughly democratic republican manner, with equality for all nations and languages fully guaranteed.

All nations composing Russia must have full right freely to separate and to form independent states. Denial of such a right and failure to take measures that guarantee its practical realisation, are tantamount to supporting the policy of seizures and annexations. Only recognition by the proletariat of the right of nations for separation guarantees full solidarity of the workers of different nations and contributes to a real democratic rapprochement of nations.

The conflict that has now risen between Finland and the Russian Provisional Government shows with particular clarity that denial of the right of free separation leads to direct continuation of the tsarist policy.

It is not permissible to confuse the question of the right of nations to free separation with the question of the advisability of this or that nation forming a separate state at this or that moment. This latter question must be solved by the party of the proletariat in every particular case with full independence, with a view to the interests of the entire social development and the interests of the class struggle of the proletariat for Socialism.

The party demands far-going regional autonomy; abolition of control from above; abolition of a compulsory state language; drawing of the boundary lines of self-governing and autonomous regions on the basis of consideration by the local population itself of economic and ethnic conditions, of the national composition of the populations, etc.

The party of the proletariat decidedly rejects the so-called "national culture autonomy," *i. e.*, the plan to eliminate the schools, etc., from state jurisdiction and to place it under something like national diets. Autonomy of national culture draws artificial lines of adherence to "national cultures" between workers who live in the same locality and even work in the same enterprises, *i. e.*, it strengthens the connection between the workers and the bourgeois culture of the respective nations, whereas the task of Social-Democracy consists in strengthening the international culture of the world proletariat.

The party demands the inclusion into the constitution of a fundamental law declaring void any privileges of one of the nations and any encroachments on the rights of national minorities.

The interests of the working class demand the merging of the workers of

all nationalities of Russia into the same proletarian organisations, whether
political, trade union, co-operative or educational, etc.   Only such a merging
in the same organisations of the workers of various nationalities will enable
the proletariat to wage a victorious struggle against international capital and
bourgeois nationalism.

7. ON UNITING THE INTERNATIONALISTS AGAINST THE PETTY-BOURGEOIS DE-FENCIST BLOC

Whereas, (1) the party of the Socialists-Revolutionists and the party of
the Social-Democratic Mensheviks, etc., have, in an overwhelming majority,
gone over to the position of "revolutionary defencism," i. e., the position of
supporting the imperialist war (voting in favour of the loan and supporting
the Provisional Government which represents the interests of capital);

And whereas, (2) these parties in all their policies defend the interests
and the point of view of the petty bourgeoisie and thus corrupt the proletariat
with bourgeois influence by trying to persuade it that it is possible, by means
of agreements, "control," participation in the cabinet, etc., to change the
course of the imperialist policy of the government and to divert it from the
road of counter-revolutionary encroachments on liberty;

And whereas, (3) this policy nurtures and enhances the naïvely trustful
attitude of the masses towards the capitalists at a time when such attitude is
the chief obstacle to the further development of the revolution, and is the
source of a possible victory over the revolution on the part of the landowner
and bourgeois counter-revolution,—

Now, therefore, the Conference decides that

1. Unity with parties and groups that pursue this policy is absolutely
impossible; and,

2. That rapprochement and unity with groups and trends that are following
an internationalist tone in practice, are necessary on the basis of breaking
with the policy of the petty-bourgeois betrayal of Socialism.

8. THE SITUATION WITHIN THE INTERNATIONAL AND THE TASKS OF THE R.S.-D.L.P.

Under the conditions of a peaceful period that began after 1871, when the
national bourgeois revolutions in most of the countries of Western Europe
had been fully completed, a period when the colonial policy was developing,
etc., there was formed, toward the end of the nineteenth century, an opportunist tendency in most of the parties of the Second International (1889-1914).
The social bases of opportunism are:

1. A labour aristocracy, a comparatively thin layer of workers who are
bought by their bourgeoisie which "sacrifices" some crumbs from its profits
to bribe them;

2. Petty-bourgeois "fellow-travellers" of Social-Democracy, drawn to the
latter not by its Socialist programme but by its democratic demands.

In most of the European workers' parties opportunism gained the upper
hand before the beginning of the present war.   With the beginning of the
imperialist war in 1914, opportunism turned into social-chauvinism, into
"defencism."   The defencists proclaimed "national defence" in the predatory
imperialist war and perpetrated a betrayal of the cause of the working class.
Opportunism caused the collapse of the Second International.

During the war three main tendencies were developed inside the world labour movement:

1. The "defencists" of all countries broke with Socialism; they became a tool of their respective imperialist governments; they helped the imperialist governments to prolong the war; in practice they became class enemies of the proletariat;

2. The "centre," whose main leaders are Kautsky and Haase in Germany, Longuet and Pressemane in France, Axelrod and others in Russia, Robert Grimm in Switzerland, Turati and others in Italy, have substituted pacifism for revolutionary Socialism. The "centre" does not call the workers to overthrow the capitalist governments, but it tries to persuade the present imperialist *governments* to conclude a democratic peace. Vacillating as it does between internationalism and defencism, not advocating in war time a revolutionary struggle of the workers against their governments, the "centre" insists on unity with the defencists on an international scale without drawing the necessary conclusions from the split that occurred in the Social-Democratic parties, a split that has taken place even in a country like Germany;

3. The revolutionary internationalists who have started a struggle against the war in all countries in spite of martial law and an iron-clad régime. Such are the groups of Karl Liebknecht and that of the *Arbeiterpolitik* in Germany; MacLean, Tom Mann, the Left Wing of the British Socialist Party and the Independent Labour Party in England; Loriot (the Secretary of the Committee for the Establishment of International Connections) and his comrades in France; the Left Wing of the Socialist Party in Italy; the comrades grouped around the Viennese Karl Marx Club in Austria; the Socialist Labour Party and the group publishing the periodical *Internationalist* in the United States of America; the party that has broken with the "defencists" and which is led by Comrades Höglund and others in Sweden; the Tribunist Party (Pannekoek, Roland-Holst, Gorter and others) in Holland; the comrades grouped around the periodical *Youth International* in Switzerland. The tendency that is at the present moment represented by the above-named groups has started a struggle against the capitalists of the respective countries during and in spite of the war, it has broken with the respective "defencists" and it has started a struggle against the "centre." This is the only tendency that has remained loyal to Socialism. The Socialist future belongs to this tendency alone.

The majority in Zimmerwald and Kienthal belonged to the "centre." This weakened the Zimmerwald bloc from the very start. The Zimmerwald bloc as a whole rejected the proposal made by its Left section relative to calling the workers of all countries to an immediately revolutionary struggle against their governments. The Zimmerwald bloc refused to recognise the necessity of a straight split with the social-chauvinists' majority of the old official parties and thus it weakened the Zimmerwald movement. The Kienthal Conference in words condemned both bourgeois and Socialist pacifism, in reality, however, the majority of the parties and groups that belong to the Zimmerwald bloc continue a policy of social-chauvinism. The vacillating tactics of the Zimmerwald majority have brought about a situation where in some countries Zimmerwald is already beginning to serve as a brake on the revolutionary movement.

The task of our party, operating as it does in a country where the revolution started earlier than in other countries, is to take the initiative of creating the Third International which is finally to break with "defencism" and to wage a decisive struggle against the middle-of-the-road policy of the "centre" as well.

The Conference is against the plan of the so-called "reconstruction of the International" by means of a mutual amnesty of the leaders of "defencist" parties. The Conference warns against organising international congresses with the participation of the social-chauvinists.

Our party remains in the Zimmerwald bloc with the aim of defending the tactics of the Zimmerwald Left Wing there, and it authorises the Central Committee immediately to take steps leading to the establishment of the Third International.

The new Socialist International can be created only by the workers themselves, by their revolutionary struggle in their own countries. The Conference decidedly protests against the attempts of the Berne International Socialist Commission to enter into an agreement with the organisers of the Stockholm Conference, the social-patriots Troelstra, Branting and others, in whom the Socialist proletariat can have no political confidence.

The Conference decides to take part in the International conference of the Zimmerwaldists scheduled for May 31 and authorises the Central Committee to organise a delegation to that conference.

9. The Present Political Situation

The World War, brought about by the struggle of world trusts and bank capital for domination over the world market, has already resulted in a mass destruction of material values, in an exhaustion of production forces, and in such a growth of war industry that even the production of an absolutely necessary minimum of goods for consumption and means of production proves impossible.

Thus the present war has brought humanity to a blind alley; it has placed it on the brink of ruin.

The objective conditions for a Socialist revolution that undoubtedly existed even before the war in the more developed and advanced countries, have been and are ripening with tremendous rapidity as a result of the war. The crowding-out and ruin of small and medium-sized economic enterprises is proceeding at an accelerated pace. The concentration and internationalisation of capital are making gigantic strides, monopoly capitalism is changing into state monopoly capitalism. Social regulation of production and distribution is, under the pressure of circumstances, being introduced in many countries. Some are introducing universal labour service.

When private property in the means of production is retained, all these steps towards a greater monopolisation and nationalisation of production are inevitably accompanied by an increased exploitation of the labouring masses, by an increase of oppression, by a growing difficulty in offering resistance to the exploiters, by a growth of reaction and military despotism. At the same time these steps lead to a gigantic increase in the profits of large capitalists at the expense of all the other strata of the population; they deliver the labouring masses to the bondage of capitalists through tributes imposed on them in the form of billions of interest to be paid on war loans for many decades to come. The same measures, however, when private property in the means of production has been abolished, when state power has completely passed into the hands of the proletariat, are the guaranty for the success of a transformation of society that will do away with the exploitation of man by man and insure the well-being of every one and all.

On the other hand, the forecast of the Socialists of the whole world who unanimously declared in the Basle Manifesto of 1912 the inevitability of a proletarian revolution in connection with the imperialist war that was then approaching and is now raging, that forecast has been fully confirmed by the course of events.

The Russian Revolution is only the first stage of the first of the proletarian revolutions that are inevitably being brought about by the war.

In all the countries there grows a rebellious spirit among large masses of the people against the capitalist class, and there grows the consciousness of the proletariat that only the passing of power into its hands, and the abolition of private property in the means of production, will save humanity from ruin.

In all the countries, especially in the most advanced of them, England and Germany, hundreds of Socialists who have not gone over to the side of "their" national bourgeoisie, have been thrown into prison by the governments of capitalism who have thus given an object lesson that they are afraid of the proletarian revolution that is growing in the depths of the masses of the people. The rise of the revolution in Germany is seen both in the mass struggles which have assumed particularly large proportions in the last weeks, and in the growth of fraternisation between the German and the Russian soldiers at the front.

Thus, fraternal confidence and a fraternal unity among the workers of the various countries, the very same workers who, at present, are exterminating each other for the interests of the capitalists, is gradually being restored. This, in its turn, will create prerequisites for concerted revolutionary actions of the workers of the various countries. Only such actions are capable of guaranteeing the development of the world Socialist revolution according to the best conceived plan, and the success of such a revolution on the most unfailing basis.

The proletariat of Russia operating in one of the most backward countries of Europe, surrounded by a vast petty peasant population, cannot make its aim the immediate realisation of a Socialist transformation.

Yet it would be a grave error to infer from the foregoing that the proletariat must support the bourgeoisie, or that we must keep our activities within the boundaries acceptable to the petty bourgeoisie, or that the proletariat must renounce its leading rôle in the matter of explaining to the people the imperative urgency of a number of measures that are ripe to be put into practice and that lead to Socialism.

Such inference would be in practice equivalent to going over to the side of the bourgeoisie.

Such steps are, first, nationalisation of the land. Such a measure which does not directly overstep the boundaries of the bourgeois system would, at the same time, be a hard blow to private property in the means of production, and to the same degree it would strengthen the influence of the Socialist proletariat over the semi-proletarians of the village.

Such measures are, further, the establishment of government control over all the banks which are to be united into a single central bank, also control over insurance companies and the large capitalist syndicates (for example, the sugar syndicate, the coal syndicate, the metal syndicate, etc.), all this to be accompanied by a change to a more just and progressive taxation of income and property. Economic conditions are ripe for such measures. From the technical point of view they can be carried out immediately. From the political point of view they are likely to get the support of the overwhelming majority of the peasants who in every respect will gain by such reforms.

The Soviets of Workers', Soldiers', Peasants', and other Deputies now covering Russia with an ever-growing network would introduce not only the above measures but also universal labour service, for the character of these institutions guarantees, on the one hand, that all these reforms would be introduced only in so far as an overwhelming majority of the people has realised clearly and firmly their practical necessity, on the other hand, the character of these institutions guarantees, not a realisation of reforms through a system of police and officials, but a voluntary participation of organised and armed masses of the proletariat and the peasantry in regulating their own economic life. All the measures just indicated as well as others of the same nature could and should be not merely discussed and prepared so that they might be carried out on a national scale in case the proletarians and semi-proletarians gain power, but, whenever opportunity presents itself, should be carried into life immediately by local revolutionary organs of people's power.

In carrying out the above measures it is necessary to exercise extreme circumspection and caution and to win a solid majority of the population as well as its intelligent conviction that the country is ready for the practical introduction of this or that measure, but it is in this direction that we must rivet the attention and the efforts of the class-conscious vanguard of the proletarian masses who are in duty bound to help the peasant masses find an escape from the present economic chaos.

10. The Soviets of Workers' and Soldiers' Deputies

Having discussed the reports and communications of the comrades who work in the Soviets of Workers' and Soldiers' Deputies in various localities of Russia, the Conference establishes the following:

In a whole series of provincial localities the revolution progresses by the proletariat and the peasantry organising on their own initiative into Soviets; by removing, on their own initiative, old local authorities; by the creation of a proletarian and peasant militia; by the passage of all lands into the hands of the peasantry; by the introduction of the control of the workers over the factories; by the introduction of the eight-hour work-day; by increasing the wages; by insuring undiminished production; by establishing a control of the workers over the distribution of supplies, etc.

This growth, in scope and intensity, of the revolution in the provinces marks, on the one hand, the growth of a movement towards giving over all power to the Soviets and towards control by the workers and peasants themselves over production; on the other hand, it marks the preparation, on an all-Russian scale, of forces for the second stage of the revolution which must give over all state power into the hands of Soviets or other organs expressing directly the will of the majority of the people (organs of local self-government, the Constituent Assembly, etc.).

In the capitals and in a few other large cities, the task of the assumption of state power by the Soviets offers the greatest difficulties and requires an especially prolonged preparation of the forces of the proletariat. Here the largest forces of the bourgeoisie are concentrated. Here there is more apparent a policy of agreement with the bourgeoisie, a policy that often thwarts the revolutionary initiative of the masses and weakens their independence; a circumstance which is particularly dangerous in view of the leading rôle of those Soviets locally.

It is, therefore, the task of the proletarian party on the one hand to support in every possible way the indicated development of the revolution locally, on the other hand to conduct a systematic struggle inside of the

Soviets (by means of propaganda and new elections) for the victory of the proletarian line; to concentrate all its efforts and all its attention on the mass of workers and soldiers; to draw a line of demarcation between proletarian and petty-bourgeois policy, between the internationalist policy on the one hand and the defencist and opportunist policy on the other; to organise and arm the workers; to prepare their forces for the next stage of the revolution. The Conference reiterates the necessity of comprehensive activity within the Soviets of Workers' and Soldiers' Deputies, of increasing the number of Soviets, of increasing their power, of welding together, within the Soviets, the proletarian internationalist groups of our party.

Soldatskaia Pravda, No. 13, May 16, 1917.

11. THE REVISION OF THE PARTY PROGRAMME

The Conference recognises as imperative the revision of the party programme along the following lines:

1. Evaluating imperialism and the epoch of imperialist wars in connection with the approaching Socialist revolution; struggle with the distortion of Marxism by the so-called defencists who have forgotten Marx's slogan, "The workers have no fatherland";

2. Amending the theses and the paragraphs dealing with the state; such amendment to be in the nature of a demand for a democratic proletarian-peasant republic (*i.e.*, a type of state functioning without police, without a standing army and without a privileged bureaucracy) and not for a bourgeois-parliamentary republic;

3. Eliminating or amending the obsolete portions of the political programme;

4. Recasting a number of points in the political minimum programme so as to point out with greater precision more consistent democratic demands;

5. Completely recasting in very many places the out-of-date economic portion of the minimum programme and points relating to popular education;

6. Recasting the agrarian programme in conformity with the adopted resolution on the agrarian question;

7. Inserting a demand for the nationalisation of a number of syndicates already ripe for such a step;

8. Adding a characterisation of the main currents in contemporary Socialism.

The Conference directs the Central Committee to work out, on the basis of the above suggestions, a draft for a party programme. This is to be carried out within two months and is to be submitted for ratification to the party congress. The Conference calls upon all organisations and all members of the party to consider drafts of the programme, to correct them, and to work out counter-proposals.

12. DRAFT OF RESOLUTION ON NATIONAL QUESTION SUBMITTED BY G. PIATAKOV
IN THE NAME OF THE SECTION ON THE NATIONAL QUESTION

The policy of national oppression, being an inheritance of autocracy and monarchy, is supported by the rich landowners, the capitalists and the petty bourgeoisie in their attempt to safeguard their class privileges and to sow discord among workers of different nationalities.

Modern imperialism, by strengthening the tendency towards subjugating weak peoples, is a new factor leading to a sharpening of national oppression.

In so far as removal of national oppression is at all possible in capitalist society, it is possible only when the state is organised and governed in a thoroughly democratic republican manner, with equality for all nationalities and languages fully guaranteed.

The R.S.-D.L.P. demands such a system. At the same time it strives towards a far-going regional autonomy; abolition of control from above; abolition of a compulsory state language; drawing of the boundary-lines of self-governing and autonomous regions on the basis of consideration by the local population itself of economic and ethnic conditions, of the national composition of the population, etc. It demands the inclusion into the constitution of a fundamental law declaring void any privileges of one of the nationalities and any encroachments on the rights of national minorities.

The party warns, however, against assuming that the realisation of those measures may solve the national question. The only effective method of solving it is the method of a Socialist revolution under the slogan, "Down with boundaries!" for only thus can one do away with imperialism,—this new factor leading to a sharpening of national oppression.

The party also warns against anti-proletarian methods of "solving" the national question.

It rejects the so-called "national culture autonomy," *i. e.*, the plan to eliminate the schools, etc., from state jurisdiction and to place it under something like national diets. This plan draws artificial lines of adherence to national cultures between workers who live in the same locality and even work in the same enterprises, *i. e.*, it strengthens the connections between the workers and the bourgeois culture of the respective nations, whereas the task of Social-Democracy consists in strengthening the international culture of the world proletariat.

It also rejects in principle the splitting up of large state formations into small national states. Waging an active revolutionary struggle against every kind of national oppression and against the forcible retention by the bourgeoisie of one or the other nation within the framework of a given state, the party at the same time conducts a vigorous propaganda among the proletariat and among those strata of the population of the oppressed nation that follow the proletariat, to the effect that the formation of national states under conditions of an imperialist epoch, *i. e.*, on the eve of the Socialist revolution, is a harmful and reactionary utopia. On the other hand, the international party of the proletariat, having a majority on an international scale, cannot heed the will of the majority of a nation, if that will is at variance with the will of its proletarian minority.

Proceeding from the above considerations, the Conference of the R.S.-D.L.P. declares that

Whereas (1) "the right of nations to self-determination" is a mere phrase without any definite meaning;

And whereas (2) this phrase is interpreted as meaning much more than is thought of in the ranks of revolutionary Social-Democracy, particularly

(a) in regions inhabited by so-called oppressed nations;

(b) in times of imperialist wars;

And whereas (3) it is the task of Social-Democracy, as far as the national question is concerned, not to proclaim abstract rights, but to determine those principles on which it considers necessary to base the mutual relations of nations,—

Therefore the Conference, considering itself as lacking in authority to change the party programme, and considering the question insufficiently analysed, proposes to the local organisations to prepare themselves for the coming party congress which shall have to undertake a change of the programme. As far as the Conference is concerned, it assumes that paragraph 9 of our programme should be eliminated and, instead, while retaining paragraph 8, specific indications should be given, as to which forms of national existence in general, and which forms of existence for the nations now composing the Russian state in particular, the R.S.-D.L.P. shall actually strive for.

As to the structure of proletarian organisations, the interests of the working class demand the merging of the workers of all nationalities of Russia into the same proletarian organisations, whether political, trade union, co-operative or educational, etc. Only such a merging in the same organisations of the workers of various nationalities will enable the proletariat to wage a victorious struggle against international capital and bourgeois nationalism.

Petrograd City Conference and All-Russian Conference, April and May, 1917. 1st part, 1925.

Istpart, 1925.

XI

COMMENTS ON THE GENERAL (THEORETICAL) PART OF THE PROGRAMME MADE AT THE SECTION ON PROGRAMME DURING THE APRIL CONFERENCE *

THE Section on the Revision of the Party Programme came to the conclusion that the mere *adding* of Comrade Lenin's preliminary draft to the general part of the programme would mean to create a mechanical combination out of keeping with the latter. Hence the Section expressed itself in favour of recasting the entire general part of our programme in conformity with the propositions expressed by Comrade Lenin in his preliminary draft and taking into account the arguments advanced at the sessions of the Section.

To carry this out, the Section, at its general meeting, elected a sub-committee of three. The sub-committee came to the following conclusions:

1. The first paragraph of the programme must be recast to mean that "a close bond of unity" is created not only by the exchange of commodities but also by the export of capital, by the struggle for an economic territory, in general by a number of economic processes of recent times. While the exchange of commodities has led to the establishment of such "bonds of unity" directly, the export of capital, etc., lead to it as a result of a complex struggle of various contradictory tendencies brought about by these processes. Emphasise that modern capitalism brings about a levelling of the peculiarities of capitalism in the various countries, creates common methods and common aims, etc. (In favour, Bogolepov and Sokolnikov.)

2. Paragraph 2 retains the old wording (unanimous).

3. Paragraph 3 to be recast in accordance with the most recent data on the economic rôle of syndicates and trusts; substantiate the statement as to the world passing to the most recent phase of finance capital. Formulate the end of the paragraph more categorically (eliminating "more or less").

4. Amplify paragraph 4 by mentioning the tendency of capital to utilise, in ever-growing proportions, the labour of backward uncivilised peoples (two for, and one against).

* See page 380, Book I of this volume.

5. The fifth paragraph needs fundamental recasting. Add observations on the export of capital, the struggle for economic territories, the commercial policy of finance capital at home and abroad, the sharpening of competition and the rivalry between the capital of various nations aspiring to world hegemony. Crises and depressions sharpen this rivalry still more. Explain the proposition that we have entered an era of imperialist wars; add that military conflicts are inevitable.

In the statements on crises, strike out "more or less" and substitute "and depressions." As to the expression "over-production," part of the comrades moved that it be avoided as lacking in precision. At the end of the paragraph it was proposed to eliminate the word "sometimes" and to substitute for it "at the present time" (Oppokov, Bogolepov, Sokolnikov).

6. In paragraph 6 make reference to mounting cost of living, to impoverishment, financial control, decrease in real wages, etc. (Attempts at enslavement of labour.) (Unanimous.)

7. Amplify second part of paragraph. It is necessary to mention the influence of finance capital and banks on concentration of production, the trend towards state regulation of production and distribution, the formation of interstate economic coalitions. There comes into being what practically amounts to a dictatorship of finance capital which, in the course of a powerful clash of forces in present-day society, must inevitably be replaced by a dictatorship of the proletariat. (Oppokov, Sokolnikov, Bogolepov.)

8. Paragraph 8 remains.

9. It is proposed to formulate the ninth paragraph approximately as follows: "A necessary prerequisite of this social revolution is the dictatorship of the proletariat, i. e., the conquest by the proletariat of such political power as would enable it to suppress every resistance on the part of the exploiters. Setting itself the task of preparing the proletariat, in all possible ways and without delay, for the conquest of political power which will enable it to introduce the economic measures which are the essence of the social revolution, international Social-Democracy organises the proletariat into an independent political party opposed to all the bourgeois parties; it gives direction to all the expressions of class struggle on its part; it reveals to it the irreconcilable clash of interests of the exploiters and the exploited, and makes it clear that a proletarian Socialist revolution becomes, in consequence of objective conditions, a problem for the present historic period, and that only such a revolution can lead humanity out of the blind alley into which it was driven by imperialism and imperialist wars. Whatever the difficulties of the revolution and its possible failures, whatever even the waves of counter-revolution, the final victory of the proletariat is unavoidable. Simultaneously with this, the party of the proletariat reveals to the entire mass of the other toilers and exploited the hopelessness of their situation in capitalist society and the necessity of a social revolution that would free them from the oppression by capital. Revolutionary Social-Democracy, the party of the working class, calls into its ranks all strata of the toiling and exploited population in so far as they make the standpoint of the proletariat their own."

These comments were made and found correct by the sub-committee of the Section (Bogolepov, Oppokov, Sokolnikov).

They were to be reported to the plenary session of the Section.

G. OPPOKOV, *Chairman of the Section.*

Materials for the Revision of the Party Programme, Petrograd, 1917.

XII

DECLARATION MADE AT THE FIRST ALL-RUSSIAN CONGRESS OF SOVIETS CONCERNING THE OFFENSIVE *

WE, the undersigned fractions, groups and individual delegates to the Congress, consider it necessary for the Congress to take up as its first order of business a question upon which devolves the fate not only of all the other activities of the Congress, but—in the full and precise meaning of the word— the fate of the whole Russian Revolution, namely, the question of the military offensive that is being prepared for the immediate future. That such an offensive has been decided upon, and is to take place shortly, is evident from numerous undisputed facts and declarations that can be verified by anybody, from the formation of Death Battalions, from the disbanding of certain regiments, and, directly, from Minister Kerensky's reference in his explanation as to the reasons for prohibiting the Ukrainian congress.

From the very essence of all the circumstances of the present situation it follows that an offensive at the front, dictated by the magnates of Allied imperialism, pursues a purely political aim: To relegate to the background and completely to wipe out from the minds of large masses of the people the memory of the diplomatic negotiations with the Allies which resulted in revealing the out-and-out imperialist character of that grouping which was participated in by pre-revolutionary Russia (the question of Albania, Greece, Persia, the replies and declarations of the Allied diplomats).

Having confronted the people and the army (which does not know for the sake of which international aims it is called on at present to shed its blood) with the fact of the offensive and all its consequences, the counter-revolutionary circles of Russia hope, among other things, that the offensive will cause a concentration of power in the hands of the military-diplomatic and capitalist groups which are bound up with English, French, and American imperialism, and will free them of the necessity to reckon in the future with the organised will of Russian democracy.

It is obviously in anticipation of such a change in the interrelation of forces in favour of the propertied classes that Rodzianko calls his June 16 men ** into Petrograd, hoping that the old Imperial Duma may be successfully utilised to counteract the Soviet of Workers' and Soldiers' Deputies and to help guarantee a policy of firm and vigorous imperialism, vigorous, in the first place, against the revolution and democracy.

The counter-revolutionary initiators of the offensive, operating behind the scenes and not shrinking even before what the congress of the party of the Socialists-Revolutionists correctly termed "military adventure," consciously try to play up the decomposition of the army, a phenomenon caused by all the circumstances of the internal and international situation of the country. For this purpose they are putting into the minds of the despairing elements of democracy the fundamentally erroneous idea that an offensive, by the very fact of its taking place, may "regenerate" the army and thus compensate by mechanical means for the absence of a definite programme of action in the matter of terminating the war. It is obvious, however, that such an offensive can only disorganise the army utterly by opposing certain of its sections to others.

* See page 203 of this book.
** See note 246.

Under such conditions, a grave historic responsibility rests upon the Congress of Soviets of Workers' and Soldiers' Deputies. The Congress cannot let pass in silence an attack on the international revolutionary struggle for peace, on the conquered and organised positions of Russian democracy, an attack that is being openly prepared and thoroughly organised. The Congress must either immediately repel the counter-revolutionary onslaught for which the road is to be cleared by the offensive, or else take upon itself, openly and fully, the responsibility for such a policy.

In warning the working class, the army and the peasantry of this danger looming over the country, we insist that the question be taken up as the first point on the agenda of the Congress.

Delegate of the Minsk Soviet of Workers' and Soldiers' Deputies, Posern.

Bureau of the Congress Fraction of the R.S.-D.L.P. (Bolsheviks).

Bureau of the United Social-Democrats-Internationalists.

Pravda, No. 73, June 20, 1917.

XIII

STATEMENT MADE BEFORE THE ALL-RUSSIAN CONGRESS OF THE SOVIETS CONCERNING THE BAN PLACED ON THE JUNE 23, 1917, DEMONSTRATION *

On June 22 the All-Russian Congress decreed to prohibit a peaceful political manifestation of the Petrograd workers and soldiers, which manifestation our party had been planning to direct. As the cause for such an extraordinary violation of the will of the Petrograd proletariat the leaders of the Congress pointed out the imminent danger of the demonstration being taken advantage of by the organised forces of the counter-revolution. We have not had at our disposal the information about those plans known to the Executive Committee of the Petrograd Soviet of Workers' and Soldiers' Deputies. But in view of such an interpretation alleged to be the cause of the ban, we found it necessary on our part to appeal to the workers and soldiers of Petrograd urging them to give up the manifestation.

After your delegates have visited the factories and regiments, there can be no doubt in your mind as to the fact that if the demonstration has not taken place, it was due not to your ban, but to our party abandoning the plan.

It was reasonable to assume and expect that, after this, you would place on your agenda an investigation of the counter-revolutionary plot you had referred to in justifying your ban on the demonstration. In practice, however, you are powerless against the counter-revolution which, you say, is lurking, you can do nothing because you are bound to the Russian and "Allied" imperialists with whom you dare not break.

Instead, you have placed on your agenda a trial of our party. In the name of the commission appointed by you, Citizen Dan has introduced the draft of a resolution which condemns our party for "secret" actions (*i. e.*, actions independent of the official majority of the Soviet), for street manifestations without the permit of the Soviet (*i. e.*, in essence, without the permit of the Provisional Government) and which threatens offenders with exclusion from the ranks of the Soviet.

On this occasion we deem it necessary to declare that, entering the Soviet

* See page 250 of this book.

and fighting for the passing of all power to it, we have not renounced for a single moment in favour of a hostile majority of the Soviet our right, independently and freely, to utilise all liberties for the purpose of mobilising the working masses under the banner of our proletarian class party. We categorically decline, also for the future, to impose on ourselves such anti-democratic limitations. Even if all state power were to pass wholly into the hands of the Soviet—and we stand for this—and the Soviet were to attempt to put fetters on our propaganda,—this would compel us, not to submit passively, but to face prison and other penalties in the name of the ideas of international Socialism which separate us from you.

In reality the leaders of the Congress went even further. Tsereteli declared Dan's resolution to be insufficient and therefore inoperative. Tsereteli accuses our party, not of a violation of discipline, but of a direct proletarian and military *plot* against the Provisional Government and the Congress that supports it. This new and sweeping accusation is not only out of keeping with the reasons officially advanced against the demonstration of the day before yesterday, but it is also in crass contradiction to Dan's resolution introduced to-day. Still, Minister Tsereteli does not dare to draw from his own accusation the conclusion that it is necessary to investigate the alleged plot, which he needed only to be able to advance a programme of an obviously counter-revolutionary character. It is necessary, says Tsereteli, to take away the arms from those who threaten with these arms the Government of "revolutionary democracy." In other words, the fable of a military plot was presented by the member of the Provisional Government to justify the disarming of the Petrograd proletariat and the disbandment of the Petrograd garrison.

The meaning and significance of these measures are self-evident. What is planned is the disarming of the revolutionary vanguard,—a measure that has always been resorted to by the bourgeois counter-revolution when it felt its inability to cope with the tasks advanced by the revolution and with the growing resentment of the labouring masses. Citizen Tsereteli and those who direct him are hardly ignorant of the fact that never in history have the working masses given up without struggle the arms they had received at the hand of the revolution. Consequently, the ruling bourgeoisie and its "Socialist" Ministers are provoking civil war around the fundamental point which has always been the stake in the test of strength between the bourgeoisie and the working class,—and they are aware of what they are doing.

Fully aware of all the consequences which such a provocation policy may lead to, we expose before the All-Russian Congress and the masses of the people, in the first place the proletarian masses that stand behind the Congress, this attack on the revolution that is now being prepared behind the scenes by the Provisional Government. We have quit the sessions of the special commission which is considering measures against the freedom of propaganda and is preparing the disarming of the workers.

The revolution is passing through a moment of supreme danger. We call upon the workers to be firm and watchful.

Central Committee R.S.-D.L.P.

Bureau of the Bolshevik Fraction of the All-Russian Congress of Soviets

The entire Fraction of the Bolsheviks has subscribed to this Declaration
June 24, 1917.

Pravda, No. 80, June 26, 1917.

BIBLIOGRAPHY

LIST OF BOOKS, PERIODICALS AND NEWSPAPERS CITED BY LENIN IN THIS VOLUME

A. Books

Engels, Friedrich, *Preface* to the third German edition of Marx' *The Civil War in France.*—I 50.

—— Letter to August Bebel of March 18-28, 1875 (reprinted by Bebel in his autobiography, *Aus Meinem Leben*, Vol. I, pp. 318-324, Stuttgart, 1910). —I 50, 139.

—— *Zur Kritik des sozialdemokratischen Programmentwurfs*, 1891, published in the *Neue Zeit*, Vol. XX, 1901-02, Book I.—I 328; II 152.

Hobson, J. A., *Imperialism*, London, 1902.—I 320.

Ilyin, V. (Lenin's pseudonym), *Twelve Years*, Collected Essays, Vol. I, *Two Tendencies in Russian Marxism and the Russian Social-Democracy* (Russian), Petersburg, 1908.—I 127.

—— *Imperialism as the Final Stage of Capitalism*, Petrograd, 1917.—I 320.

Marx, Karl, *The Civil War in France.*—I 50, 140.

—— *The Critique of the Gotha Programme.* (Written 1875, first published in the *Neue Zeit*, Vol. IX, 1890-91, Book I).—I 154.

—— *The Communist Manifesto.*—I 154.

Plekhanov, G., *Anarchism and Socialism.* (First published in German by the *Vorwärts* Verlag, Berlin, 1894).—I 125.

Zinoviev, G. and Lenin, N., *Socialism and the War*, Geneva, 1915.—I 71, 176, 190, 213.

B. Newspapers and Periodicals

Birzhevya Viedomosti, No. 16,195, May 4, 1917, evening paper, "Evening Session of the Three Highest Ministries."—I 260.

Corriere della Sera (Milan), No. 88, March 29, 1917, telegram of the Petrograd Correspondent.—I 74.

Dielo Naroda, No. 23, April 26, 1917. "The Social-Democratic *Yedinstvo* on Bolshevism."—I 180, 188, 243.

—— idem, "Diplomatic Silence and Warlike Speeches."—I 182.

—— No. 25, April 28, 1917, "The Congress of Peasant Deputies."—I 219.

—— No. 26, April 29, 1917, article by Chernov, "Lenin."—I 242.

—— No. 28, May 3, 1917, editorial.—I 240.

—— idem, "A Letter from Plekhanov."—I 236.

—— No. 44, May 22, 1917, article by S. Mstislavsky.—II 146.

—— No. 48, May 26, 1917, "About Unity and Discord" (in the department "Press and Life").—II 146.

—— No. 51, May 30, 1917, "The Dispute over Peace without Annexations." —II 92, 138.

—— No. 57, June 7, 1917, "Three Replies."—II 146.

—— No. 59, June 9, 1917, appeal to vote for the Socialists-Revolutionists.— II 155.

—— idem, "Silence Is Golden."—II 155.

—— No. 75, June 28, 1917, article by Chernov, "False Conclusions from a Correct Premise."—II 259.
—— No. 84, July 8, 1917, "Report of the Minister of Agriculture."—II 291.
Dien, No. 33, April 27, 1917, article by C. Ponomarev, "Arbitrary Redivision." —I 192.
—— No. 40, May 5, 1917, "The Government Crisis."—I 260.
——No. 52, May 19, 1917, article by V. Vodovozov, "Publication of the Secret Treaties."—II 66.
—— No. 86, June 29, 1917, concerning the Malinovsky affair.—II 264.
—— No. 91, July 5, 1917, "The Cadets and the Provisional Government."— II 277.
Finansovaia Gazeta, April 30, 1917, editorial, "The Lefts and the Loan."— I 227, 228.
—— May 30, 1917.—II 95.
Frankfurter Zeitung, No. 81, March 23, 1917, "The Situation in Petersburg."— I 45.
Gazeta Kopeika, No. 3131, April 27, 1917, "Requisition of Privately Owned Lands."—I 253.
L'Humanité (Paris), No. 4,729, March 28, 1917, reproduction of a telegram of the *Petit Parisien* from Petrograd.—I 76.
Izvestia of the All-Russian Soviet of Peasant Deputies, No. 10, June 1, 1917, S. Maslov's report at the Congress of Peasant Deputies.—II 103.
Izvestia of the Petrograd Soviet of Workers' and Soldiers' Deputies, No. 15, March 27, 1917, appeal to all peoples.—II 206.
—— No. 32, April 18, 1917, decision of the Petrograd Soviet on Lenin's passage through Germany.—I 104, 185, 193.
—— No. 43, April 30, 1917, editorial.—I 223, 243.
—— No. 55, May 15, 1917, appeal to the Socialists of the world.—II 30.
—— No. 60, May 20, 1917, "The Opponents of the New Government."—II 68.
—— No. 62, May 23, 1917.—II 71, 73.
—— No. 63, May 24, 1917, "What Does the Provisional Government Want?" —II 78.
—— *idem*, resolution of the economic department of the Executive Committee of the Soviet of Workers' and Soldiers' Deputies.—II 78-79.
—— No. 67, May 29, 1917, "Without Annexations."—II 91.
——No. 68, May 30, 1917, concerning the struggle against economic chaos.—II 93.
——*idem*, concerning the re-elections to the Workers' and Soldiers' Soviet.— II 94.
—— No. 70, June 1, 1917, articles and reports on the economic chaos.—II 143.
—— No. 74, June 7, 1917, "Settling the Cronstadt Incident."—II 151.
—— No. 76, June 9, 1917, concerning the disbanding of four regiments.— II 148.
—— *idem*, the notes of the English and French governments.—II 164.
—— No. 78, June 12, 1917, communication of the Department of International Relations of the Executive Committee of the Soviet to Huysmans.—II 175.
—— No. 104, July 12, 1917, concerning the metal industry of the Moscow district.—II 301, 302.
Malenkaia Gazeta, No. 85, April 27, 1917, appeal of a group of soldiers on Lenin's passage through Germany.—I 193.
Neue Zeit, Die, XX, 1 (1901-02), Engels, "Zur Kritik des sozialdemokratischen Programmentwurfs."—I 328; II 152.
—— XXX, 2 (1912), article by Karl Kautsky, "The New Tactics."—I 49.

—— XXXV, 2 (1917), article by Karl Kautsky, "The Perspectives of the Russian Revolution."—I 63.

Neue Züricher Zeitung, No. 495, first noon edition, March 21, 1917, concerning the revolution in Russia, reprint of a telegram of the Berlin *National-zeitung* (No. 66, March 20, 1917).—I 41.

—— No. 517, first noon edition, March 24, 1917, telegram from Berlin.—I 56.

—— No. 557, first morning edition, March 30, 1917, telegram from Milan.— I 74.

Novaia Zhizn, No. 2, May 3, 1917, "Put an End to the Policy of Conquest."— I 240.

—— No. 17, May 20, 1917, "The Plans of the Coalition Government. An Interview with the New Ministers."—II 61.

—— No. 24, May 29, 1917, article by V. Bazarov, "The Conflict in the Donetz Basin."—II 86.

—— No. 30, June 6, 1917, article by Bazarov, "The Present Anarchy and the Coming Napoleon."—II 141.

—— No. 36, June 16, 1917, concerning the conference of factory committees (Avilov's resolution).—II 179.

—— No. 41, June 19, 1917. "Press Review" ("An Angry Criticism").— II 234.

—— No. 50, June 29, 1917, concerning the Malinovsky affair.—II 264.

—— No. 60, July 11, 1917, appeal to the workers by Minister of Labour Skobelev.—II 299.

—— *idem*, article by Avilov, "The Chaos in the Ministry of Commerce."— II 299.

—— No. 61, July 12, 1917, article by A. Sandomirsky, "The Struggle for the Organisation of Industry."—II 302.

Novoie Vremia, No. 14,744, April 19, 1917, concerning Lenin's arrival and his welcome.—I 104.

—— No. 14,787, June 9, 1917, "Vote for the Ticket of the People's Freedom Party."—II 154.

—— No. 14,795, June 19, 1917, article by N. Nash, "The Black Hand."— II 228.

Pravda, No. 27, April 21, 1917, article by Kamenev, "Our Differences."—I 121.

—— No. 32, April 27, 1917, correspondence from Kanavin concerning a proletarian militia.—I 229.

—— No. 33, April 28, 1917.—II 35.

—— No. 37, May 4, 1917, proclamation to the soldiers of all belligerent countries.—I 279; II 14.

—— No. 55, May 25, 1917, decision on the convocation of an international Socialist conference.—II 159.

—— No. 60, May 31, 1917.—II 138.

—— No. 68, June 10, 1917.—I 328.

—— *idem*, letter from a peasant.—II 218.

—— No. 80, June 26, 1917, declaration to the Soviet Congress.—II 250.

Rabochaia Gaseta, No. 32, April 28, 1917, "For the Return of the Emigrants."— I 242.

—— No. 35, May 3, 1917, "The Old Tune."—I 146.

—— No. 38, May 5, 1917, "An Insane Step."—I 251.

—— *idem*, "The Subordinate Officer's Widow."—I 265.

—— No. 39, May 8, 1917, report on Borgbjerg's proposal.—I 288.

—— No. 42, May 11, 1917, "The Delegation of the Finnish Social-Democracy in the Organisation Committee."—I 312; II 26.

—— No. 56, May 27, 1917, "The Country Is in Danger."—II 168.

—— No. 57, May 29, 1917, article by Cherevanin, "The Struggle for Peace and the Defence of the Country."—II 147.

—— No. 63, June 6, 1917, "The Malinovsky Affair."—II 155.

—— No. 67, June 10, 1917, "The Malinovsky Affair."—II 157.

—— *idem,* "The Notes of the French and English Governments."—II 164, 165.

—— No. 80, June 27, 1917, "Call to Order."—II 255.

—— No. 81, June 28, 1917, "Defection of the Ukraine."—II 260.

—— No. 82, June 29, 1917, "Formidable Symptoms."—II 262.

—— No. 93, July 12, 1917, article by Ivanovich, "Shall We Fear Peace?"—II 304.

Riech, No. 73, April 10, 1917, "The Provisional Government on the Tasks of the War."—I 173.

—— No. 78, April 18, 1917, "Lenin's Arrival."—I 112.

—— No. 83, April 24, 1917, Miliukov's statement.—I 173.

—— No. 85, April 26, 1917, editorial.—I 178, 180.

—— No. 86, April 27, 1917, editorial.—I 189.

—— No. 91, May 3, 1917, Plekhanov's letter.—I 236.

—— *idem,* editorial.—II 49.

—— No. 104, May 18, 1917, announcement of the formation of a central committee for the restoration and maintenance of the normal labour process in industrial enterprises.—II 53.

—— No. 107, May 22, 1917, "The Secrets of Foreign Policy."—II 64, 65.

—— *idem,* "On the Edge of the Abyss."—II 69.

—— No. 112, May 27, 1917, report of a session of the Soviet (Skobelev's speech).—II 83.

—— No. 115, May 31, 1917, report of the Kolomna-Machine Construction Co. for 1916.—II 287.

—— No. 128, June 16, 1917, editorial.—II 192.

—— No. 137, June 27, 1917, concerning the autonomy of the Ukraine.—II 254.

—— No. 141, July 1, 1917, editorial.—II 277.

—— No. 150, July 12, 1917, report on the private conference of members of the Imperial Duma.—II 306.

Russkaia Volia, May 17, 1917, evening edition, concerning the state of mind of the delegates of the Peasant Congress.—II 52.

Soldatskaia Pravda, No. 13, May 16, 1917, (Supplement), resolutions of the April Conference.—II 91, 106, 111, 158.

Sotsial-Democrat (central organ of the Bolsheviks, published in Geneva in Russian), No. 47, October 13, 1915, theses of the editors.—I 39, 40, 49, 60, 72, 76, 83, 85, 200; II 76.

—— No. 58, January 31, 1917, article by Lenin, "A Turn in World Politics."—I 19.

Sotsial-Democrat (Moscow), No. 59, letter from a peasant.—II 218.

Temps (Paris), March 20, 1917, telegram from Petrograd (Proclamation of the Soviet of Workers' Deputies).—I 41.

—— March 22, 1917, correspondence from Petrograd.—I 45.

Times (London), March 16, 1917, telegram from Petrograd.—I 36, 37, 40, 45.

Vossische Zeitung, evening edition, March 21, 1917, report from Russia via Stockholm.—I 45.

—— March 22, 1917, morning edition.—I 45.

Vecherneie Vremia, May 19, announcement of the formation of a central committee for the restoration and maintenance of the normal labour process in industrial enterprises.—II 53.

Viedomosti Obshchestvenova Gradonachelstva, May 30, 1917, lists of candidates for members of the Borough Councils of Petrograd.—II 131.

Vestnik Finansov, No. 18, May 20, 1917.—II 297.

Volia Naroda, No. 7, May 18, 1917, announcement of the formation of a central committee for the restoration, etc., of industrial enterprises.—II 53.

—— No. 31, June 17, 1917, article, "Via Zimmerwald-Berlin-Stockholm-Petrograd."—II 223.

Yedinstvo, No. 5, April 18, 1917, "Conference of the Representatives of the Social-Democratic Party on the Question of Unity."—I 109.

—— Nos. 9, 10, and 11, April 22, 24, 25, 1917, article by Plekhanov, "On Lenin's Theses and Why Deliriums Are Occasionally Interesting."—I 176.

—— No. 15, April 29, 1917, "Hands Off!"—I 243.

—— No. 18, May 3, 1917, Plekhanov's letter to the "Association of Socialist Students."—I 236.

—— No. 19, May 4, 1917, editorial.—I 251.

—— No. 20, May 5, 1917, proclamation of G. Plekhanov, Leo Deutsch and Vera Zasulich.—I 262.

—— No. 44, June 2, 1917, article by Dnevnitsky, "Enemies of the People."—II 226.

CALENDAR OF EVENTS

FROM THE BEGINNING OF MARCH TO THE MIDDLE OF JULY, 1917

March 3. Beginning of strike at the Putilov plant (Metal Works) in Petrograd.

March 8. Celebration of International Woman's Day.

March 10. General strike in Petrograd. Workers' demonstrations fired upon. Elections to Petrograd Soviet of Workers' Deputies begin.

March 11. Manifesto of Petrograd Committee of Russian Social-Democratic Labour Party (Bolsheviks) urging creation of a Provisional Revolutionary Government.

March 12. Troops going over to the side of the workers. Petrograd Soviet of Workers' Deputies formed. Executive Committee of Imperial Duma formed. Movement in Moscow begins.

March 13. General strike in Moscow. Moscow Soviet of Workers' Deputies and Committee of Public Organisations formed.

March 14. Names of provisional commissars appointed by Executive Committee of Imperial Duma made public. Order Number One issued by Petrograd Soviet of Workers' and Soldiers' Deputies. Soldiers' section of the Petrograd Soviet formed.

March 15. Nicholas II abdicates in favour of Michael Romanov. Provisional Government formed. National Rada formed in Kiev.

March 16. Michael Romanov abdicates.

March 18. *Pravda* appears in Petrograd. Petrograd Soviet calls off strike.

March 19. Strike in Petrograd ended. Military commission formed as part of Petrograd Committee of Russian Social-Democratic Labour Party (Bolsheviks).

March 20. Contact Commission formed by Executive Committee of Petrograd Soviet for dealing with Provisional Government. In an appeal to Petrograd Soviet of Workers' and Soldiers' Deputies, Petrograd Committee of R.S.-D.L.P. (Bolsheviks) urges it to introduce eight-hour work-day and to issue an appeal for peace to the proletariat of the belligerent countries. *Social-Democrat* appears in Moscow.

March 21. Nicholas II arrested. Extraordinary Investigating Commission formed by Provisional Government.

March 22. Provisional Government decrees to suppress agrarian movement in Kazan Province.

March 23. Agreement between Petrograd Soviet and Society of Manufacturers concerning introduction of eight-hour work-day and factory committees. L. B. Kamenev joins editorial staff of *Pravda.*

March 25. Soviet demonstration in Moscow.

March 27. Petrograd Soviet addresses peace manifesto to all the peoples.

March 28. Strikes in Moscow, eight-hour work-day demanded.

March 29. Petrograd City Conference of Socialist-Revolutionist Party adopts resolution directed against incipient agrarian movement and land seizures. Bolshevik fraction in Moscow Soviet proposes that eight-hour work-day be introduced by the workers' own action.

April 1. Demonstration in Kiev, autonomy for the Ukraine demanded. I. Tsereteli returns to Petrograd from exile.

April 5. Funeral of participants of March Revolution in Petrograd. Administration of Provodnik plant in Moscow arrested by workers.

April 7. Establishment of Special Conference to prepare electoral laws for Constituent Assembly. Congress of Constitutional-Democratic Party. Conference of Soviets of Workers' and Soldiers' Deputies of central industrial region in Moscow.

April 8. Provisional Government decides to issue "Liberty Loan."

April 11. All-Russian Conference of Soviets of Workers' and Soldiers' Deputies opens in Petrograd. Finnish Diet opens.

April 13. G. V. Plekhanov returns to Petrograd.

April 16. V. I. Lenin and other Bolsheviks return to Petrograd. City Conference of Bolshevik organisation in Moscow.

April 18. Russian sailors and soldiers demonstrate in Helsingfors.

April 20. Executive Committee of Petrograd Soviet votes for "Liberty Loan."

April 26. Preliminary conference of peasants' organisations and Soviets of Peasants' Deputies make arrangements for All-Russian Congress of Peasant Deputies.

April 27. Petrograd City Conference of Bolshevik organisation opens.

April 28. *Soldatskaia Pravda* appears in Petrograd. Minsk Front Congress adopts resolution on war. Moscow City Conference of Bolshevik organisation held.

April 29. Demonstration of soldiers and sailors in Petrograd protesting against baiting Lenin and Bolsheviks.

April 30. Regional Congress of Soviets of Workers', Soldiers' and Sailors' Deputies of Finland opens in Vyborg.

May 1. First-of-May street demonstrations all over Russia. Note of Foreign Minister Miliukov affirms Provisional Government's adherence to treaties with Allies.

May 2. Moscow Regional Conference of Bolsheviks opens.

May 3. Street demonstrations in Petrograd against Miliukov's note. First resolution of Bolshevik Central Committee on crisis created by Miliukov's note.

May 4. Second resolution of Bolshevik Central Committee on crisis. Demonstrations against Miliukov continued in Petrograd. Firing in the streets. Commander of Petrograd Military District, General Kornilov, orders artillery moved against demonstrators. Counter-demonstration of bourgeoisie on Nevsky Prospect. Provisional Government's interpretation of Miliukov's note. Petrograd Soviet of Workers' and Soldiers' Deputies prohibits meetings and demonstrations for two days. Meetings and demonstration of protest against Miliukov in Moscow.

May 5. Third resolution of Bolshevik Central Committee on crisis. Demonstration of 55th Reserve Regiment in Moscow against Miliukov. Petrograd Soviet of Workers' and Soldiers' Deputies votes for "Liberty Loan."

May 6. Danish Socialist Borgbjerg proposes to Executive Committee of Petrograd Soviet calling of international Socialist conference for preliminary discussion of conditions for concluding peace.

May 7-12. All-Russian April Conference of R.S.-D.L.P. (Bolsheviks) in Petrograd.

May 8. Executive Committee of Petrograd Soviet accepts Borgbjerg's proposal for calling international Socialist conference in Stockholm.

May 9. Provisional Government proclaims necessity of widening its composition (*i. e.* of forming a Coalition Government).

424 APPENDICES

May 10. Members of all four Imperial Dumas hold session in Tauride Palace in Petrograd.

May 11. Borough Soviet of Workers' and Soldiers' Deputies of Vyborg section of Petrograd decrees to organise a workers' guard.

May 13. War and Navy Minister Guchkov resigns. Soviet of Workers' and Soldiers' Deputies appeals to army urging offensive and to Socialists of all countries urging the calling of international Socialist conference.

May 14. Executive Committee of Petrograd Soviet of Workers and Soldiers' Deputies votes in favour of forming a Coalition Government. Provisional Committee of Imperial Duma votes in favour of forming a Coalition Government.

May 15. Foreign Minister Miliukov resigns.

May 17. Conference of members of Imperial Duma adopts resolution proclaiming necessity of "staunch loyalty to our valiant Allies." Miliukov and Guchkov deliver speeches. All-Russian Congress of Peasant Deputies opens.

May 18. Coalition Provisional Government formed.

May 21. All-Russian Menshevik conference adopts decision in favour of its party representatives' participation in Coalition Government. All-Russian officers' congress in Petrograd.

May 22. Congress of Constitutional-Democratic Party in Petrograd.

May 23. Vandervelde's speech on war at Congress of Peasant Deputies. Magazine *Rabotnitsa* [*Working Woman*], organ of Central Committee of Bolsheviks, appears in Petrograd.

May 27. War Minister Kerensky orders preparations for offensive. Soviet demonstration in Moscow against death sentence for Friedrich Adler.

May 28. First issue of Bolshevik paper *Okopnaia Pravda* [*Truth in the Trenches*] appears at north front.

May 30. Minister of Justice Pereverzev orders all deals in land stopped.

May 31. Minister of Commerce Konovalov resigns.

June 7. Special Conference to prepare electoral law for Constituent Assembly opens.

June 8. Minister of Justice Pereverzev rescinds order prohibiting deals in land.

June 9. A number of regiments at the front disbanded for refusal to take offensive. Elections to Borough Councils begin in Petrograd.

June 12. First conference of shop and factory committees opens in Petrograd. All-Ukrainian military congress prohibited by Kerensky.

June 15. Provisional Government decrees to banish the Swiss Social-Democrat R. Grimm from Russia. All-Russian Congress of Peasant Deputies closes.

June 16. All-Russian Congress of Soviets of Workers' and Soldiers' Deputies opens. Provisional Government issues note proposing calling of Allied conference to revise treaties relating to war aims. Former president of Imperial Duma, Rodzianko, in letter, proposes to members of Imperial Duma not to leave Petrograd in view of important political events. Provisional Government decrees question of Ukrainian autonomy must not be solved pending convocation of All-Russian Constituent Assembly.

June 17. Khaustov, Bolshevik, editor of *Okopnaia Pravda*, arrested.

June 18. Second All-Ukrainian military congress opens in Kiev.

June 19. Sailors arrest officers in Sebastopol. Gathering of delegates of ships' crews demands resignation of Admiral Kolchak, commander of Black Sea fleet.

June 20. State's Attorney of Petrograd Judicial Chamber orders Durnovo's summer estate to be vacated by organisations that had taken hold of it. All-Russian Cossacks' congress in Petrograd.

June 21. Workers of Vyborg section demonstrate against order to vacate Durnovo's estate.

June 22. All-Russian Congress of Soviets puts three days' ban on street demonstrations. Central Committee of Bolsheviks gives up demonstration called for June 23. Meetings in shops and barracks in connection with ban on demonstration.

June 23. Meetings in boroughs and military units continue.

June 24. Joint session of Executive Committee of Petrograd Soviet, Presidium of Soviet Congress and bureau of fractions discusses demonstration. Tsereteli speaks. Bolsheviks withdraw in protest. All-Ukrainian military congress issues "Universal Act on the State System of the Ukraine."

June 25. Soviet Congress calls demonstration for July 1 under its own slogans. Resolution of Soviet Congress condemns demonstration called by Bolsheviks for June 23. Bolshevik fraction of Congress protests.

June 27. Provisional Government appoints October 13 for opening of Constituent Assembly and September 30 for elections.

June 28. All-Ukrainian Central Rada organises General Secretariat as executive organ of Rada.

June 29. Kerensky, in proclamation to army and navy, orders offensive. All-Russian conference of Bolshevik military organisations in Petrograd.

June 30. Soviet Congress forms All-Russian Central Executive Committee.

July 1. Russian army begins advance at front. First successes. Very large demonstration in Petrograd under Bolshevik slogans.

July 2. Bourgeois demonstration with national banners on Nevsky Prospect in Petrograd in honour of victories of Russian army. Durnovo's estate raided by government, Anarchists arrested. Workers of Vyborg section strike in protest against raid on the Durnovo estate.

July 4. Economic Council and Chief Economic Committee established in Provisional Government. All-Russian Conference of Trade Unions opens in Petrograd.

July 5. First meeting of All-Russian Central Executive Committee.

July 6. All-Russian Conference of Constitutional-Democratic Party in Moscow.

July 8. Elections to Moscow City Council begin.

July 9. Minister of Labour Skobelev, in appeal to workers, puts ban on "actions by decision from below."

July 10. Finnish Diet passes bill "On Sovereign Rights of Finnish Diet."

July 11. All-Russian Conference of Trade Unions closes. Defeats of Russian army at the front begin.

July 14. City Conference of Bolsheviks in Petrograd. Delegation of Provisional Government, consisting of Tsereteli, Kerensky and Tereshchenko, reaches agreement with All-Ukrainian Central Rada in Kiev. Chernov introduces bill prohibiting deals in land.

EVENTS IN THE LIFE OF V. I. LENIN

FROM THE MIDDLE OF MARCH TO THE MIDDLE OF JULY, 1917

Middle of March. First news of the uprising of workers and soldiers in Petrograd, and of the victory of the Russian Revolution, finds V. I. Lenin in Zürich, Switzerland. Considering a speedy return to Russia to be his prime task, and having reasons to assume that England will not allow the emigrant-internationalists to pass, Lenin begins to seek other ways of going home.

March 16. Lenin writes a letter to Kollontai, in which, guided by the fragmentary reports of the foreign press, he makes the first analysis of the Russian Revolution.

March 17. Together with Zinoviev Lenin prepares "Draft Theses of March 17" (analysis of the perspectives of the Russian Revolution and the tasks of the Bolshevik Party).

March 19. A conference of various political groups of Russian emigrants in Switzerland considers ways and means of returning to Russia and accepts Martov's plan of returning via Germany under condition that an equal number of German and Austrian prisoners interned in Russia should be exchanged for the returning emigrants. Lenin joins in this plan. Grimm, a Swiss Socialist, is authorised to conduct necessary negotiations with the Swiss Government.

March 20. Lenin begins, for the party press, a series of "Letters from Afar," the first of which, entitled, "The First Stage of the First Revolution," he sends to the *Pravda* via Stockholm.

March 30. Lenin telegraphs to Hanecki in Stockholm requesting him to take steps through the Soviet of Workers' Deputies for the exchange of the Russian emigrants-internationalists for Germans interned in Russia. He sends through Hanecki instructions to members of the Bolshevik organisations in Russia.

March 31. Volksrecht, a Social-Democratic paper in Zürich, publishes the text of a report, "On the Tasks of the Russian Social-Democratic Labour Party in the Russian Revolution," given by Lenin before a gathering of Swiss workers. The Foreign Bureau of the Central Committee decides to go via Germany immediately, without awaiting the consent of the other emigrant party groupings, which decision Lenin telegraphs to Grimm.

April 2. In view of the equivocal position taken by Grimm on the question of the emigrants' return through Germany, Lenin removes him as negotiator, and entrusts the further conduct of negotiations to the Swiss Socialist, Platten.

April 4. Platten presents to the German Embassy in Berne an outline, prepared by Lenin, of conditions for the emigrants' passage through Germany.

April 7. Lenin goes to Berne, where he (together with Loriot, Guilbeaux and P. Levi) signs the "Report on the Passage through Germany."

April 8. A meeting of the Russian Bolsheviks departing for Russia adopts, with slight editorial changes, the text of a "Farewell Letter to the Swiss Workers" as written by Lenin. The Bolsheviks depart for Germany, Platten accompanying the car with the emigrants.

April 13. Lenin on a steamboat between Sassnitz, Germany, and Trolleborg,

Sweden. Arrives at Trolleborg late at night, departs with night train for Stockholm.

April 14. Lenin arrives in Stockholm in the morning, departs for Russia in the evening.

April 16. Arrives in Petrograd late in the evening. Is greeted at the station by a large demonstration of workers and soldiers. Makes his first speech in Russia addressing the crowd on the square in front of the Finland Station. Concludes his speech, delivered standing on an armoured motor car, with the words, "Long live a world-wide Socialist revolution!" Participates at a gathering of responsible party workers of Petrograd in Central Committee headquarters, in the former house of Kshesinskaia.

April 17. Lenin appears before the Executive Committee of the Petrograd Soviet of Workers' and Soldiers' Deputies to report on his passage through Germany. Addresses a conference of Bolshevik members of the All-Russian Conference of Soviets of Workers' and Soldiers' Deputies, defending the "theses." Repeats his address before a joint meeting of Bolsheviks and Mensheviks, members of the same Conference. Joins the editorial staff of the *Pravda,* which he edits until it is raided by the military cadets in July.

April 20. Lenin publishes the "theses" in the *Pravda,* in an article entitled "On the Tasks of the Proletariat in the Present Revolution."

April 23. Lenin addresses a meeting of soldiers in the Izmailov Regiment. Participates in a session of the Central Committee where the character of the Russian Revolution is discussed. Finishes his pamphlet, *The Tasks of the Proletariat in Our Revolution.*

End of April. Lenin writes "Letters on Tactics. First Letter. An Estimate of the Present Situation."

April 27. Lenin participates in the work of the Petrograd City Conference of the R.S.-D.L.P. of which he is elected honorary chairman. Reports, and makes concluding remarks, on the political situation before the Conference.

April 28. Lenin participates in the debates on the resolution introduced at the Petrograd Conference on the political situation.

May 1. From the Central Committee platform Lenin addresses the workers during the May Day celebration.

May 3. Lenin participates in the Central Committee session devoted to the crisis created by Miliukov's note.

May 4. Lenin participates in a Central Committee session devoted to the same question. The Central Committee adopts the resolution proposed by him.

May 5. In the morning Lenin participates in a Central Committee session devoted to the May crisis, and has his resolution adopted. In the evening, at a session of the Petrograd City Conference, Lenin participates in the discussion of the question of communal elections and introduces a resolution on that question which the Conference adopts.

May 6. Lenin gives an interview to Torniainen, editor of the Finnish Social-Democratic paper, the *Tyomies.* Finishes his "Proposed Changes in the Theoretical, Political and Several Other Parts of the Programme," prepared for the All-Russian party conference.

May 7. Lenin opens the All-Russian Conference of the R.S.-D.L.P., delivers the opening address, is elected to the Presidium, delivers a report on the political situation and on the war; in the evening session he makes the concluding speech. The Conference elects Lenin to the resolutions commission.

May 8. At the morning and evening sessions of the All-Russian Conference Lenin delivers one address on the plan of calling an international Socialist conference as proposed by Borgbjerg, and another on the Bolsheviks' attitude towards the Soviets.

May 9. Lenin participates in the work of the resolutions commission of the All-Russian Conference.

May 10. In the morning Lenin participates in the work of the sections of the All-Russian Conference; in the evening session he speaks in favour of the resolution on the war as prepared by the resolutions commission with his very active participation.

May 11. In the morning Lenin participates in the work of the resolutions commission of the Conference; in the evening he reports before the Conference on the agrarian question and on the revision of the party programme.

May 12. Lenin speaks at the Conference on the state of affairs in the International, defends the commission's resolution on the political situation, is elected to the Central Committee by 104 out of 109 votes (the largest number cast for any one of the slate) and delivers the closing speech.

May 21. Lenin makes a report on the All-Russian April Conference before a party gathering in the building of the Marine Corps in Petrograd. The gathering receives him enthusiastically.

May 23. Lenin speaks at a gathering of the interborough organisation of the R.S.-D.L.P. on the question of uniting the Bolsheviks with the Social-Democrats-Internationalists.

May 25. Lenin delivers a speech at a meeting organised by the Bolsheviks to protest against the death sentence imposed upon Friedrich Adler.

May 28. Lenin delivers a lecture on the war.

June 4. Lenin delivers an address on the agrarian question before the All-Russian Peasant Congress.

June 12. Lenin appears at a session of the Petrograd Committee of the R.S.-D.L.P. to argue against the decision of the Executive Commission of the Petrograd Committee to establish a special organ of the Petrograd Committee.

June 13. Lenin delivers an address on the control of industry before the first Petrograd conference of shop and factory committees.

June (exact date unknown). Lenin speaks at a sailors' and workers' meeting in the Marine Exercise Hall of Cronstadt.

June 17. Lenin delivers an address on the Bolshevik attitude towards the Provisional Government before the First All-Russian Congress of Soviets of Workers' and Soldiers' Deputies.

June 22. Lenin delivers an address on the war before the All-Russian Congress of Soviets. In view of the ban put by the Congress of Soviets on the demonstration planned by the Bolsheviks for June 23 and the Black Hundred danger alleged to be connected with it, Lenin, at a night session of the Central Committee, insists, and has a decision adopted, that the proposed demonstration be abandoned.

June 24. Lenin, at a session of the Petrograd Committee, speaks on the abandonment of the planned demonstration.

July 11. Lenin goes to Finland for a few days' rest.

CPSIA information can be obtained at www.ICGtesting.com
Printed in the USA
BVOW06s0409110915

417545BV00010B/69/P

9 781162 790